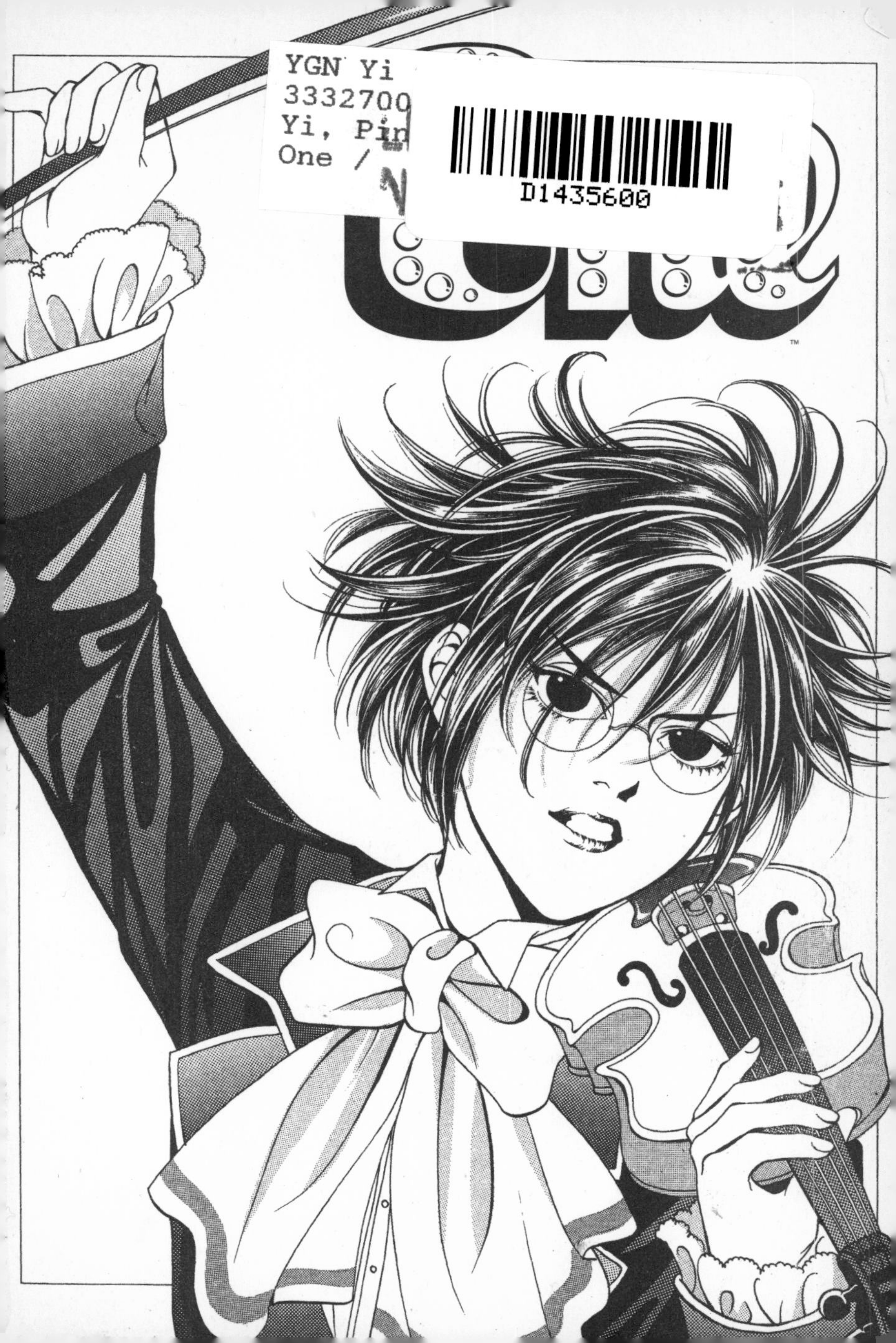

ALSO AVAILABLE FROM TOKYOPOP®

MANGA

.HACK//LEGEND OF THE TWILIGHT
@LARGE
ABENOBASHI: MAGICAL SHOPPING ARCADE
A.I. LOVE YOU
AI YORI AOSHI
ANGELIC LAYER
ARM OF KANNON
BABY BIRTH
BATTLE ROYALE
BATTLE VIXENS
BRAIN POWERED
BRIGADOON
B'TX
CANDIDATE FOR GODDESS, THE
CARDCAPTOR SAKURA
CARDCAPTOR SAKURA - MASTER OF THE CLOW
CHOBITS
CHRONICLES OF THE CURSED SWORD
CLAMP SCHOOL DETECTIVES
CLOVER
COMIC PARTY
CONFIDENTIAL CONFESSIONS
CORRECTOR YUI
COWBOY BEBOP
COWBOY BEBOP: SHOOTING STAR
CRAZY LOVE STORY
CRESCENT MOON
CULDCEPT
CYBORG 009
D•N•ANGEL
DEMON DIARY
DEMON ORORON, THE
DEUS VITAE
DIGIMON
DIGIMON TAMERS
DIGIMON ZERO TWO
DOLL
DRAGON HUNTER
DRAGON KNIGHTS
DRAGON VOICE
DREAM SAGA
DUKLYON: CLAMP SCHOOL DEFENDERS
EERIE QUEERIE!
ERICA SAKURAZAWA: COLLECTED WORKS
ET CETERA
ETERNITY
EVIL'S RETURN
FAERIES' LANDING
FAKE
FLCL
FORBIDDEN DANCE
FRUITS BASKET
G GUNDAM
GATEKEEPERS
GETBACKERS

GIRL GOT GAME
GRAVITATION
GTO
GUNDAM BLUE DESTINY
GUNDAM SEED ASTRAY
GUNDAM WING
GUNDAM WING: BATTLEFIELD OF PACIFISTS
GUNDAM WING: ENDLESS WALTZ
GUNDAM WING: THE LAST OUTPOST (G-UNIT)
HANDS OFF!
HAPPY MANIA
HARLEM BEAT
I.N.V.U.
IMMORTAL RAIN
INITIAL D
INSTANT TEEN: JUST ADD NUTS
ISLAND
JING: KING OF BANDITS
JING: KING OF BANDITS - TWILIGHT TALES
JULINE
KARE KANO
KILL ME, KISS ME
KINDAICHI CASE FILES, THE
KING OF HELL
KODOCHA: SANA'S STAGE
LAMENT OF THE LAMB
LEGAL DRUG
LEGEND OF CHUN HYANG, THE
LES BIJOUX
LOVE HINA
LUPIN III
LUPIN III: WORLD'S MOST WANTED
MAGIC KNIGHT RAYEARTH I
MAGIC KNIGHT RAYEARTH II
MAHOROMATIC: AUTOMATIC MAIDEN
MAN OF MANY FACES
MARMALADE BOY
MARS
MARS: HORSE WITH NO NAME
METROID
MINK
MIRACLE GIRLS
MIYUKI-CHAN IN WONDERLAND
MODEL
ONE
ONE I LOVE, THE
PARADISE KISS
PARASYTE
PASSION FRUIT
PEACH GIRL
PEACH GIRL: CHANGE OF HEART
PET SHOP OF HORRORS
PITA-TEN
PLANET LADDER
PLANETES
PRIEST

02.03.04T

ALSO AVAILABLE FROM TOKYOPOP®

PRINCESS AI
PSYCHIC ACADEMY
RAGNAROK
RAVE MASTER
REALITY CHECK
REBIRTH
REBOUND
REMOTE
RISING STARS OF MANGA
SABER MARIONETTE J
SAILOR MOON
SAINT TAIL
SAIYUKI
SAMURAI DEEPER KYO
SAMURAI GIRL REAL BOUT HIGH SCHOOL
SCRYED
SEIKAI TRILOGY, THE
SGT. FROG
SHAOLIN SISTERS
SHIRAHIME-SYO: SNOW GODDESS TALES
SHUTTERBOX
SKULL MAN, THE
SMUGGLER
SNOW DROP
SORCERER HUNTERS
STONE
SUIKODEN III
SUKI
THREADS OF TIME
TOKYO BABYLON
TOKYO MEW MEW
TRAMPS LIKE US
TREASURE CHESS
UNDER THE GLASS MOON
VAMPIRE GAME
VISION OF ESCAFLOWNE, THE
WARRIORS OF TAO
WILD ACT
WISH
WORLD OF HARTZ
X-DAY
ZODIAC P.I.

NOVELS

CLAMP SCHOOL PARANORMAL INVESTIGATORS
KARMA CLUB
SAILOR MOON
SLAYERS

ART BOOKS

ART OF CARDCAPTOR SAKURA
ART OF MAGIC KNIGHT RAYEARTH, THE
PEACH: MIWA UEDA ILLUSTRATIONS

ANIME GUIDES

COWBOY BEBOP
GUNDAM TECHNICAL MANUALS
SAILOR MOON SCOUT GUIDES

TOKYOPOP KIDS

STRAY SHEEP

CINE-MANGA™

ALADDIN
ASTRO BOY
CARDCAPTORS
CONFESSIONS OF A TEENAGE DRAMA QUEEN
DUEL MASTERS
FAIRLY ODDPARENTS, THE
FAMILY GUY
FINDING NEMO
G.I. JOE SPY TROOPS
JACKIE CHAN ADVENTURES
JIMMY NEUTRON: BOY GENIUS, THE ADVENTURES OF
KIM POSSIBLE
LILO & STITCH
LIZZIE MCGUIRE
LIZZIE MCGUIRE MOVIE, THE
MALCOLM IN THE MIDDLE
POWER RANGERS: NINJA STORM
SHREK 2
SPONGEBOB SQUAREPANTS
SPY KIDS 2
SPY KIDS 3-D: GAME OVER
TEENAGE MUTANT NINJA TURTLES
THAT'S SO RAVEN
TRANSFORMERS: ARMADA
TRANSFORMERS: ENERGON

For more
information visit
www.TOKYOPOP.com

02.03.04T

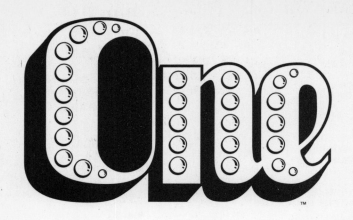

Volume 1

Los Angeles • Tokyo • London

Translator - Sunah Kim Schultz
English Adaptation - Dan Bova
Associate Editor - Troy Lewter
Retouch and Lettering - Christina R. Siri
Cover Layout - Harlan Harris
Graphic Designer - Monalisa de Asis

Editor - Bryce P. Coleman
Digital Imaging Manager - Chris Buford
Pre-Press Manager - Antonio DePietro
Production Managers - Jennifer Miller, Mutsumi Miyazaki
Art Director - Matt Alford
Managing Editor - Jill Freshney
VP of Production - Ron Klamert
President & C.O.O. - John Parker
Publisher & C.E.O. - Stuart Levy

E-mail: info@TOKYOPOP.com
Come visit us online at www.TOKYOPOP.com

A  Manga

TOKYOPOP Inc.
5900 Wilshire Blvd. Suite 2000
Los Angeles, CA 90036

One Vol. 1

ISBN: 1-59182-752-3

First TOKYOPOP printing: April 2004

10 9 8 7 6 5 4 3 2 1

Printed in the USA

CONTENTS

•ONE VOLUME 1•

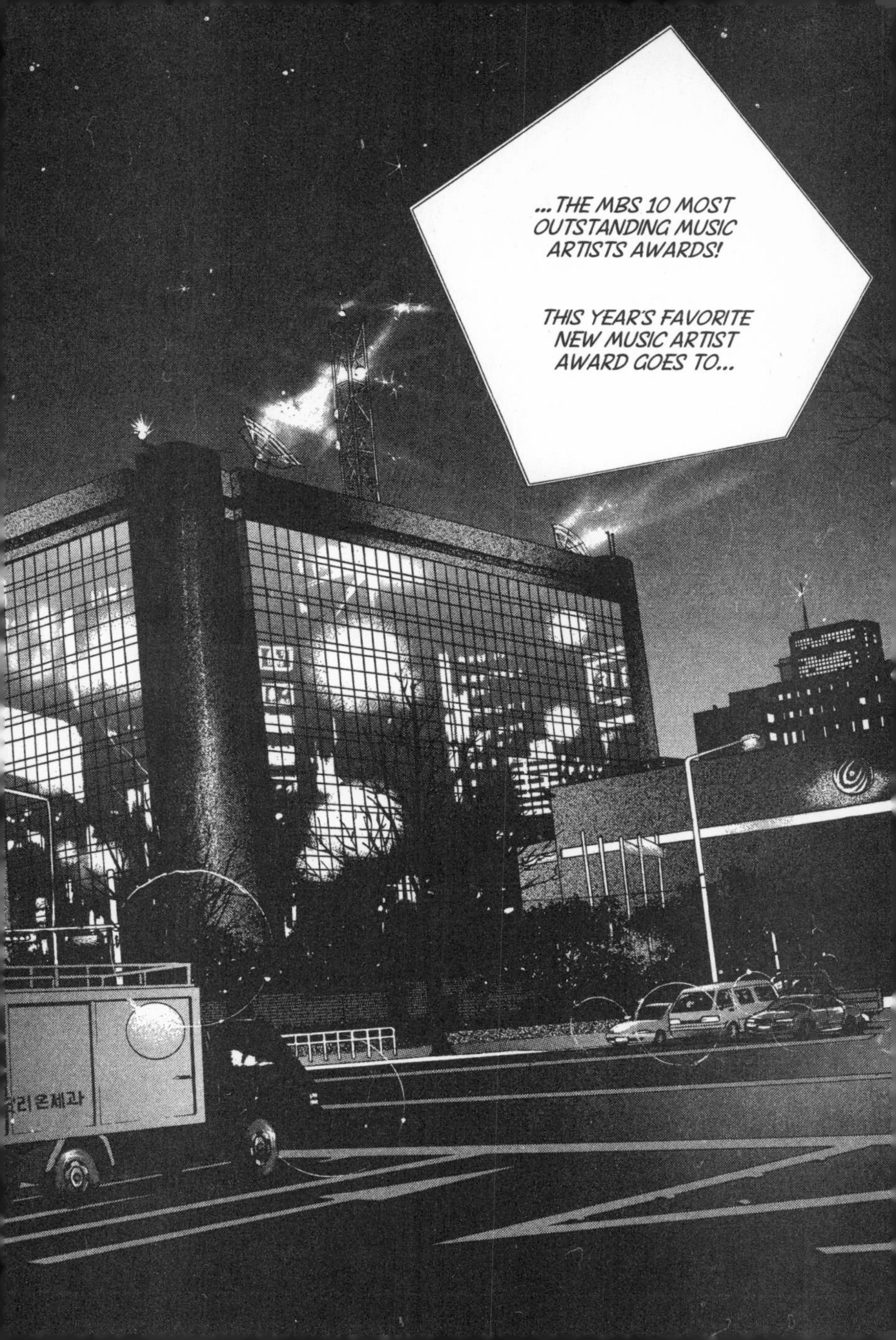
...THE MBS 10 MOST OUTSTANDING MUSIC ARTISTS AWARDS!
THIS YEAR'S FAVORITE NEW MUSIC ARTIST AWARD GOES TO...

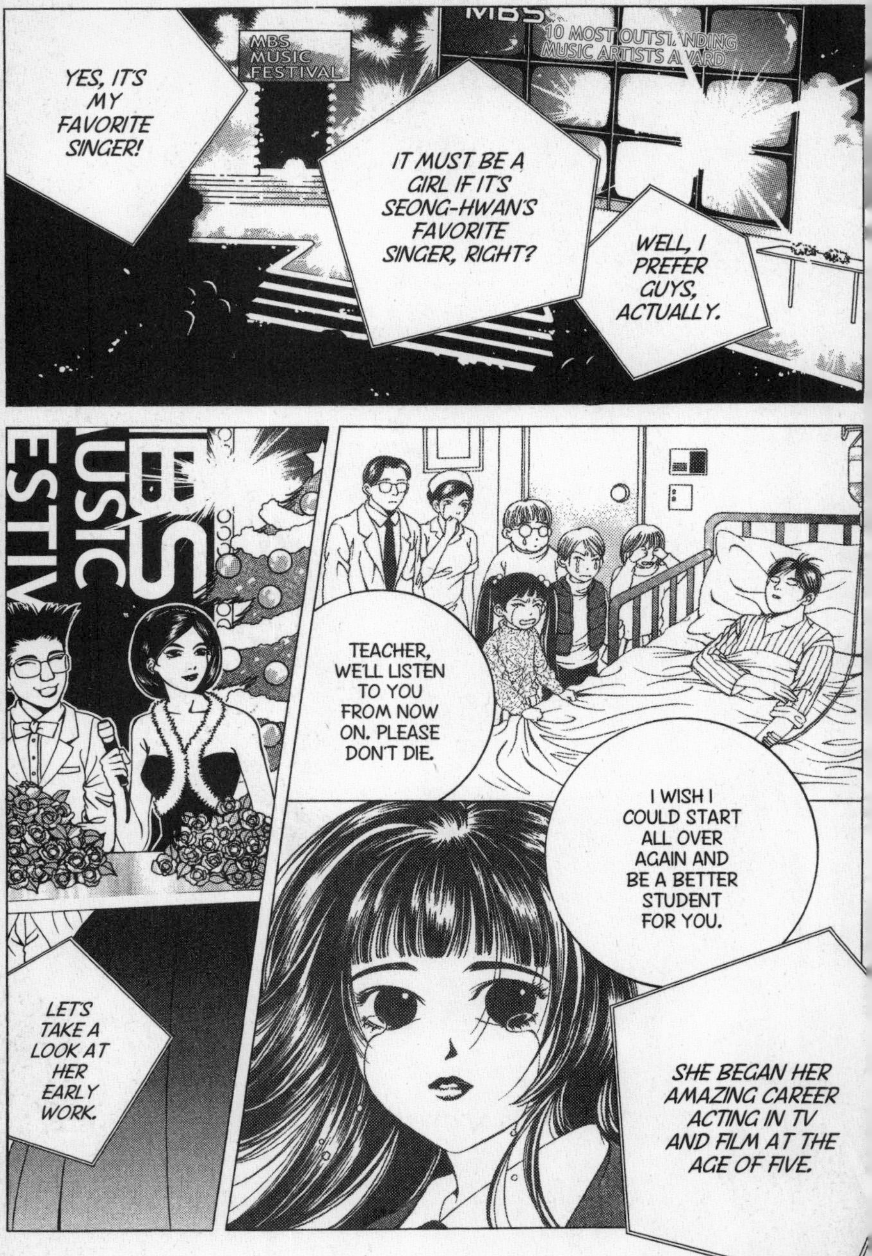
MBS
MBS MUSIC FESTIVAL
10 MOST OUTSTANDING MUSIC ARTISTS AWARD
YES, IT'S MY FAVORITE SINGER!
IT MUST BE A GIRL IF IT'S SEONG-HWAN'S FAVORITE SINGER, RIGHT?
WELL, I PREFER GUYS, ACTUALLY.
MBS MUSIC FESTIV
LET'S TAKE A LOOK AT HER EARLY WORK.
TEACHER, WE'LL LISTEN TO YOU FROM NOW ON. PLEASE DON'T DIE.
I WISH I COULD START ALL OVER AGAIN AND BE A BETTER STUDENT FOR YOU.
SHE BEGAN HER AMAZING CAREER ACTING IN TV AND FILM AT THE AGE OF FIVE.

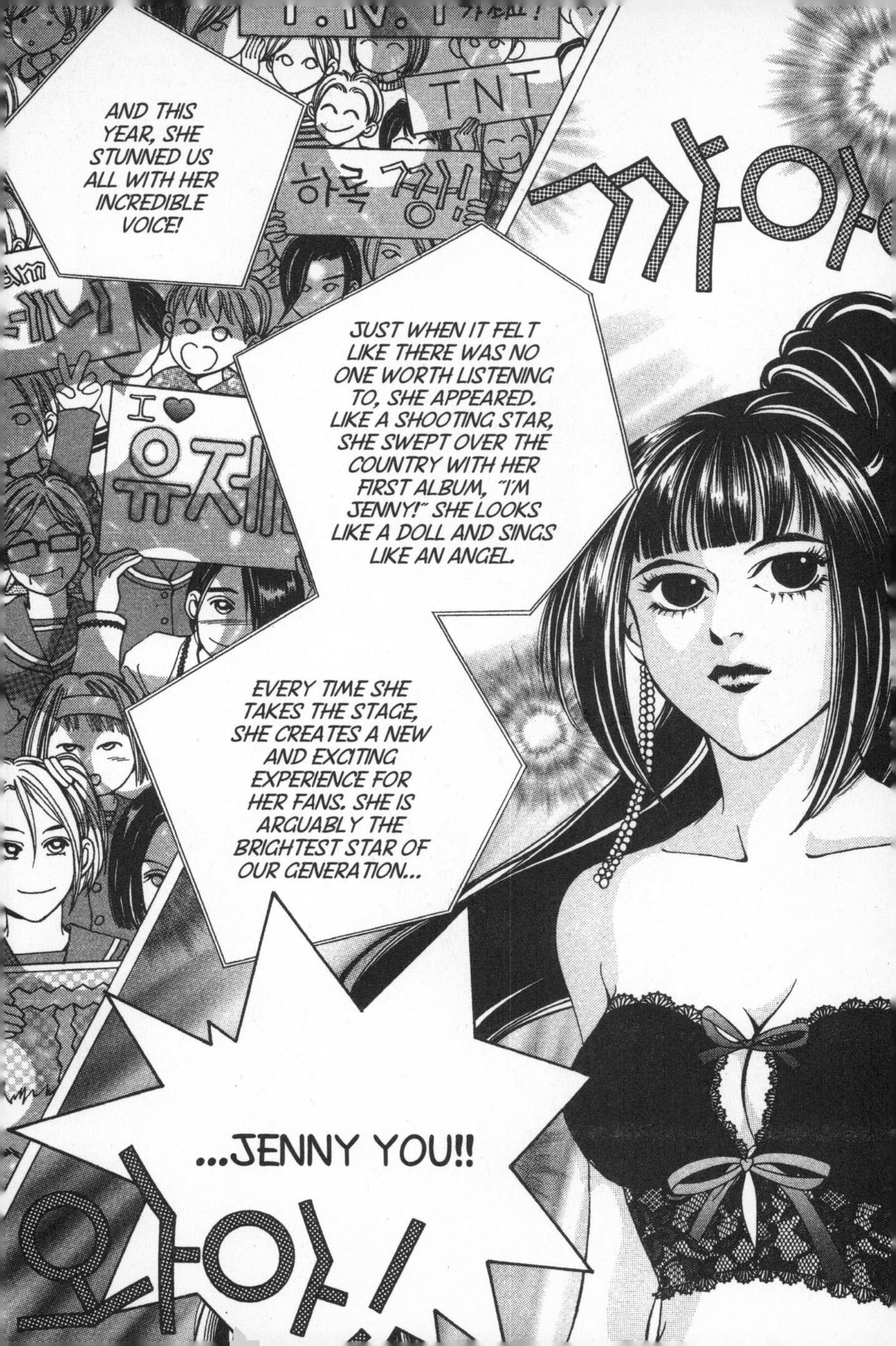
AND THIS YEAR, SHE STUNNED US ALL WITH HER INCREDIBLE VOICE!
TNT
꺄아아
JUST WHEN IT FELT LIKE THERE WAS NO ONE WORTH LISTENING TO, SHE APPEARED. LIKE A SHOOTING STAR, SHE SWEPT OVER THE COUNTRY WITH HER FIRST ALBUM, "I'M JENNY!" SHE LOOKS LIKE A DOLL AND SINGS LIKE AN ANGEL.
EVERY TIME SHE TAKES THE STAGE, SHE CREATES A NEW AND EXCITING EXPERIENCE FOR HER FANS. SHE IS ARGUABLY THE BRIGHTEST STAR OF OUR GENERATION...
...JENNY YOU!!
와아아!

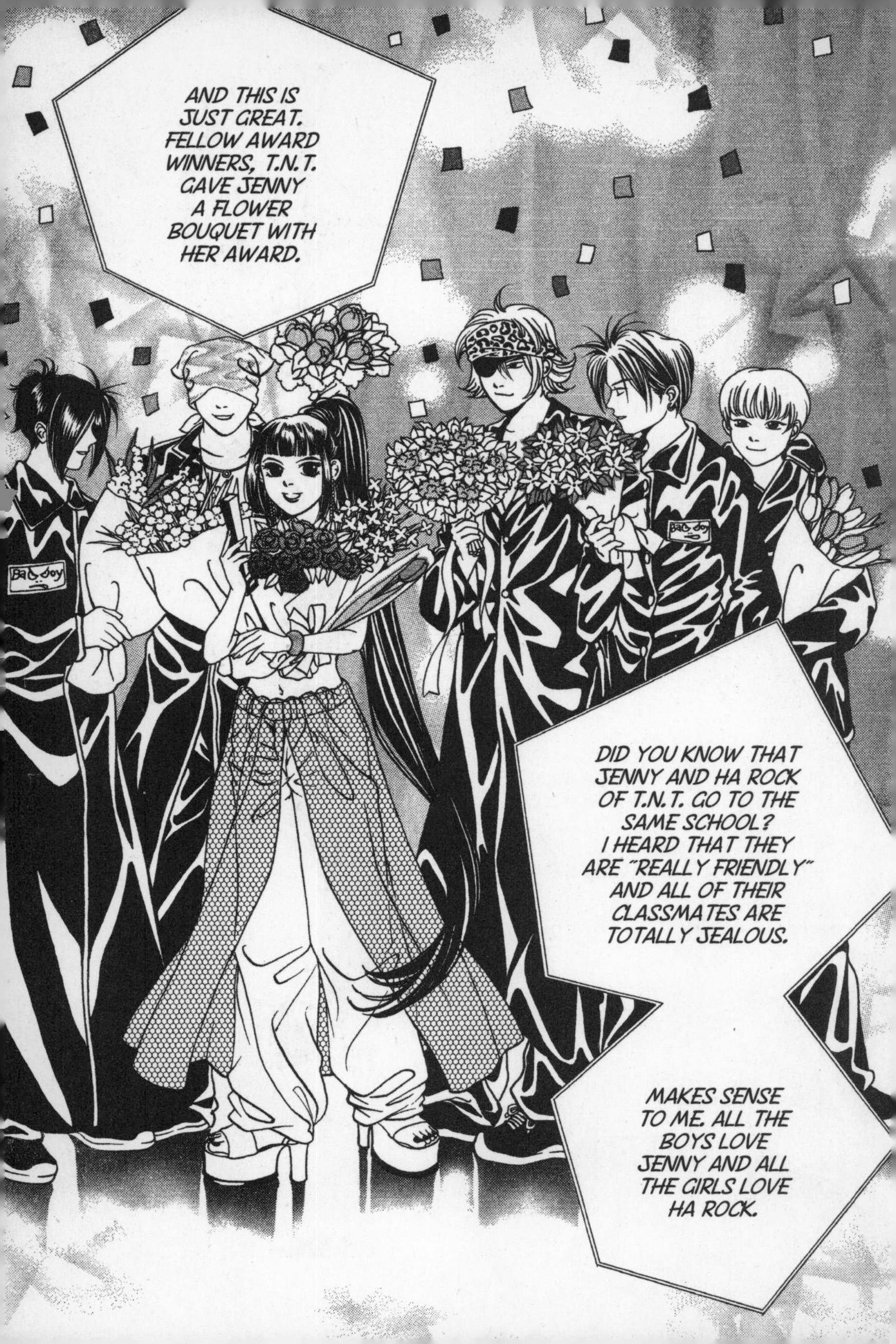
AND THIS IS JUST GREAT. FELLOW AWARD WINNERS, T.N.T. GAVE JENNY A FLOWER BOUQUET WITH HER AWARD.
DID YOU KNOW THAT JENNY AND HA ROCK OF T.N.T. GO TO THE SAME SCHOOL? I HEARD THAT THEY ARE "REALLY FRIENDLY" AND ALL OF THEIR CLASSMATES ARE TOTALLY JEALOUS.
MAKES SENSE TO ME. ALL THE BOYS LOVE JENNY AND ALL THE GIRLS LOVE HA ROCK.

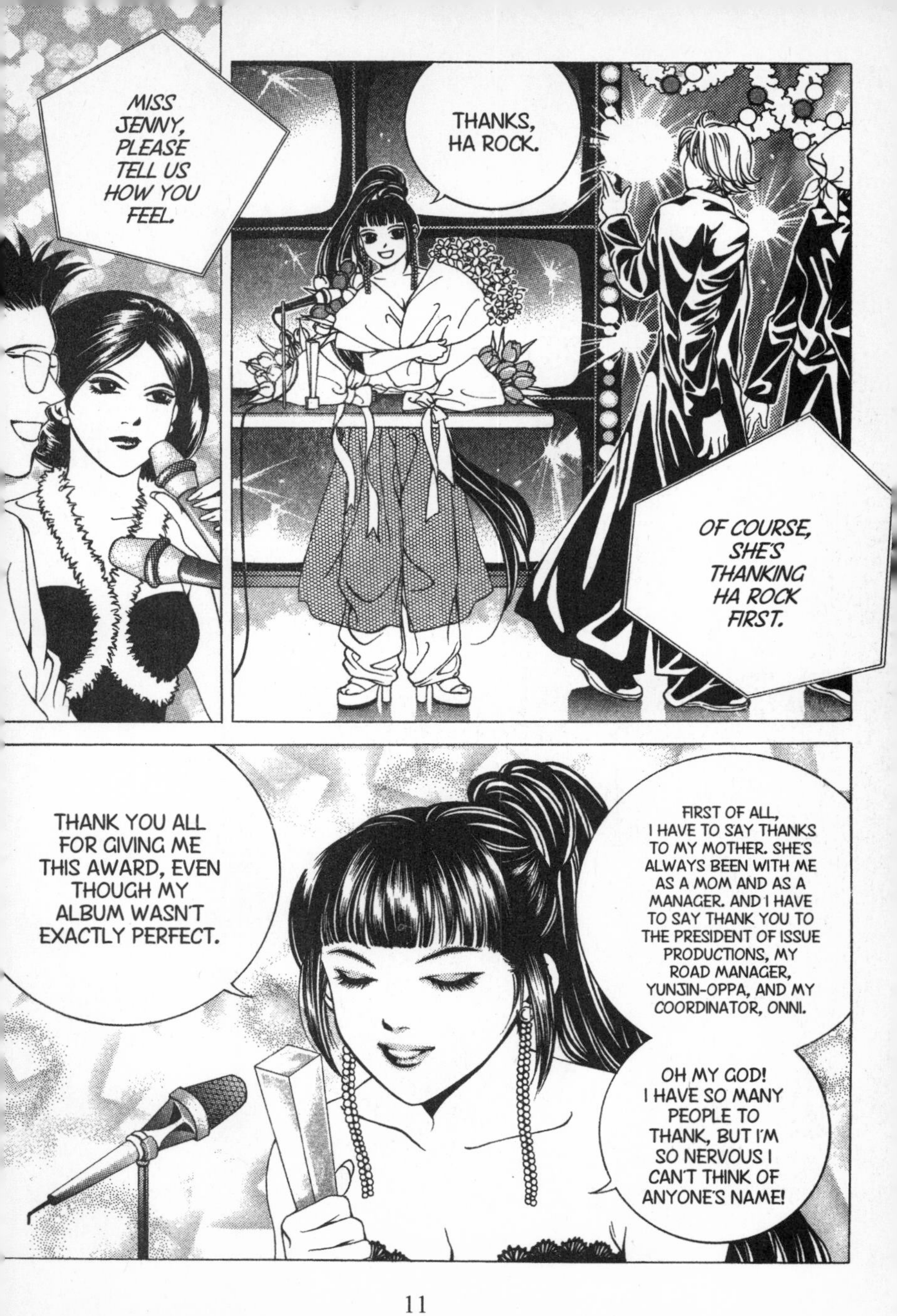
MISS JENNY, PLEASE TELL US HOW YOU FEEL.
THANKS, HA ROCK.
OF COURSE, SHE'S THANKING HA ROCK FIRST.
THANK YOU ALL FOR GIVING ME THIS AWARD, EVEN THOUGH MY ALBUM WASN'T EXACTLY PERFECT.
FIRST OF ALL, I HAVE TO SAY THANKS TO MY MOTHER. SHE'S ALWAYS BEEN WITH ME AS A MOM AND AS A MANAGER. AND I HAVE TO SAY THANK YOU TO THE PRESIDENT OF ISSUE PRODUCTIONS, MY ROAD MANAGER, YUNJIN-OPPA, AND MY COORDINATOR, ONNI.
OH MY GOD! I HAVE SO MANY PEOPLE TO THANK, BUT I'M SO NERVOUS I CAN'T THINK OF ANYONE'S NAME!

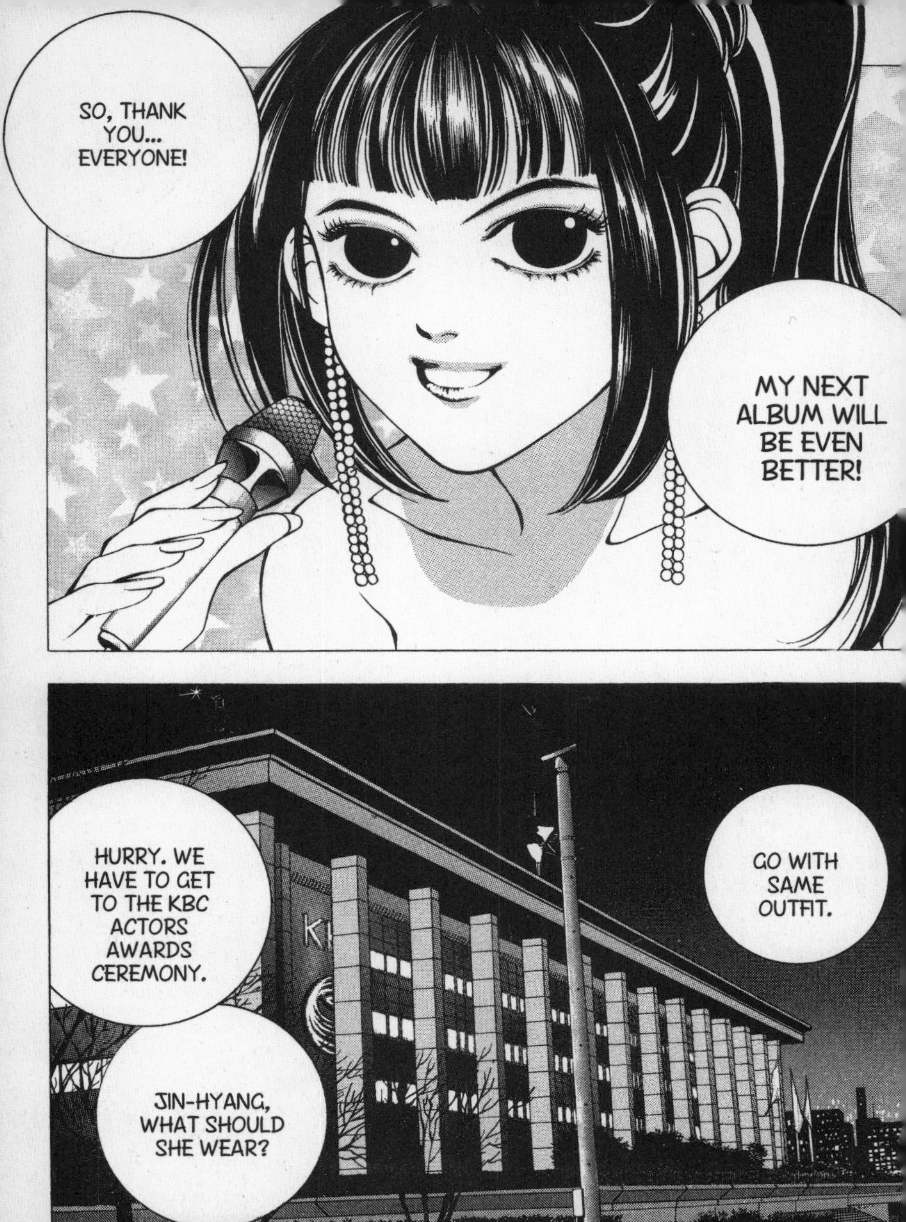

SO, THANK YOU... EVERYONE!
MY NEXT ALBUM WILL BE EVEN BETTER!
HURRY. WE HAVE TO GET TO THE KBC ACTORS AWARDS CEREMONY.
JIN-HYANG, WHAT SHOULD SHE WEAR?
GO WITH SAME OUTFIT.

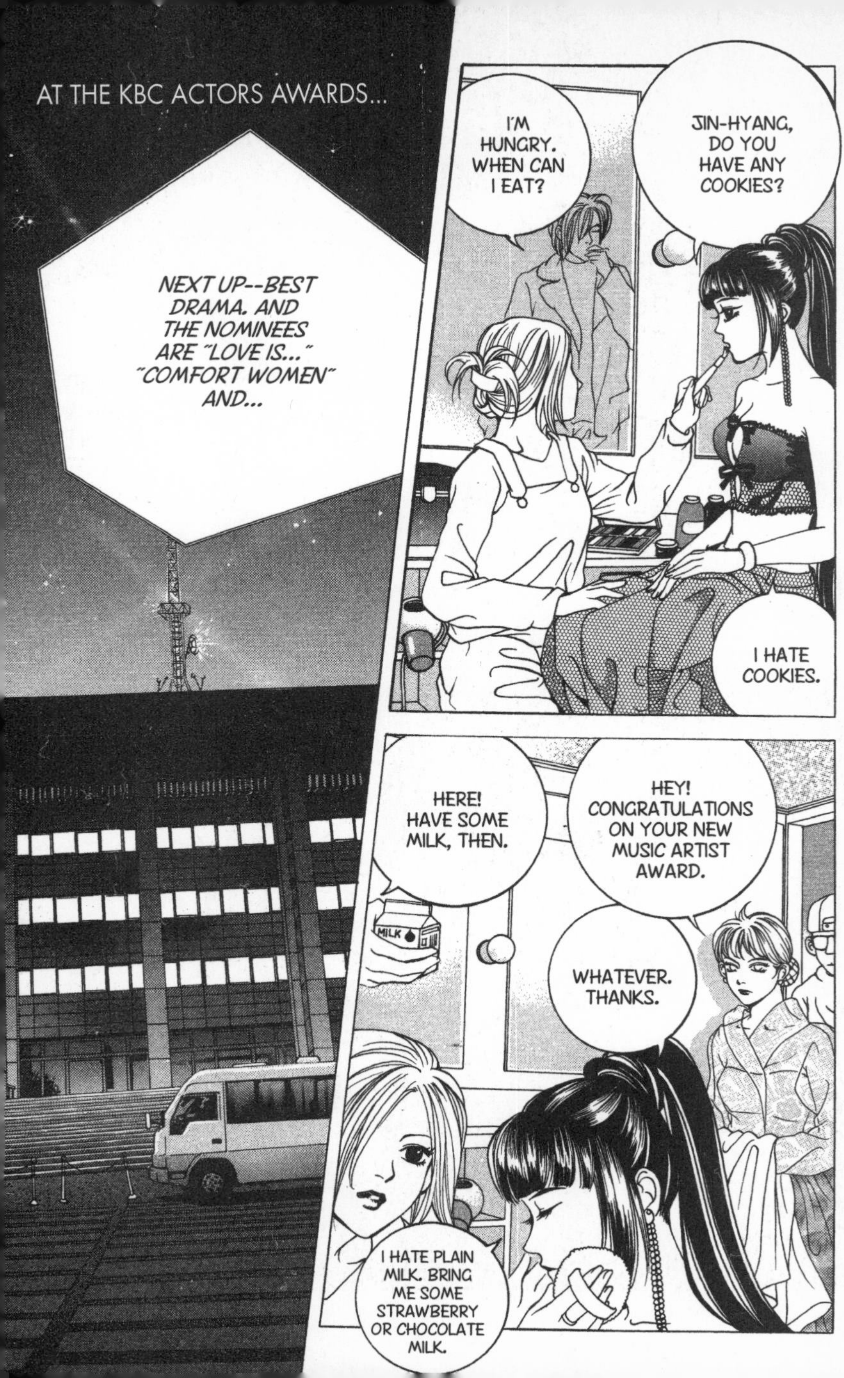
AT THE KBC ACTORS AWARDS...
NEXT UP--BEST DRAMA. AND THE NOMINEES ARE "LOVE IS..." "COMFORT WOMEN" AND...
I'M HUNGRY. WHEN CAN I EAT?
JIN-HYANG, DO YOU HAVE ANY COOKIES?
I HATE COOKIES.
HERE! HAVE SOME MILK, THEN.
MILK
HEY! CONGRATULATIONS ON YOUR NEW MUSIC ARTIST AWARD.
WHATEVER. THANKS.
I HATE PLAIN MILK. BRING ME SOME STRAWBERRY OR CHOCOLATE MILK.

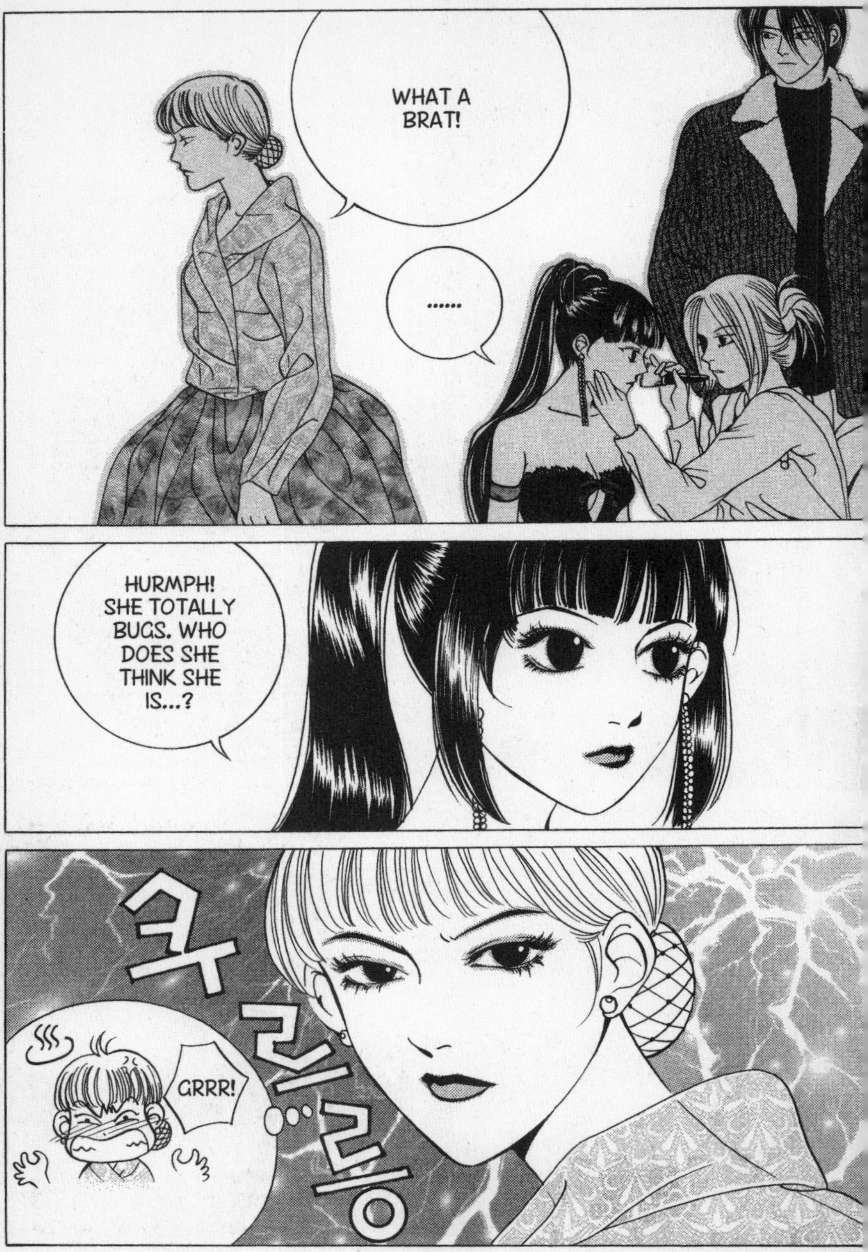
WHAT A BRAT!
......
HURMPH! SHE TOTALLY BUGS. WHO DOES SHE THINK SHE IS...?
GRRR!

MR. YUNJIN, DOES SHE SPEAK TO EVERYONE THAT WAY?

YEAH...

APOLOGIZE TO HER!

I STARTED MY ACTING CAREER WHEN I WAS HER AGE, BUT I WASN'T A MONSTER LIKE THAT.

I'M SORRY. SHE REALLY NEEDS TO GROW UP...

BLEAHHH.

JENNY, PLEASE WATCH YOUR MOUTH. YOU'RE MAKING THINGS VERY DIFFICULT.

YOU KNOW WHO MISS JIHAE IS. WHY WERE YOU SO BITCHY TO HER?

LIKE I CARE.

HOW OLD IS SHE, ANYWAY? ISN'T SHE ALMOST 30?

SHE'S OVER 30.

15

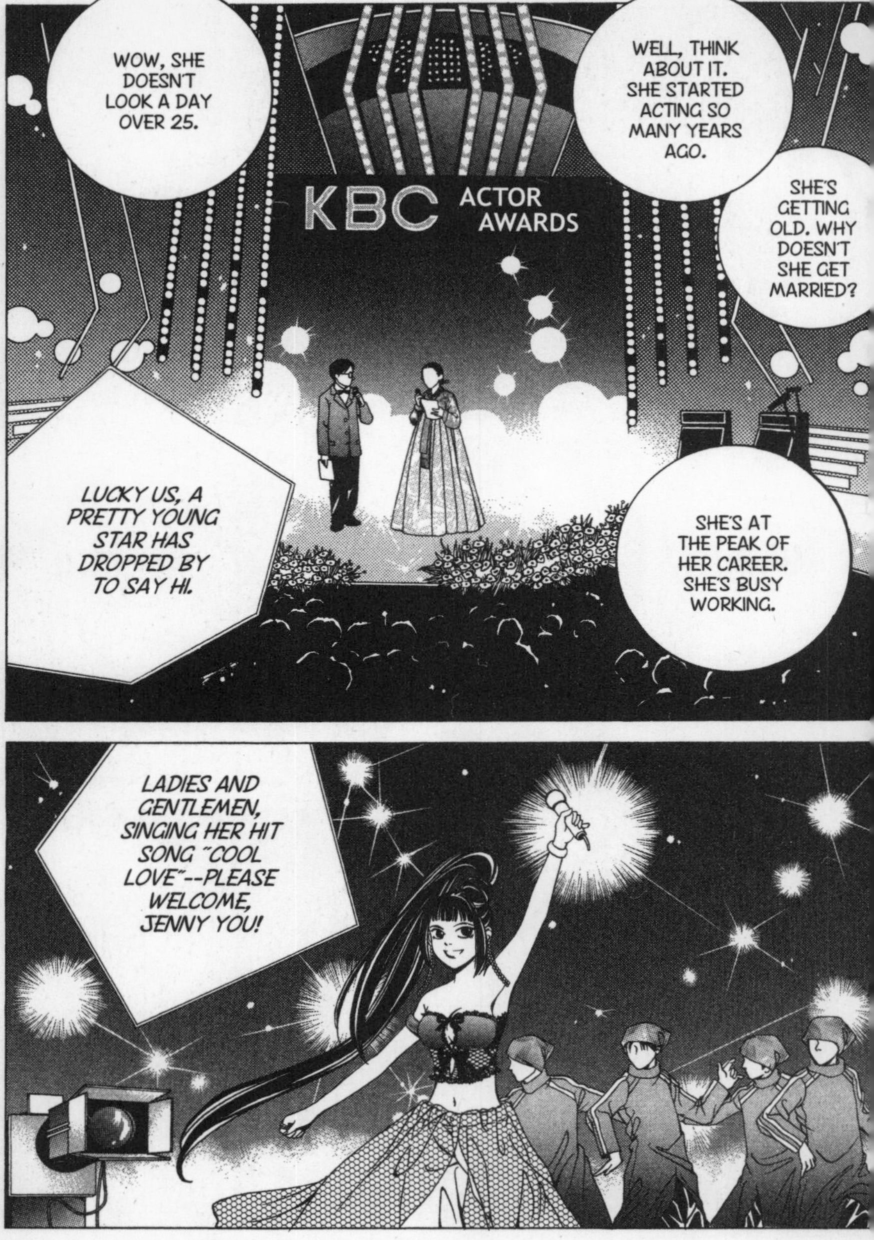
WOW, SHE DOESN'T LOOK A DAY OVER 25.
KBC ACTOR AWARDS
WELL, THINK ABOUT IT. SHE STARTED ACTING SO MANY YEARS AGO.
SHE'S GETTING OLD. WHY DOESN'T SHE GET MARRIED?
LUCKY US, A PRETTY YOUNG STAR HAS DROPPED BY TO SAY HI.
SHE'S AT THE PEAK OF HER CAREER. SHE'S BUSY WORKING.
LADIES AND GENTLEMEN, SINGING HER HIT SONG "COOL LOVE"--PLEASE WELCOME, JENNY YOU!

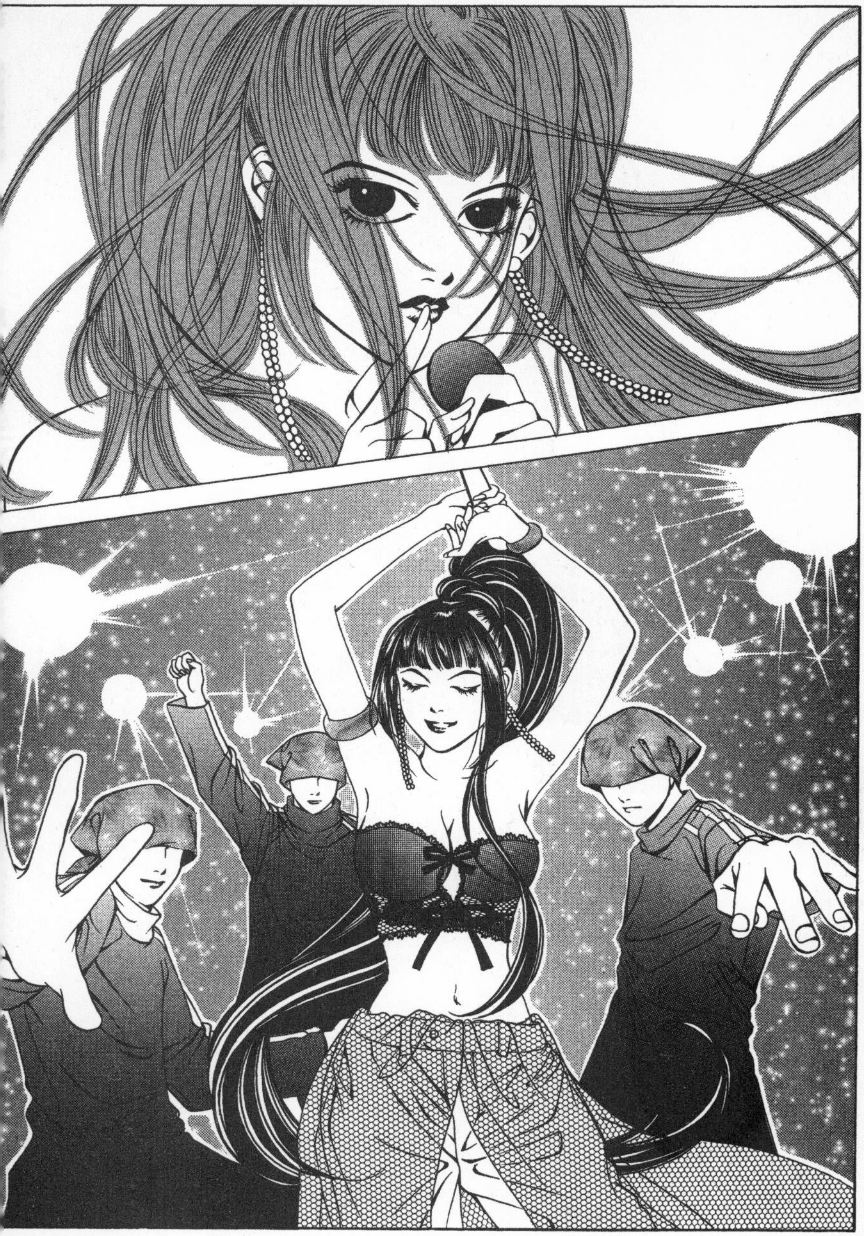

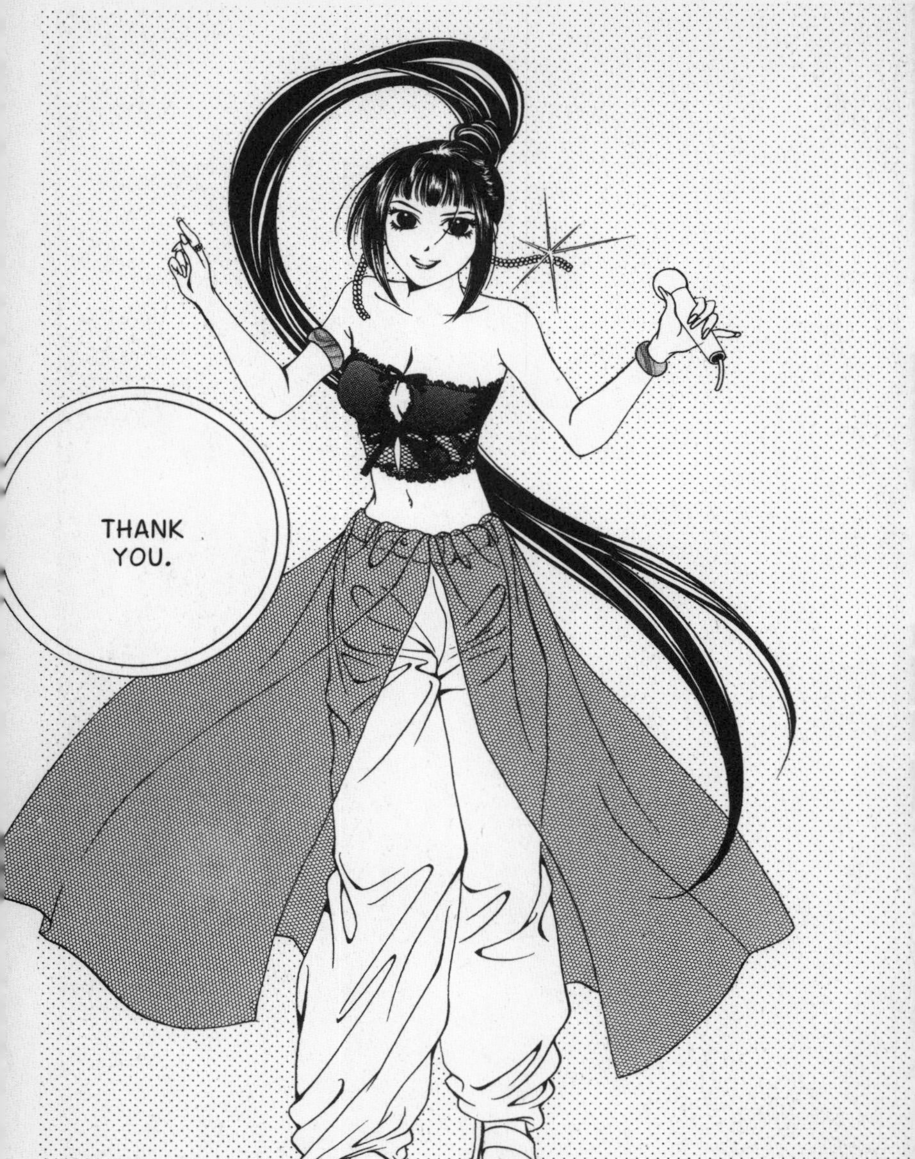
THANK YOU.

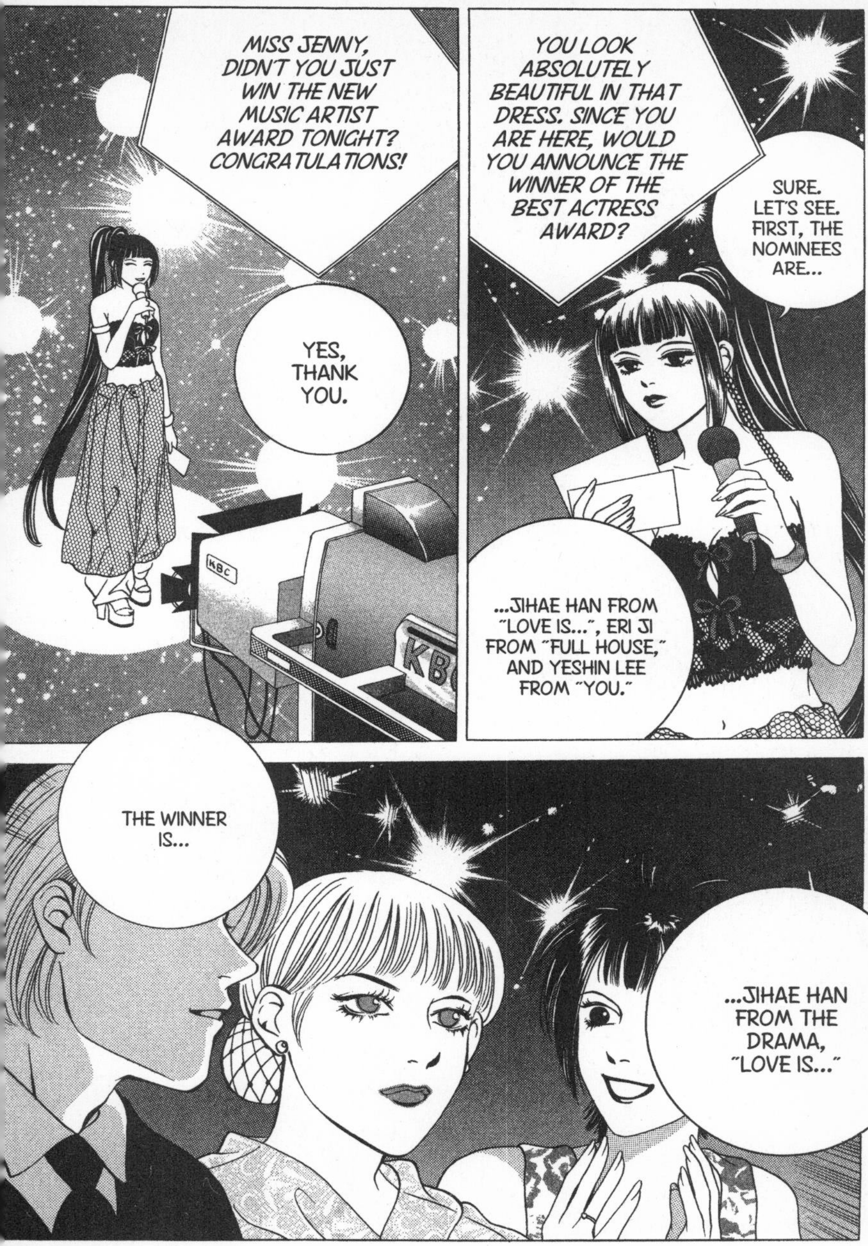
MISS JENNY, DIDN'T YOU JUST WIN THE NEW MUSIC ARTIST AWARD TONIGHT? CONGRATULATIONS!
YES, THANK YOU.
YOU LOOK ABSOLUTELY BEAUTIFUL IN THAT DRESS. SINCE YOU ARE HERE, WOULD YOU ANNOUNCE THE WINNER OF THE BEST ACTRESS AWARD?
SURE. LET'S SEE. FIRST, THE NOMINEES ARE...
...JIHAE HAN FROM "LOVE IS...", ERI JI FROM "FULL HOUSE," AND YESHIN LEE FROM "YOU."
THE WINNER IS...
...JIHAE HAN FROM THE DRAMA, "LOVE IS..."

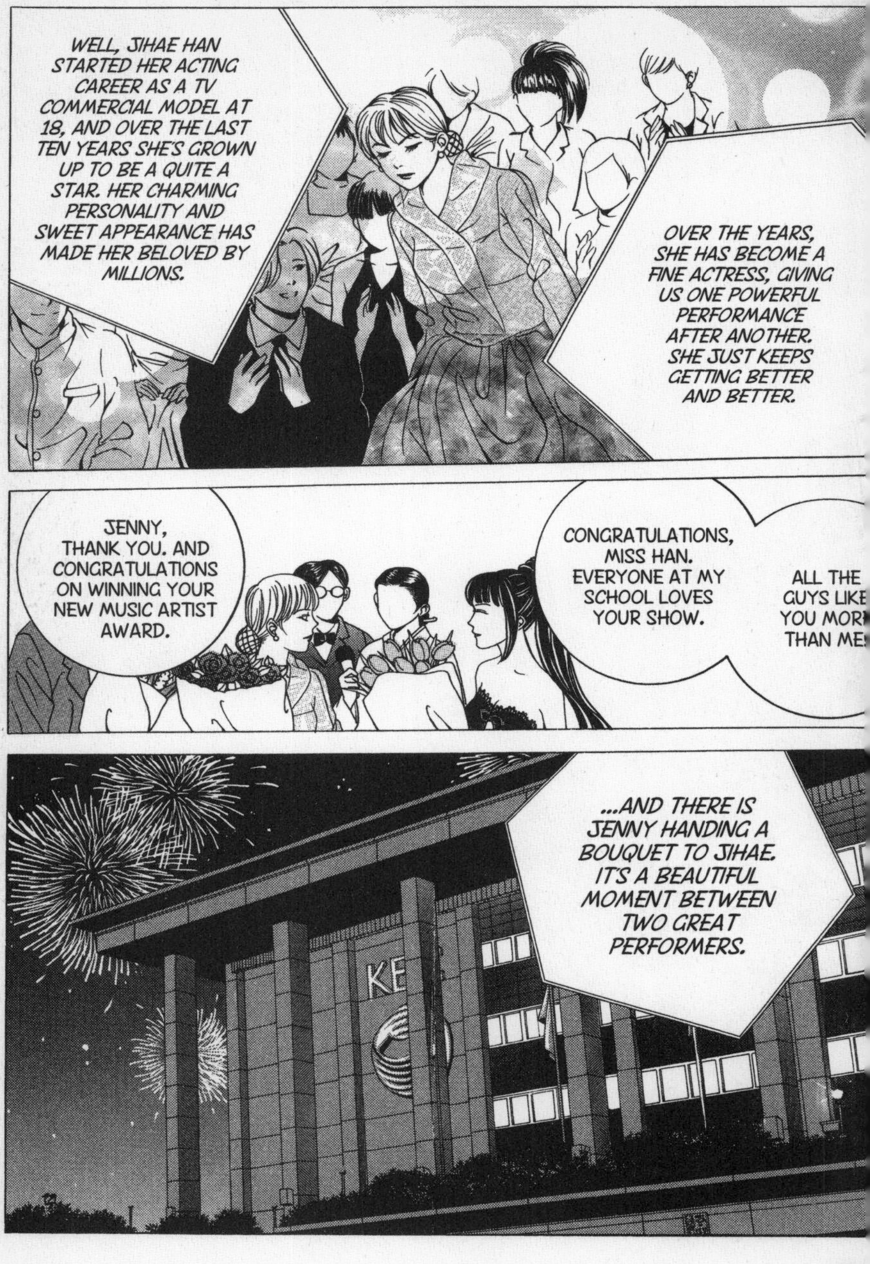
WELL, JIHAE HAN STARTED HER ACTING CAREER AS A TV COMMERCIAL MODEL AT 18, AND OVER THE LAST TEN YEARS SHE'S GROWN UP TO BE A QUITE A STAR. HER CHARMING PERSONALITY AND SWEET APPEARANCE HAS MADE HER BELOVED BY MILLIONS.
OVER THE YEARS, SHE HAS BECOME A FINE ACTRESS, GIVING US ONE POWERFUL PERFORMANCE AFTER ANOTHER. SHE JUST KEEPS GETTING BETTER AND BETTER.
JENNY, THANK YOU. AND CONGRATULATIONS ON WINNING YOUR NEW MUSIC ARTIST AWARD.
CONGRATULATIONS, MISS HAN. EVERYONE AT MY SCHOOL LOVES YOUR SHOW.
ALL THE GUYS LIKE YOU MOR THAN ME
...AND THERE IS JENNY HANDING A BOUQUET TO JIHAE. IT'S A BEAUTIFUL MOMENT BETWEEN TWO GREAT PERFORMERS.
KE

SECTION 1
A SNAIL AND AN ACORN

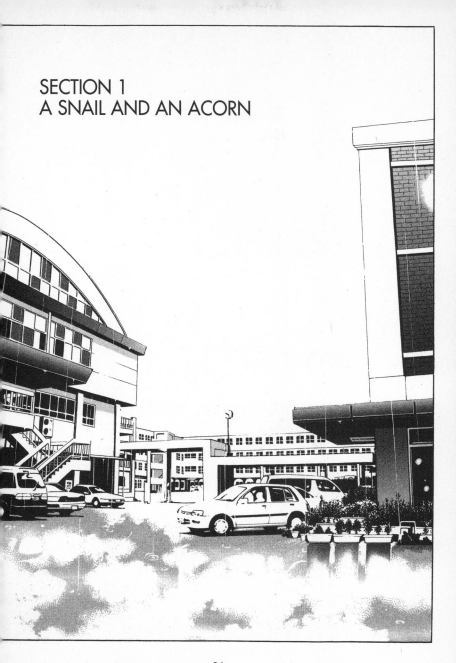

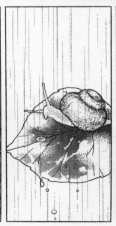

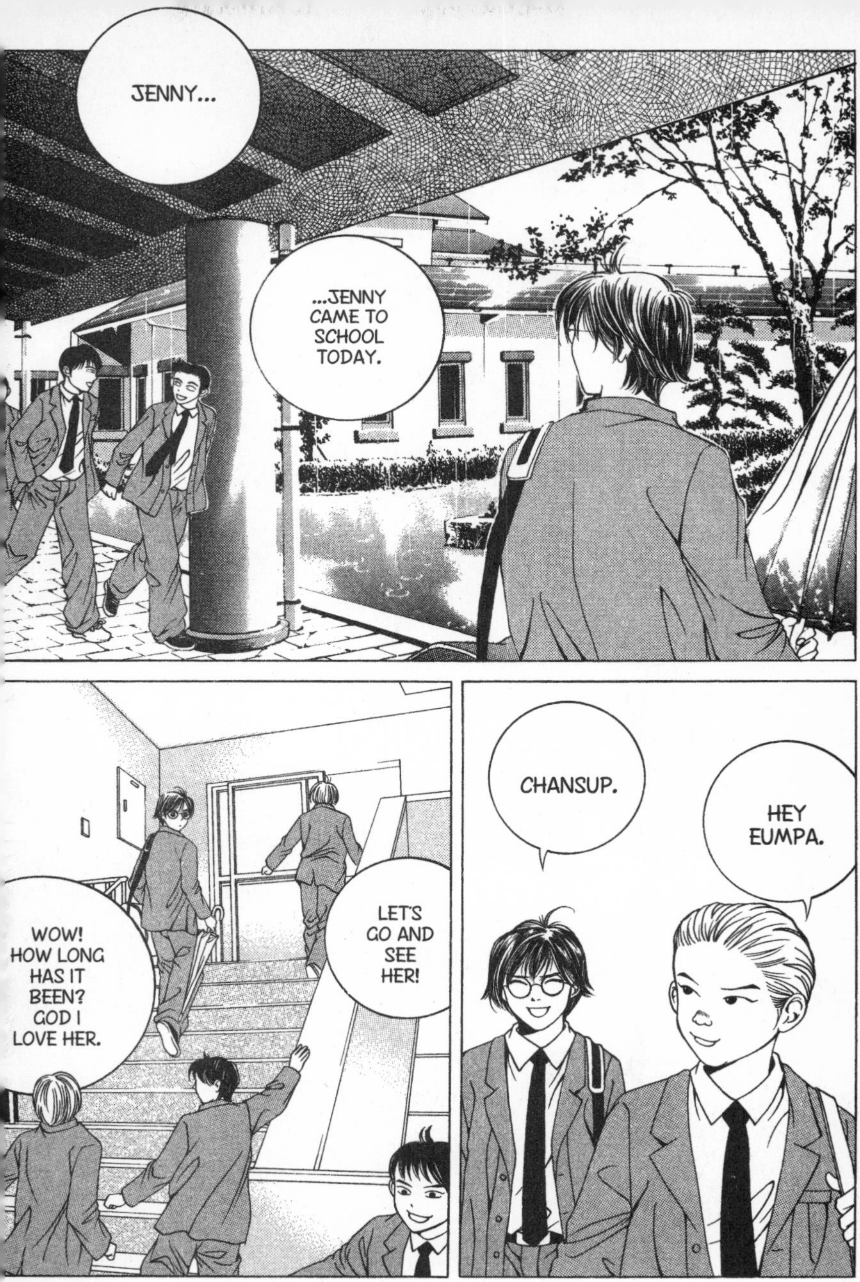
JENNY...
...JENNY CAME TO SCHOOL TODAY.
WOW! HOW LONG HAS IT BEEN? GOD I LOVE HER.
LET'S GO AND SEE HER!
CHANSUP.
HEY EUMPA.

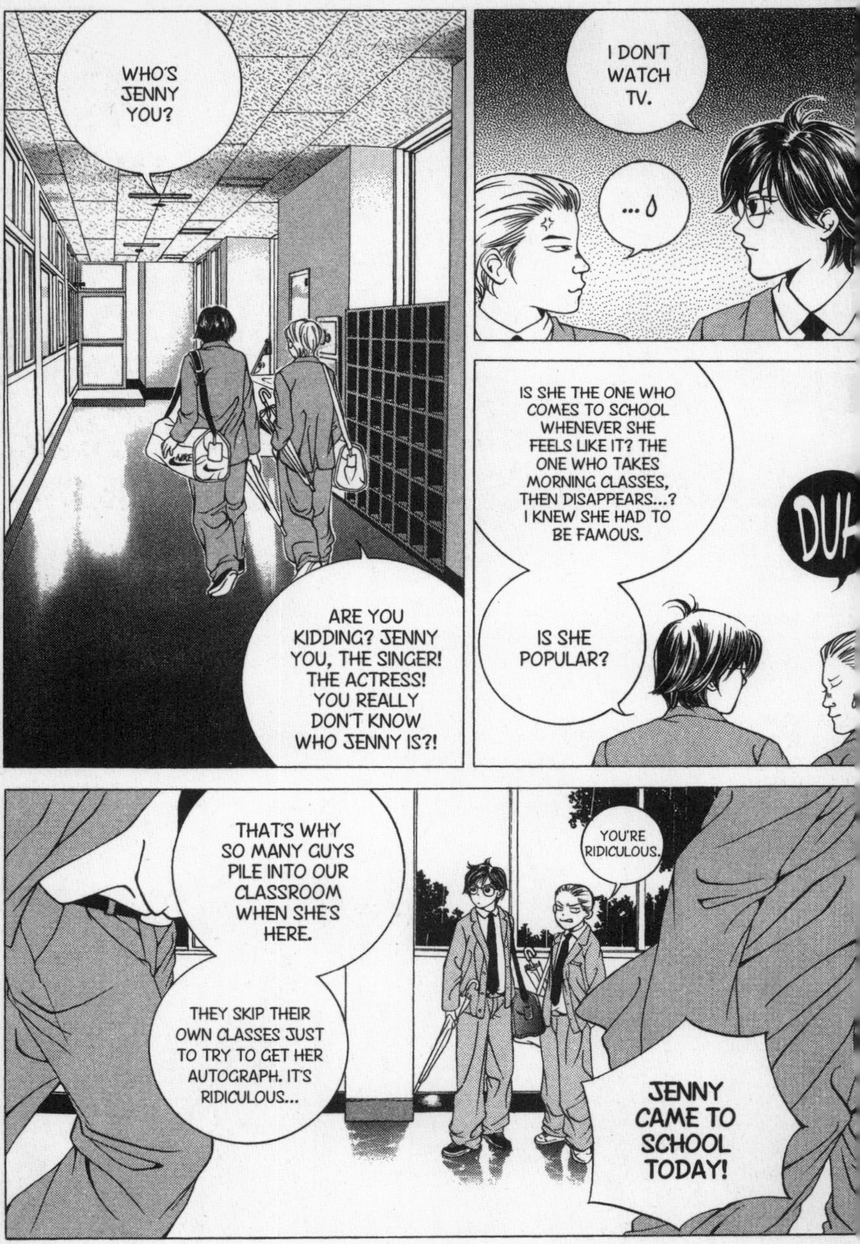
WHO'S JENNY YOU?
ARE YOU KIDDING? JENNY YOU, THE SINGER! THE ACTRESS! YOU REALLY DON'T KNOW WHO JENNY IS?!
I DON'T WATCH TV.
...
IS SHE THE ONE WHO COMES TO SCHOOL WHENEVER SHE FEELS LIKE IT? THE ONE WHO TAKES MORNING CLASSES, THEN DISAPPEARS...? I KNEW SHE HAD TO BE FAMOUS.
IS SHE POPULAR?
THAT'S WHY SO MANY GUYS PILE INTO OUR CLASSROOM WHEN SHE'S HERE.
THEY SKIP THEIR OWN CLASSES JUST TO TRY TO GET HER AUTOGRAPH. IT'S RIDICULOUS...
YOU'RE RIDICULOUS.
JENNY CAME TO SCHOOL TODAY!

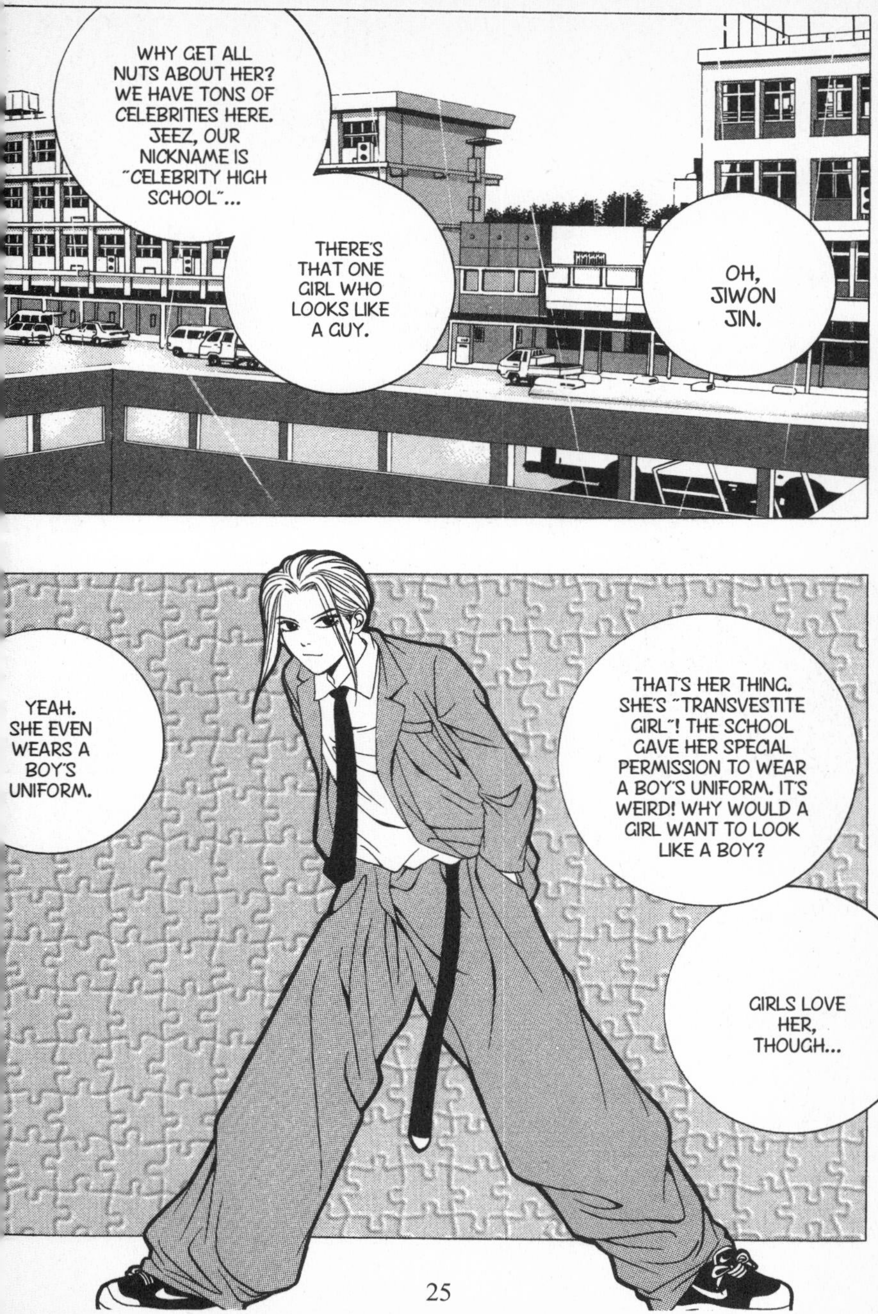
WHY GET ALL NUTS ABOUT HER? WE HAVE TONS OF CELEBRITIES HERE. JEEZ, OUR NICKNAME IS "CELEBRITY HIGH SCHOOL"...
THERE'S THAT ONE GIRL WHO LOOKS LIKE A GUY.
OH, JIWON JIN.
YEAH. SHE EVEN WEARS A BOY'S UNIFORM.
THAT'S HER THING. SHE'S "TRANSVESTITE GIRL"! THE SCHOOL GAVE HER SPECIAL PERMISSION TO WEAR A BOY'S UNIFORM. IT'S WEIRD! WHY WOULD A GIRL WANT TO LOOK LIKE A BOY?
GIRLS LOVE HER, THOUGH...

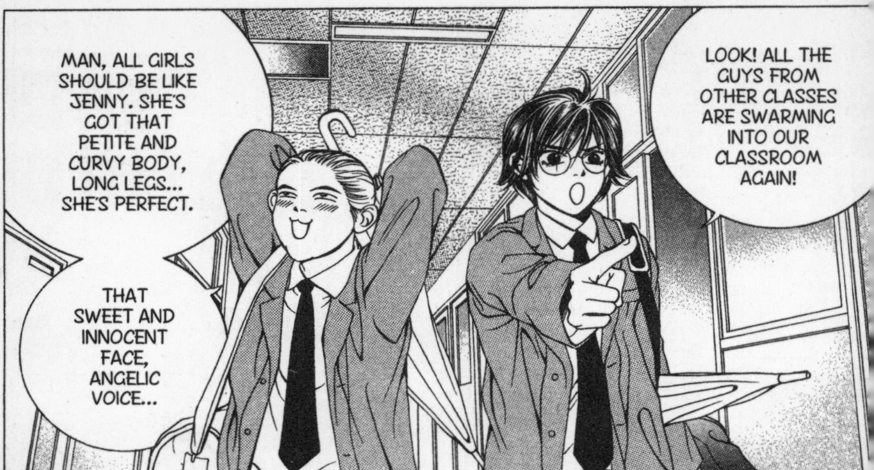
MAN, ALL GIRLS SHOULD BE LIKE JENNY. SHE'S GOT THAT PETITE AND CURVY BODY, LONG LEGS... SHE'S PERFECT.
THAT SWEET AND INNOCENT FACE, ANGELIC VOICE...
LOOK! ALL THE GUYS FROM OTHER CLASSES ARE SWARMING INTO OUR CLASSROOM AGAIN!

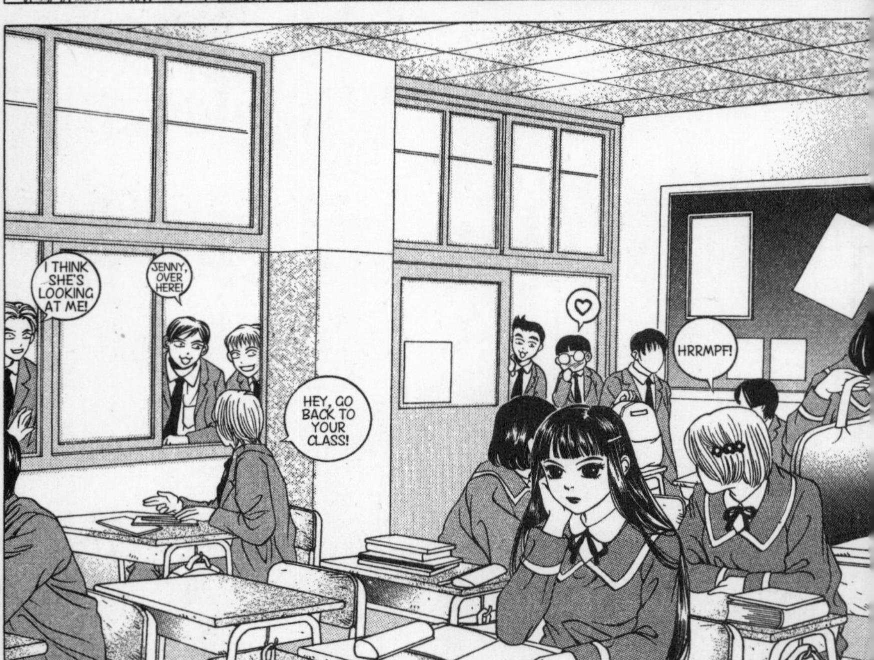
I THINK SHE'S LOOKING AT ME!
JENNY, OVER HERE!
HEY, GO BACK TO YOUR CLASS!
♡
HRRMPF!

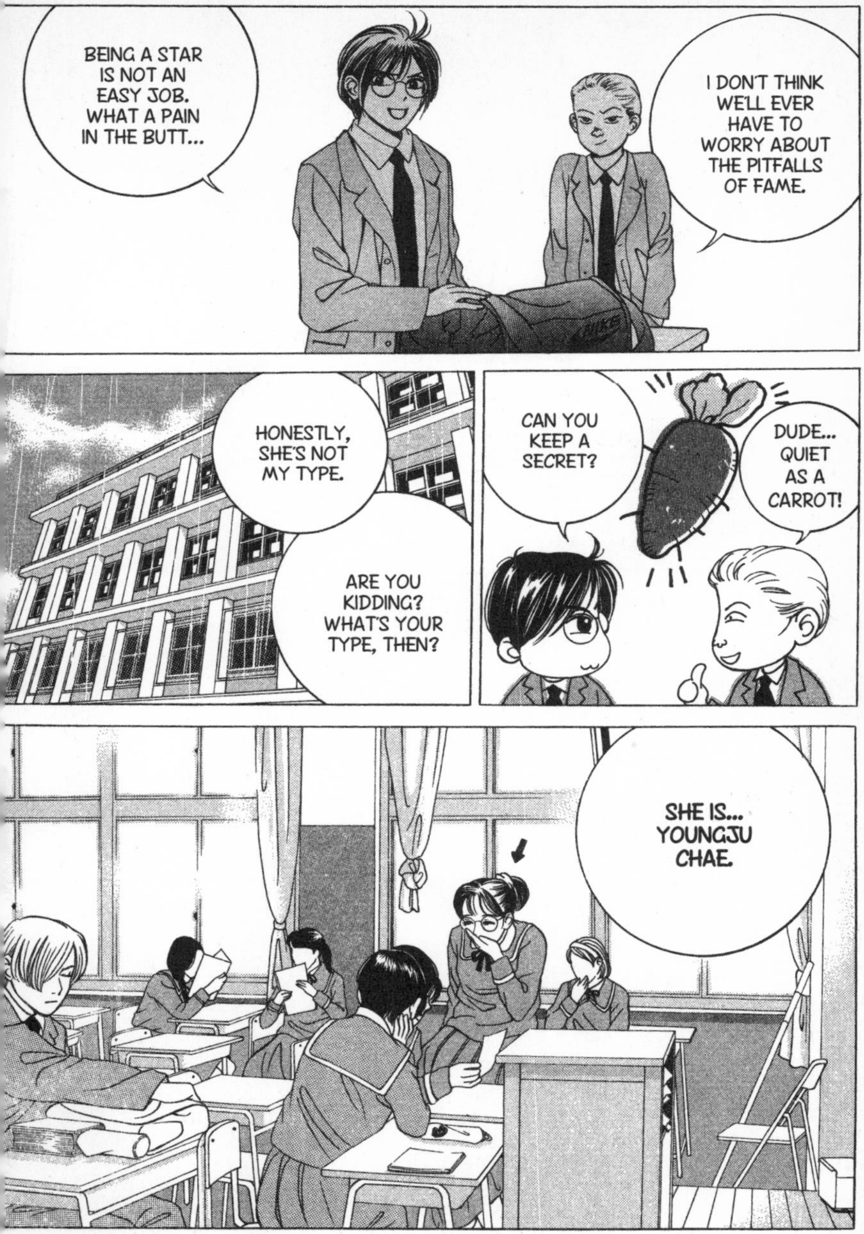
BEING A STAR IS NOT AN EASY JOB. WHAT A PAIN IN THE BUTT...
I DON'T THINK WE'LL EVER HAVE TO WORRY ABOUT THE PITFALLS OF FAME.
HONESTLY, SHE'S NOT MY TYPE.
ARE YOU KIDDING? WHAT'S YOUR TYPE, THEN?
CAN YOU KEEP A SECRET?
DUDE... QUIET AS A CARROT!
SHE IS... YOUNGJU CHAE.

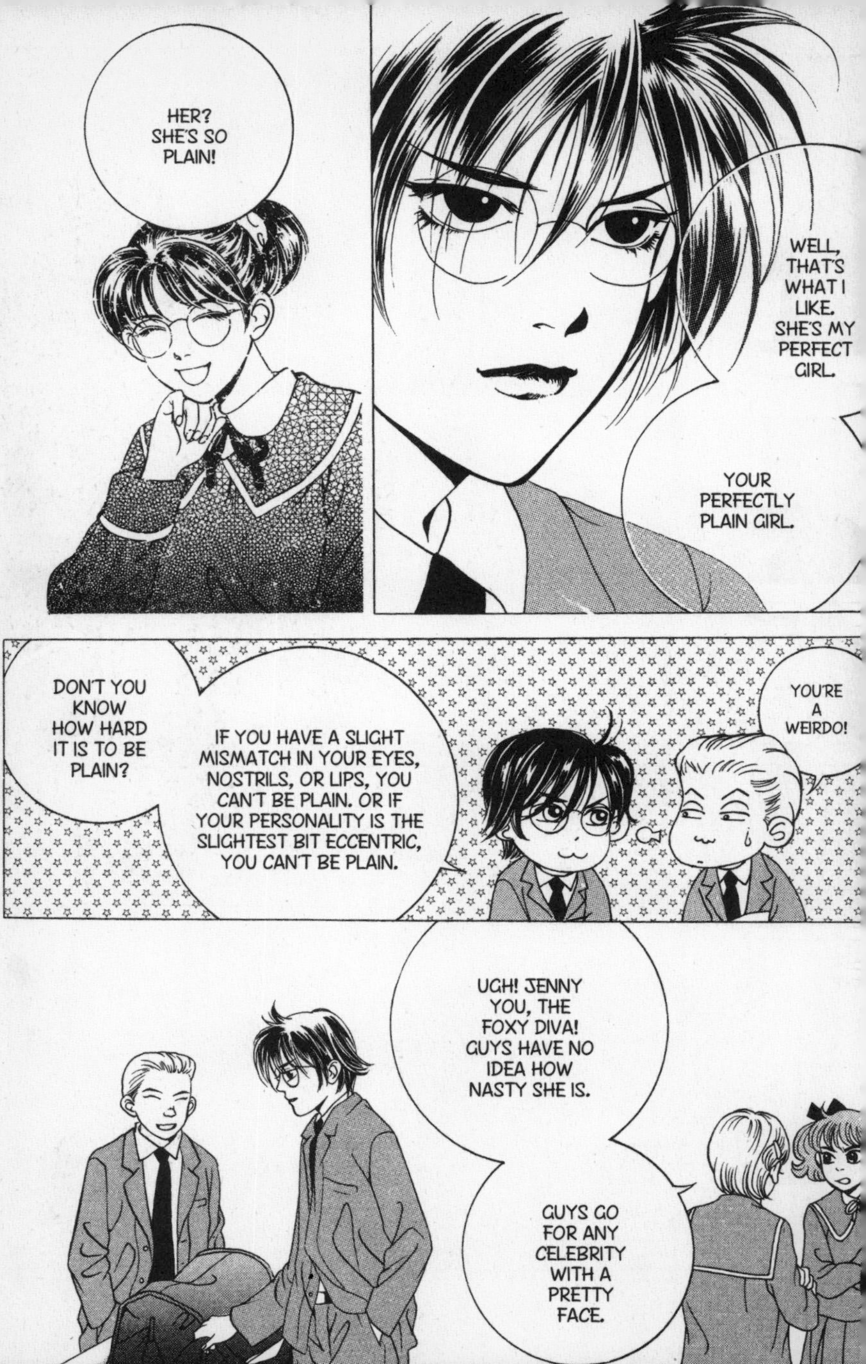
HER? SHE'S SO PLAIN!
WELL, THAT'S WHAT I LIKE. SHE'S MY PERFECT GIRL.
YOUR PERFECTLY PLAIN GIRL.
DON'T YOU KNOW HOW HARD IT IS TO BE PLAIN?
IF YOU HAVE A SLIGHT MISMATCH IN YOUR EYES, NOSTRILS, OR LIPS, YOU CAN'T BE PLAIN. OR IF YOUR PERSONALITY IS THE SLIGHTEST BIT ECCENTRIC, YOU CAN'T BE PLAIN.
YOU'RE A WEIRDO!
UGH! JENNY YOU, THE FOXY DIVA! GUYS HAVE NO IDEA HOW NASTY SHE IS.
GUYS GO FOR ANY CELEBRITY WITH A PRETTY FACE.

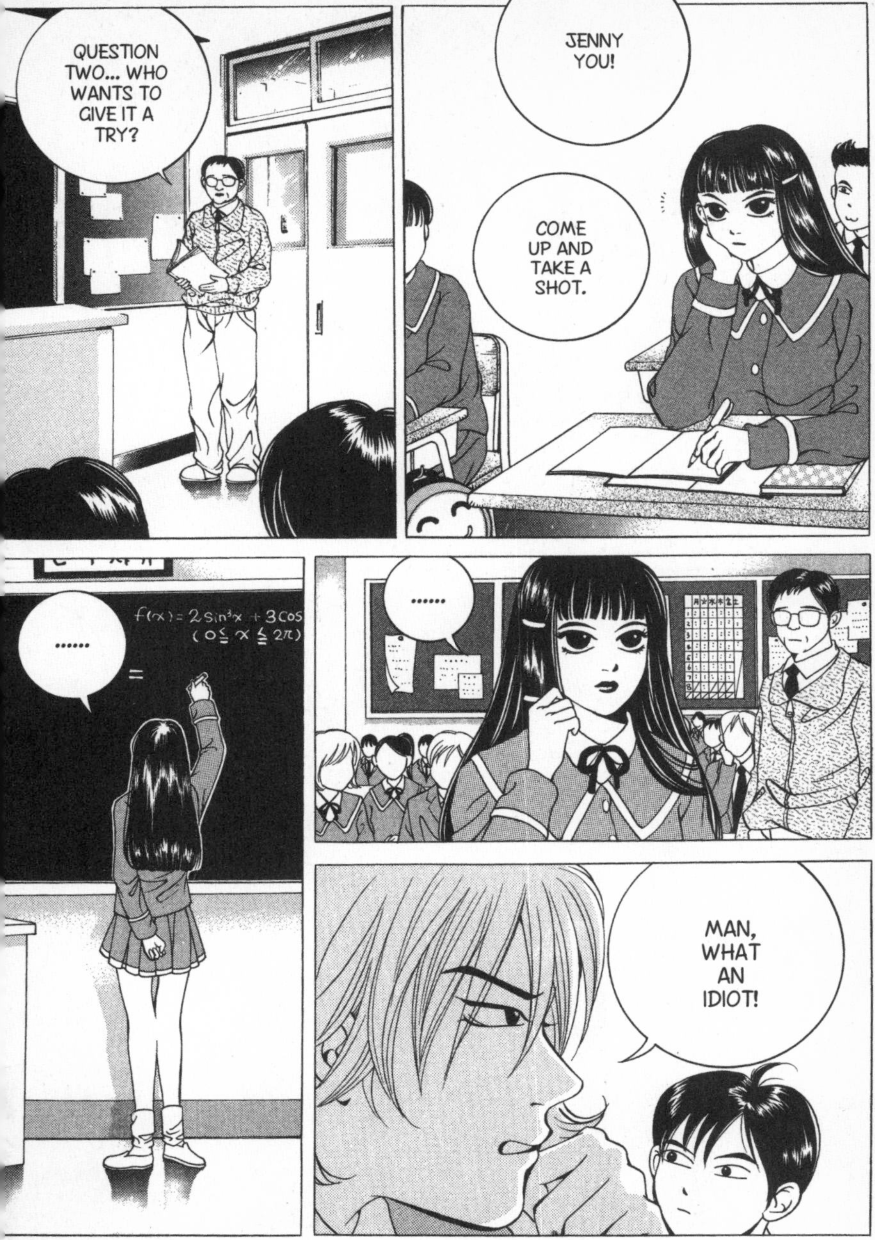
QUESTION TWO... WHO WANTS TO GIVE IT A TRY?
JENNY YOU!
COME UP AND TAKE A SHOT.
......
f(x) = 2sin³x + 3cos
(0 ≦ x ≦ 2π)
=
......
MAN, WHAT AN IDIOT!

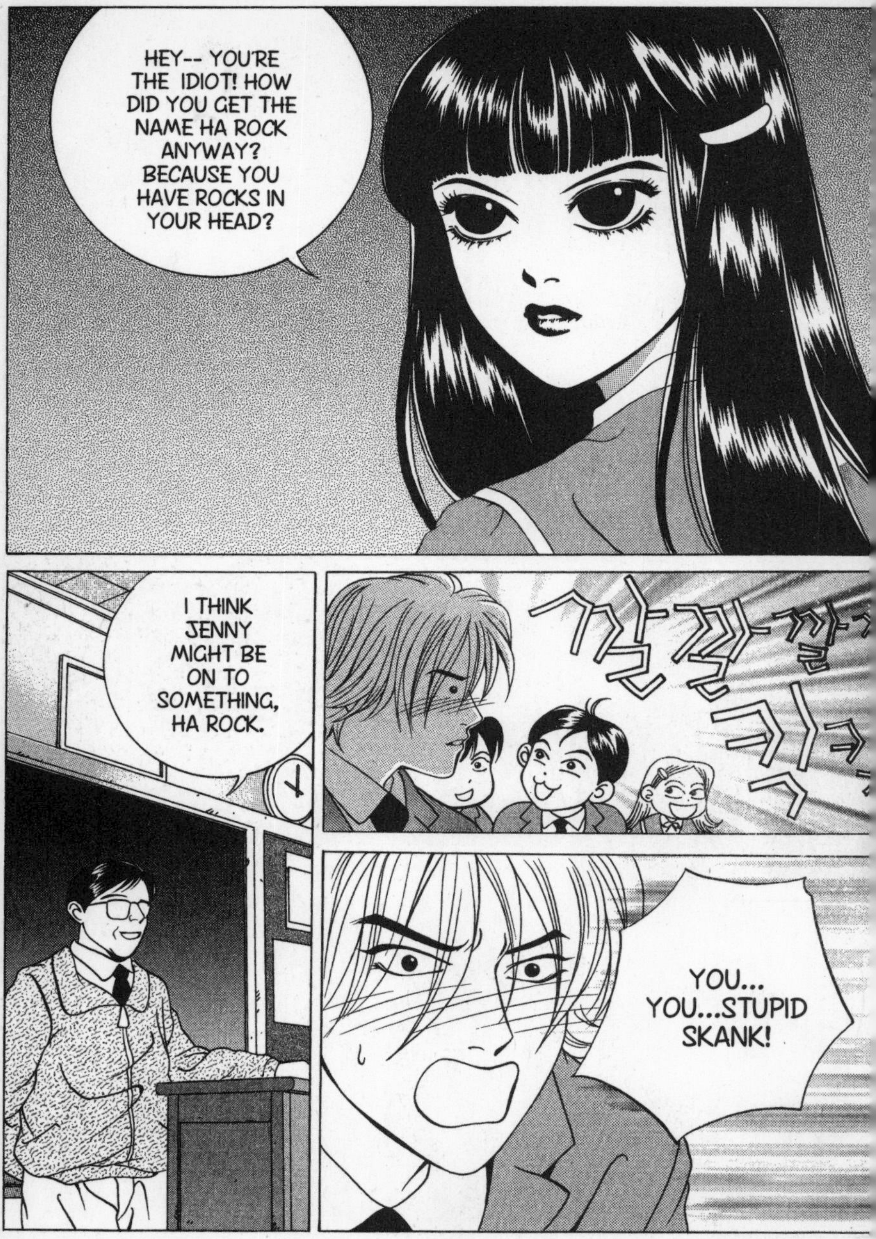
HEY-- YOU'RE THE IDIOT! HOW DID YOU GET THE NAME HA ROCK ANYWAY? BECAUSE YOU HAVE ROCKS IN YOUR HEAD?
I THINK JENNY MIGHT BE ON TO SOMETHING, HA ROCK.
YOU... YOU...STUPID SKANK!

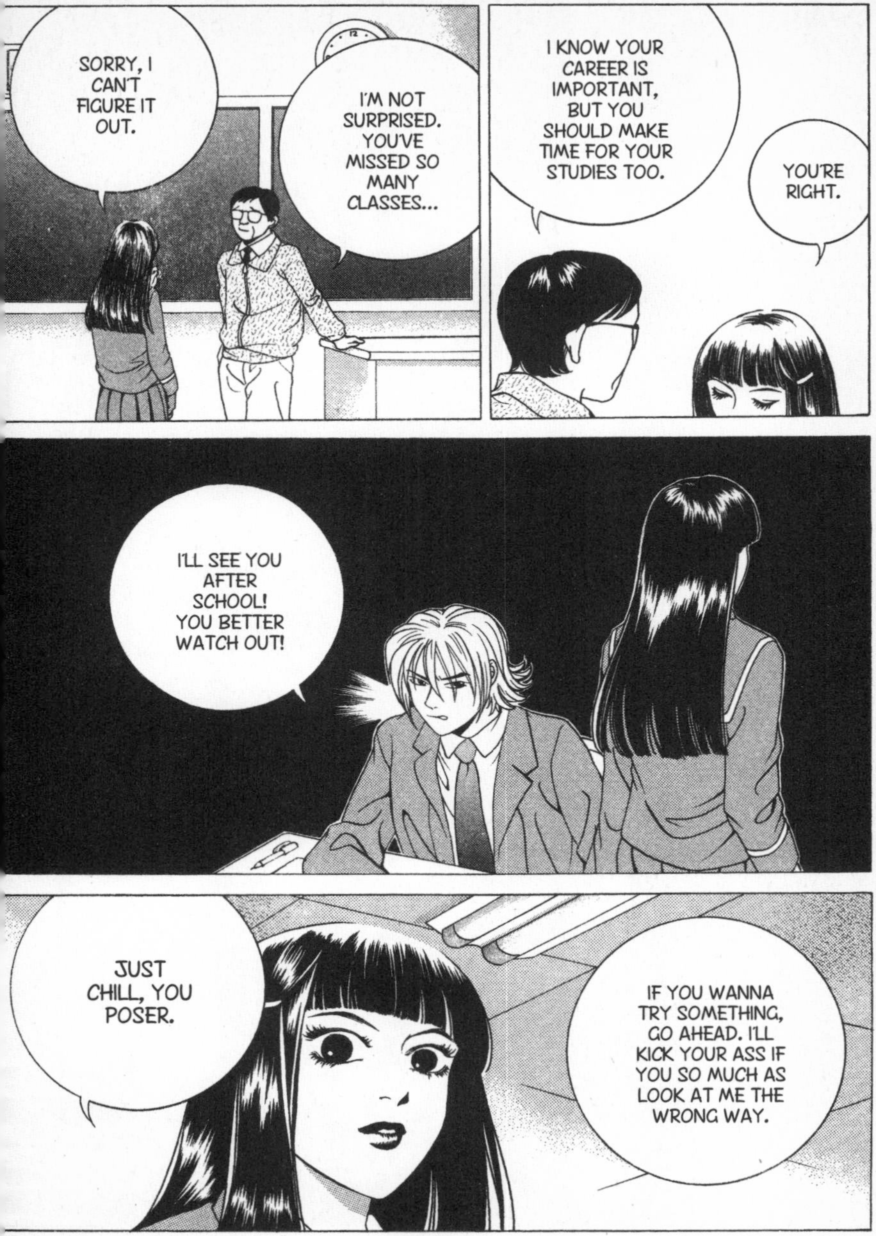
SORRY, I CAN'T FIGURE IT OUT.
I'M NOT SURPRISED. YOU'VE MISSED SO MANY CLASSES...
I KNOW YOUR CAREER IS IMPORTANT, BUT YOU SHOULD MAKE TIME FOR YOUR STUDIES TOO.
YOU'RE RIGHT.
I'LL SEE YOU AFTER SCHOOL! YOU BETTER WATCH OUT!
JUST CHILL, YOU POSER.
IF YOU WANNA TRY SOMETHING, GO AHEAD. I'LL KICK YOUR ASS IF YOU SO MUCH AS LOOK AT ME THE WRONG WAY.

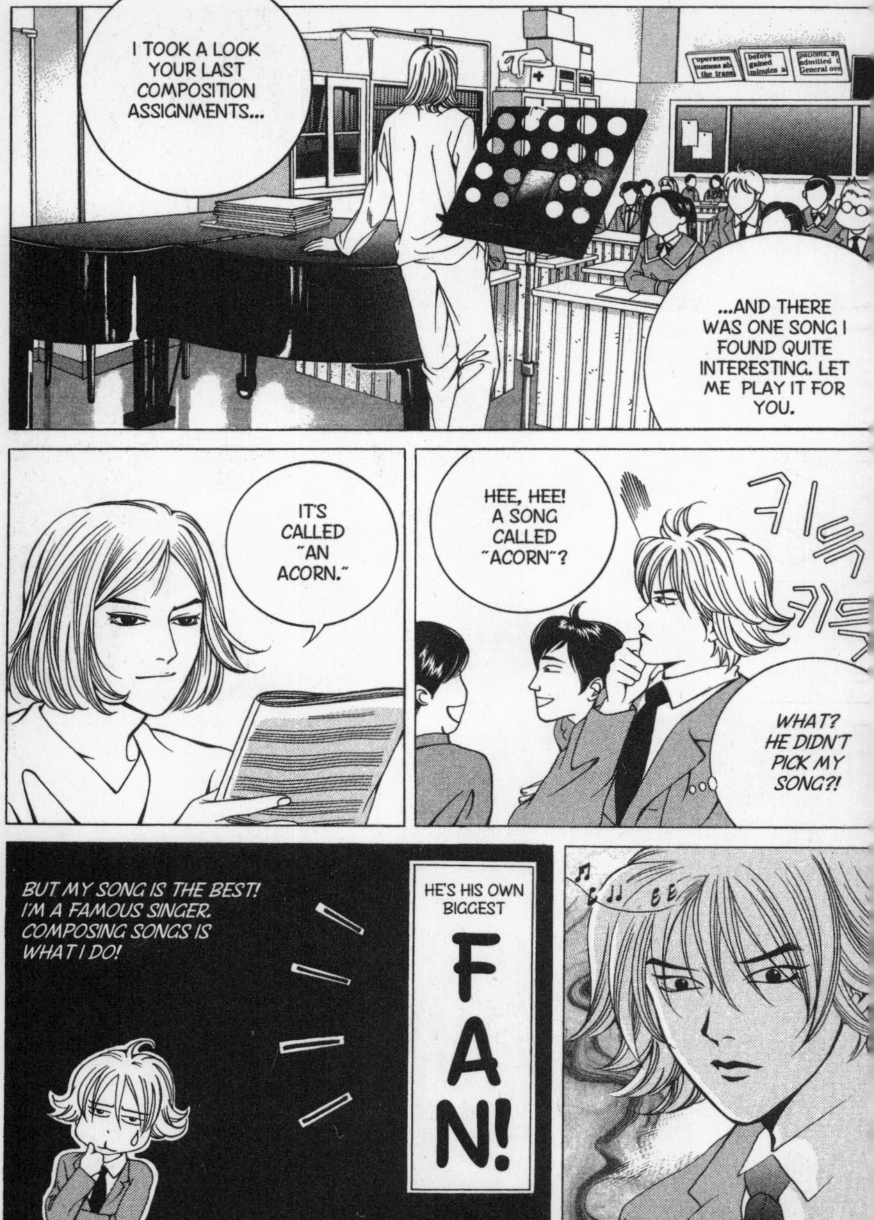
I TOOK A LOOK YOUR LAST COMPOSITION ASSIGNMENTS...
...AND THERE WAS ONE SONG I FOUND QUITE INTERESTING. LET ME PLAY IT FOR YOU.
IT'S CALLED "AN ACORN."
HEE, HEE! A SONG CALLED "ACORN"?
WHAT? HE DIDN'T PICK MY SONG?!
BUT MY SONG IS THE BEST! I'M A FAMOUS SINGER. COMPOSING SONGS IS WHAT I DO!
HE'S HIS OWN BIGGEST FAN!

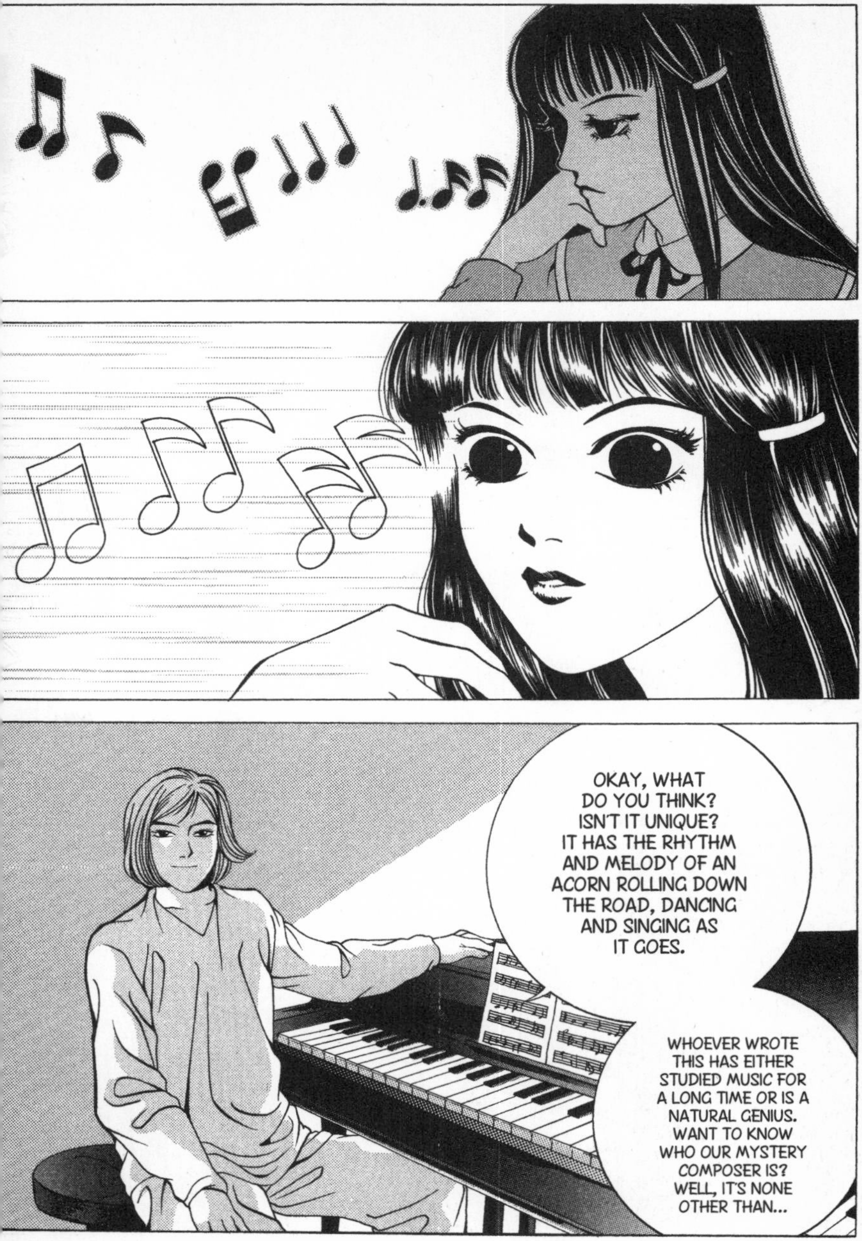
OKAY, WHAT DO YOU THINK? ISN'T IT UNIQUE? IT HAS THE RHYTHM AND MELODY OF AN ACORN ROLLING DOWN THE ROAD, DANCING AND SINGING AS IT GOES.
WHOEVER WROTE THIS HAS EITHER STUDIED MUSIC FOR A LONG TIME OR IS A NATURAL GENIUS. WANT TO KNOW WHO OUR MYSTERY COMPOSER IS? WELL, IT'S NONE OTHER THAN...

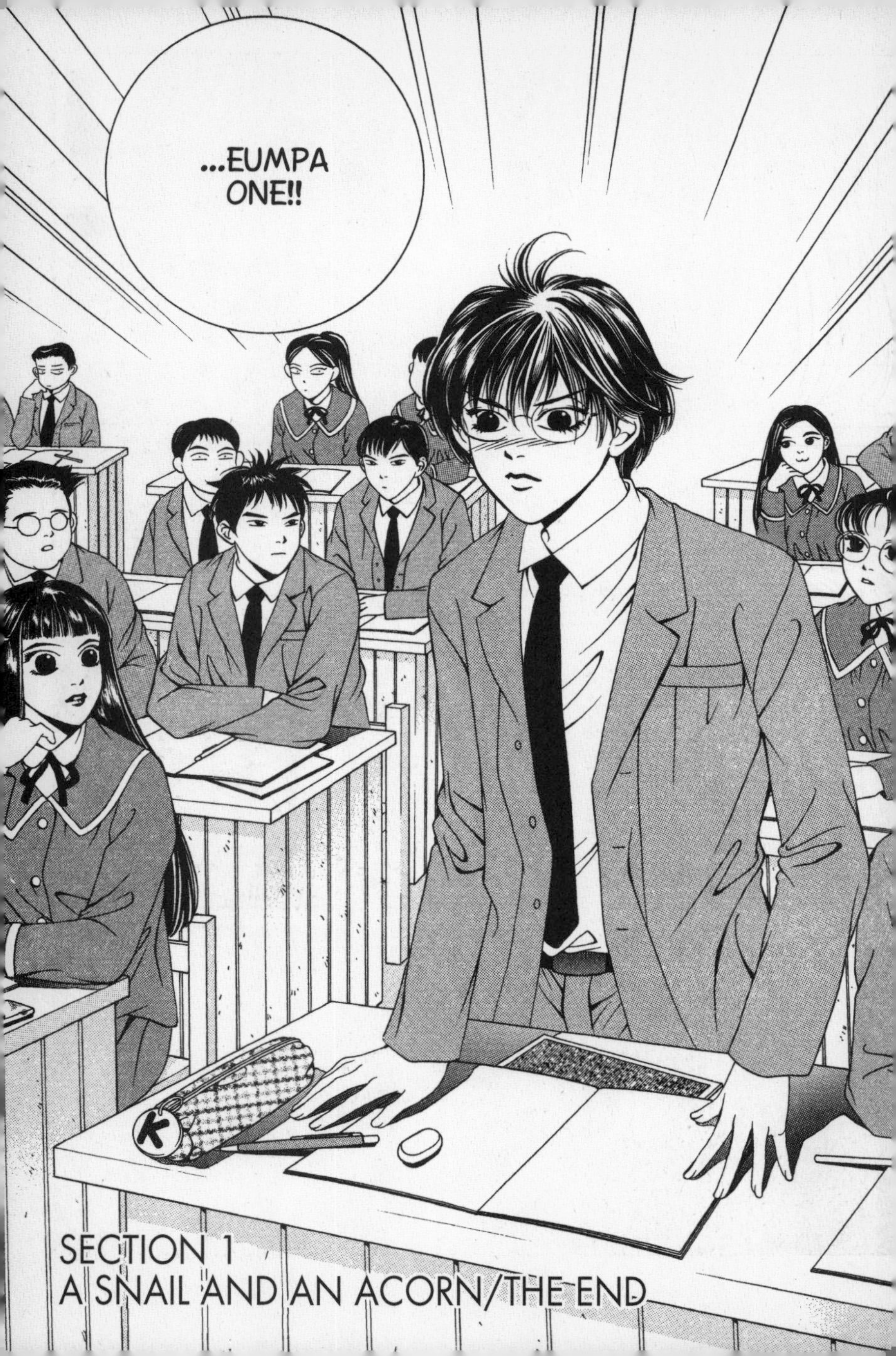
...EUMPA ONE!!
SECTION 1
A SNAIL AND AN ACORN/THE END

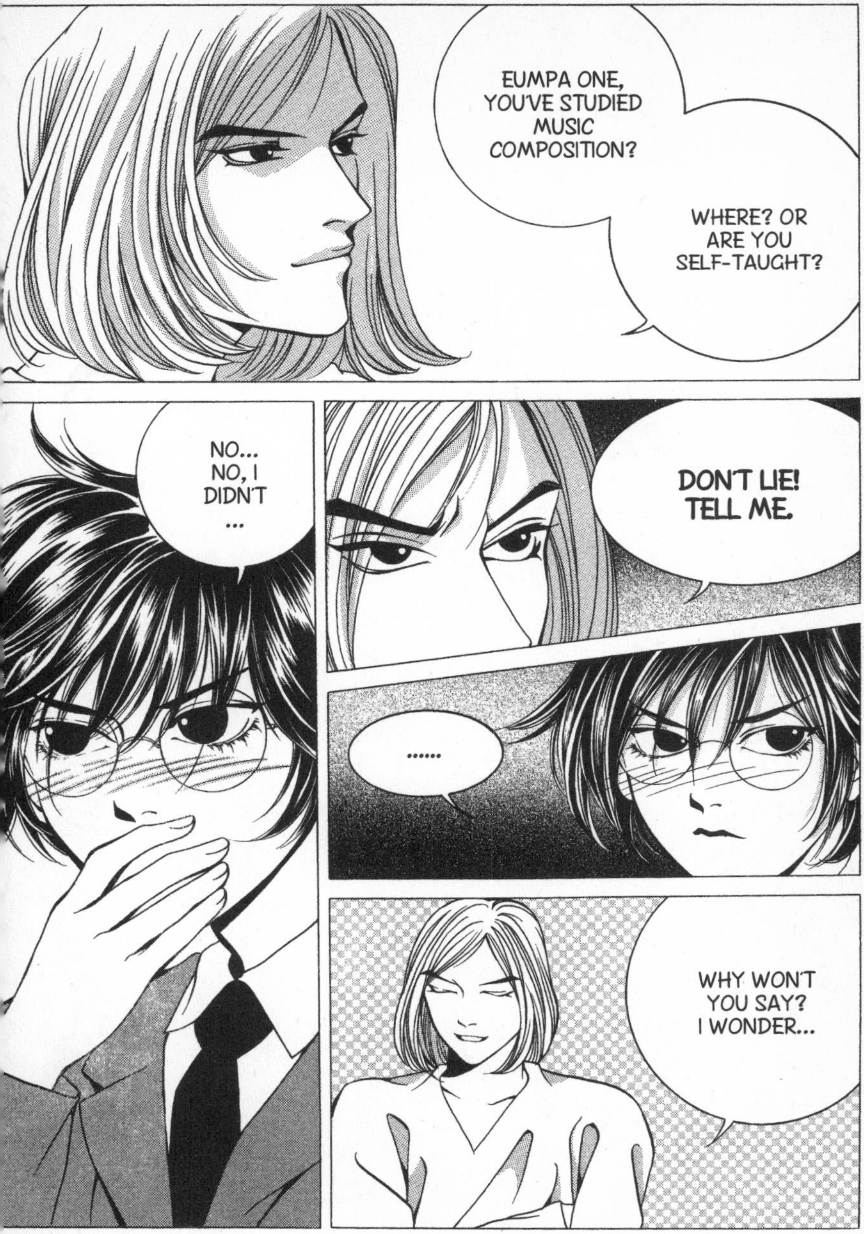
EUMPA ONE, YOU'VE STUDIED MUSIC COMPOSITION?
WHERE? OR ARE YOU SELF-TAUGHT?
NO... NO, I DIDN'T ...
DON'T LIE! TELL ME.
......
WHY WON'T YOU SAY? I WONDER...

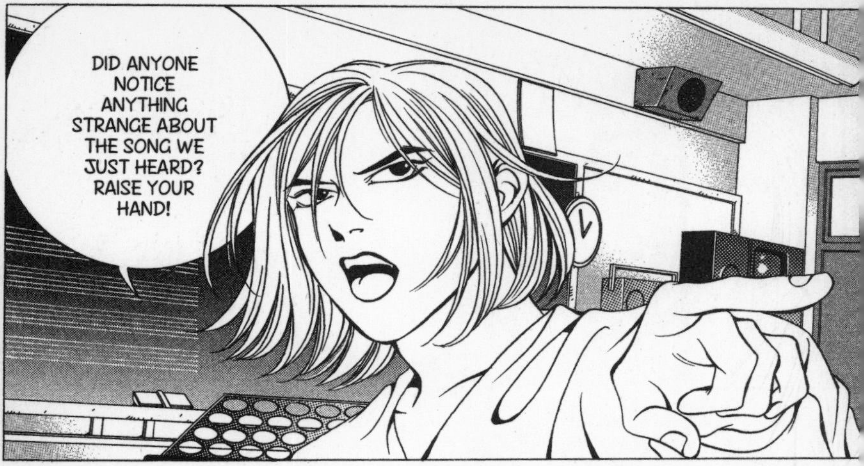
DID ANYONE NOTICE ANYTHING STRANGE ABOUT THE SONG WE JUST HEARD? RAISE YOUR HAND!

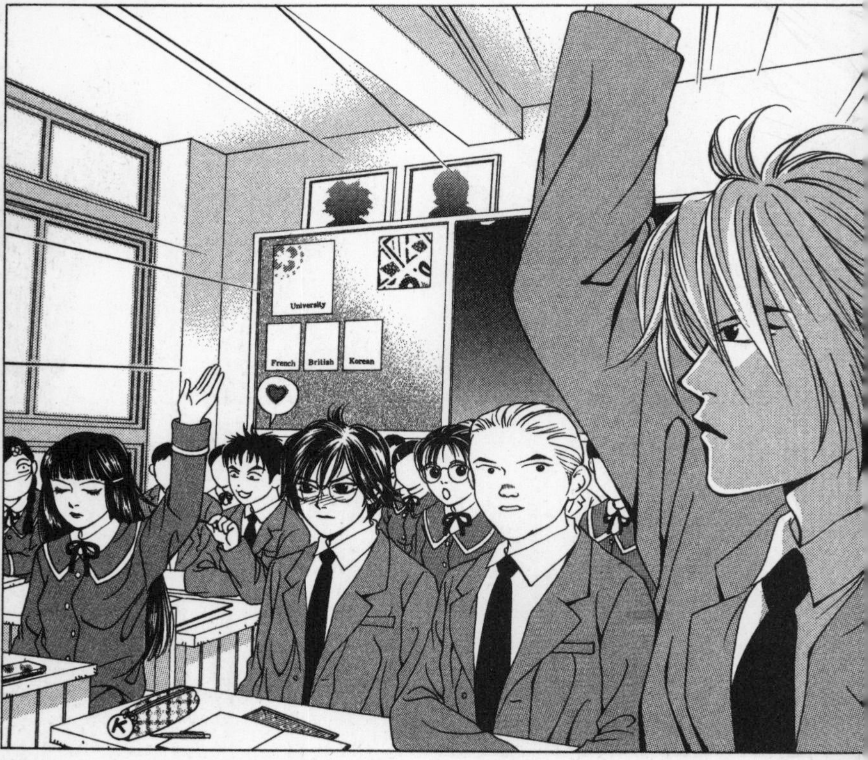
University
French
British
Korean

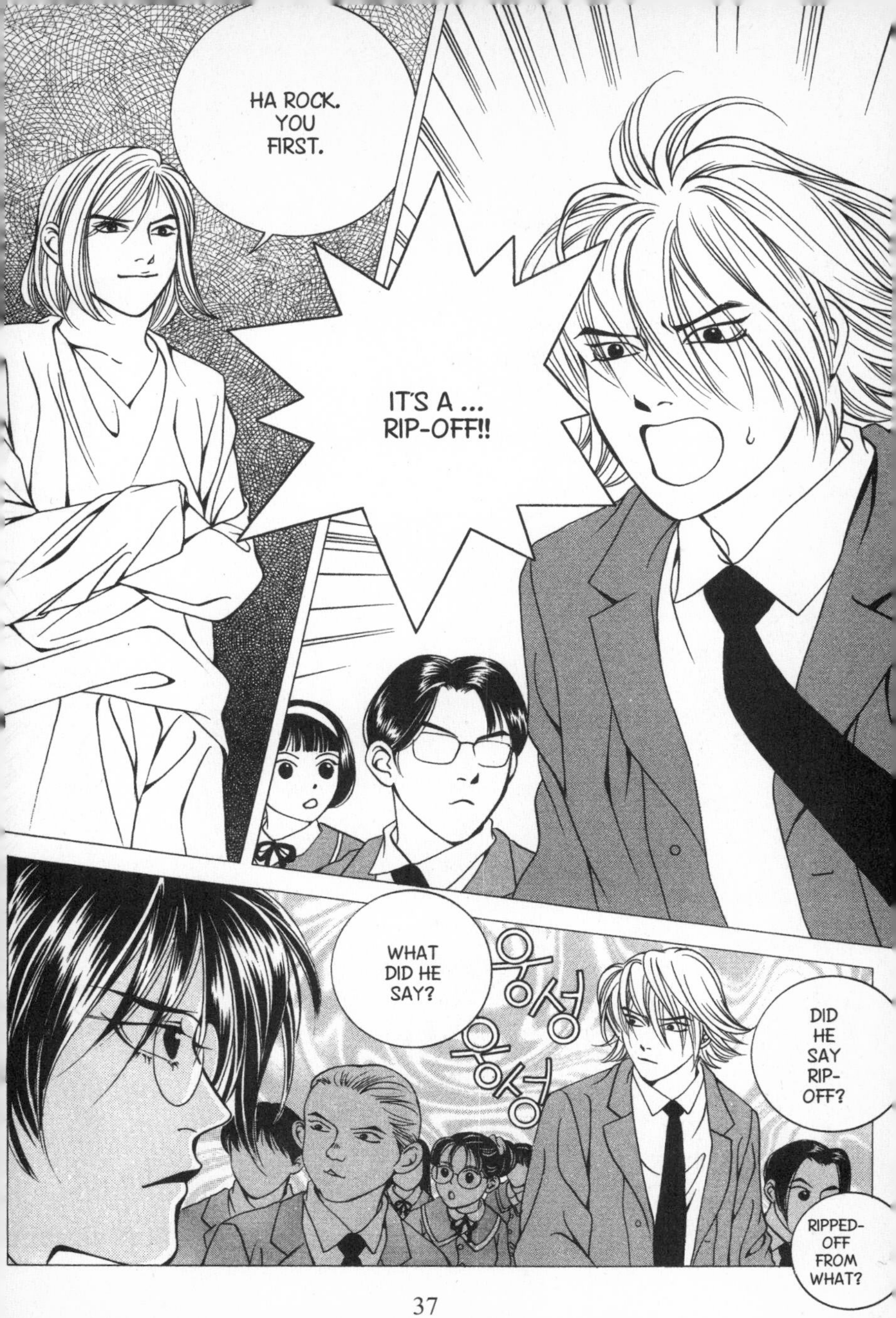
HA ROCK. YOU FIRST.
IT'S A ... RIP-OFF!!
WHAT DID HE SAY?
웅성웅성
DID HE SAY RIP-OFF?
RIPPED-OFF FROM WHAT?

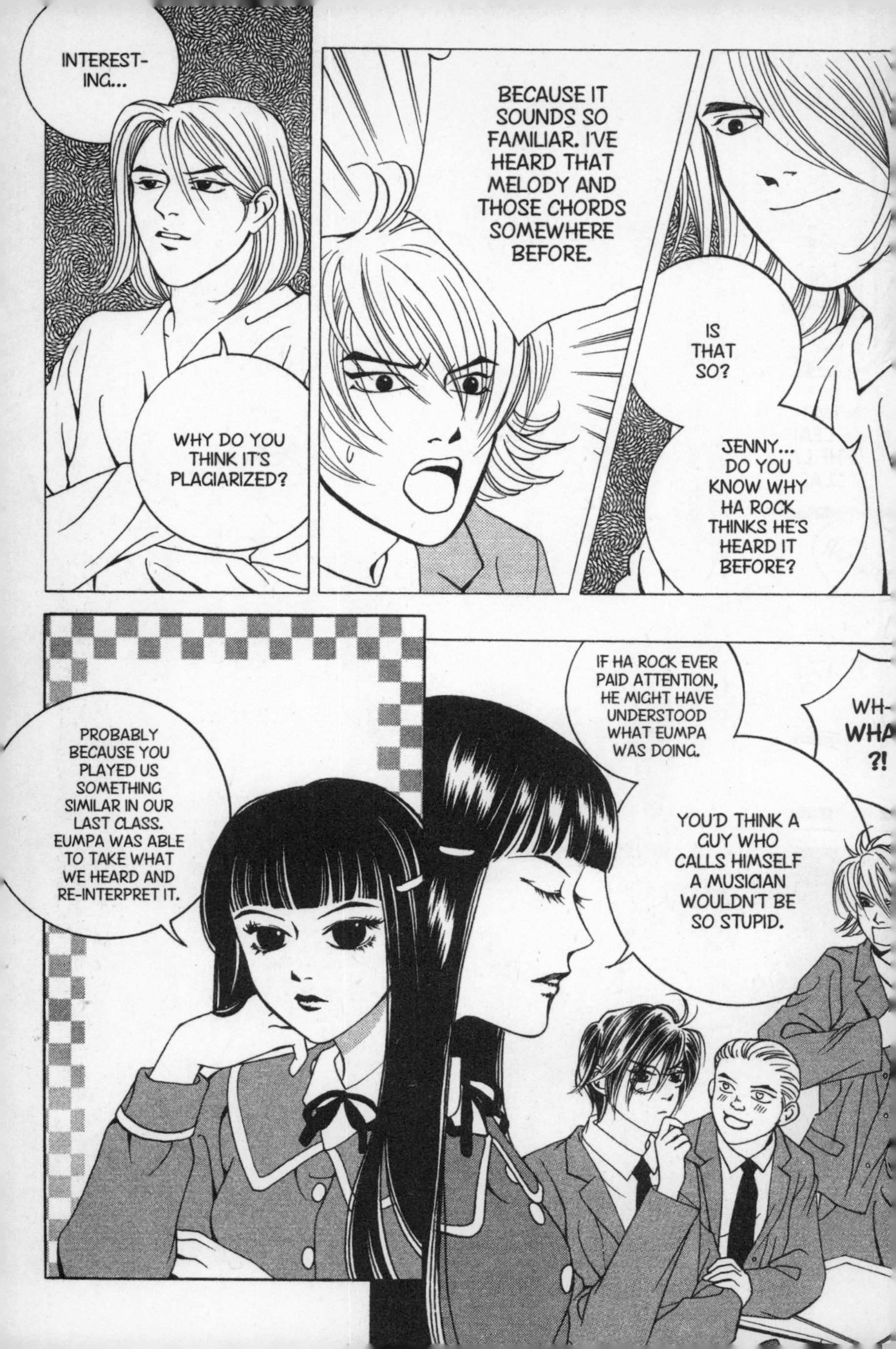
INTEREST-ING...
WHY DO YOU THINK IT'S PLAGIARIZED?
BECAUSE IT SOUNDS SO FAMILIAR. I'VE HEARD THAT MELODY AND THOSE CHORDS SOMEWHERE BEFORE.
IS THAT SO?
JENNY... DO YOU KNOW WHY HA ROCK THINKS HE'S HEARD IT BEFORE?
PROBABLY BECAUSE YOU PLAYED US SOMETHING SIMILAR IN OUR LAST CLASS. EUMPA WAS ABLE TO TAKE WHAT WE HEARD AND RE-INTERPRET IT.
IF HA ROCK EVER PAID ATTENTION, HE MIGHT HAVE UNDERSTOOD WHAT EUMPA WAS DOING.
YOU'D THINK A GUY WHO CALLS HIMSELF A MUSICIAN WOULDN'T BE SO STUPID.
WH- WHA ?!

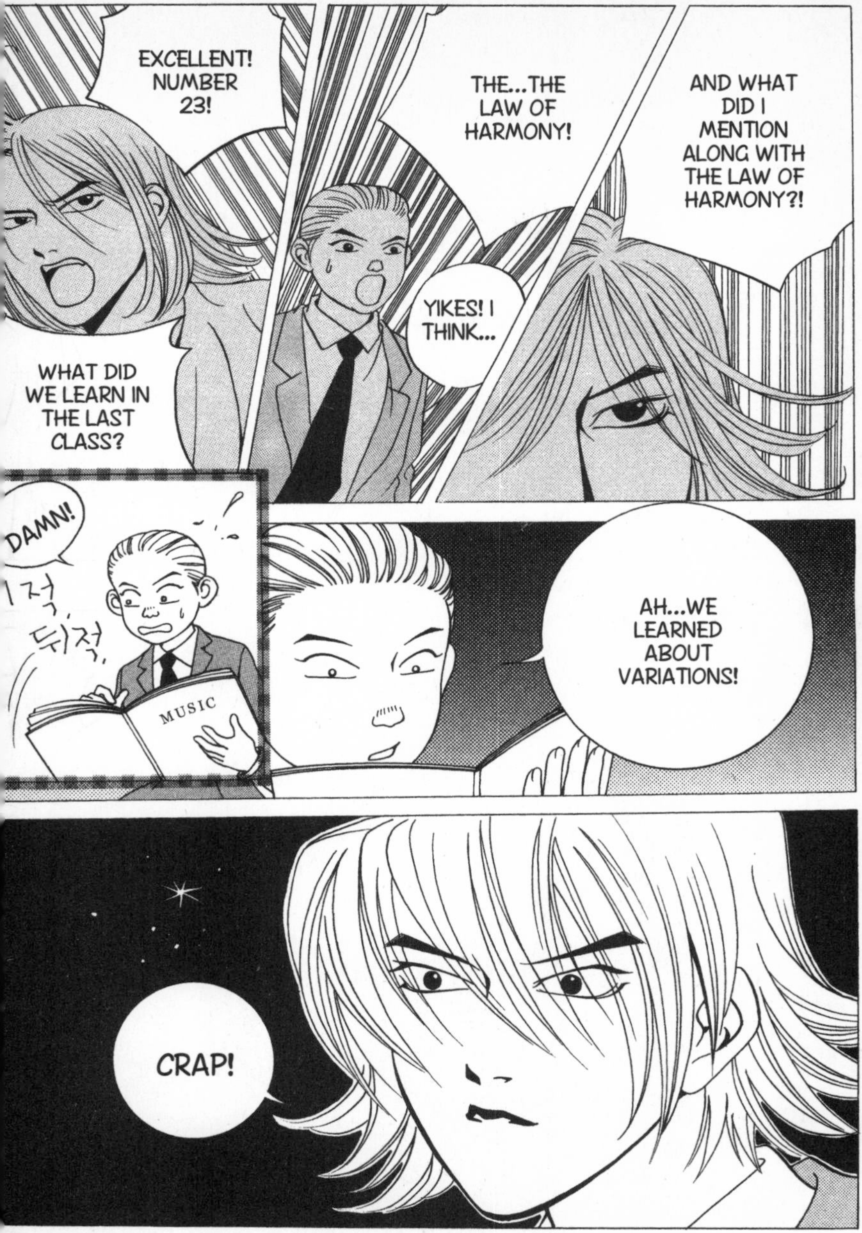
EXCELLENT! NUMBER 23!
WHAT DID WE LEARN IN THE LAST CLASS?
THE...THE LAW OF HARMONY!
YIKES! I THINK...
AND WHAT DID I MENTION ALONG WITH THE LAW OF HARMONY?!
DAMN!
적, 뒤적,
MUSIC
AH...WE LEARNED ABOUT VARIATIONS!
CRAP!

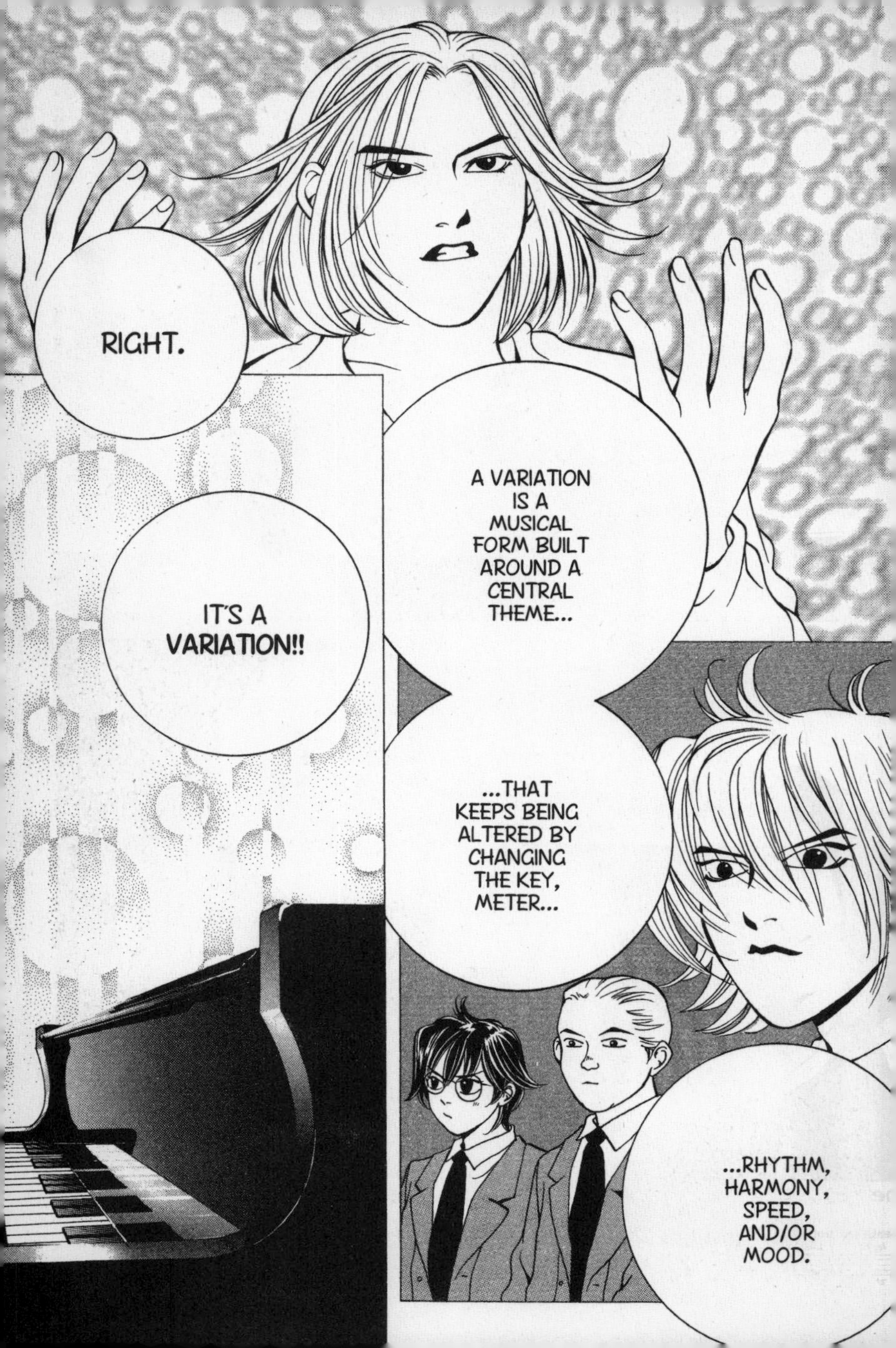
RIGHT.
IT'S A VARIATION!!
A VARIATION IS A MUSICAL FORM BUILT AROUND A CENTRAL THEME...
...THAT KEEPS BEING ALTERED BY CHANGING THE KEY, METER...
...RHYTHM, HARMONY, SPEED, AND/OR MOOD.

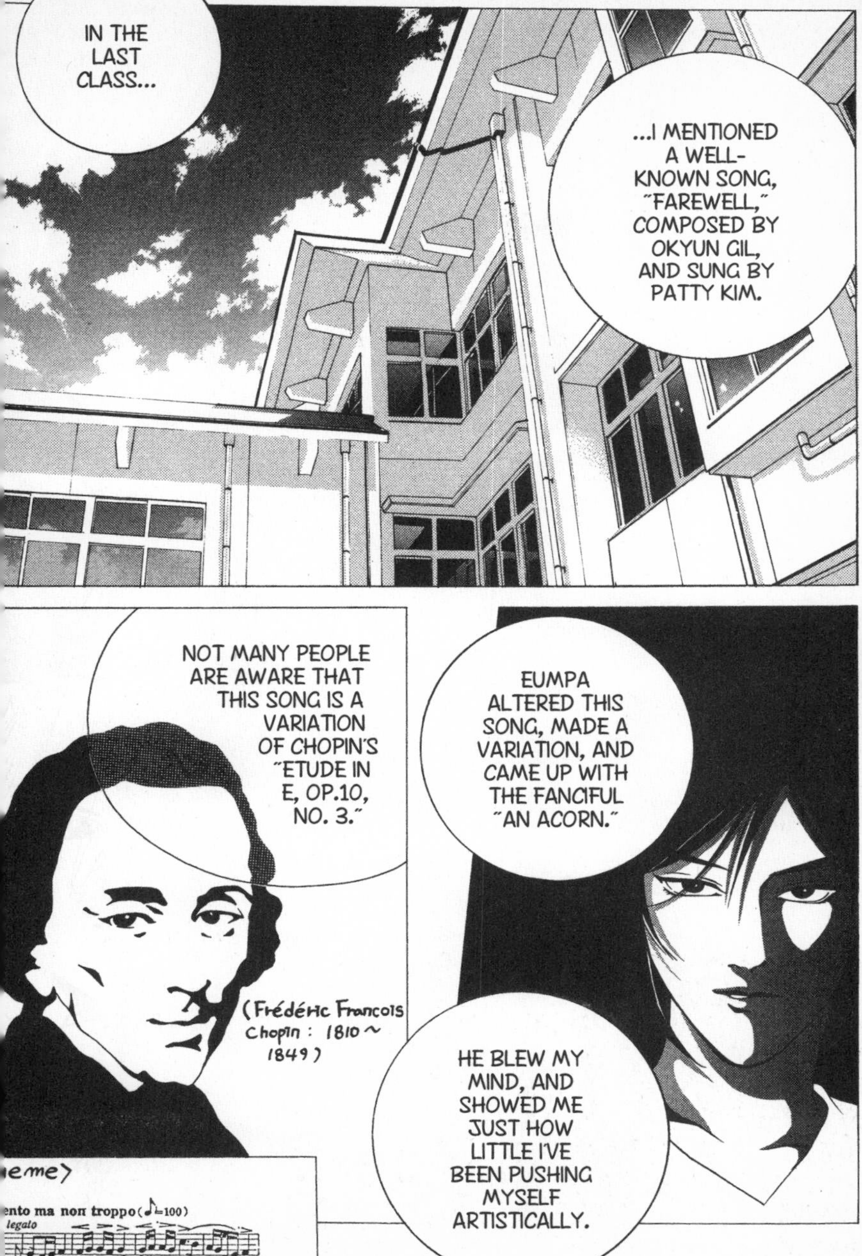
IN THE LAST CLASS...
...I MENTIONED A WELL-KNOWN SONG, "FAREWELL," COMPOSED BY OKYUN GIL, AND SUNG BY PATTY KIM.
NOT MANY PEOPLE ARE AWARE THAT THIS SONG IS A VARIATION OF CHOPIN'S "ETUDE IN E, OP.10, NO. 3."
(Frédéric Francois Chopin : 1810 ~ 1849)
eme>
ento ma non troppo (♪=100)
legato
EUMPA ALTERED THIS SONG, MADE A VARIATION, AND CAME UP WITH THE FANCIFUL "AN ACORN."
HE BLEW MY MIND, AND SHOWED ME JUST HOW LITTLE I'VE BEEN PUSHING MYSELF ARTISTICALLY.

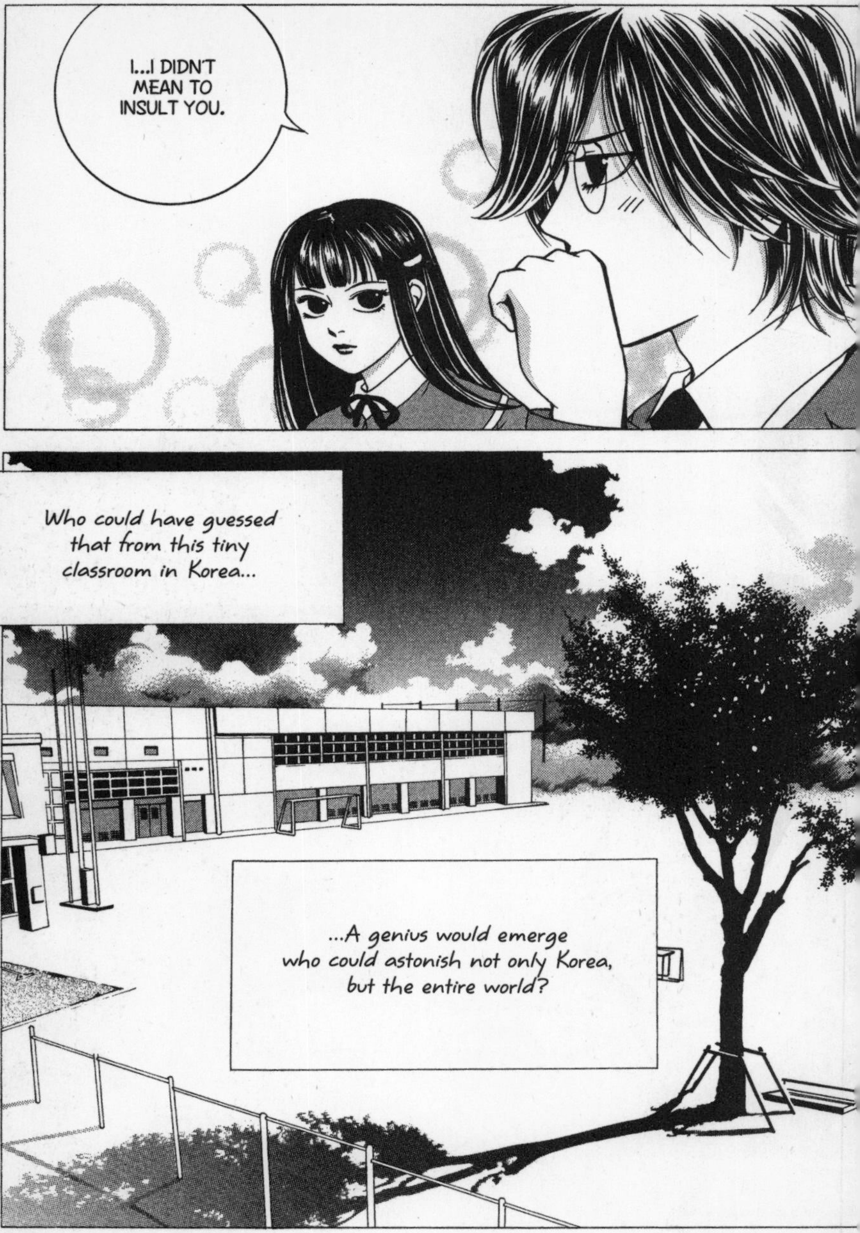
I...I DIDN'T MEAN TO INSULT YOU.
Who could have guessed that from this tiny classroom in Korea...
...A genius would emerge who could astonish not only Korea, but the entire world?

SECTION 2
INTRO

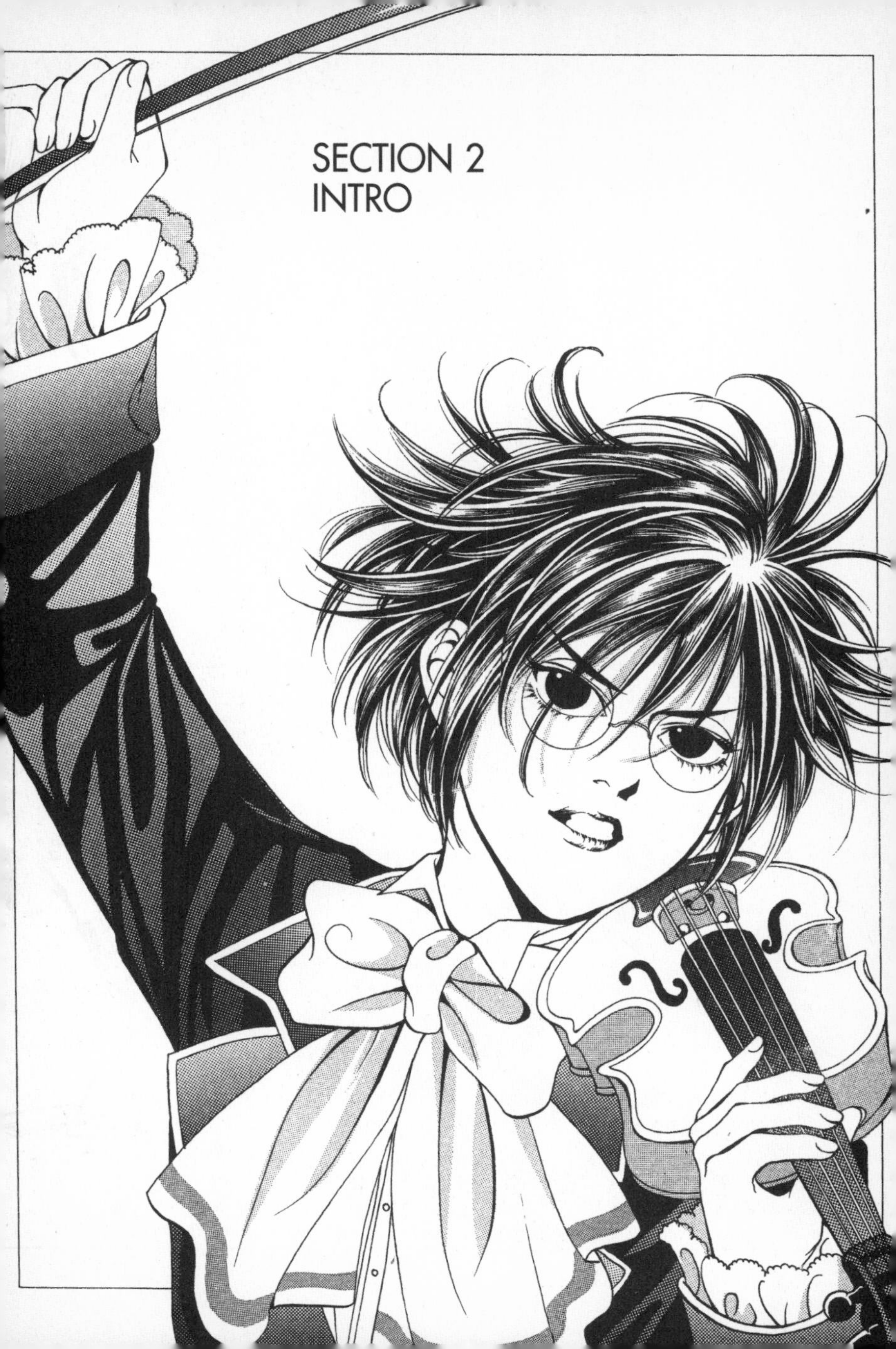

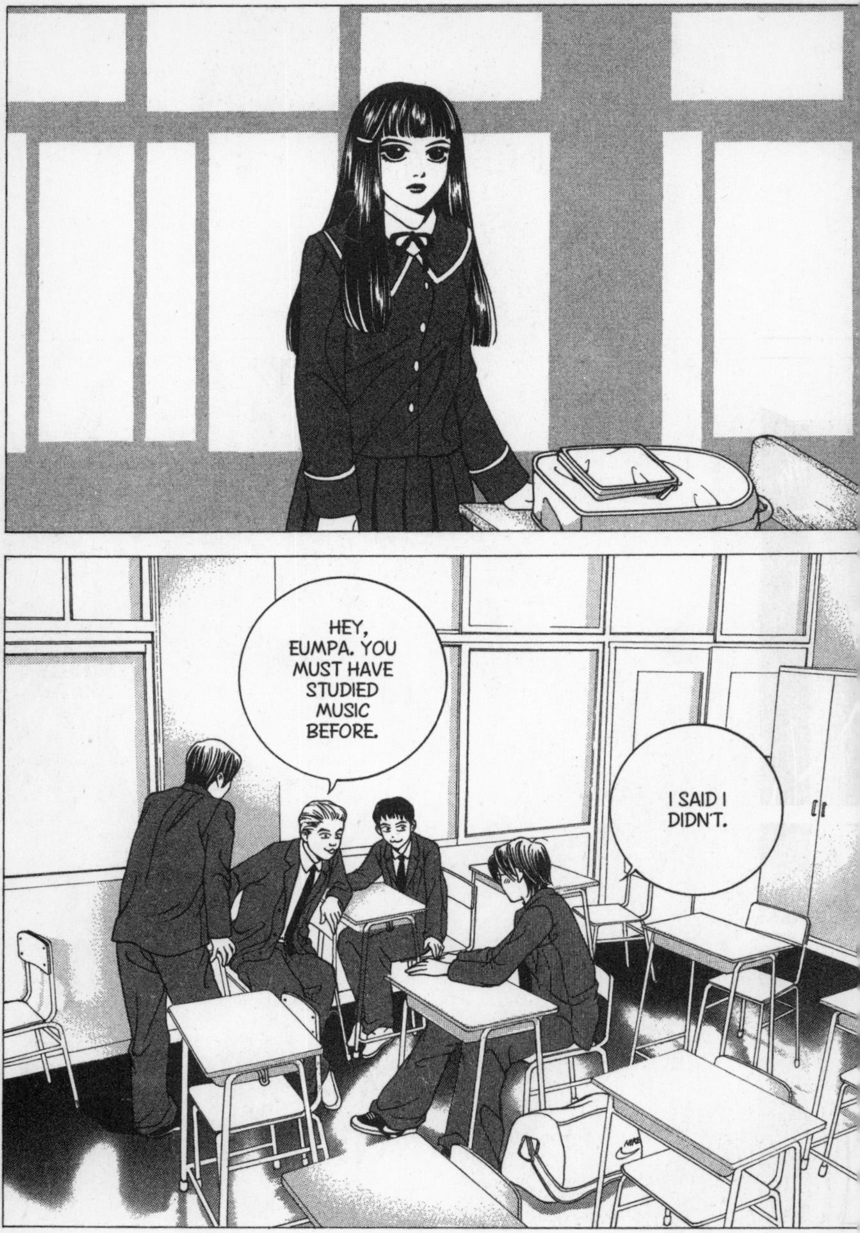
HEY, EUMPA. YOU MUST HAVE STUDIED MUSIC BEFORE.
I SAID I DIDN'T.

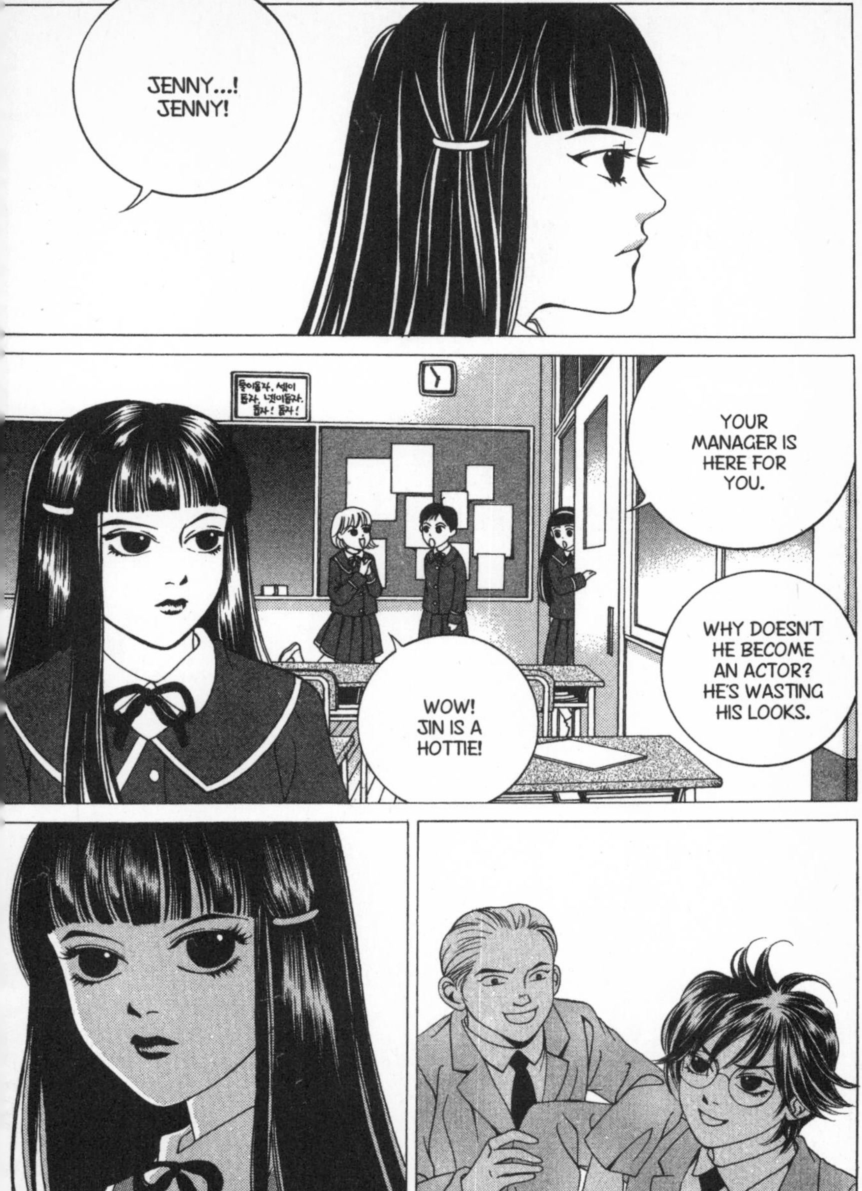
JENNY...! JENNY!
YOUR MANAGER IS HERE FOR YOU.
WHY DOESN'T HE BECOME AN ACTOR? HE'S WASTING HIS LOOKS.
WOW! JIN IS A HOTTIE!

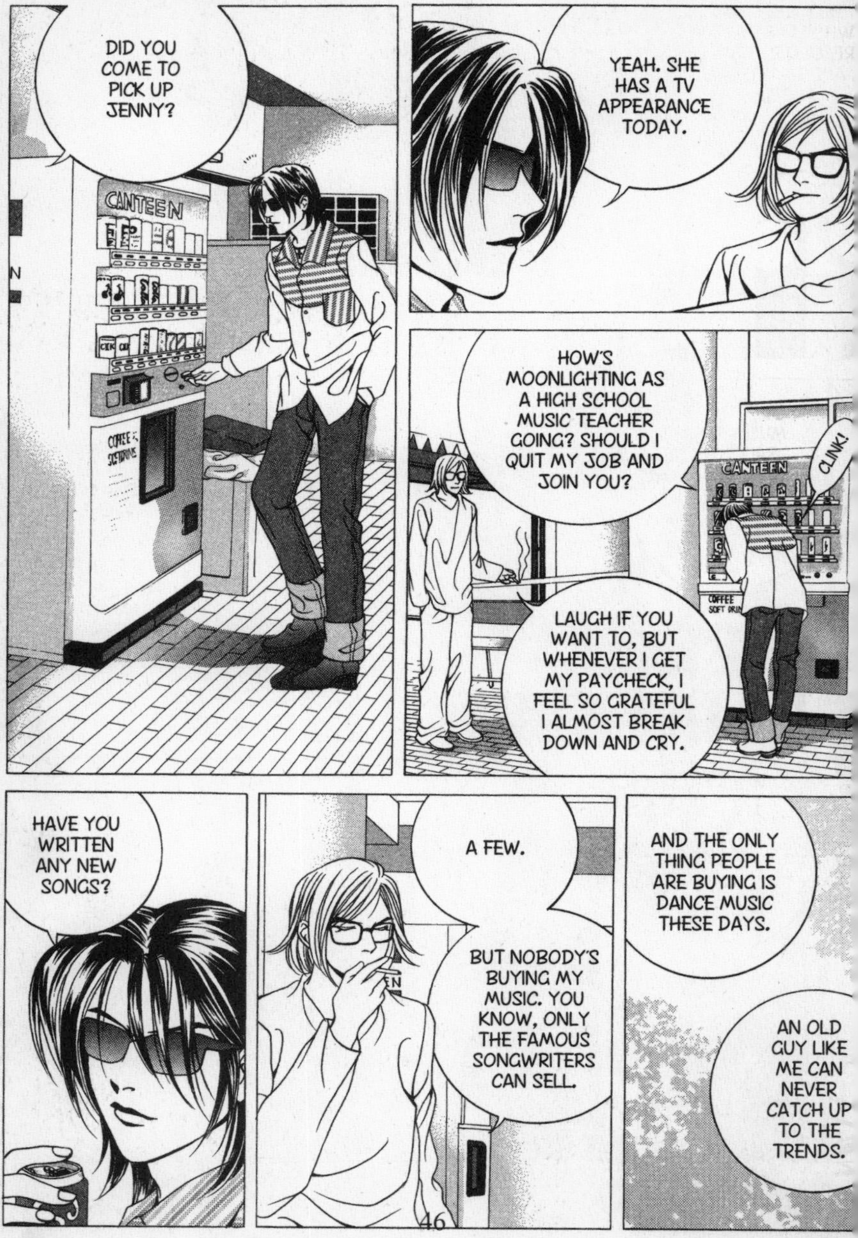
DID YOU COME TO PICK UP JENNY?
CANTEEN
YEAH. SHE HAS A TV APPEARANCE TODAY.
HOW'S MOONLIGHTING AS A HIGH SCHOOL MUSIC TEACHER GOING? SHOULD I QUIT MY JOB AND JOIN YOU?
CANTEEN
CLINK!
LAUGH IF YOU WANT TO, BUT WHENEVER I GET MY PAYCHECK, I FEEL SO GRATEFUL I ALMOST BREAK DOWN AND CRY.
HAVE YOU WRITTEN ANY NEW SONGS?
A FEW.
BUT NOBODY'S BUYING MY MUSIC. YOU KNOW, ONLY THE FAMOUS SONGWRITERS CAN SELL.
AND THE ONLY THING PEOPLE ARE BUYING IS DANCE MUSIC THESE DAYS.
AN OLD GUY LIKE ME CAN NEVER CATCH UP TO THE TRENDS.

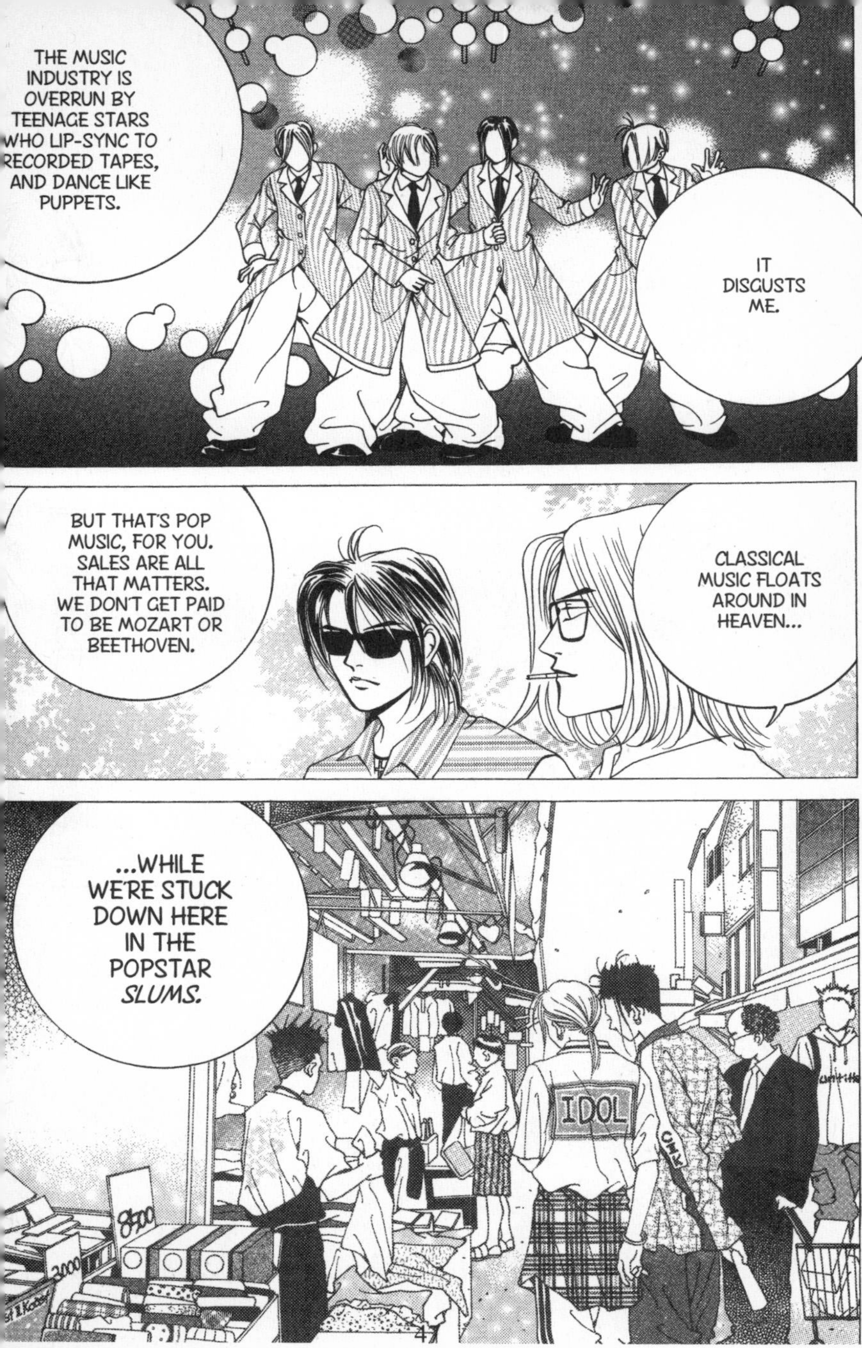
THE MUSIC INDUSTRY IS OVERRUN BY TEENAGE STARS WHO LIP-SYNC TO RECORDED TAPES, AND DANCE LIKE PUPPETS.
IT DISGUSTS ME.
BUT THAT'S POP MUSIC, FOR YOU. SALES ARE ALL THAT MATTERS. WE DON'T GET PAID TO BE MOZART OR BEETHOVEN.
CLASSICAL MUSIC FLOATS AROUND IN HEAVEN...
...WHILE WE'RE STUCK DOWN HERE IN THE POPSTAR *SLUMS.*
IDOL
3000

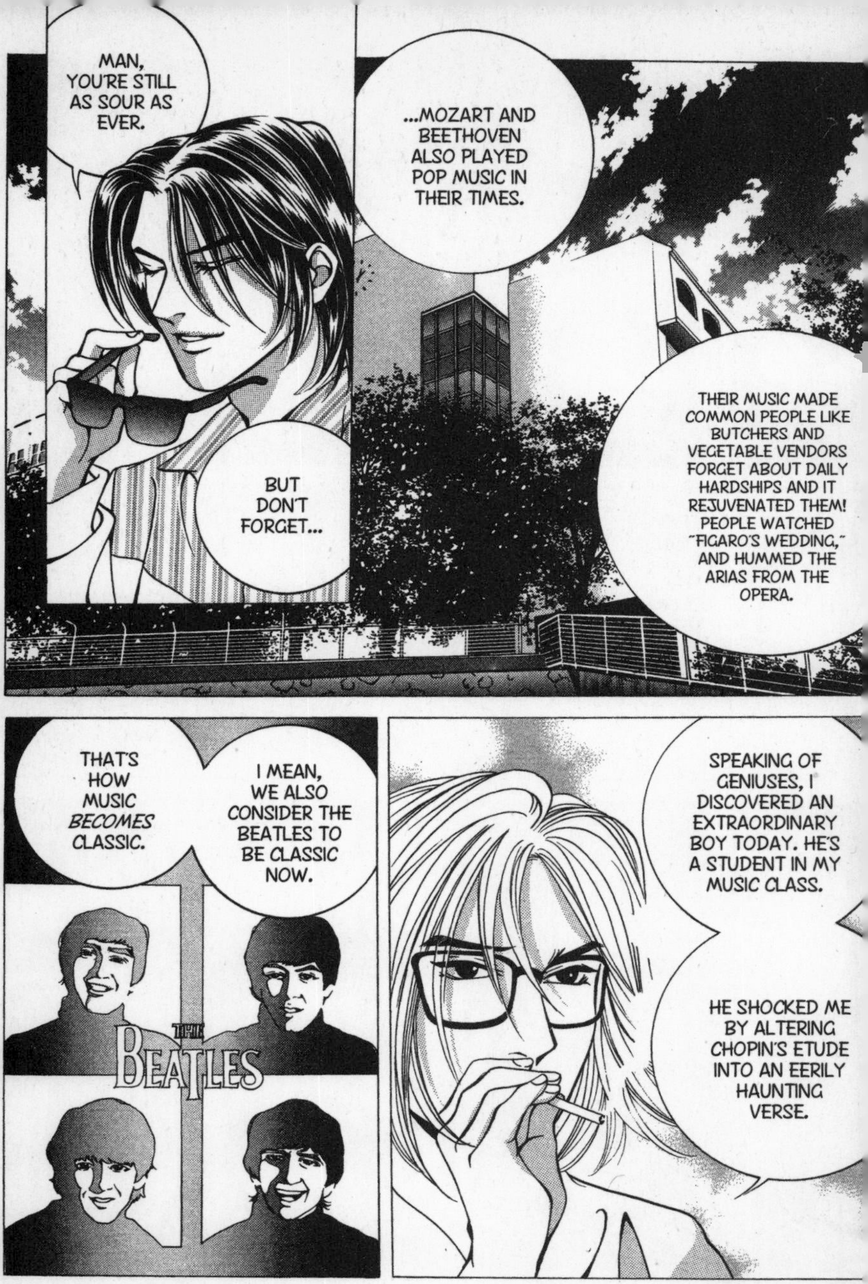

MAN, YOU'RE STILL AS SOUR AS EVER.
BUT DON'T FORGET...
...MOZART AND BEETHOVEN ALSO PLAYED POP MUSIC IN THEIR TIMES.
THEIR MUSIC MADE COMMON PEOPLE LIKE BUTCHERS AND VEGETABLE VENDORS FORGET ABOUT DAILY HARDSHIPS AND IT REJUVENATED THEM! PEOPLE WATCHED "FIGARO'S WEDDING," AND HUMMED THE ARIAS FROM THE OPERA.
THAT'S HOW MUSIC *BECOMES* CLASSIC.
I MEAN, WE ALSO CONSIDER THE BEATLES TO BE CLASSIC NOW.
THE BEATLES
SPEAKING OF GENIUSES, I DISCOVERED AN EXTRAORDINARY BOY TODAY. HE'S A STUDENT IN MY MUSIC CLASS.
HE SHOCKED ME BY ALTERING CHOPIN'S ETUDE INTO AN EERILY HAUNTING VERSE.

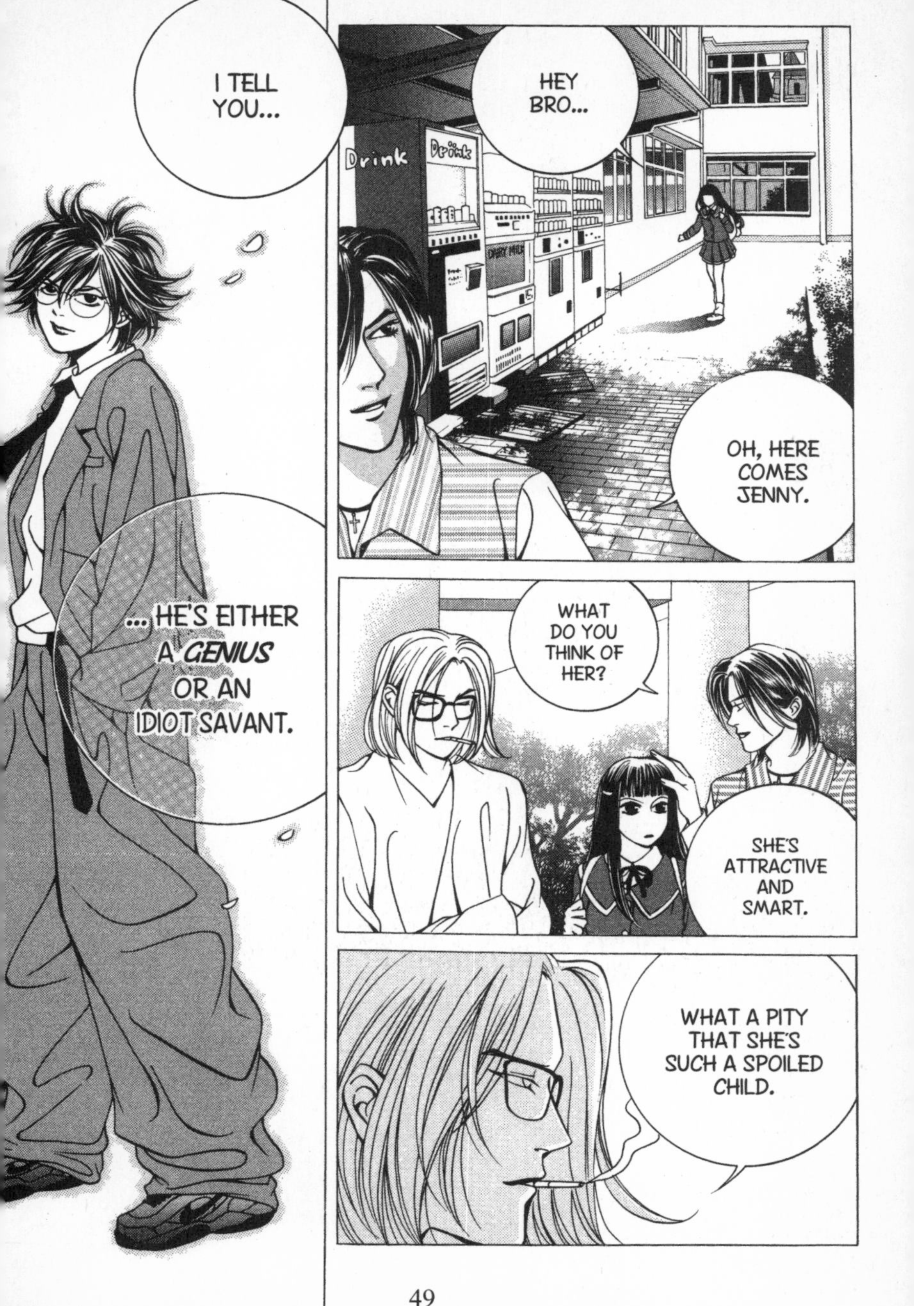
I TELL YOU...
... HE'S EITHER A *GENIUS* OR AN IDIOT SAVANT.
Drink
Drink
HEY BRO...
OH, HERE COMES JENNY.
WHAT DO YOU THINK OF HER?
SHE'S ATTRACTIVE AND SMART.
WHAT A PITY THAT SHE'S SUCH A SPOILED CHILD.

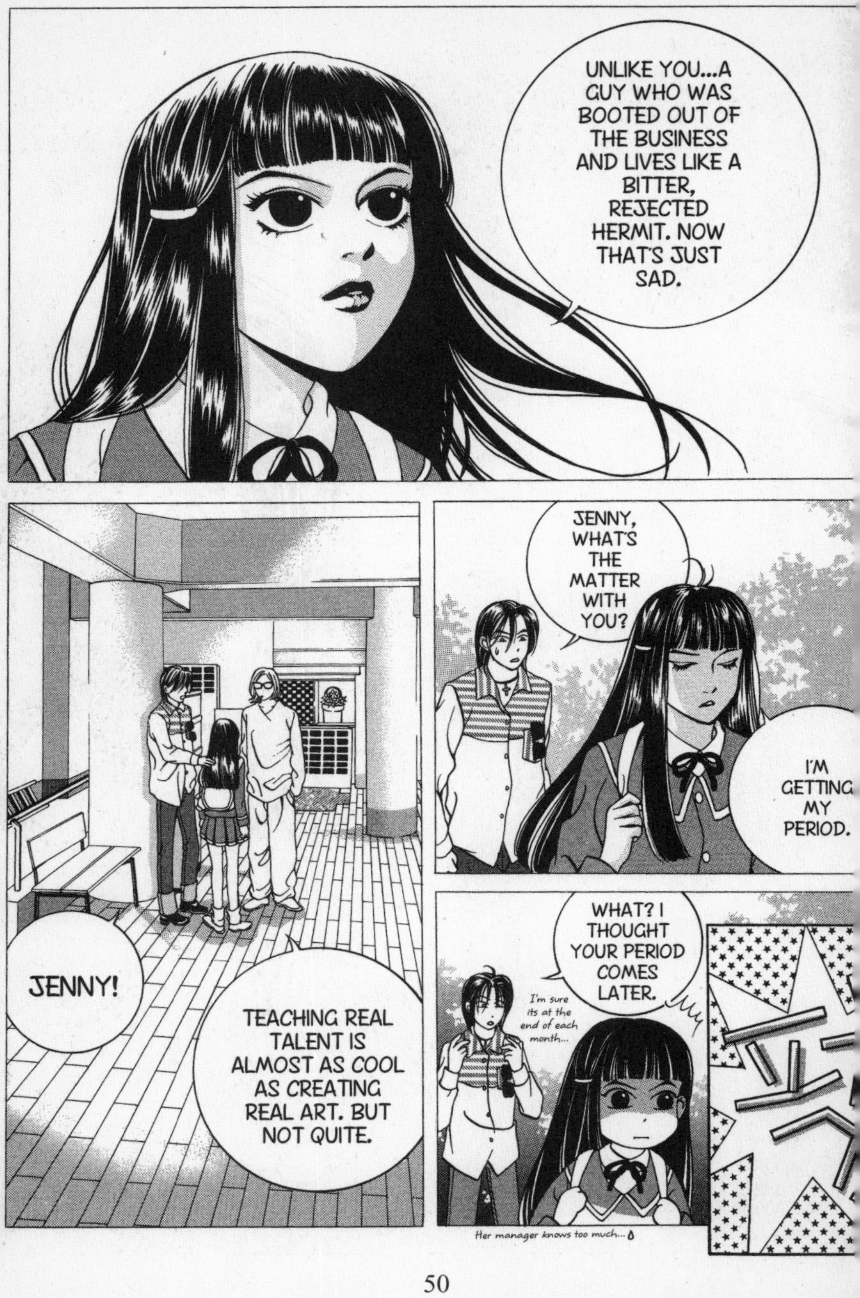
UNLIKE YOU...A GUY WHO WAS BOOTED OUT OF THE BUSINESS AND LIVES LIKE A BITTER, REJECTED HERMIT. NOW THAT'S JUST SAD.
JENNY!
TEACHING REAL TALENT IS ALMOST AS COOL AS CREATING REAL ART. BUT NOT QUITE.
JENNY, WHAT'S THE MATTER WITH YOU?
I'M GETTING MY PERIOD.
WHAT? I THOUGHT YOUR PERIOD COMES LATER.
I'm sure its at the end of each month...
Her manager knows too much...

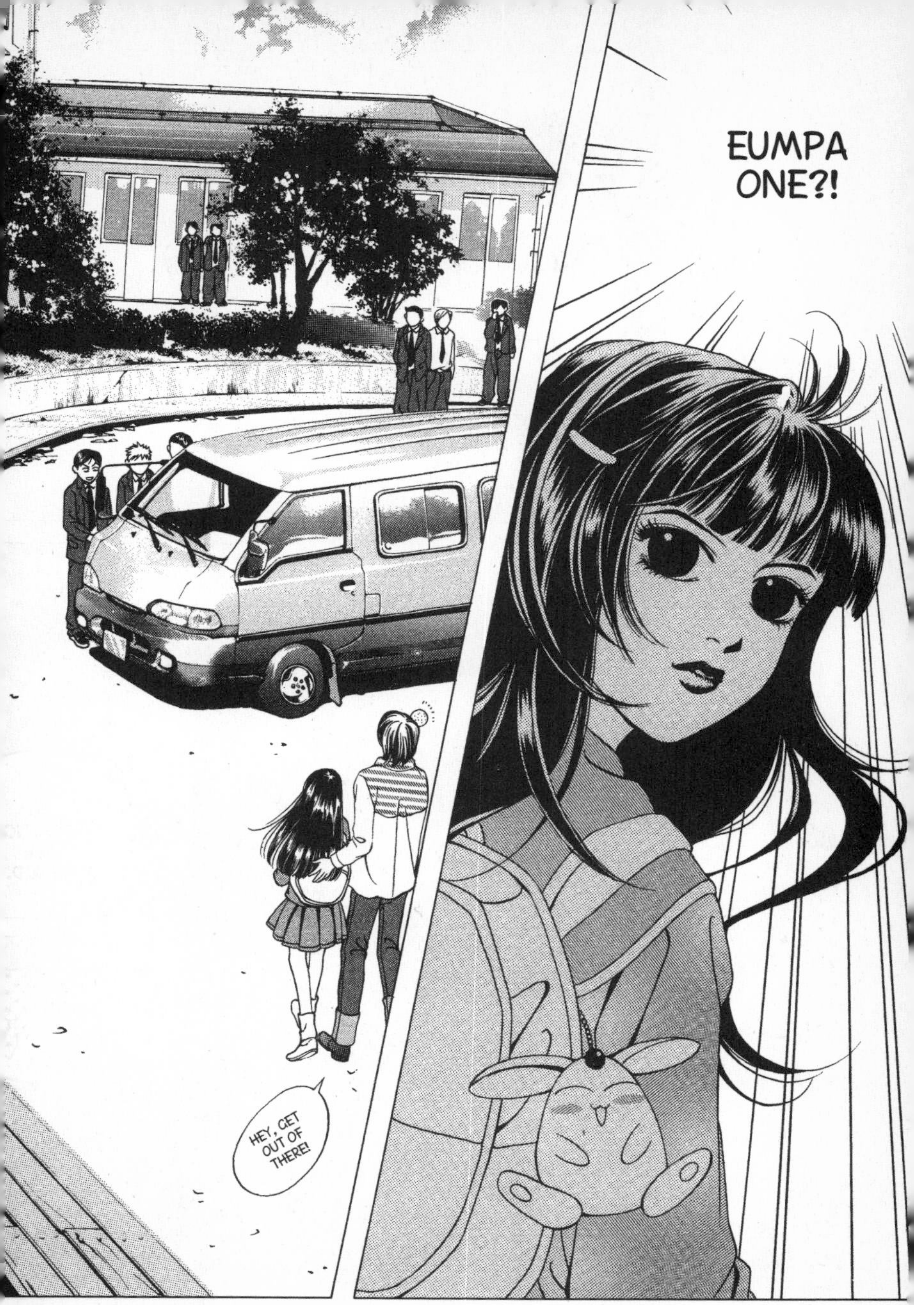
HEY, GET OUT OF THERE!
EUMPA ONE?!

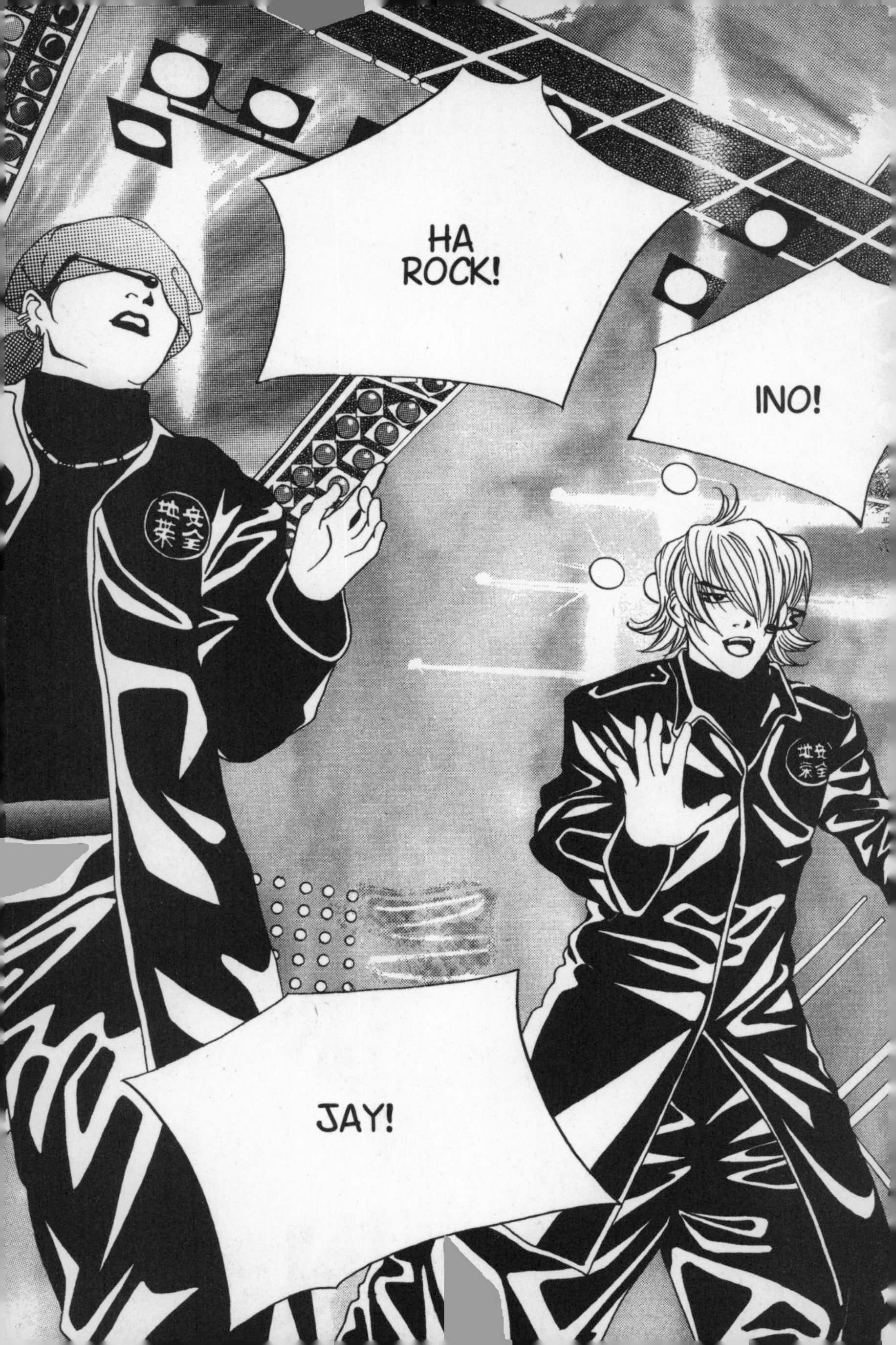
HA ROCK!
INO!
JAY!

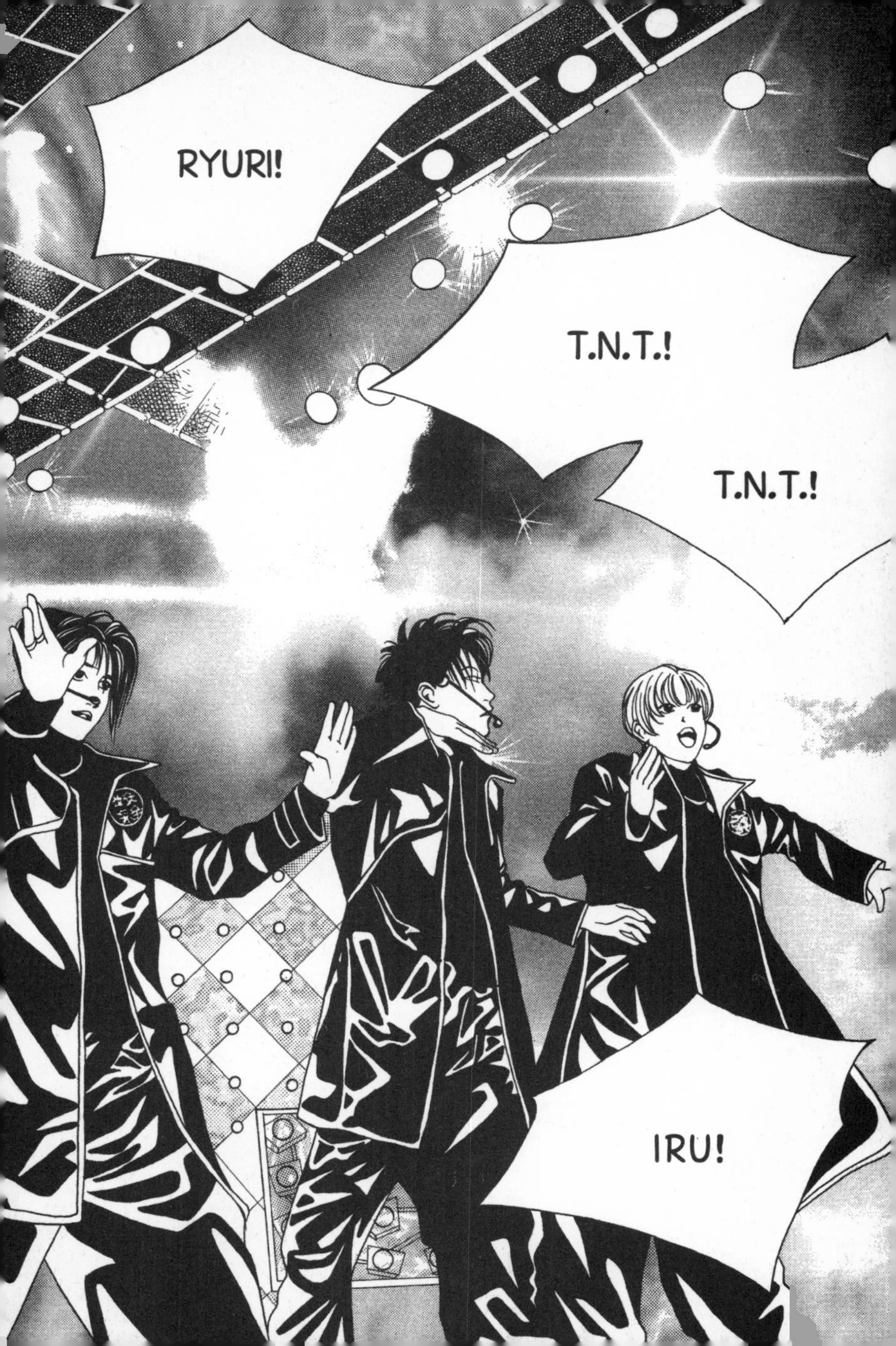
RYURI!
T.N.T.!
T.N.T.!
IRU!

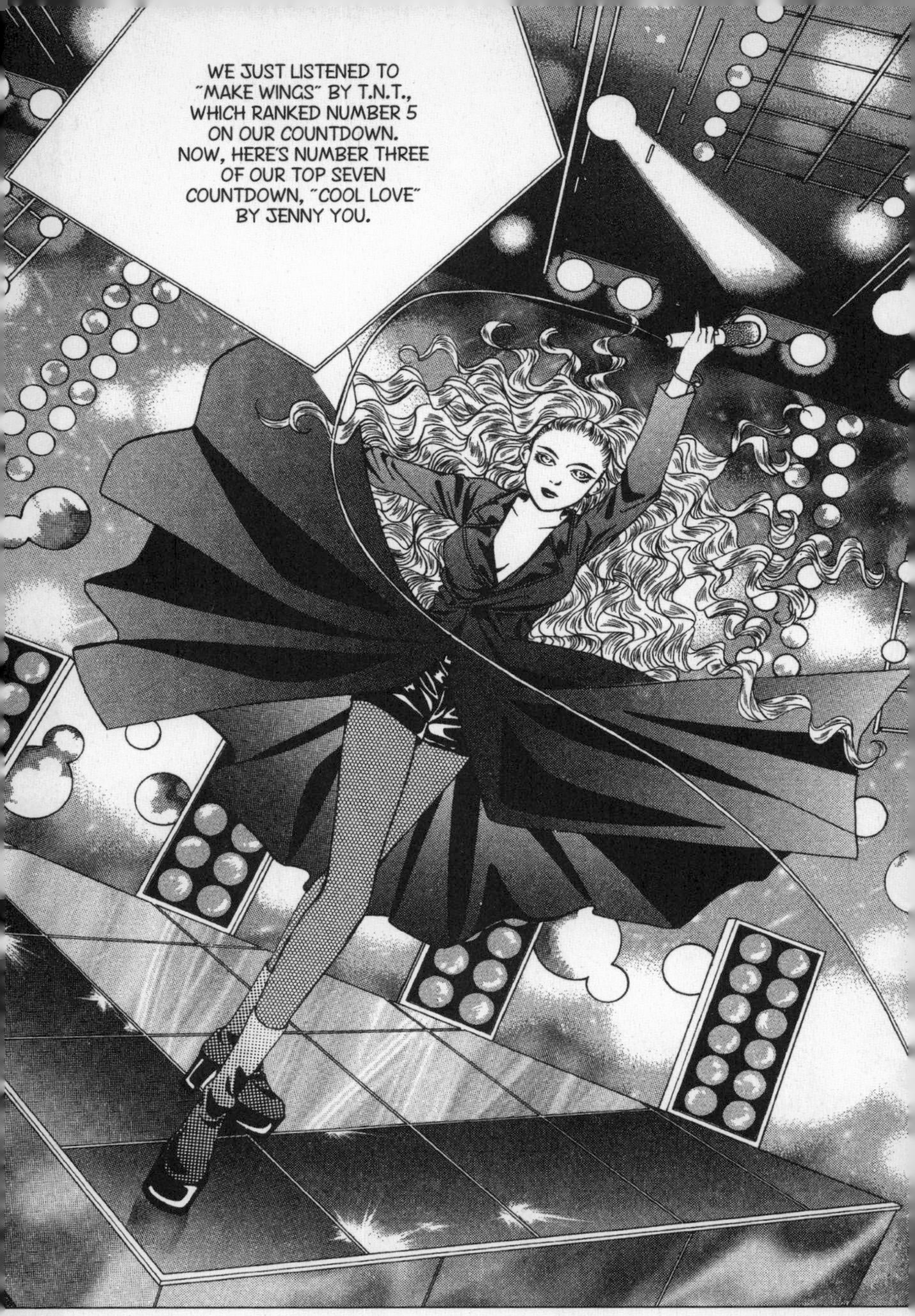
WE JUST LISTENED TO "MAKE WINGS" BY T.N.T., WHICH RANKED NUMBER 5 ON OUR COUNTDOWN. NOW, HERE'S NUMBER THREE OF OUR TOP SEVEN COUNTDOWN, "COOL LOVE" BY JENNY YOU.

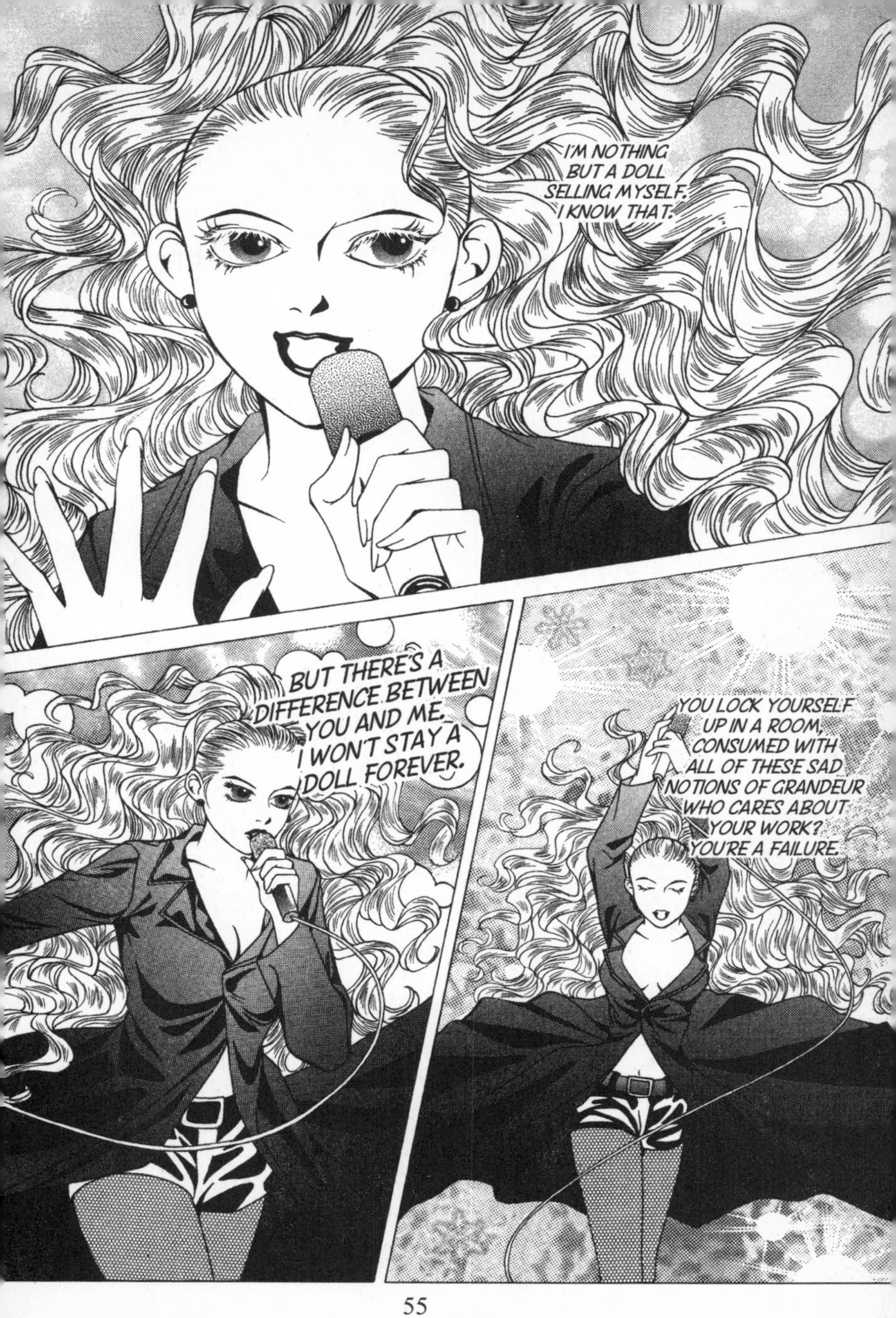
I'M NOTHING BUT A DOLL SELLING MYSELF. I KNOW THAT.
BUT THERE'S A DIFFERENCE BETWEEN YOU AND ME. I WON'T STAY A DOLL FOREVER.
YOU LOCK YOURSELF UP IN A ROOM, CONSUMED WITH ALL OF THESE SAD NOTIONS OF GRANDEUR WHO CARES ABOUT YOUR WORK? YOU'RE A FAILURE.

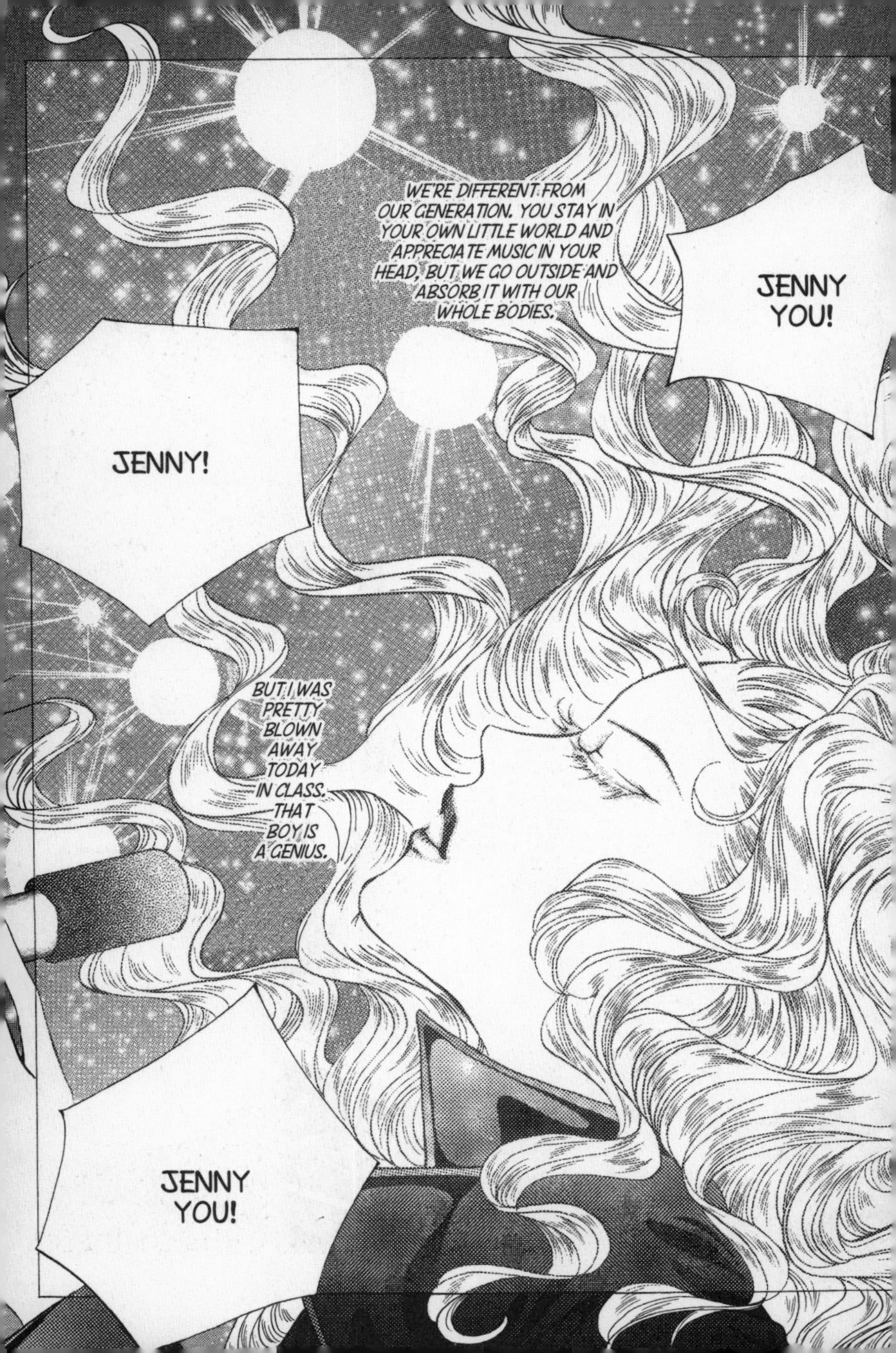
WE'RE DIFFERENT FROM OUR GENERATION. YOU STAY IN YOUR OWN LITTLE WORLD AND APPRECIATE MUSIC IN YOUR HEAD, BUT WE GO OUTSIDE AND ABSORB IT WITH OUR WHOLE BODIES.
JENNY YOU!
JENNY!
BUT I WAS PRETTY BLOWN AWAY TODAY IN CLASS. THAT BOY IS A GENIUS.
JENNY YOU!

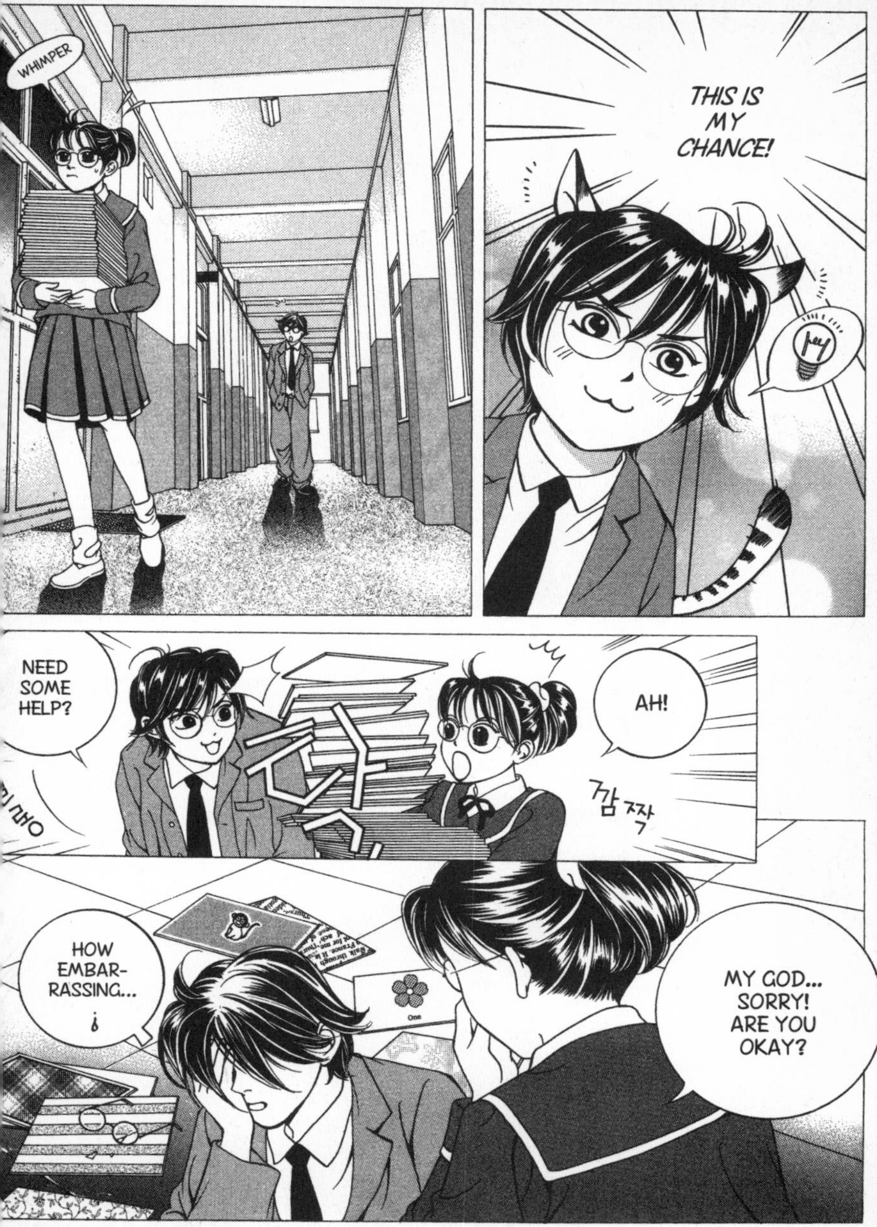
WHIMPER
THIS IS MY CHANCE!
NEED SOME HELP?
AH!
깜짝
HOW EMBAR-RASSING...
¡
MY GOD... SORRY! ARE YOU OKAY?

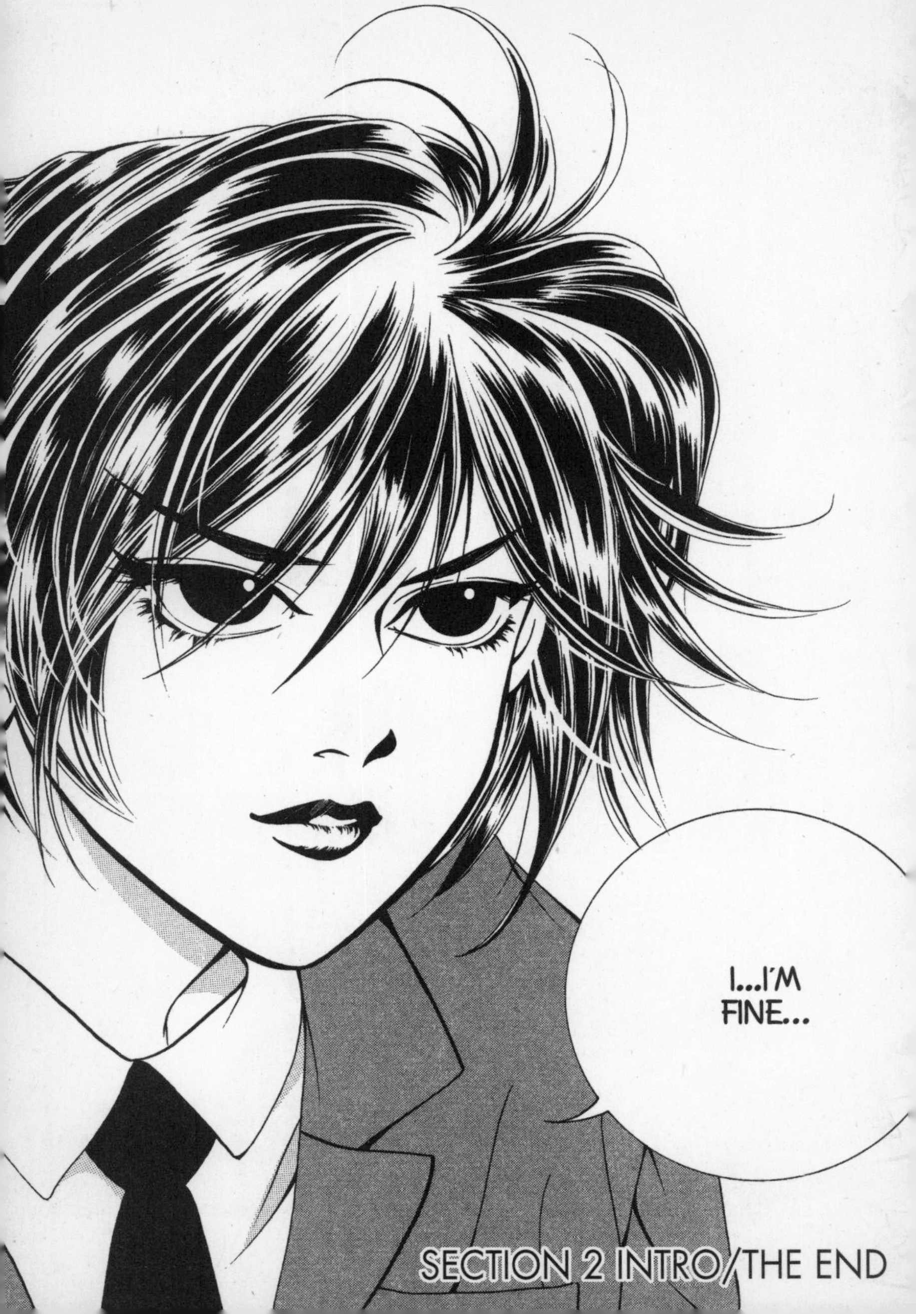
I...I'M FINE...
SECTION 2 INTRO/THE END

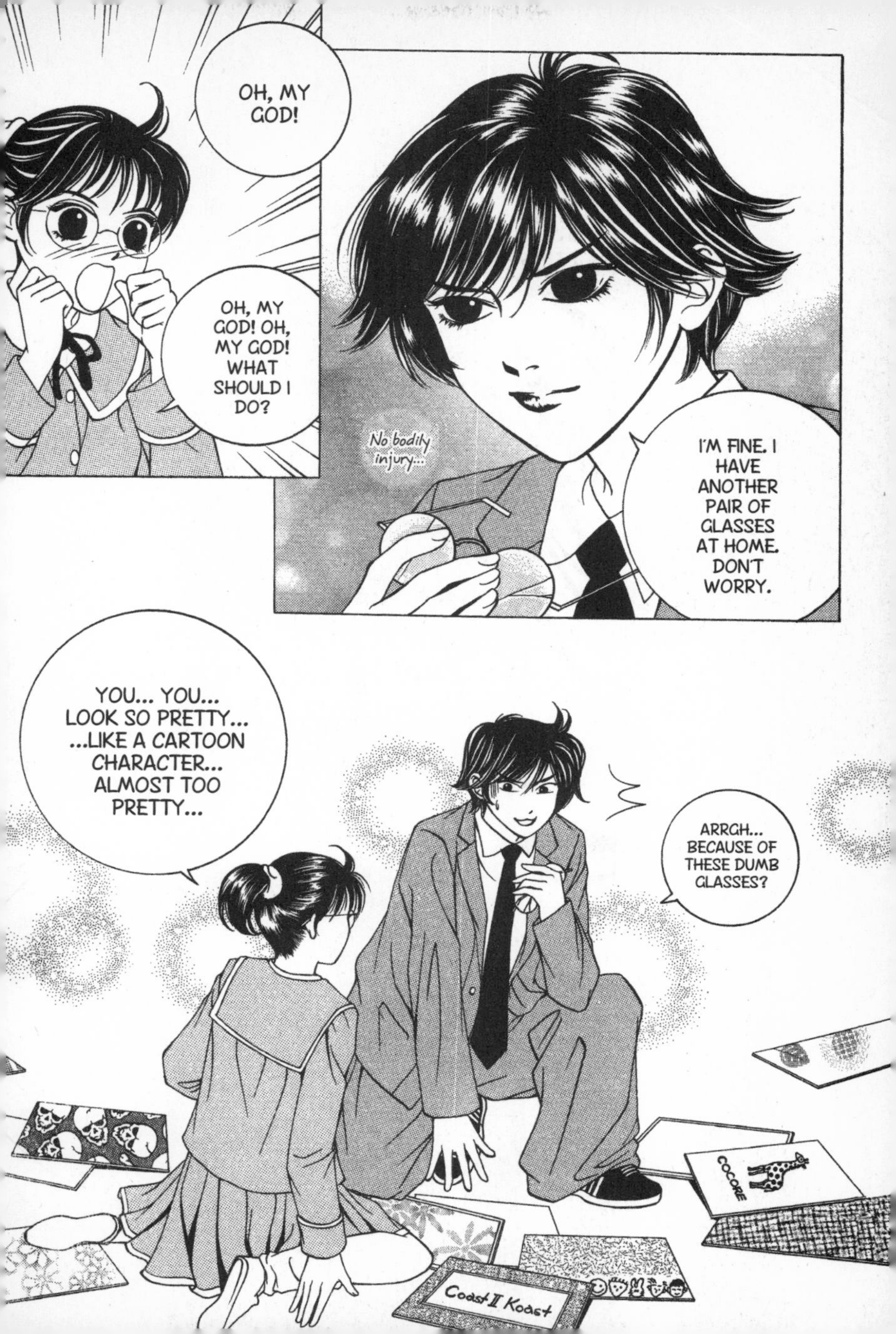
OH, MY GOD!
OH, MY GOD! OH, MY GOD! WHAT SHOULD I DO?
No bodily injury...
I'M FINE. I HAVE ANOTHER PAIR OF GLASSES AT HOME. DON'T WORRY.
YOU... YOU... LOOK SO PRETTY... ...LIKE A CARTOON CHARACTER... ALMOST TOO PRETTY...
ARRGH... BECAUSE OF THESE DUMB GLASSES?
COCORE
Coast II Koast

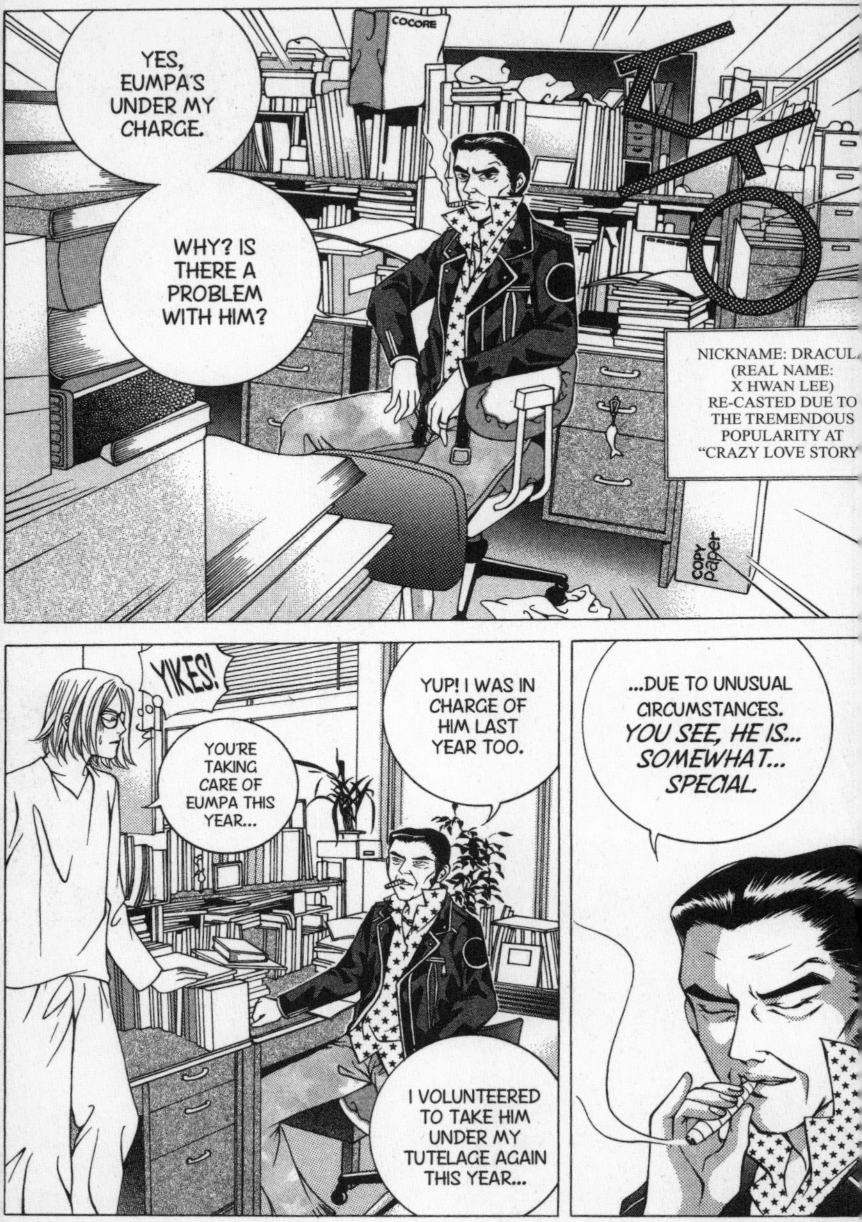
COCORE
YES, EUMPA'S UNDER MY CHARGE.
WHY? IS THERE A PROBLEM WITH HIM?
NICKNAME: DRACUL
(REAL NAME: X HWAN LEE)
RE-CASTED DUE TO THE TREMENDOUS POPULARITY AT
“CRAZY LOVE STORY
COPY Paper
YIKES!
YOU'RE TAKING CARE OF EUMPA THIS YEAR...
YUP! I WAS IN CHARGE OF HIM LAST YEAR TOO.
I VOLUNTEERED TO TAKE HIM UNDER MY TUTELAGE AGAIN THIS YEAR...
...DUE TO UNUSUAL CIRCUMSTANCES.
YOU SEE, HE IS... SOMEWHAT... SPECIAL.

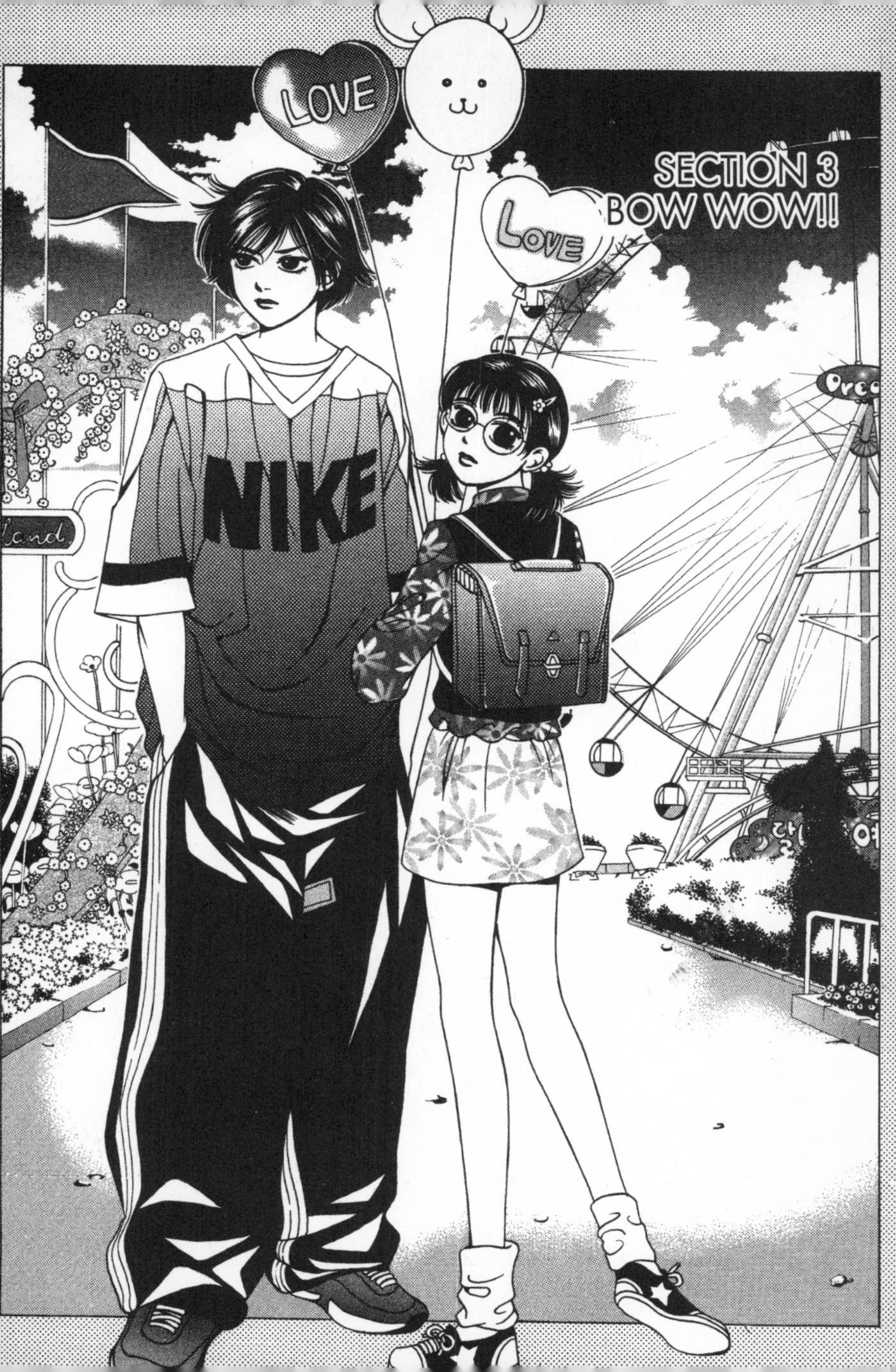
LOVE
LOVE
SECTION 3
BOW WOW!!
NIKE

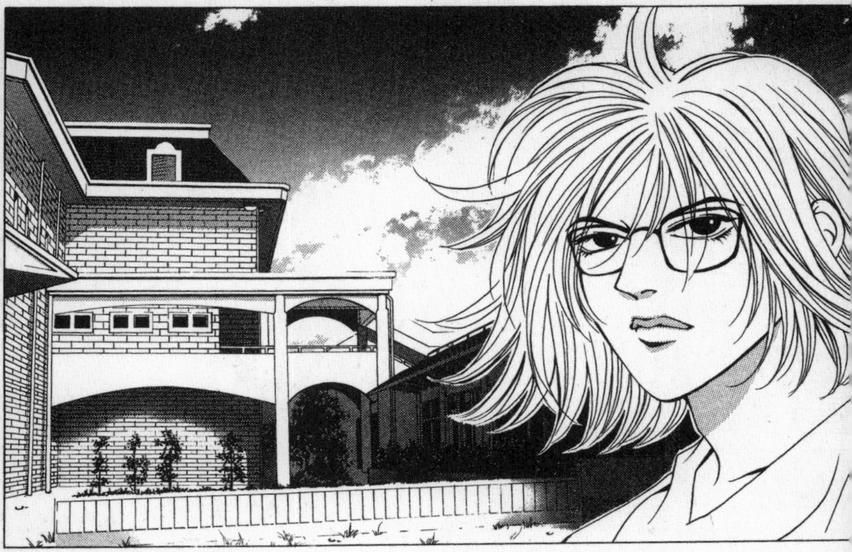

WOOJAE HA (30) :
CLASSICAL MUSIC COMPOSER AND SINGER. GRADUATED FROM SEOUL NATIONAL UNIVERSITY. MAJORED IN PIANO. COMBINING POP SONGS WITH CLASSICAL INSTRUMENTS SUCH AS VIOLIN AND CELLO, HE PRODUCED HIS DEBUT ALBUM, "RU'S SONG," WHICH CREATED A BIG SENSATION AND BROKE EVERY EXISTING SALES RECORD. UNFORTUNATELY, HE GOT WRITER'S BLOCK AND EVENTUALLY RETIRED FROM THE MUSIC INDUSTRY. HE CURRENTLY TEACHES MUSIC TO HIGH SCHOOL STUDENTS, WAITING FOR INSPIRATION. HE'S SOMEWHAT PESSIMISTIC AND TWISTED. BLOOD-TYPE: A.

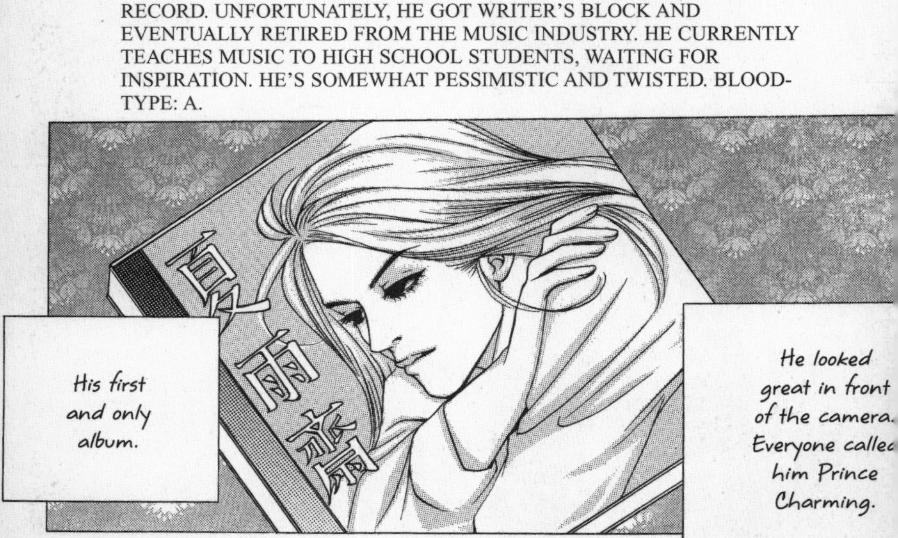
His first and only album.
He looked great in front of the camera. Everyone called him Prince Charming.

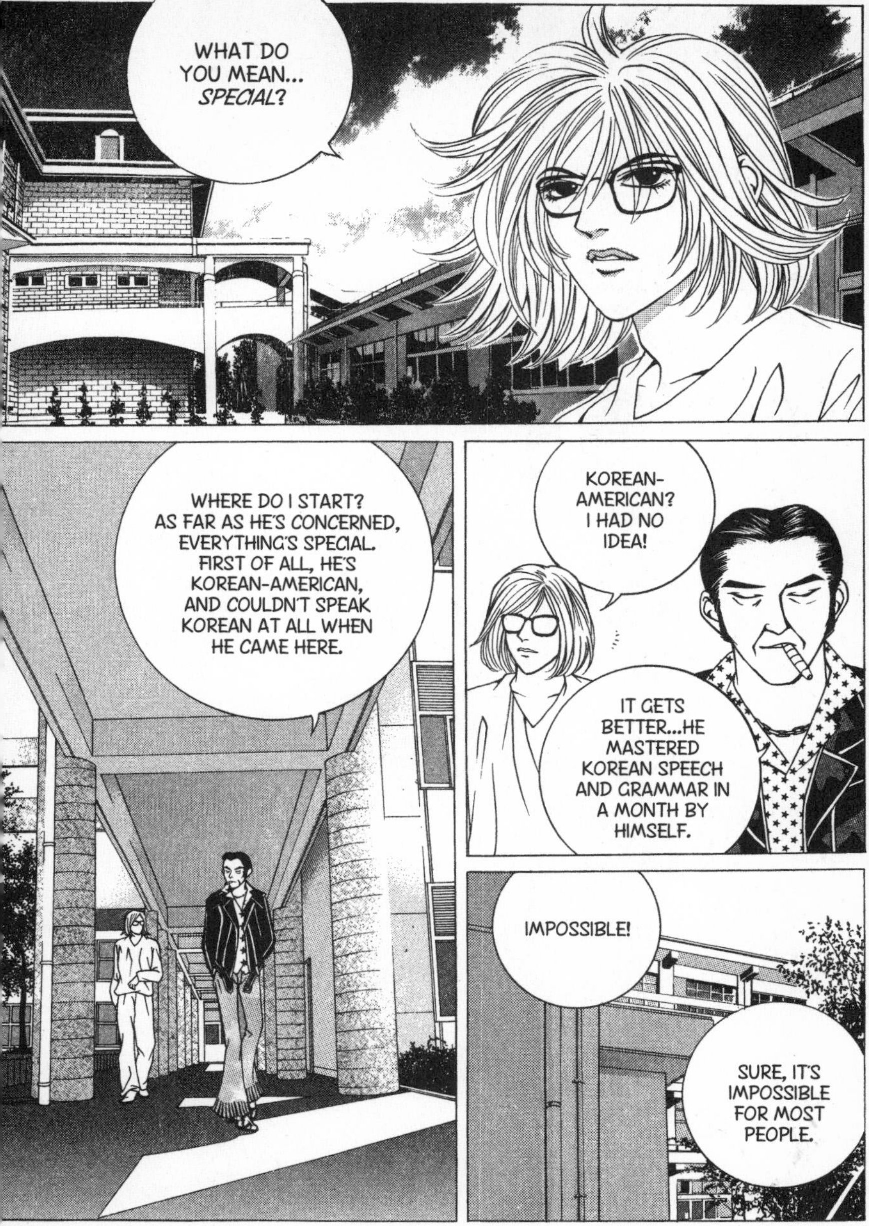

WHAT DO YOU MEAN... *SPECIAL?*
WHERE DO I START? AS FAR AS HE'S CONCERNED, EVERYTHING'S SPECIAL. FIRST OF ALL, HE'S KOREAN-AMERICAN, AND COULDN'T SPEAK KOREAN AT ALL WHEN HE CAME HERE.
KOREAN-AMERICAN? I HAD NO IDEA!
IT GETS BETTER...HE MASTERED KOREAN SPEECH AND GRAMMAR IN A MONTH BY HIMSELF.
IMPOSSIBLE!
SURE, IT'S IMPOSSIBLE FOR MOST PEOPLE.

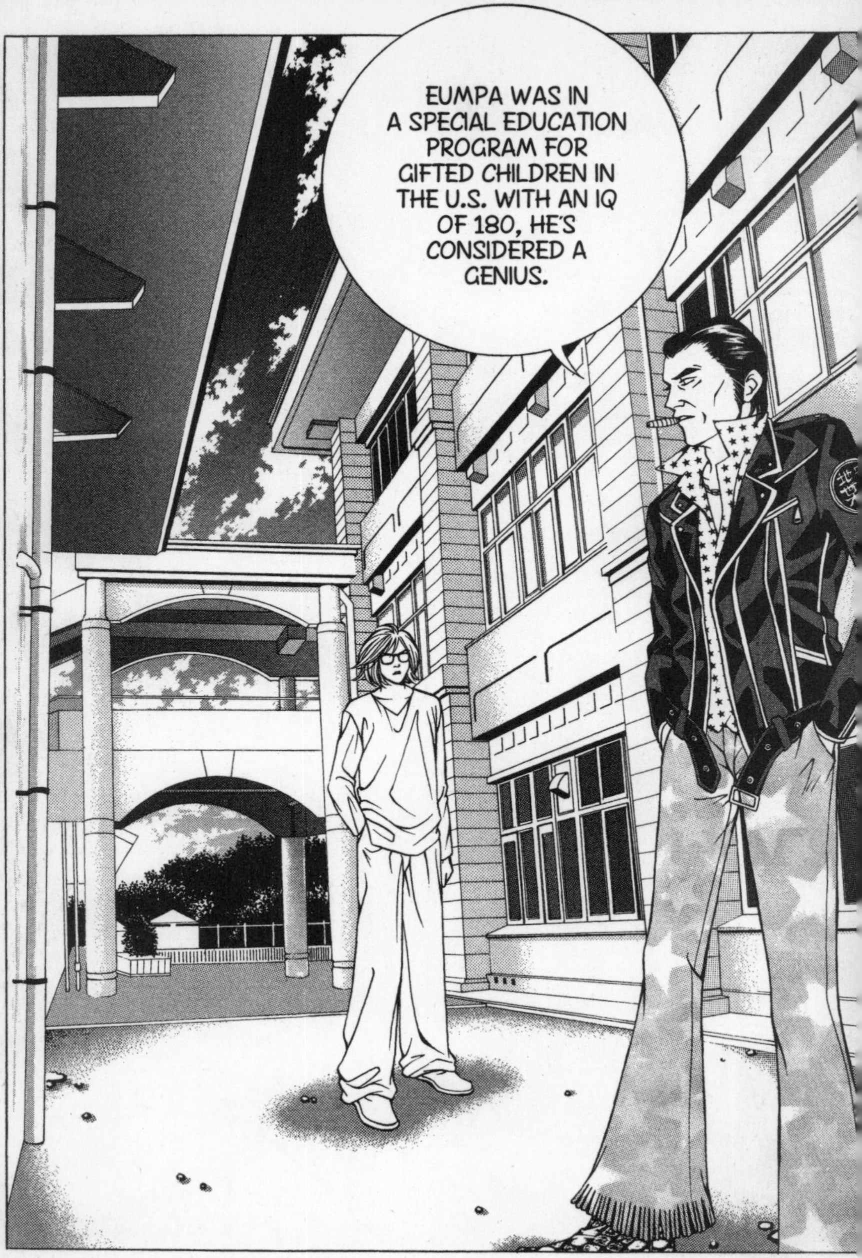
EUMPA WAS IN A SPECIAL EDUCATION PROGRAM FOR GIFTED CHILDREN IN THE U.S. WITH AN IQ OF 180, HE'S CONSIDERED A GENIUS.

SUPER MAN

I LOOK LIKE A CARTOON? BUT CARTOON CHARACTERS ARE NOT PRETTY!

ROMANCE CARTOONS! DON'T YOU READ ROMANCE COMICS?

WHAT'RE ROMANCE COMICS?

AHHH... Laider, Jimmy, Sungmu, Myoungil, Maru, Hosu, Rauds, Shin-Chan...

THEY'RE FOR GIRLS! THEY'RE VERY NICE AND SWEET BOOKS WITH STORIES ABOUT HANDSOME MEN AND BEAUTIFUL GIRLS.

HANDSOME MEN? BEAUTIFUL GIRLS?

I'M HUGE FAN OF COMICS. DON'T YOU LIKE THEM?

I guess I should pretend I do.

I LIKE COMIC BOOKS VERY MUCH.

He's never read a comic book in his life.

I SHOULD START READING THESE ROMANCE BOOKS, TOO.

I'm going to have to do a lot of reading quick!

65

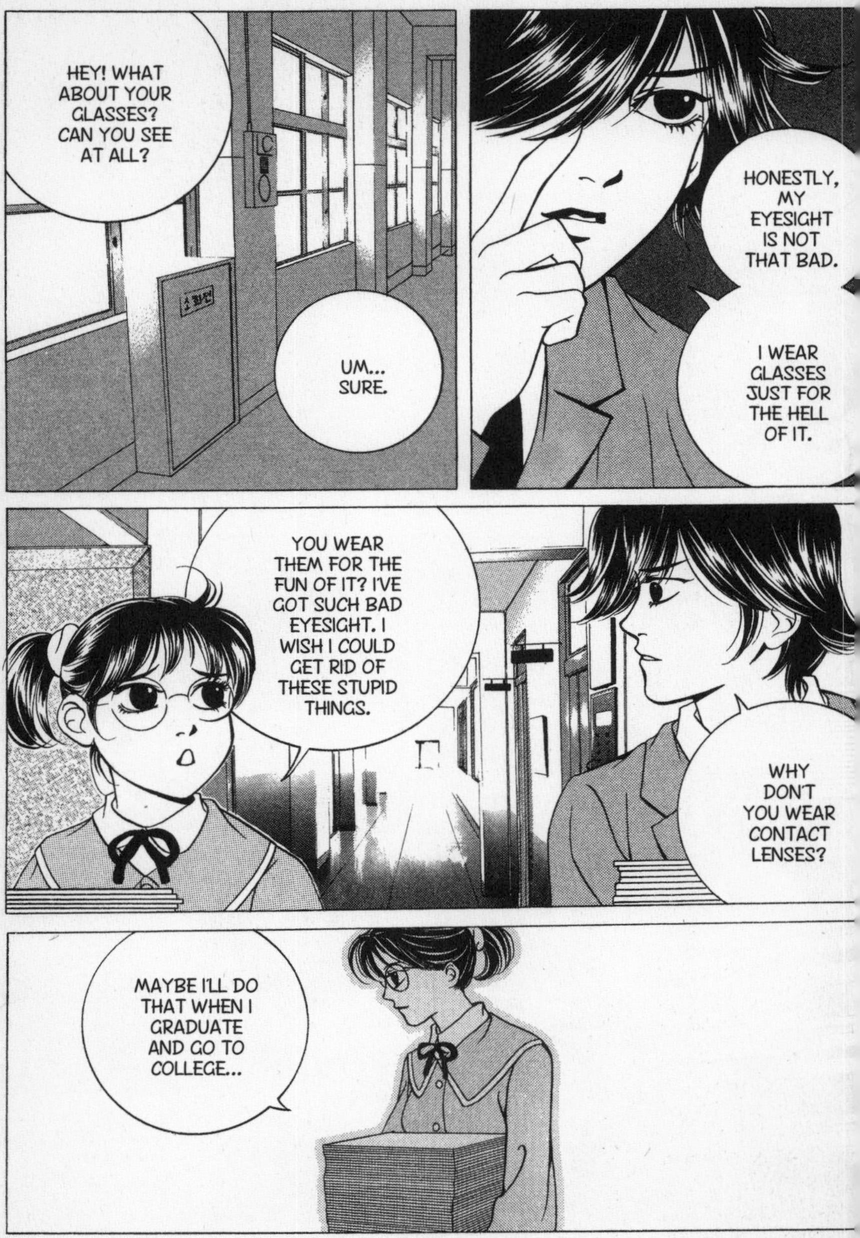
HEY! WHAT ABOUT YOUR GLASSES? CAN YOU SEE AT ALL?
UM... SURE.
HONESTLY, MY EYESIGHT IS NOT THAT BAD.
I WEAR GLASSES JUST FOR THE HELL OF IT.
YOU WEAR THEM FOR THE FUN OF IT? I'VE GOT SUCH BAD EYESIGHT. I WISH I COULD GET RID OF THESE STUPID THINGS.
WHY DON'T YOU WEAR CONTACT LENSES?
MAYBE I'LL DO THAT WHEN I GRADUATE AND GO TO COLLEGE...

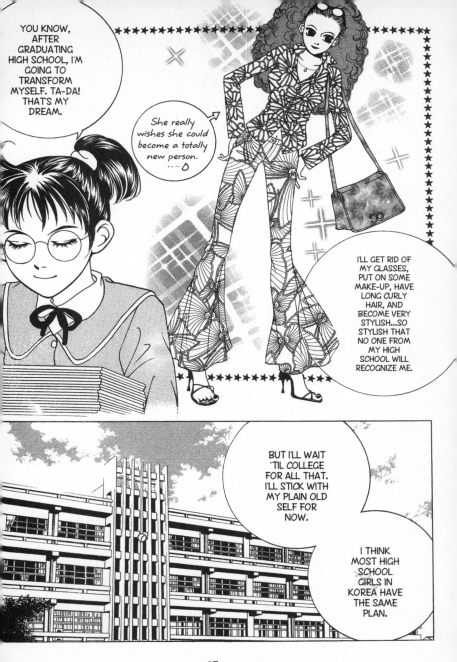

YOU KNOW, AFTER GRADUATING HIGH SCHOOL, I'M GOING TO TRANSFORM MYSELF. TA-DA! THAT'S MY DREAM.

She really wishes she could become a totally new person. ....◊

I'LL GET RID OF MY GLASSES, PUT ON SOME MAKE-UP, HAVE LONG CURLY HAIR, AND BECOME VERY STYLISH...SO STYLISH THAT NO ONE FROM MY HIGH SCHOOL WILL RECOGNIZE ME.

BUT I'LL WAIT 'TIL COLLEGE FOR ALL THAT. I'LL STICK WITH MY PLAIN OLD SELF FOR NOW.

I THINK MOST HIGH SCHOOL GIRLS IN KOREA HAVE THE SAME PLAN.

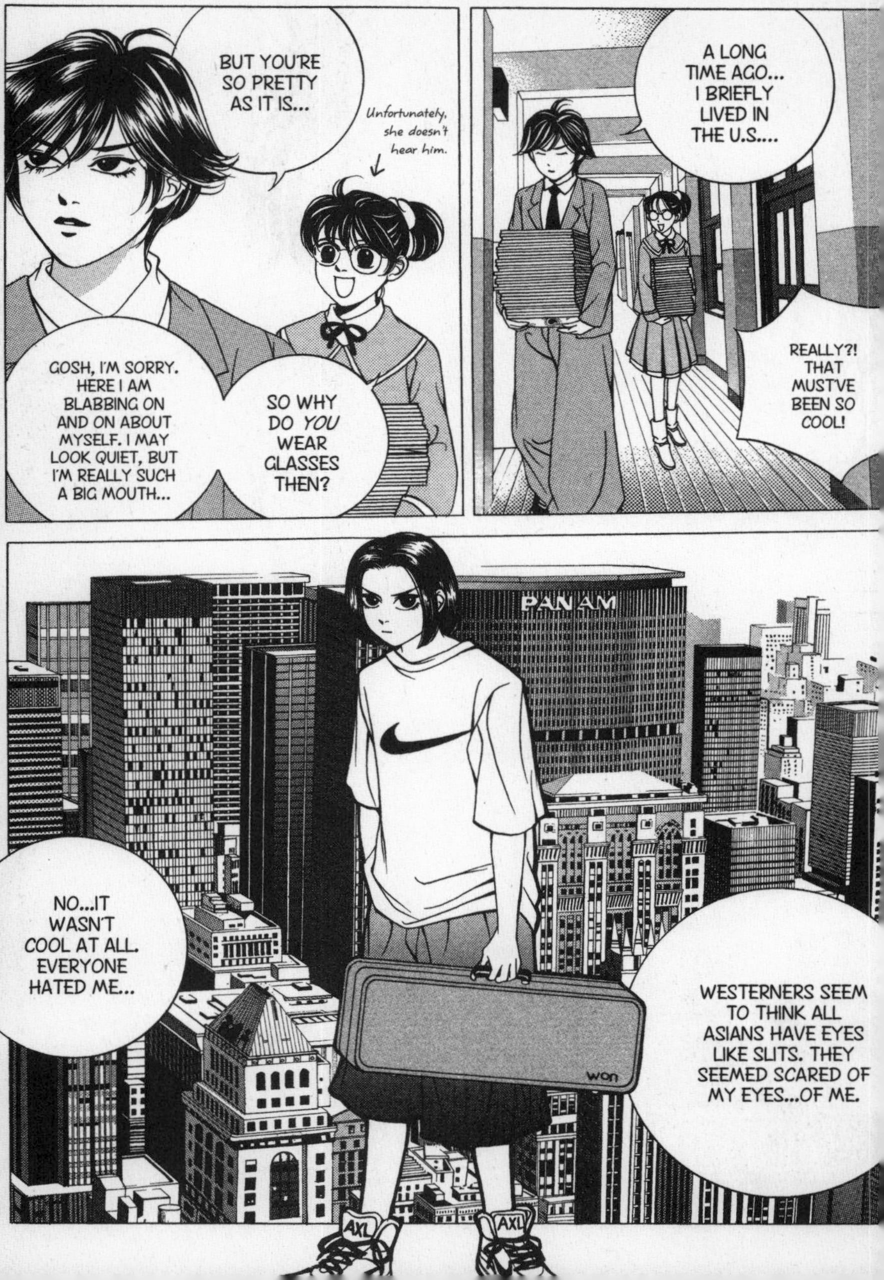
BUT YOU'RE SO PRETTY AS IT IS...
Unfortunately, she doesn't hear him.
GOSH, I'M SORRY. HERE I AM BLABBING ON AND ON ABOUT MYSELF. I MAY LOOK QUIET, BUT I'M REALLY SUCH A BIG MOUTH...
SO WHY DO *YOU* WEAR GLASSES THEN?
A LONG TIME AGO... I BRIEFLY LIVED IN THE U.S....
REALLY?! THAT MUSTVE BEEN SO COOL!
PAN AM
NO...IT WASN'T COOL AT ALL. EVERYONE HATED ME...
won
WESTERNERS SEEM TO THINK ALL ASIANS HAVE EYES LIKE SLITS. THEY SEEMED SCARED OF MY EYES...OF ME.
AXL
AXL

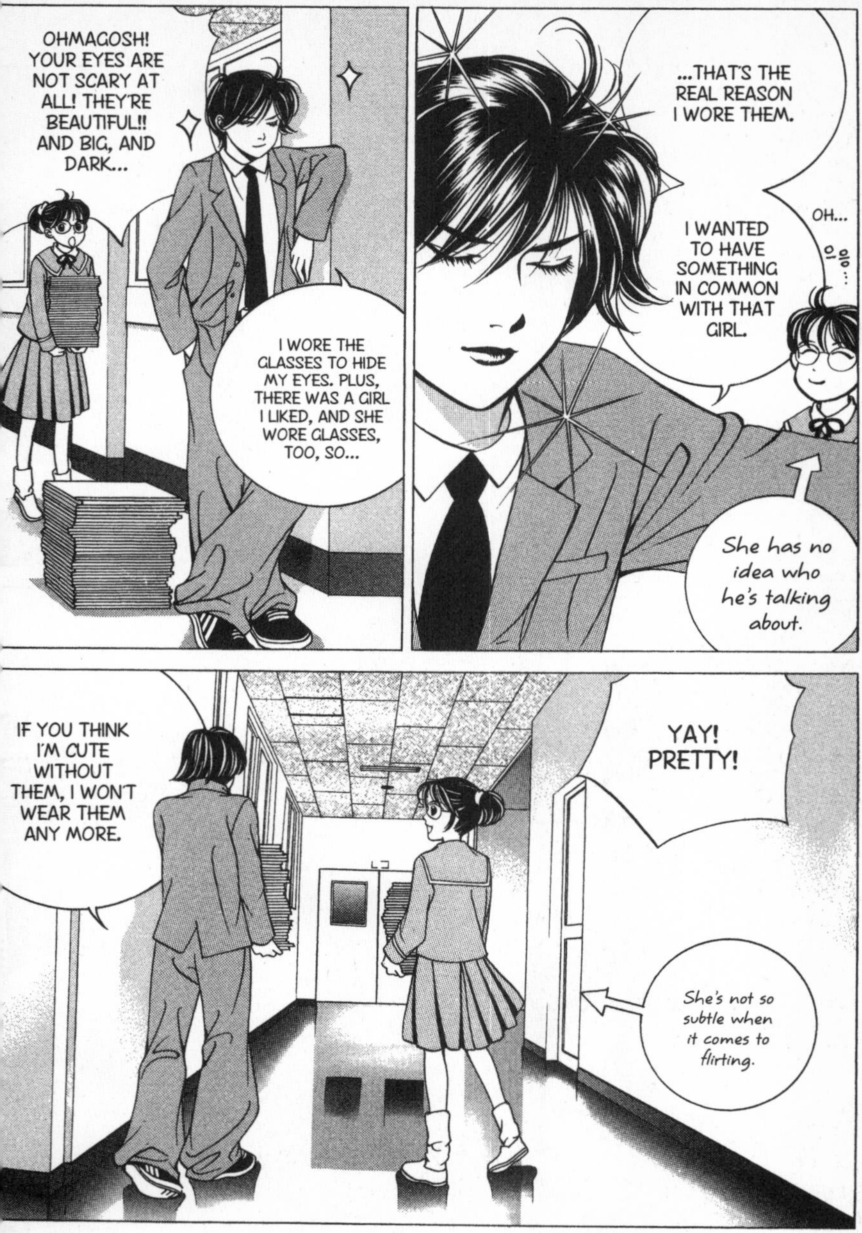
OHMAGOSH! YOUR EYES ARE NOT SCARY AT ALL! THEY'RE BEAUTIFUL!! AND BIG, AND DARK...
I WORE THE GLASSES TO HIDE MY EYES. PLUS, THERE WAS A GIRL I LIKED, AND SHE WORE GLASSES, TOO, SO...
...THAT'S THE REAL REASON I WORE THEM.
I WANTED TO HAVE SOMETHING IN COMMON WITH THAT GIRL.
OH...
이잉...
She has no idea who he's talking about.
IF YOU THINK I'M CUTE WITHOUT THEM, I WON'T WEAR THEM ANY MORE.
YAY! PRETTY!
She's not so subtle when it comes to flirting.

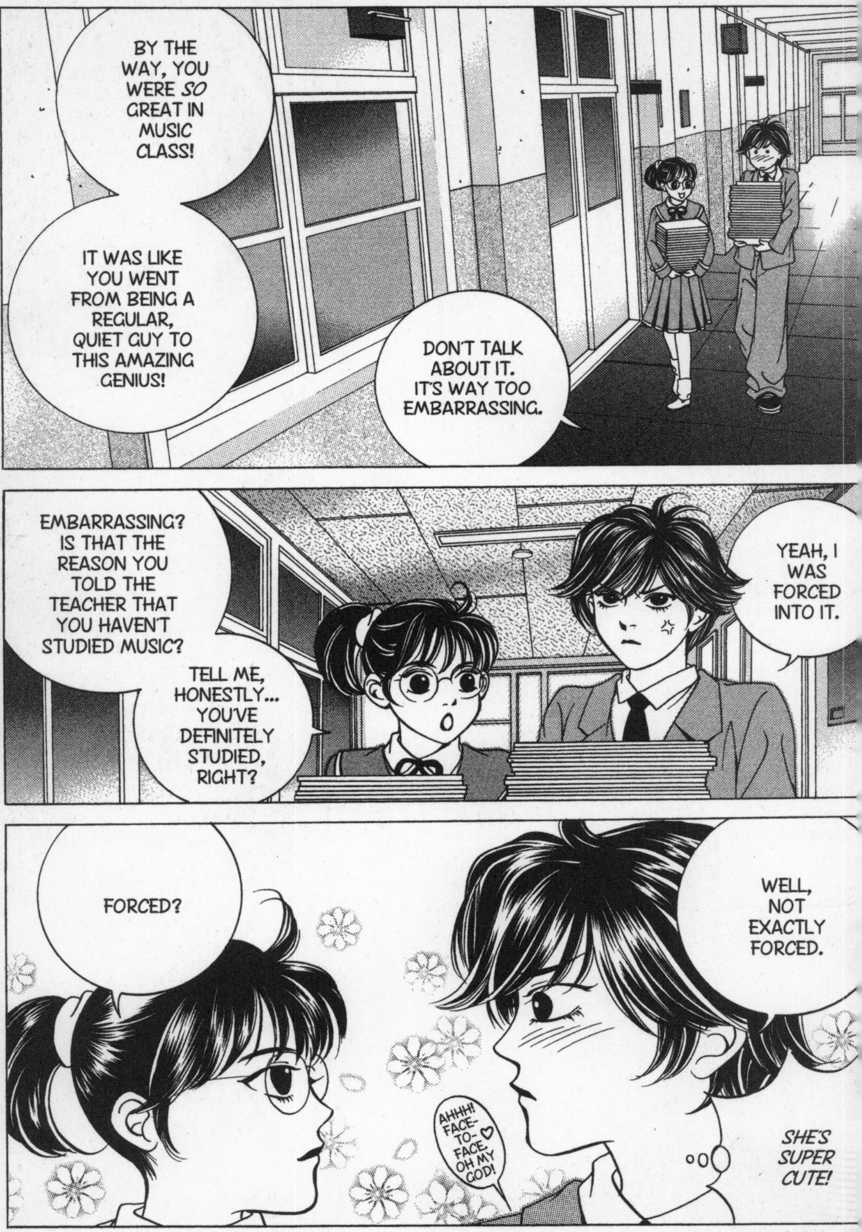
BY THE WAY, YOU WERE *SO* GREAT IN MUSIC CLASS!
IT WAS LIKE YOU WENT FROM BEING A REGULAR, QUIET GUY TO THIS AMAZING GENIUS!
DON'T TALK ABOUT IT. IT'S WAY TOO EMBARRASSING.
EMBARRASSING? IS THAT THE REASON YOU TOLD THE TEACHER THAT YOU HAVEN'T STUDIED MUSIC?
TELL ME, HONESTLY... YOU'VE DEFINITELY STUDIED, RIGHT?
YEAH, I WAS FORCED INTO IT.
FORCED?
AHHH! FACE-TO-FACE♡ OH MY GOD!
WELL, NOT EXACTLY FORCED.
SHE'S SUPER CUTE!

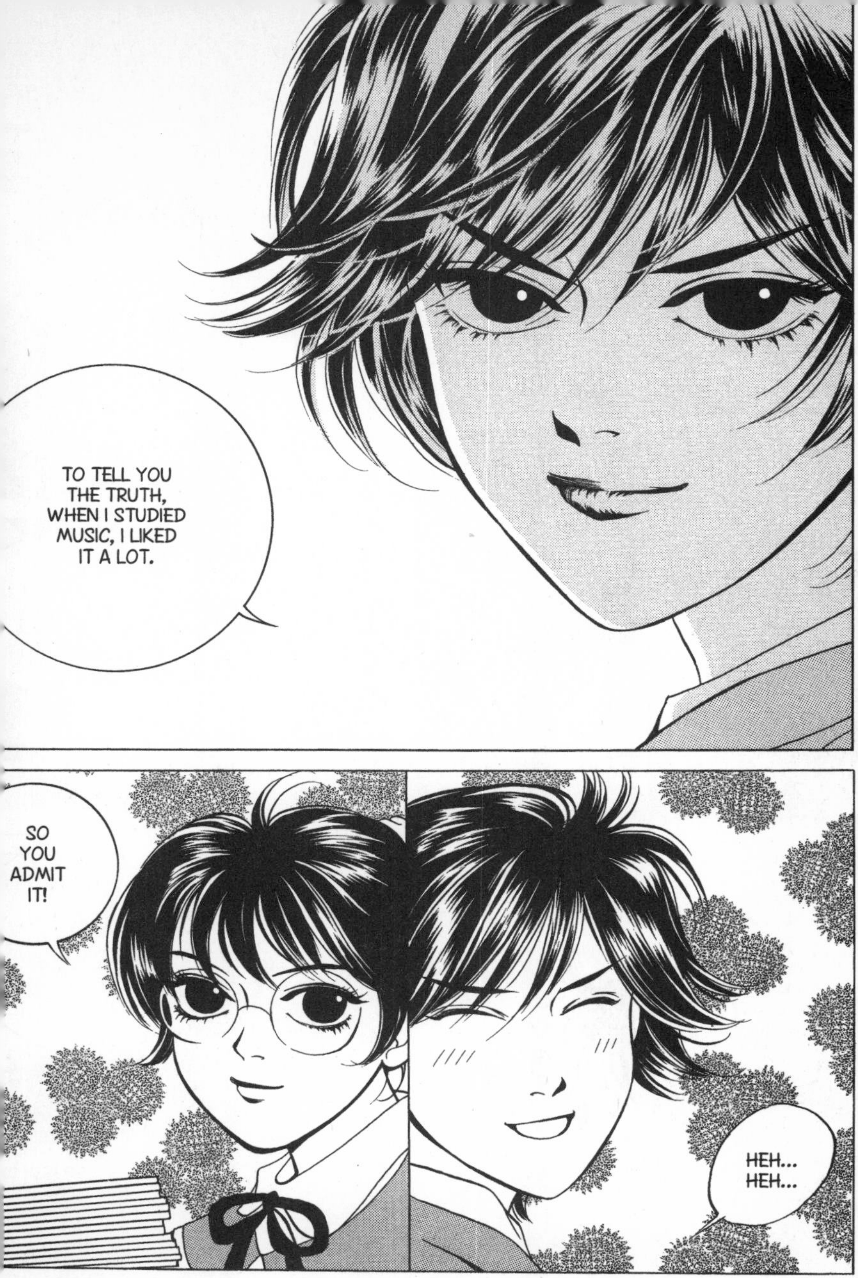
TO TELL YOU THE TRUTH, WHEN I STUDIED MUSIC, I LIKED IT A LOT.
SO YOU ADMIT IT!
HEH... HEH...

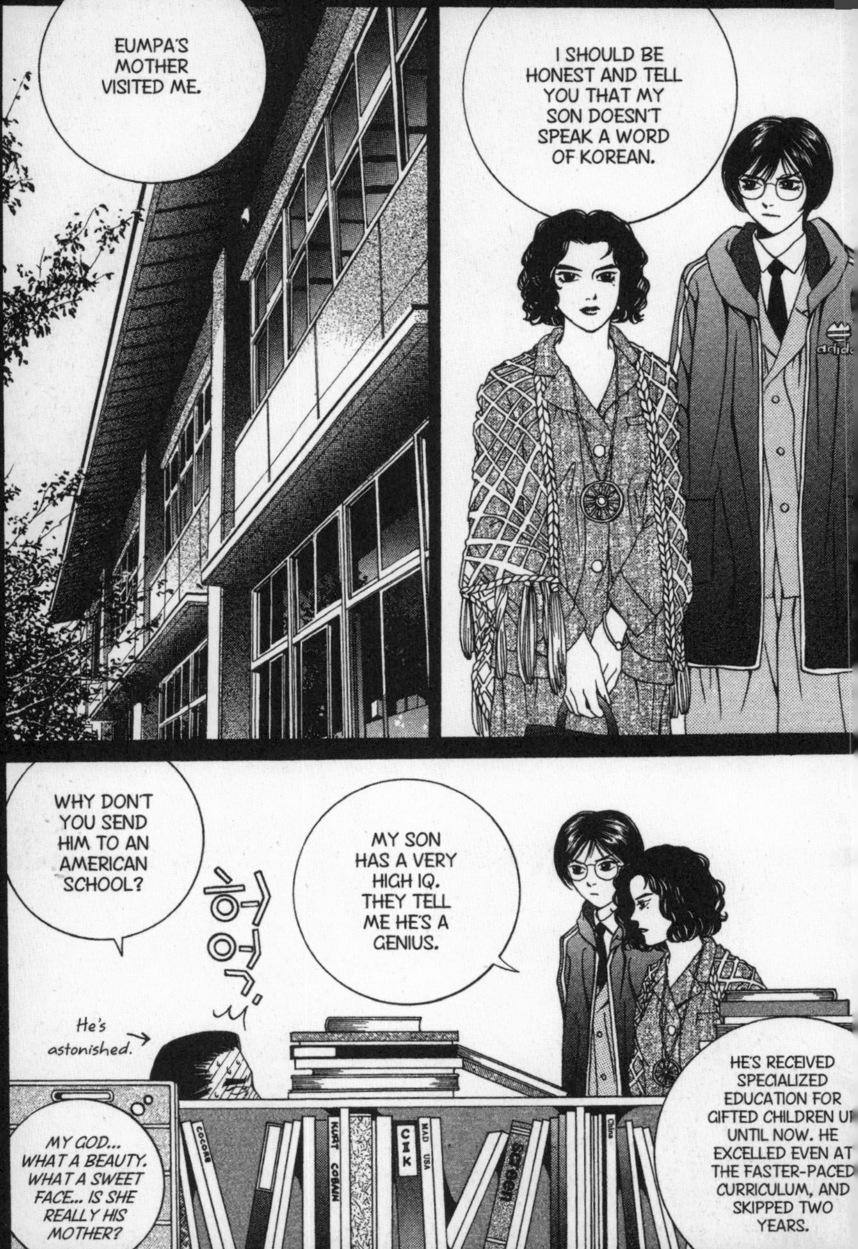
EUMPA'S MOTHER VISITED ME.
I SHOULD BE HONEST AND TELL YOU THAT MY SON DOESN'T SPEAK A WORD OF KOREAN.
WHY DON'T YOU SEND HIM TO AN AMERICAN SCHOOL?
MY SON HAS A VERY HIGH IQ. THEY TELL ME HE'S A GENIUS.
He's astonished.
MY GOD... WHAT A BEAUTY. WHAT A SWEET FACE... IS SHE REALLY HIS MOTHER?
HE'S RECEIVED SPECIALIZED EDUCATION FOR GIFTED CHILDREN U UNTIL NOW. HE EXCELLED EVEN AT THE FASTER-PACED CURRICULUM, AND SKIPPED TWO YEARS.

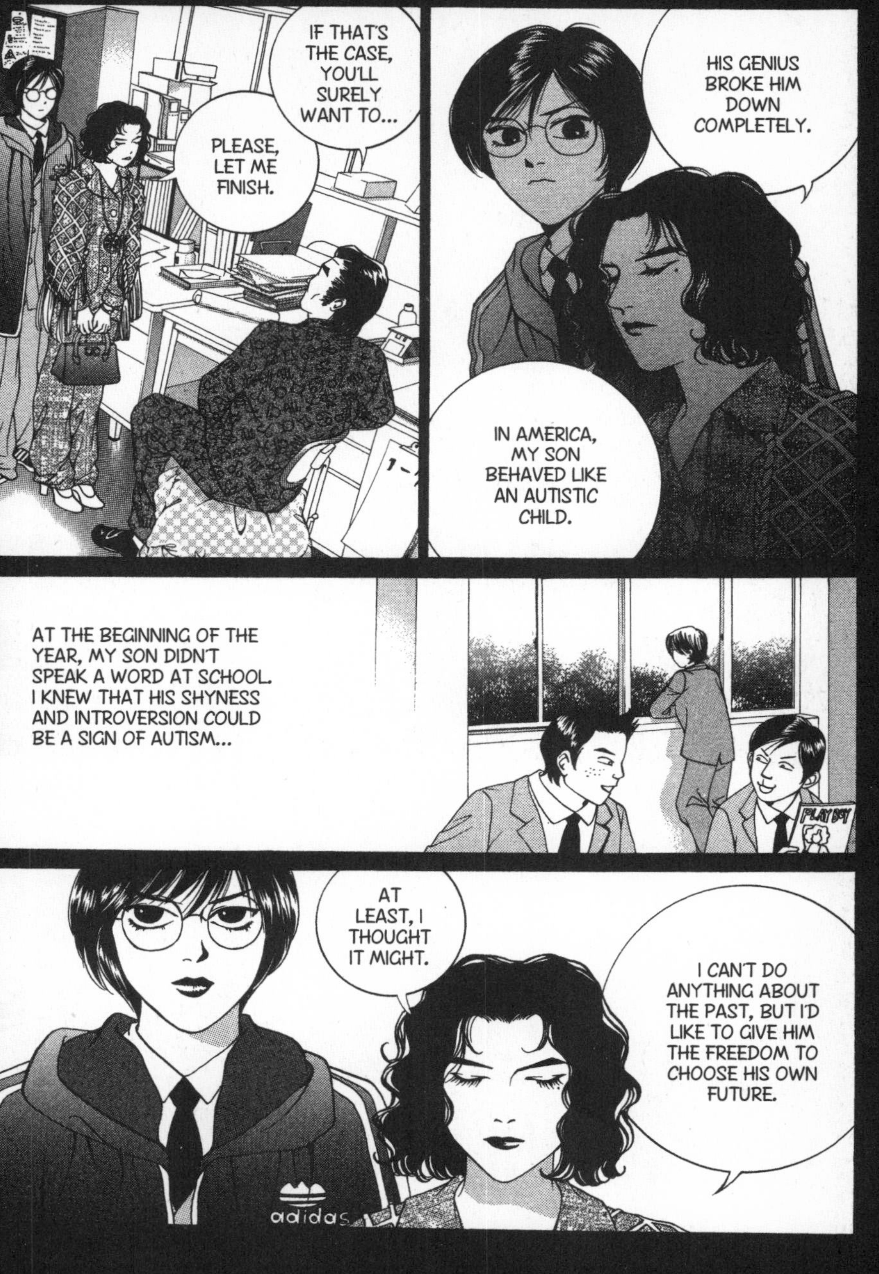
IF THAT'S THE CASE, YOU'LL SURELY WANT TO...
PLEASE, LET ME FINISH.
HIS GENIUS BROKE HIM DOWN COMPLETELY.
IN AMERICA, MY SON BEHAVED LIKE AN AUTISTIC CHILD.
AT THE BEGINNING OF THE YEAR, MY SON DIDN'T SPEAK A WORD AT SCHOOL. I KNEW THAT HIS SHYNESS AND INTROVERSION COULD BE A SIGN OF AUTISM...
PLAY BOY
AT LEAST, I THOUGHT IT MIGHT.
I CAN'T DO ANYTHING ABOUT THE PAST, BUT I'D LIKE TO GIVE HIM THE FREEDOM TO CHOOSE HIS OWN FUTURE.
adidas

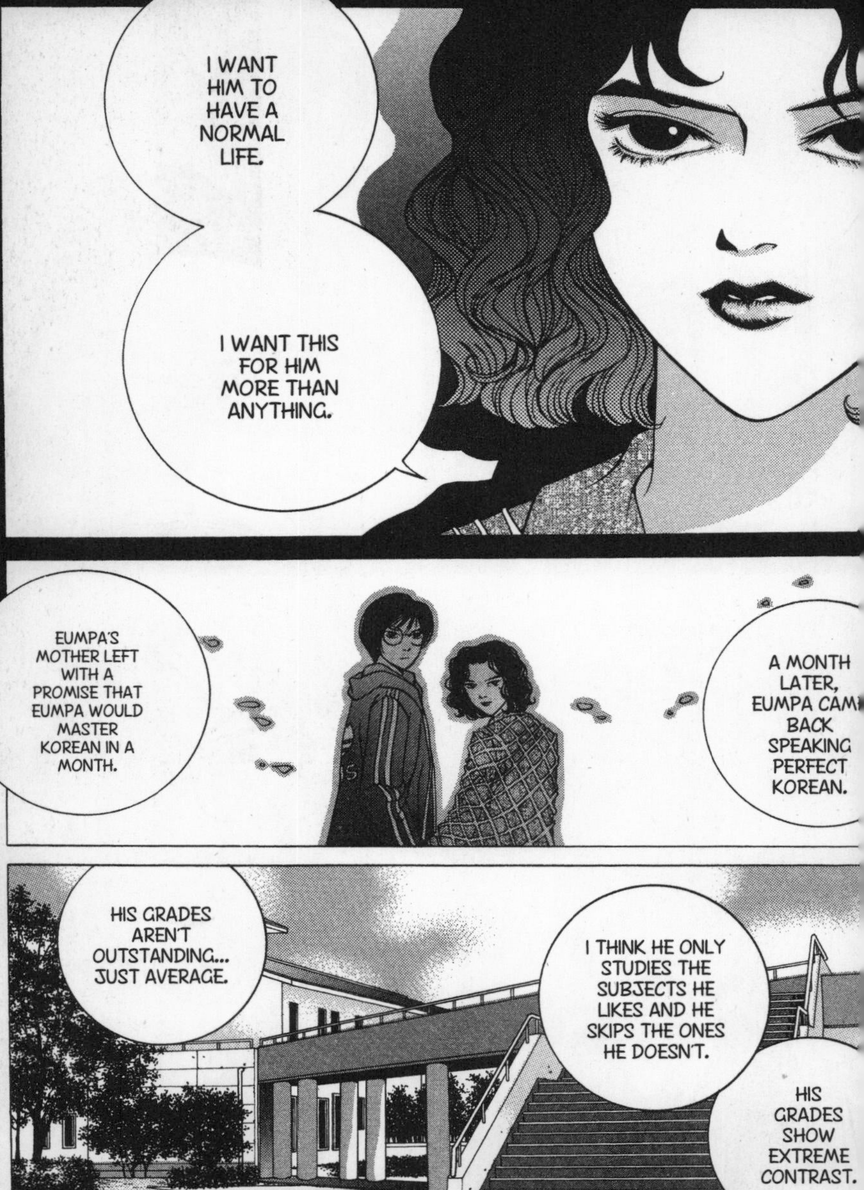
I WANT HIM TO HAVE A NORMAL LIFE.
I WANT THIS FOR HIM MORE THAN ANYTHING.
EUMPA'S MOTHER LEFT WITH A PROMISE THAT EUMPA WOULD MASTER KOREAN IN A MONTH.
A MONTH LATER, EUMPA CAM BACK SPEAKING PERFECT KOREAN.
HIS GRADES AREN'T OUTSTANDING... JUST AVERAGE.
I THINK HE ONLY STUDIES THE SUBJECTS HE LIKES AND HE SKIPS THE ONES HE DOESN'T.
HIS GRADES SHOW EXTREME CONTRAST.

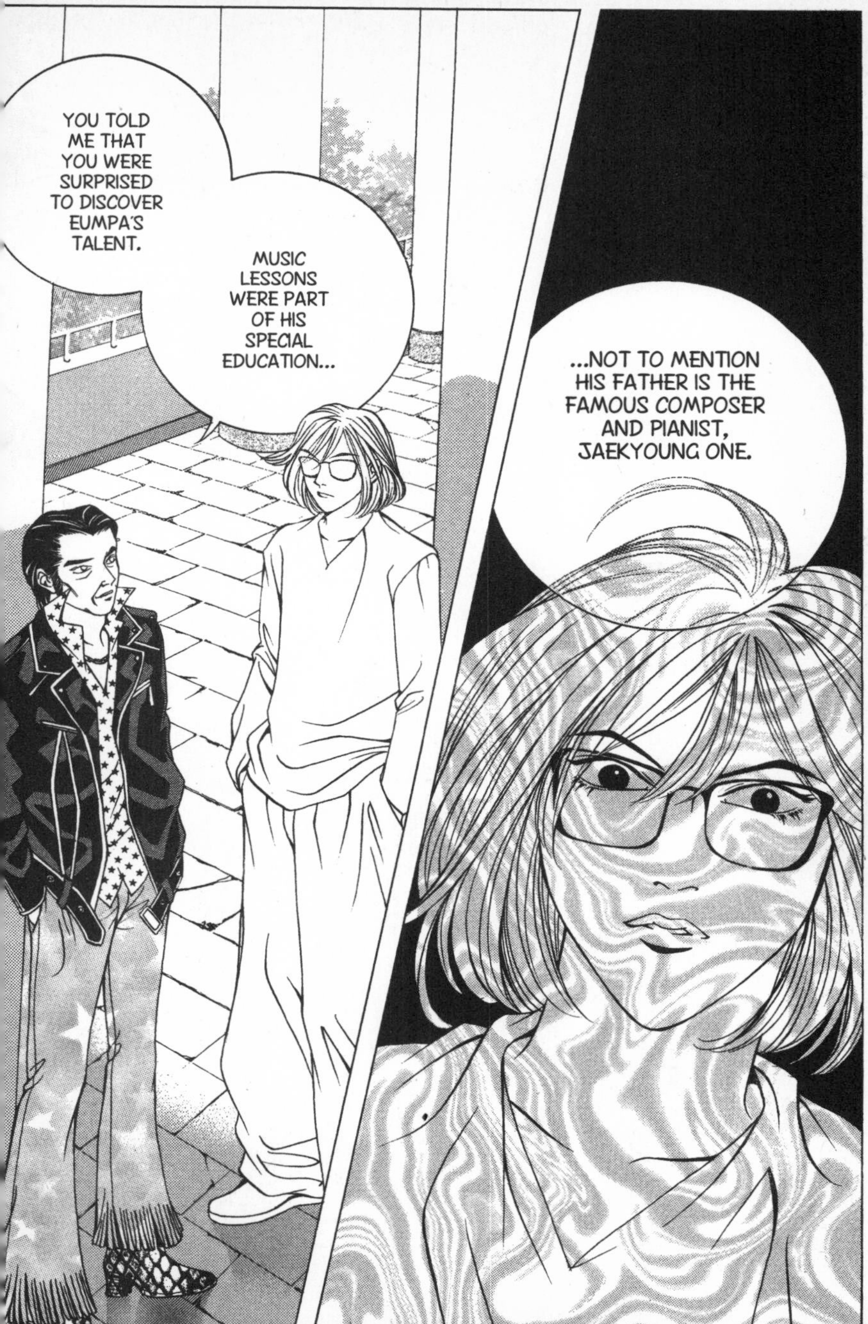
YOU TOLD ME THAT YOU WERE SURPRISED TO DISCOVER EUMPA'S TALENT.
MUSIC LESSONS WERE PART OF HIS SPECIAL EDUCATION...
...NOT TO MENTION HIS FATHER IS THE FAMOUS COMPOSER AND PIANIST, JAEKYOUNG ONE.

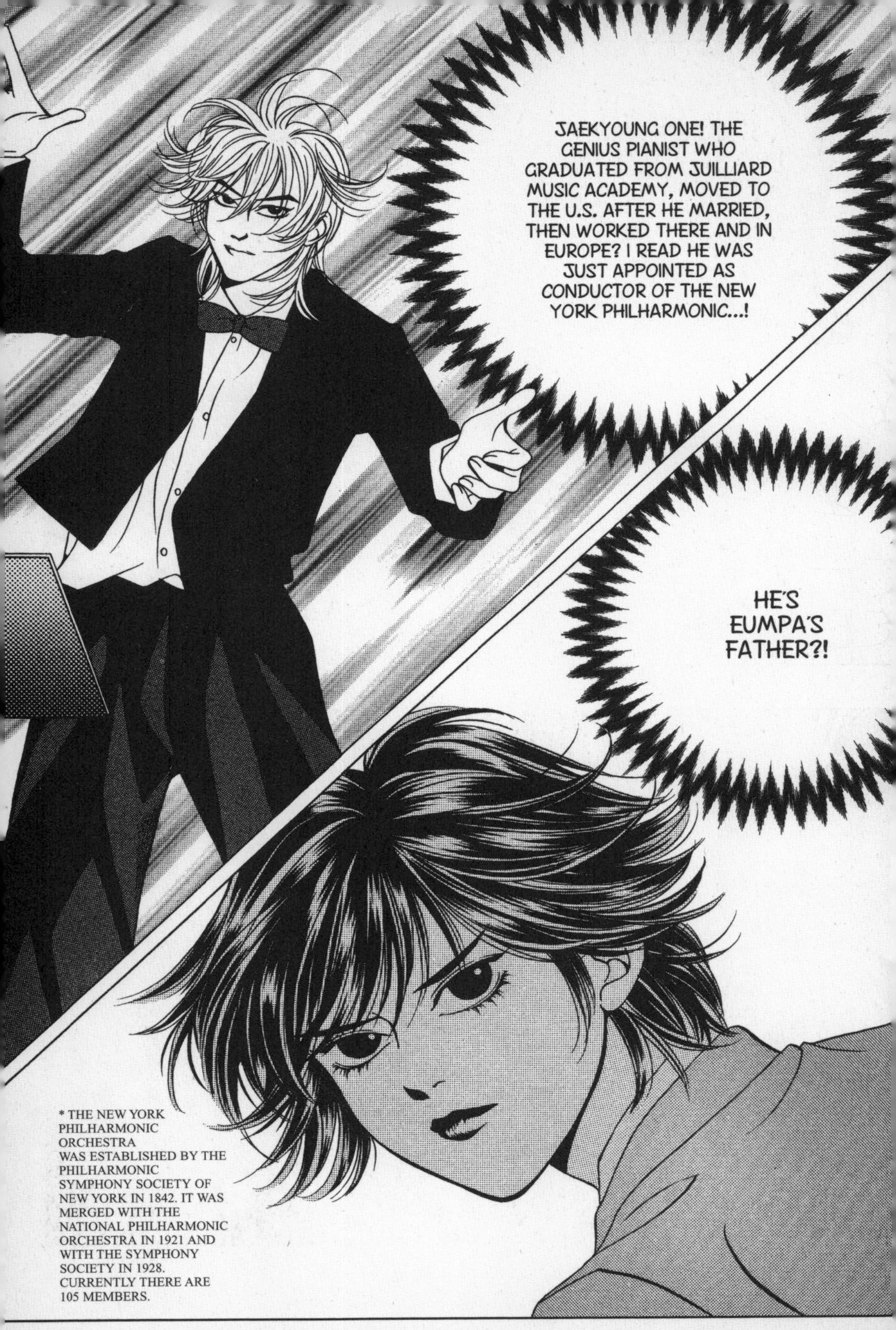
JAEKYOUNG ONE! THE GENIUS PIANIST WHO GRADUATED FROM JUILLIARD MUSIC ACADEMY, MOVED TO THE U.S. AFTER HE MARRIED, THEN WORKED THERE AND IN EUROPE? I READ HE WAS JUST APPOINTED AS CONDUCTOR OF THE NEW YORK PHILHARMONIC...!
HE'S EUMPA'S FATHER?!

* THE NEW YORK PHILHARMONIC ORCHESTRA WAS ESTABLISHED BY THE PHILHARMONIC SYMPHONY SOCIETY OF NEW YORK IN 1842. IT WAS MERGED WITH THE NATIONAL PHILHARMONIC ORCHESTRA IN 1921 AND WITH THE SYMPHONY SOCIETY IN 1928. CURRENTLY THERE ARE 105 MEMBERS.

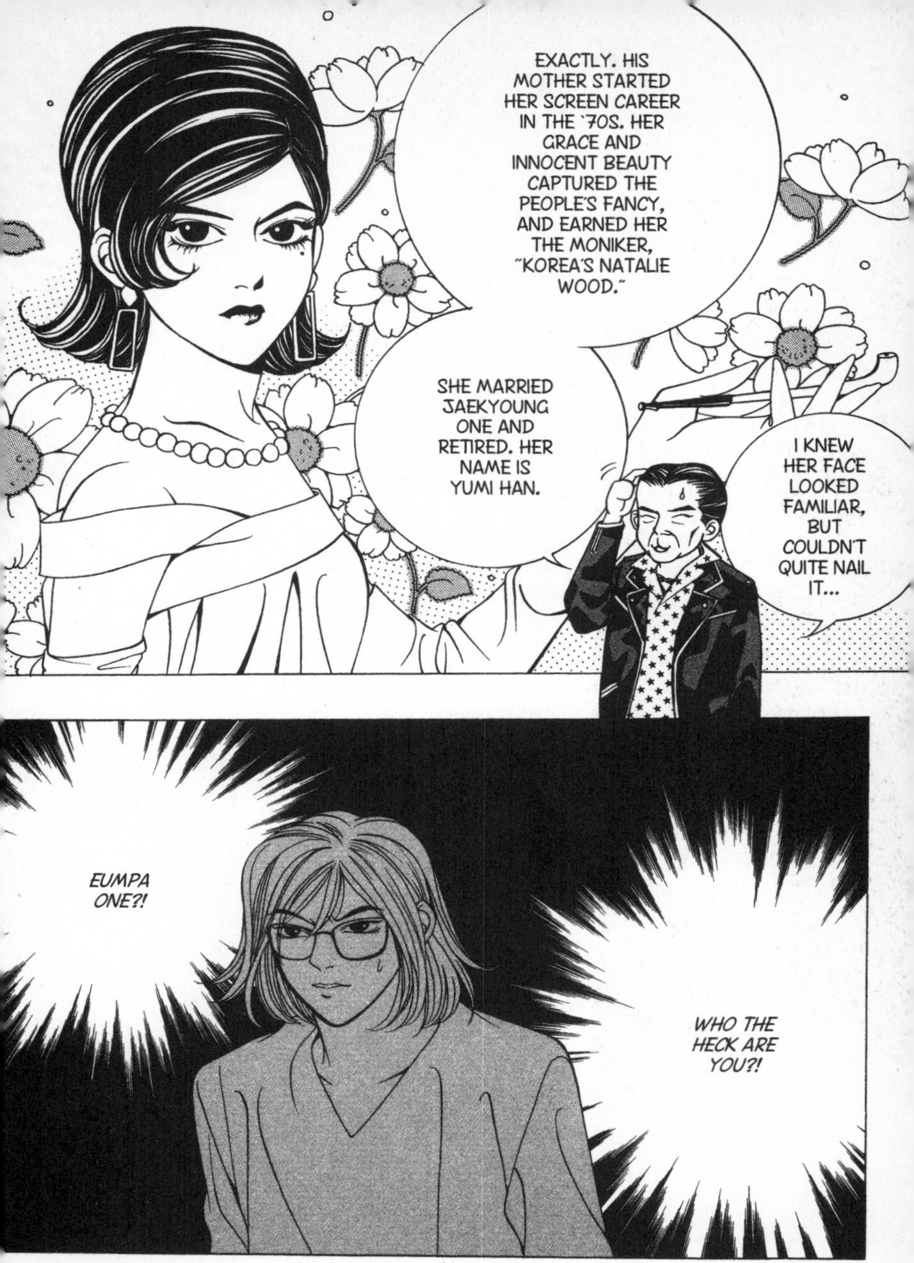

EXACTLY. HIS MOTHER STARTED HER SCREEN CAREER IN THE '70S. HER GRACE AND INNOCENT BEAUTY CAPTURED THE PEOPLE'S FANCY, AND EARNED HER THE MONIKER, "KOREA'S NATALIE WOOD."
SHE MARRIED JAEKYOUNG ONE AND RETIRED. HER NAME IS YUMI HAN.
I KNEW HER FACE LOOKED FAMILIAR, BUT COULDN'T QUITE NAIL IT...
EUMPA ONE?!
WHO THE HECK ARE YOU?!

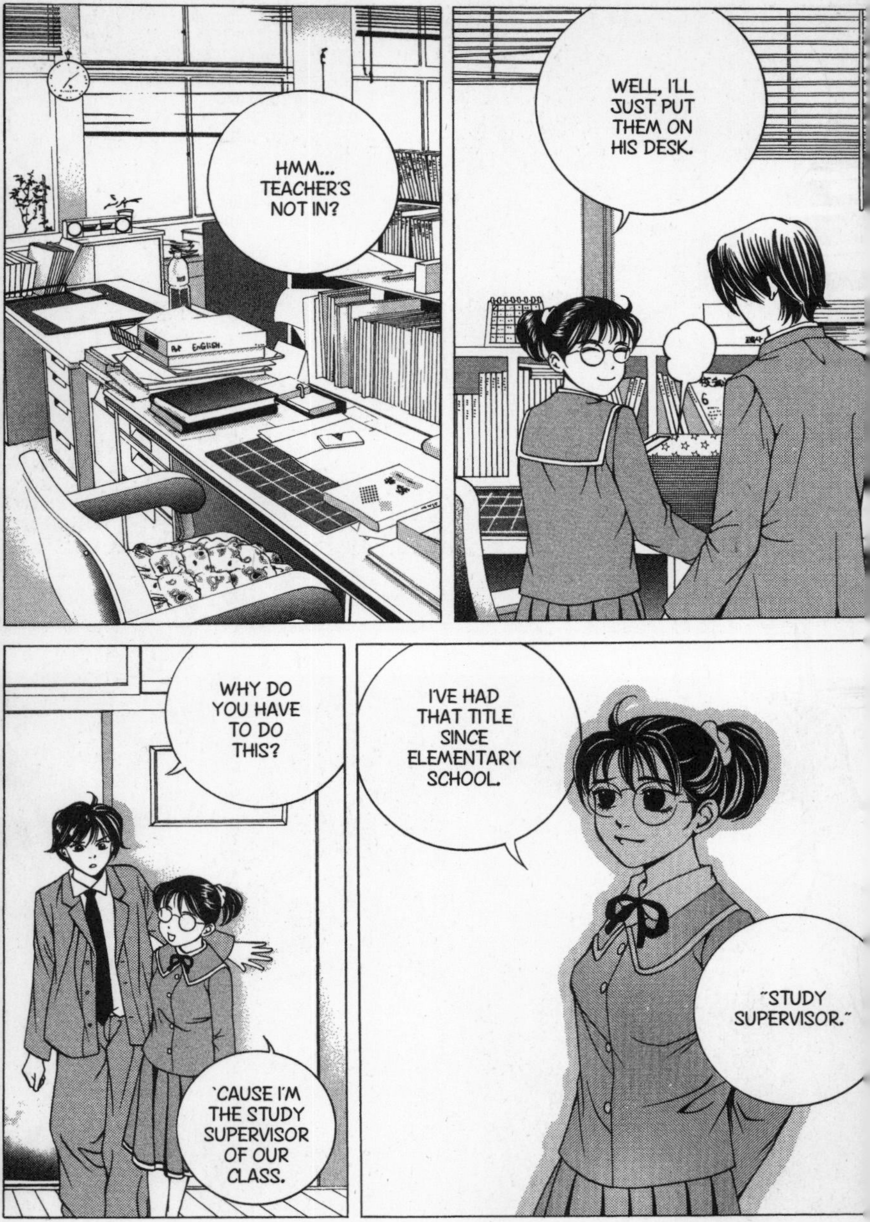
HMM... TEACHER'S NOT IN?
WELL, I'LL JUST PUT THEM ON HIS DESK.
WHY DO YOU HAVE TO DO THIS?
'CAUSE I'M THE STUDY SUPERVISOR OF OUR CLASS.
I'VE HAD THAT TITLE SINCE ELEMENTARY SCHOOL.
"STUDY SUPERVISOR."

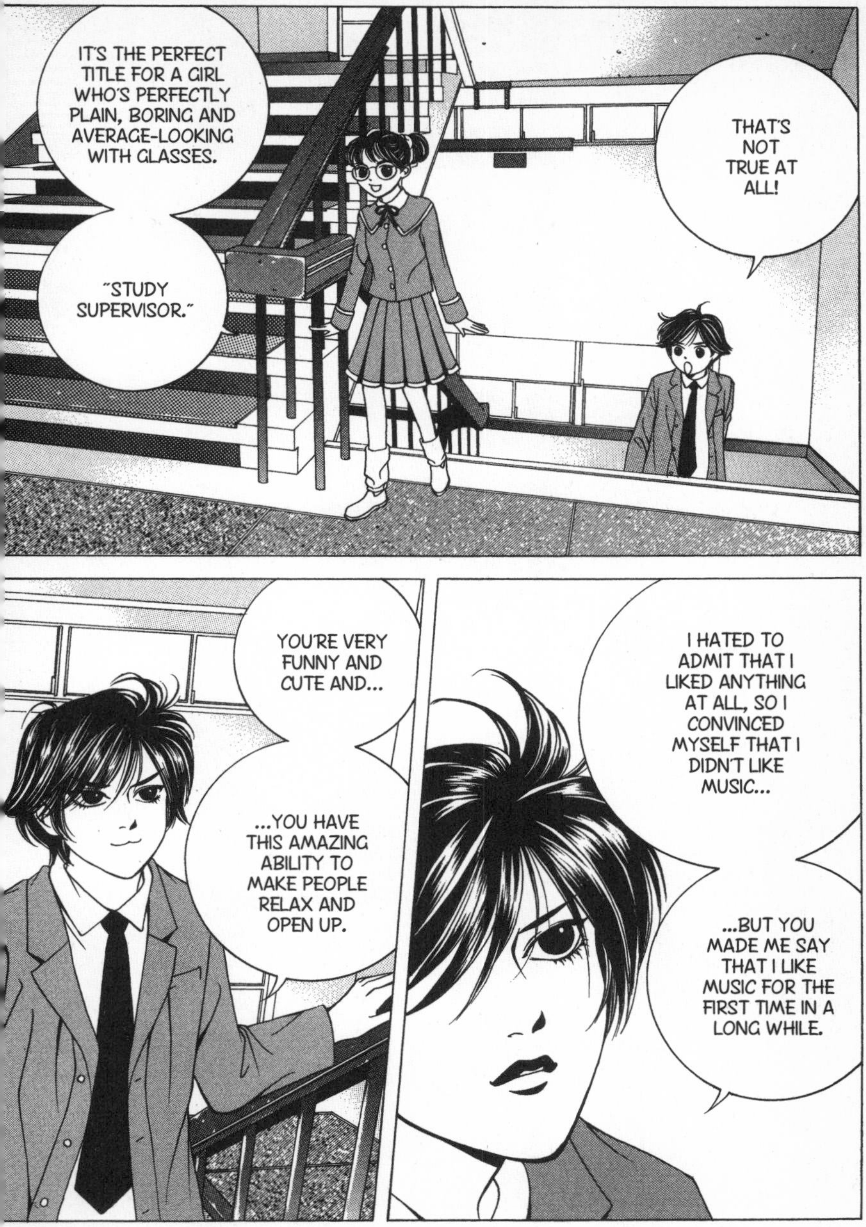
IT'S THE PERFECT TITLE FOR A GIRL WHO'S PERFECTLY PLAIN, BORING AND AVERAGE-LOOKING WITH GLASSES.
"STUDY SUPERVISOR."
THAT'S NOT TRUE AT ALL!
YOU'RE VERY FUNNY AND CUTE AND...
...YOU HAVE THIS AMAZING ABILITY TO MAKE PEOPLE RELAX AND OPEN UP.
I HATED TO ADMIT THAT I LIKED ANYTHING AT ALL, SO I CONVINCED MYSELF THAT I DIDN'T LIKE MUSIC...
...BUT YOU MADE ME SAY THAT I LIKE MUSIC FOR THE FIRST TIME IN A LONG WHILE.

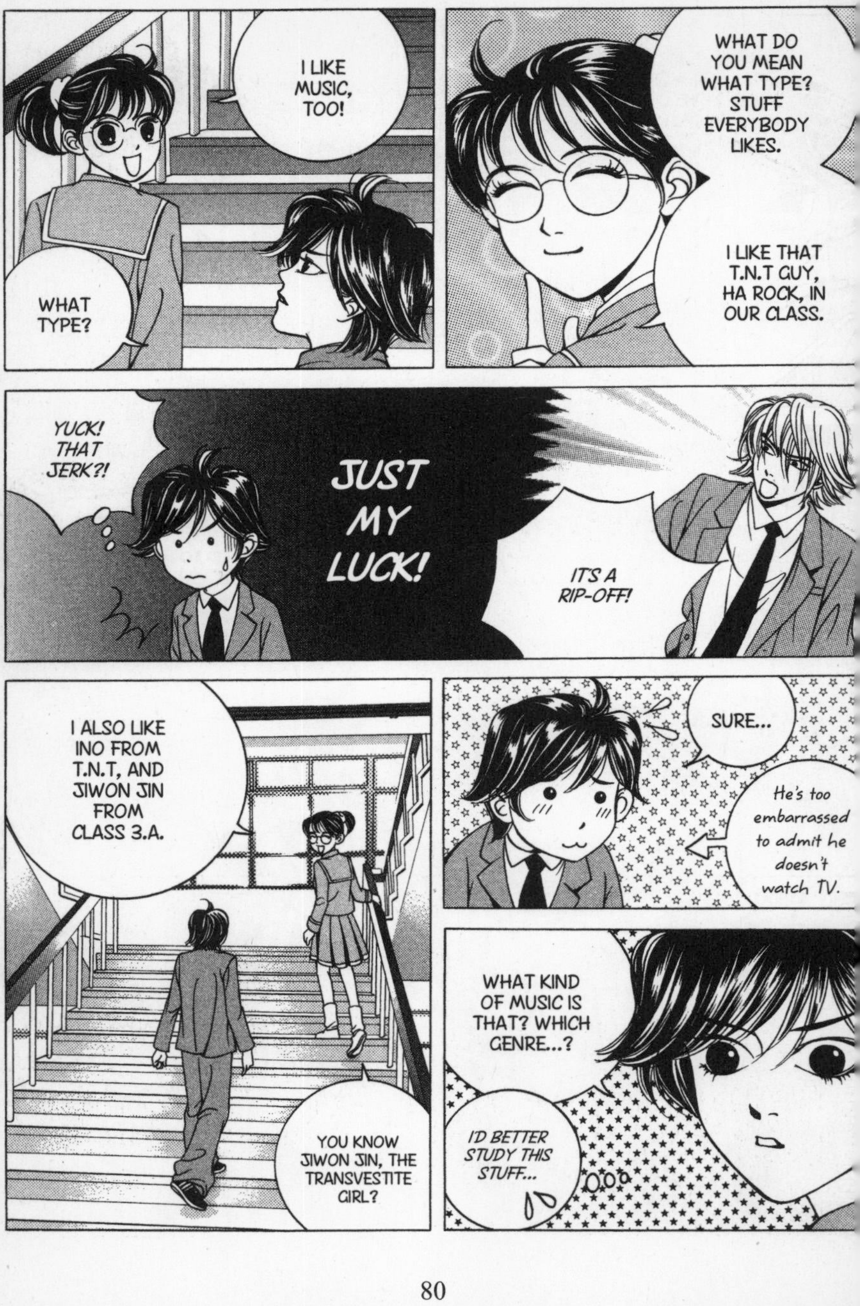
I LIKE MUSIC, TOO!
WHAT TYPE?
WHAT DO YOU MEAN WHAT TYPE? STUFF EVERYBODY LIKES.
I LIKE THAT T.N.T GUY, HA ROCK, IN OUR CLASS.
YUCK! THAT JERK?!
JUST MY LUCK!
IT'S A RIP-OFF!
I ALSO LIKE INO FROM T.N.T, AND JIWON JIN FROM CLASS 3.A.
YOU KNOW JIWON JIN, THE TRANSVESTITE GIRL?
SURE...
He's too embarrassed to admit he doesn't watch TV.
WHAT KIND OF MUSIC IS THAT? WHICH GENRE...?
I'D BETTER STUDY THIS STUFF...

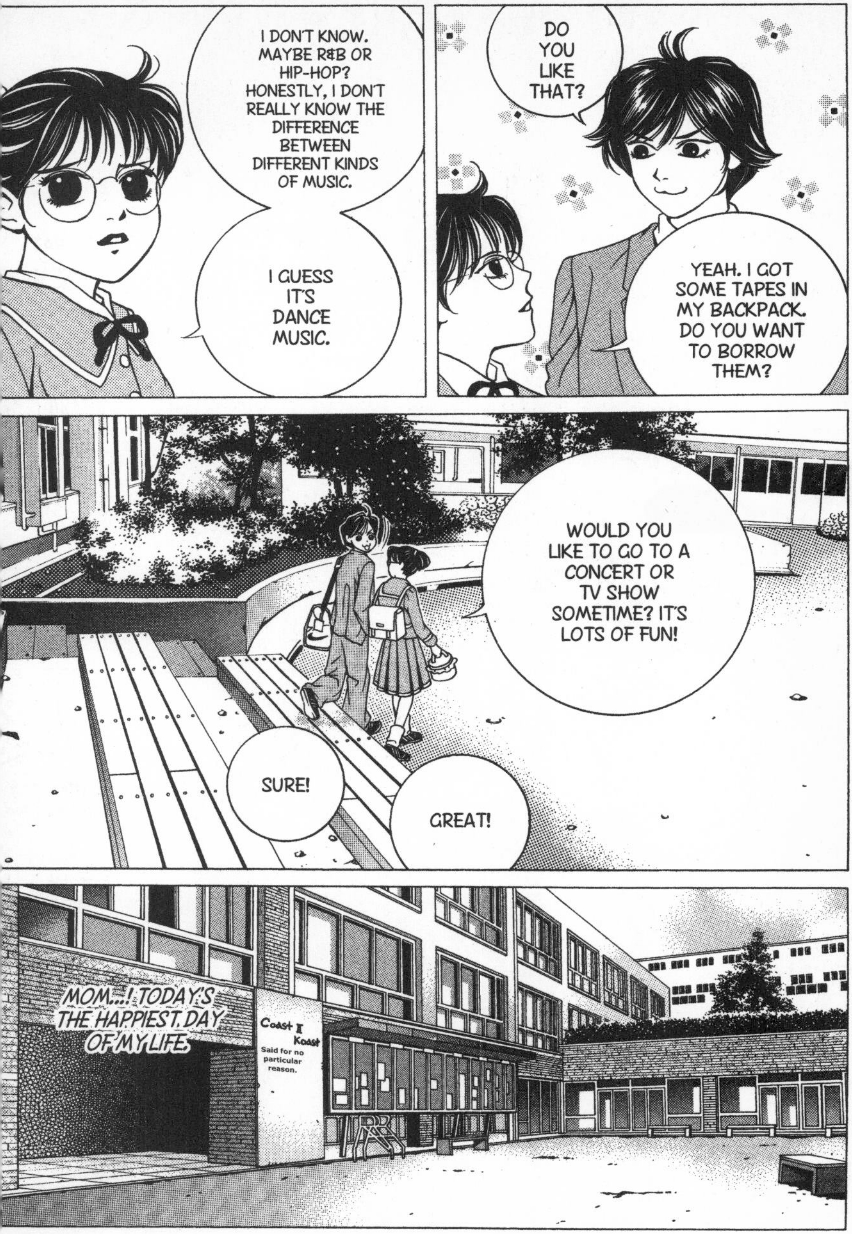
I DON'T KNOW. MAYBE R&B OR HIP-HOP? HONESTLY, I DON'T REALLY KNOW THE DIFFERENCE BETWEEN DIFFERENT KINDS OF MUSIC.
I GUESS IT'S DANCE MUSIC.
DO YOU LIKE THAT?
YEAH. I GOT SOME TAPES IN MY BACKPACK. DO YOU WANT TO BORROW THEM?
WOULD YOU LIKE TO GO TO A CONCERT OR TV SHOW SOMETIME? IT'S LOTS OF FUN!
SURE!
GREAT!
MOM...! TODAY'S THE HAPPIEST DAY OF MY LIFE.
Coast II Koast
Said for no particular reason.

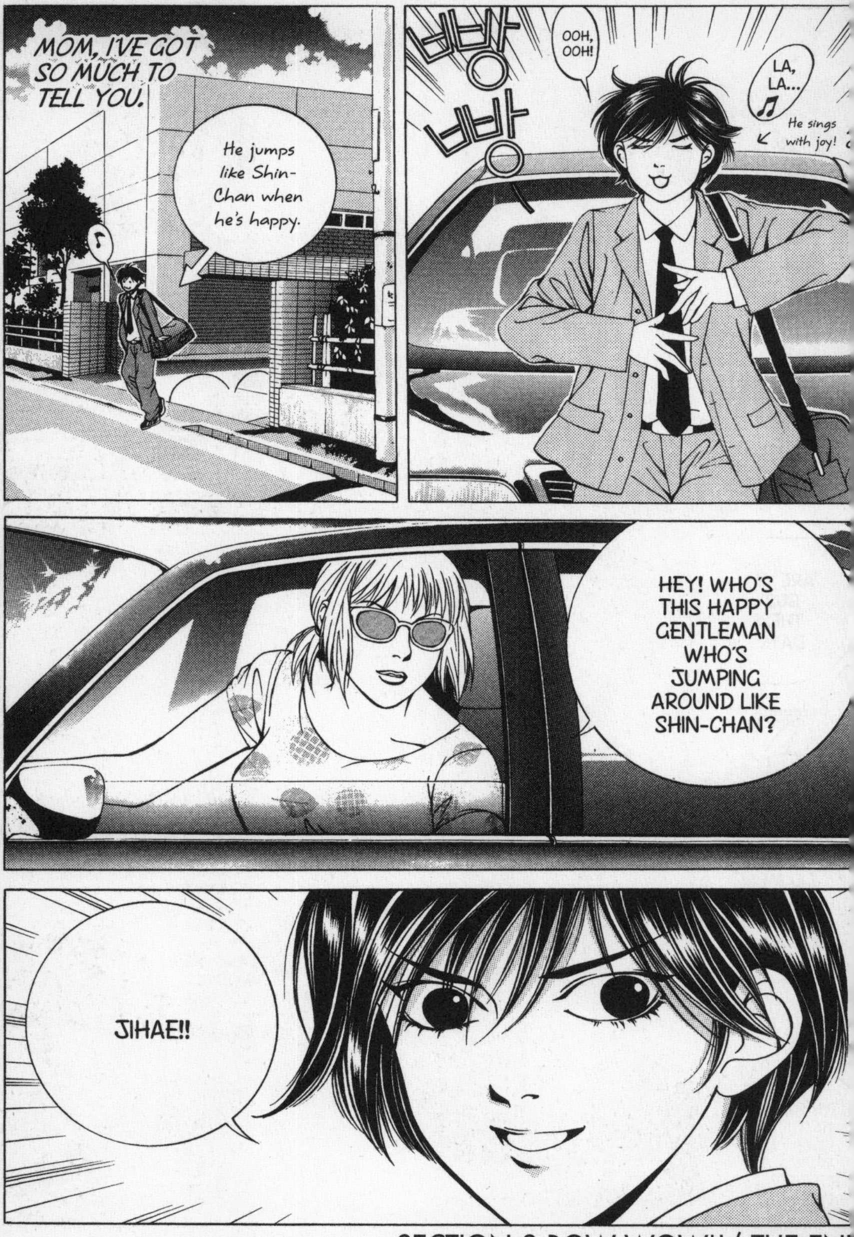
MOM, I'VE GOT SO MUCH TO TELL YOU.
He jumps like Shin-Chan when he's happy.
OOH, OOH!
LA, LA...
He sings with joy!
HEY! WHO'S THIS HAPPY GENTLEMAN WHO'S JUMPING AROUND LIKE SHIN-CHAN?
JIHAE!!

SECTION 3 BOW WOW!!/ THE END

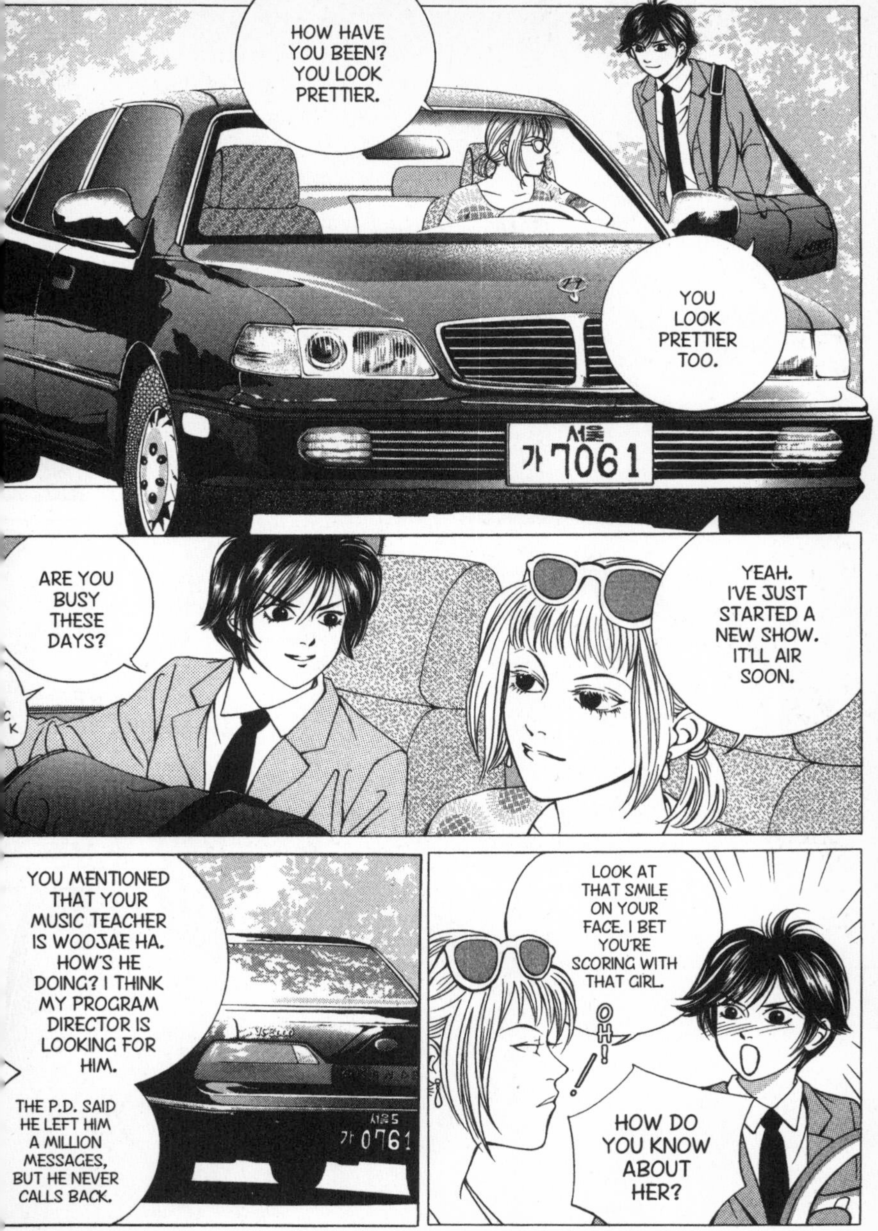
HOW HAVE YOU BEEN? YOU LOOK PRETTIER.
YOU LOOK PRETTIER TOO.
서울
가7061
ARE YOU BUSY THESE DAYS?
YEAH. I'VE JUST STARTED A NEW SHOW. IT'LL AIR SOON.
YOU MENTIONED THAT YOUR MUSIC TEACHER IS WOOJAE HA. HOW'S HE DOING? I THINK MY PROGRAM DIRECTOR IS LOOKING FOR HIM.
THE P.D. SAID HE LEFT HIM A MILLION MESSAGES, BUT HE NEVER CALLS BACK.
LOOK AT THAT SMILE ON YOUR FACE. I BET YOU'RE SCORING WITH THAT GIRL.
OH!
!
HOW DO YOU KNOW ABOUT HER?

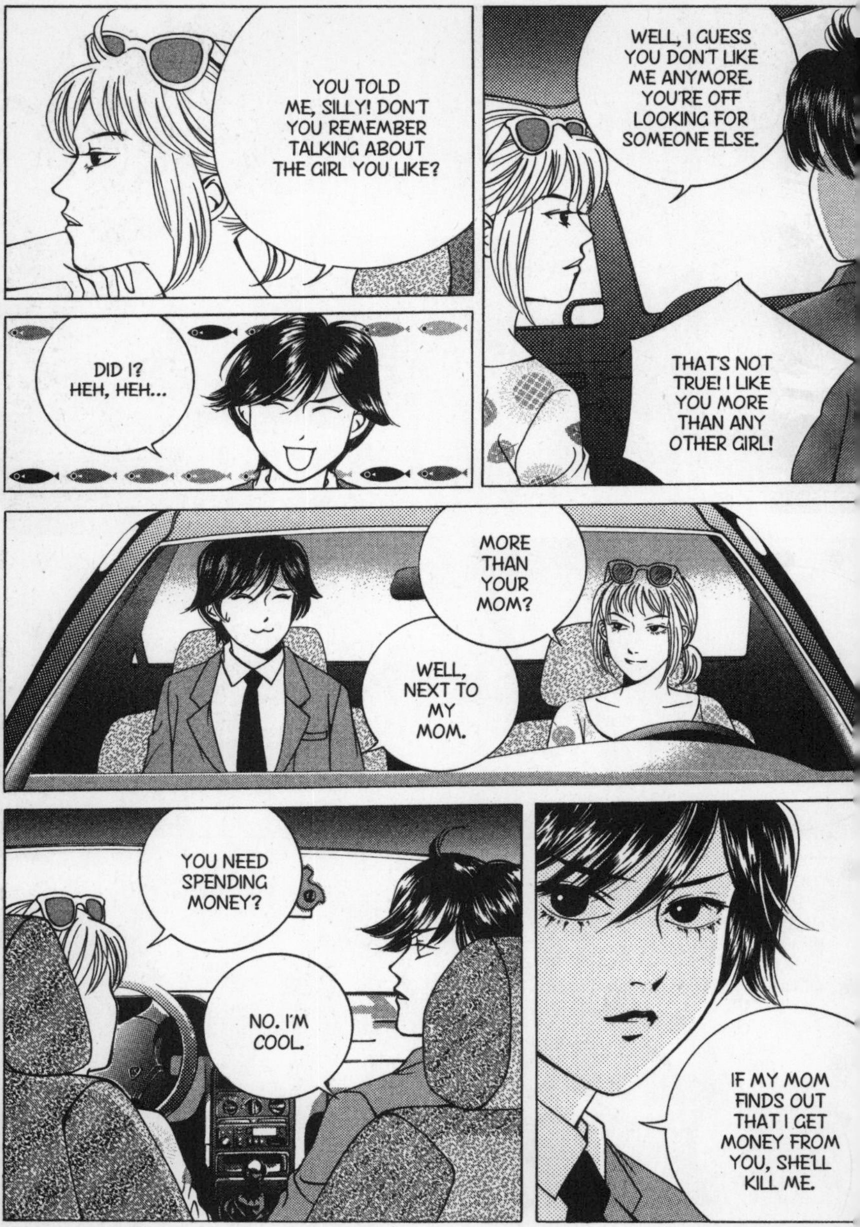
YOU TOLD ME, SILLY! DON'T YOU REMEMBER TALKING ABOUT THE GIRL YOU LIKE?
DID I? HEH, HEH...
WELL, I GUESS YOU DON'T LIKE ME ANYMORE. YOU'RE OFF LOOKING FOR SOMEONE ELSE.
THAT'S NOT TRUE! I LIKE YOU MORE THAN ANY OTHER GIRL!
MORE THAN YOUR MOM?
WELL, NEXT TO MY MOM.
YOU NEED SPENDING MONEY?
NO. I'M COOL.
IF MY MOM FINDS OUT THAT I GET MONEY FROM YOU, SHE'LL KILL ME.

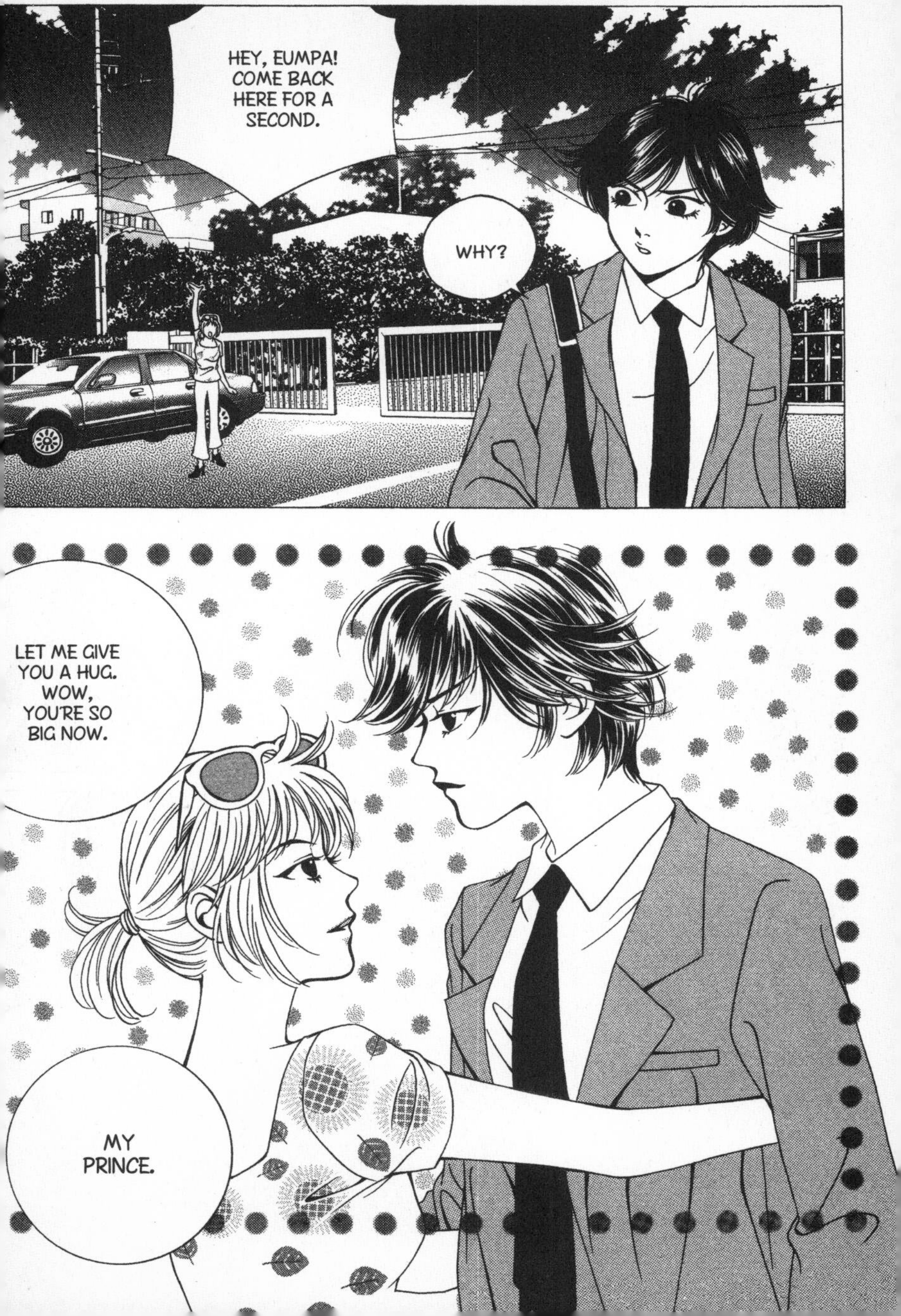
HEY, EUMPA! COME BACK HERE FOR A SECOND.
WHY?
LET ME GIVE YOU A HUG. WOW, YOU'RE SO BIG NOW.
MY PRINCE.

JIHAE HAN
(FEMALE: 30-SOMETHING?)

AT 18, SHE MADE HER DEBUT AS A COMMERCIAL MODEL. SHE MADE SO MANY COMMERCIALS THAT THEY CALLED HER "THE COMMERCIAL FAIRY." LATER, SHE BROKE INTO FILM AND TELEVISION. IN THE BEGINNING, ALL ANYONE CARED ABOUT WAS HER LOOKS. AFTER RETURNING FROM STUDYING IN THE U.S., SHE WAS ABLE TO SHOW A GREAT RANGE OF ACTING ABILITY. SHE QUICKLY BECAME RESPECTED AS AN ACTRESS. ALTHOUGH SHE WAS IN HER EARLY 30S, SHE LOOKED 10 YEARS YOUNGER. PEOPLE COULDN'T BELIEVE HOW SHE COULD APPEAR SO YOUNG, AND GAVE HER A NEW NICKNAME - "WITCH." THIS COULD HAVE HAD SOMETHING TO DO WITH HER ATTITUDE. SHE MIGHT HAVE LOOKED SWEET AND DELICATE AND INNOCENT, BUT SHE'S A NOTORIOUS DIVA! SHE HAS WHAT THEY CALL "PRINCESS SYNDROME." SHE AND JENNY ARE DEFINITELY CUT FROM THE SAME CLOTH. SHE ACTS LIKE A SWEETHEART, BUT SHE ENJOYS HARD ROCK. SHE SEEMS TO THINK THE WORLD REVOLVES AROUND HER.

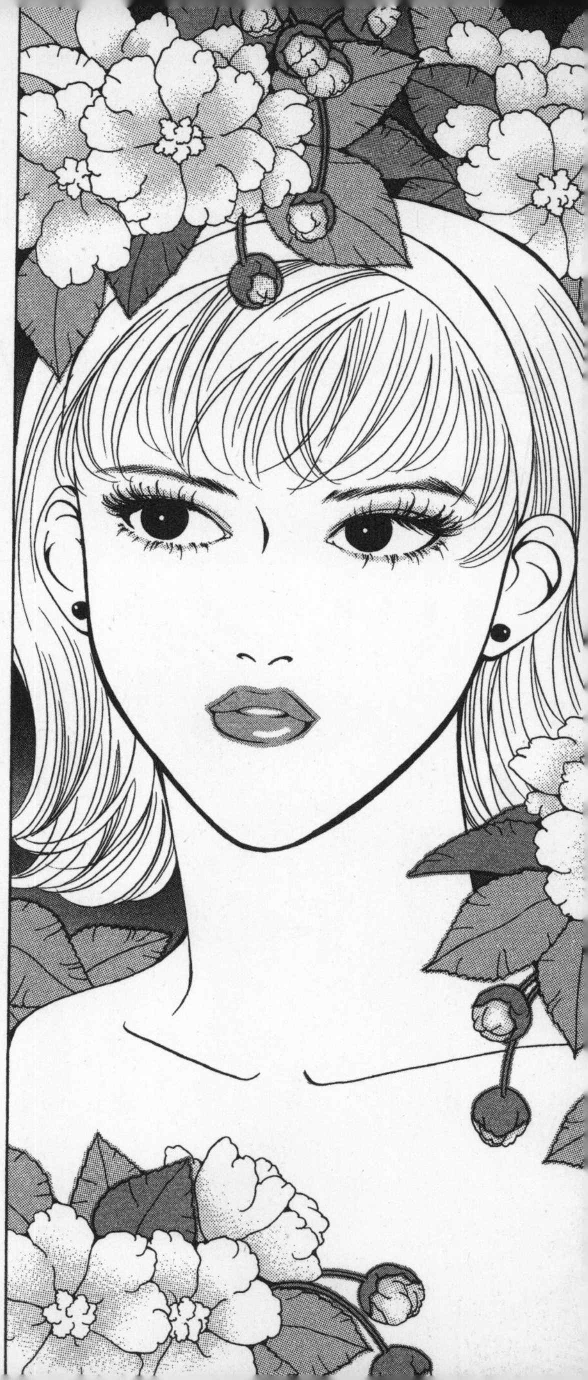

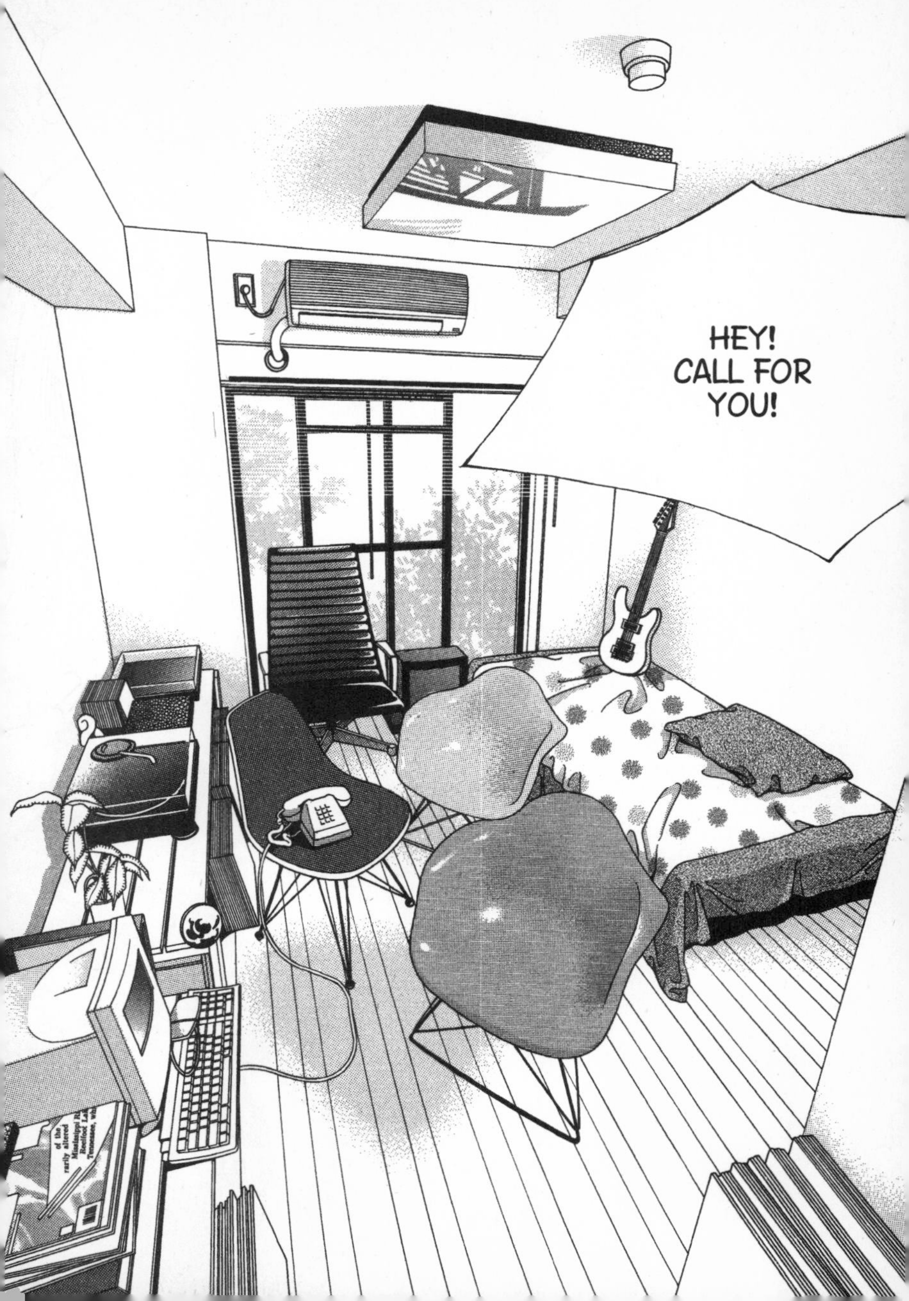
HEY! CALL FOR YOU!

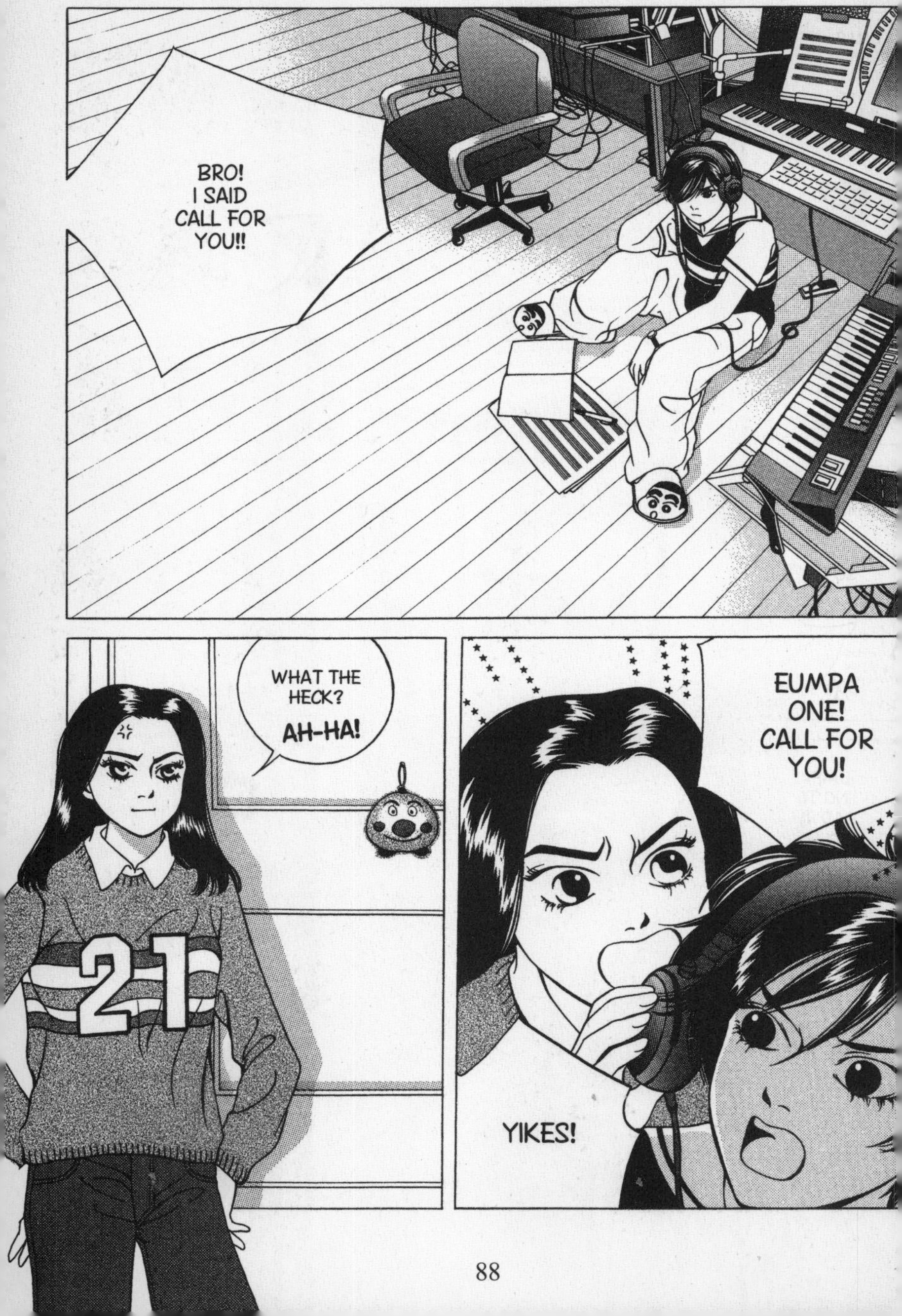
BRO! I SAID CALL FOR YOU!!
WHAT THE HECK? AH-HA!
EUMPA ONE! CALL FOR YOU!
YIKES!

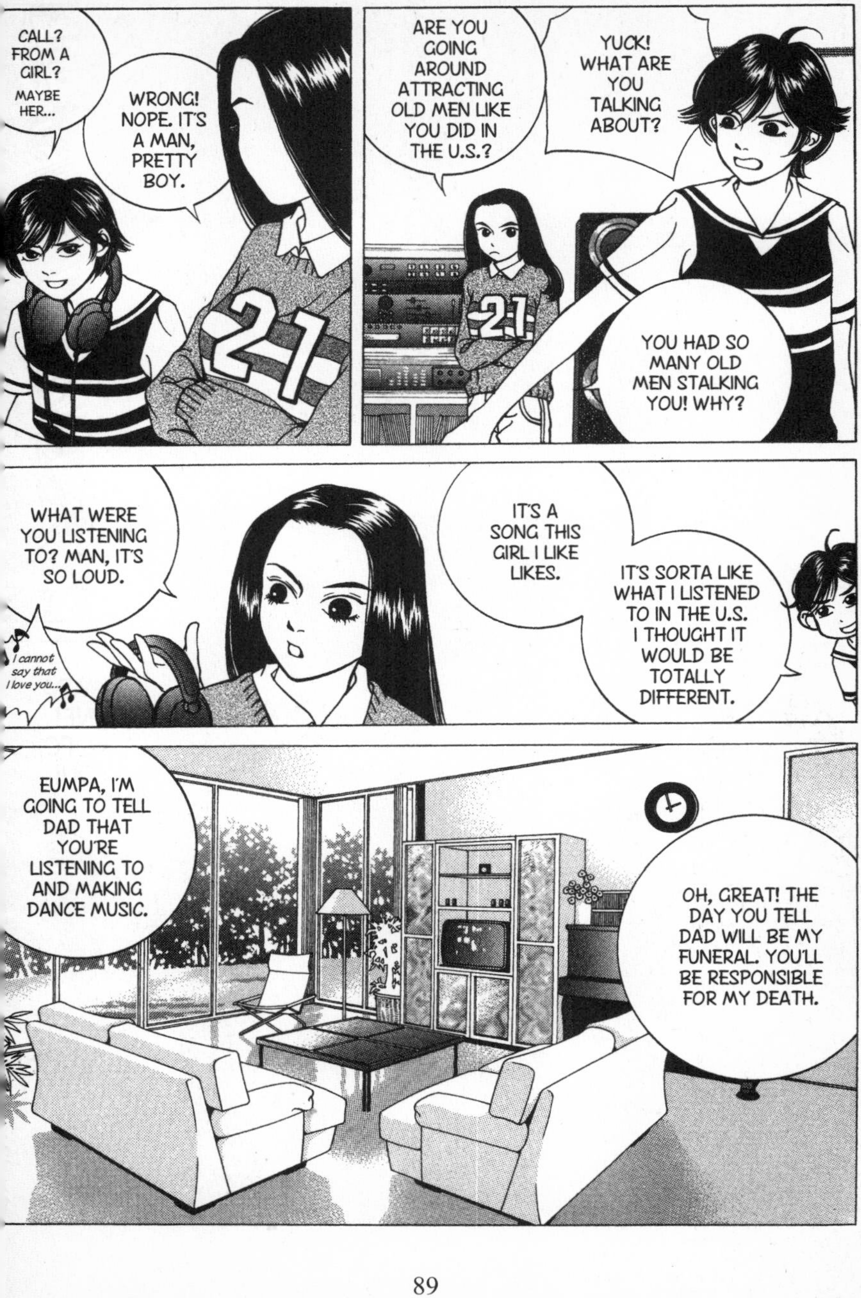
CALL? FROM A GIRL?
MAYBE HER...
WRONG! NOPE. IT'S A MAN, PRETTY BOY.
ARE YOU GOING AROUND ATTRACTING OLD MEN LIKE YOU DID IN THE U.S.?
YUCK! WHAT ARE YOU TALKING ABOUT?
YOU HAD SO MANY OLD MEN STALKING YOU! WHY?
WHAT WERE YOU LISTENING TO? MAN, IT'S SO LOUD.
I cannot say that I love you...
IT'S A SONG THIS GIRL I LIKE LIKES.
IT'S SORTA LIKE WHAT I LISTENED TO IN THE U.S. I THOUGHT IT WOULD BE TOTALLY DIFFERENT.
EUMPA, I'M GOING TO TELL DAD THAT YOU'RE LISTENING TO AND MAKING DANCE MUSIC.
OH, GREAT! THE DAY YOU TELL DAD WILL BE MY FUNERAL. YOU'LL BE RESPONSIBLE FOR MY DEATH.

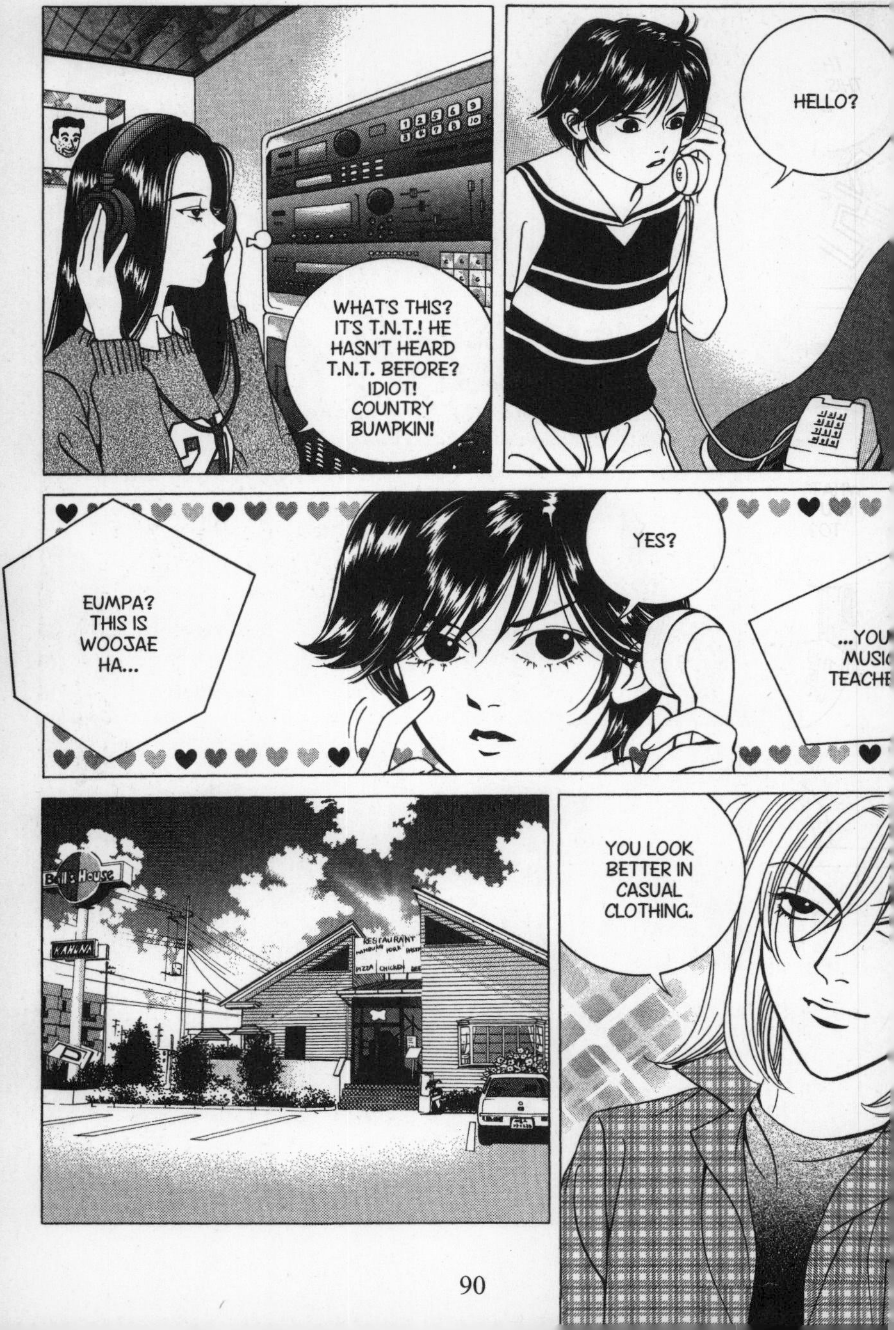
WHAT'S THIS? IT'S T.N.T.! HE HASN'T HEARD T.N.T. BEFORE? IDIOT! COUNTRY BUMPKIN!
HELLO?
EUMPA? THIS IS WOOJAE HA...
YES?
...YOU MUSIC TEACHE
YOU LOOK BETTER IN CASUAL CLOTHING.

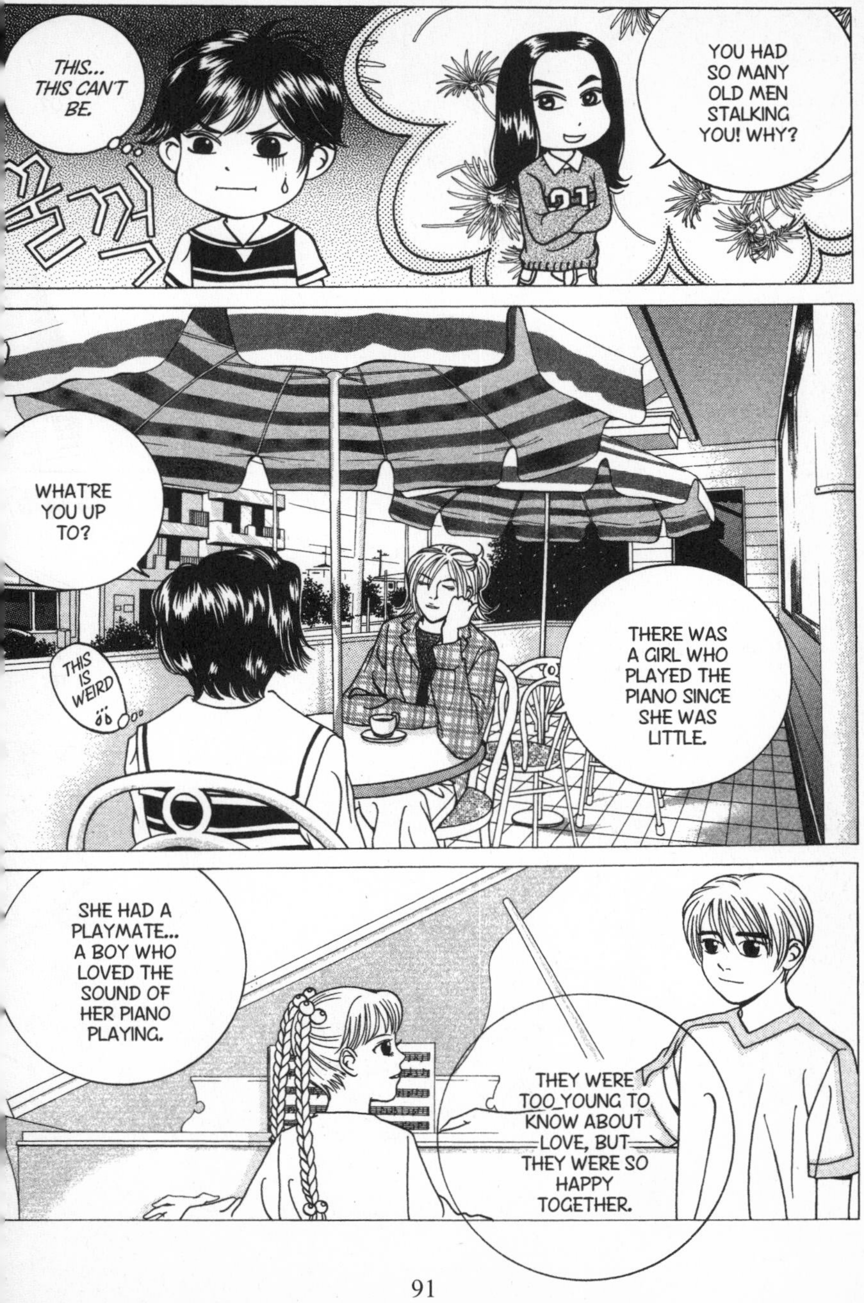
THIS... THIS CAN'T BE.
YOU HAD SO MANY OLD MEN STALKING YOU! WHY?
WHAT'RE YOU UP TO?
THIS IS WEIRD...
THERE WAS A GIRL WHO PLAYED THE PIANO SINCE SHE WAS LITTLE.
SHE HAD A PLAYMATE... A BOY WHO LOVED THE SOUND OF HER PIANO PLAYING.
THEY WERE TOO YOUNG TO KNOW ABOUT LOVE, BUT THEY WERE SO HAPPY TOGETHER.

BUT THEY HAD TO PART BECAUSE THE GIRL'S FAMILY WAS MOVING TO ANOTHER COUNTRY.

BEFORE SHE LEFT, THE GIRL GAVE THE BOY A RECORDING OF BACH THAT THEY ENJOYED SO MUCH.

WHAT ARE YOU TALKING ABOUT?

BEAR WITH ME... TIME PASSED, AND THE GIRL BECAME A WOMAN. SHE PURSUED HER PIANO STUDIES. SHE MET A FELLOW PIANIST, FELL IN LOVE AND BECAME ENGAGED.

THEN, SHE CAME BACK TO KOREA WITH HER FIANCÉ.

ONE DAY, SHE RAN INTO THE BOY, NOW FULLY GROWN.

I THI... I SE... WHE... THIS... THI... GOIN...

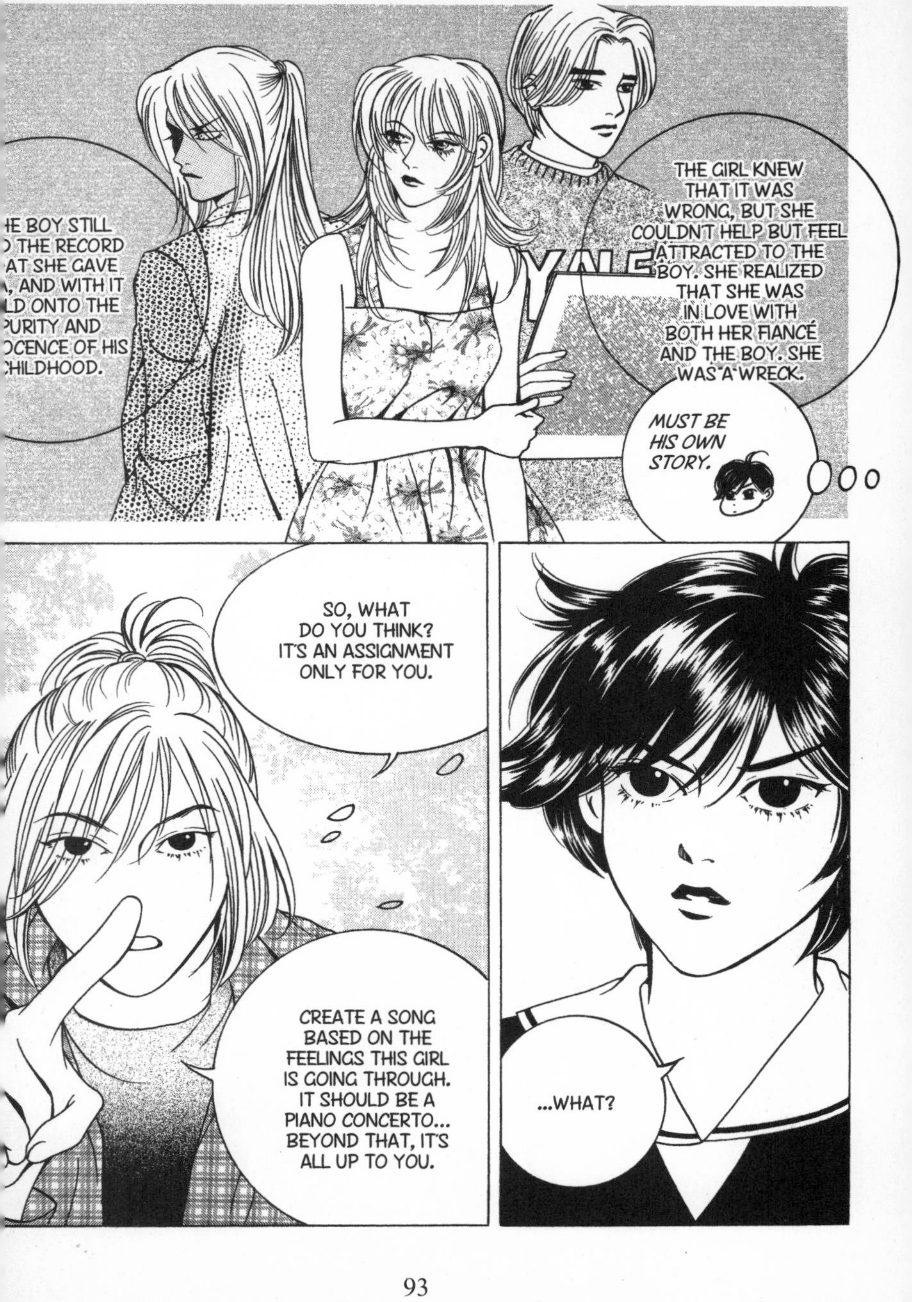
HE BOY STILL D THE RECORD AT SHE GAVE , AND WITH IT LD ONTO THE PURITY AND OCENCE OF HIS CHILDHOOD.
THE GIRL KNEW THAT IT WAS WRONG, BUT SHE COULDN'T HELP BUT FEEL ATTRACTED TO THE BOY. SHE REALIZED THAT SHE WAS IN LOVE WITH BOTH HER FIANCÉ AND THE BOY. SHE WAS A WRECK.
MUST BE HIS OWN STORY.
SO, WHAT DO YOU THINK? IT'S AN ASSIGNMENT ONLY FOR YOU.
CREATE A SONG BASED ON THE FEELINGS THIS GIRL IS GOING THROUGH. IT SHOULD BE A PIANO CONCERTO... BEYOND THAT, IT'S ALL UP TO YOU.
...WHAT?

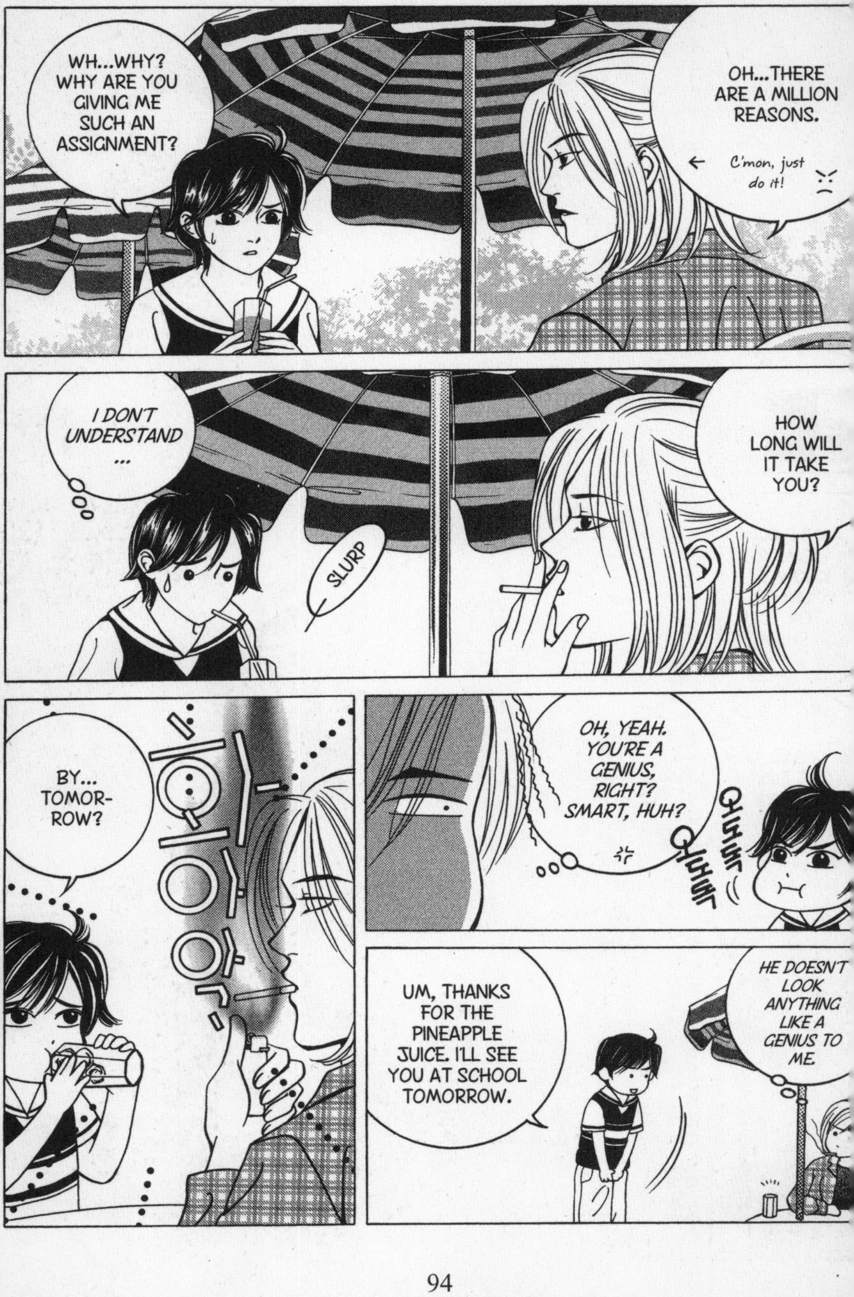

WH...WHY? WHY ARE YOU GIVING ME SUCH AN ASSIGNMENT?
OH...THERE ARE A MILLION REASONS.
← C'mon, just do it!
I DON'T UNDERSTAND ...
SLURP
HOW LONG WILL IT TAKE YOU?
BY... TOMOR-ROW?
OH, YEAH. YOU'RE A GENIUS, RIGHT? SMART, HUH?
UM, THANKS FOR THE PINEAPPLE JUICE. I'LL SEE YOU AT SCHOOL TOMORROW.
HE DOESN'T LOOK ANYTHING LIKE A GENIUS TO ME.

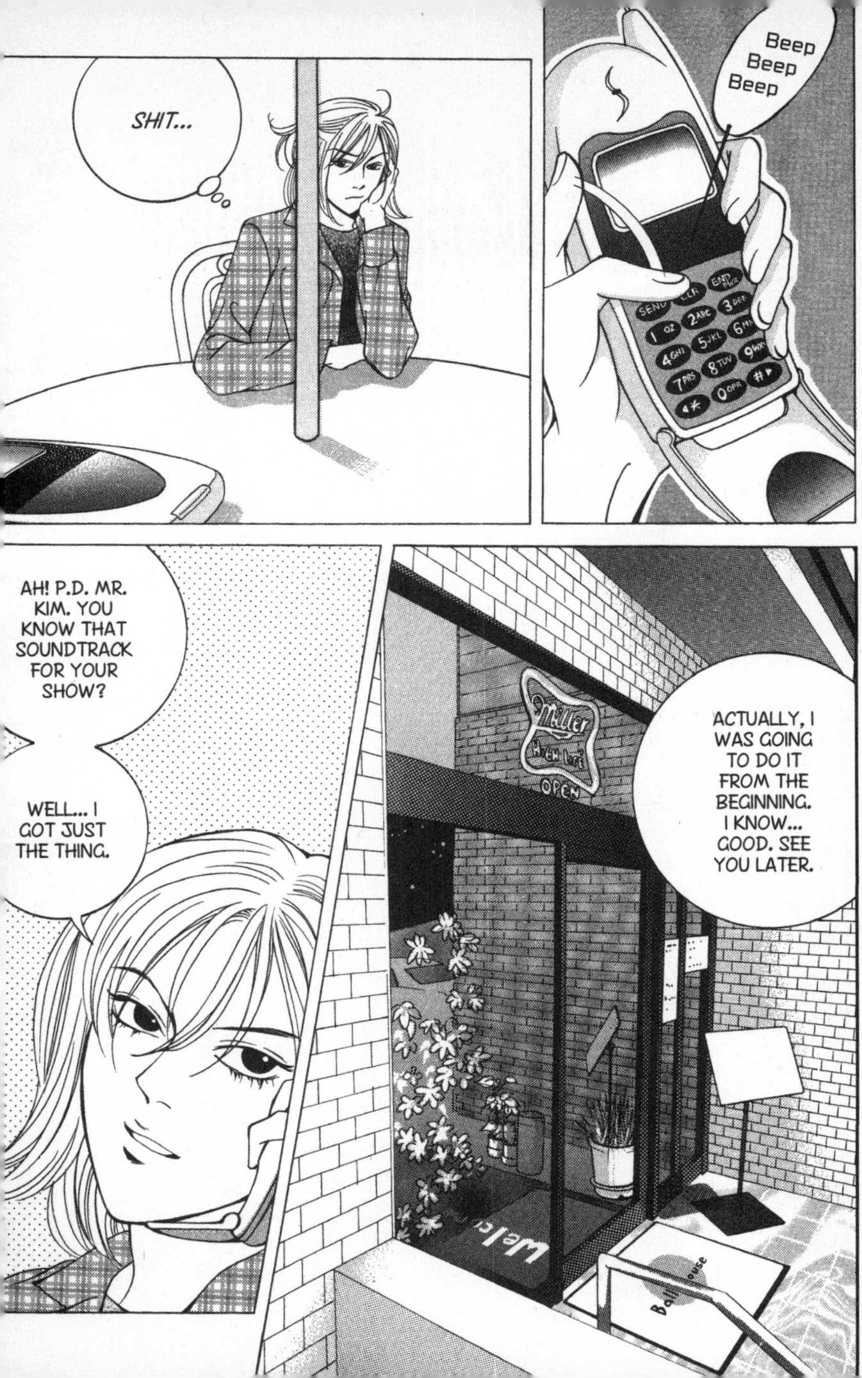
SHIT...
Beep
Beep
Beep
AH! P.D. MR. KIM. YOU KNOW THAT SOUNDTRACK FOR YOUR SHOW?
WELL... I GOT JUST THE THING.
OPEN
ACTUALLY, I WAS GOING TO DO IT FROM THE BEGINNING. I KNOW... GOOD. SEE YOU LATER.

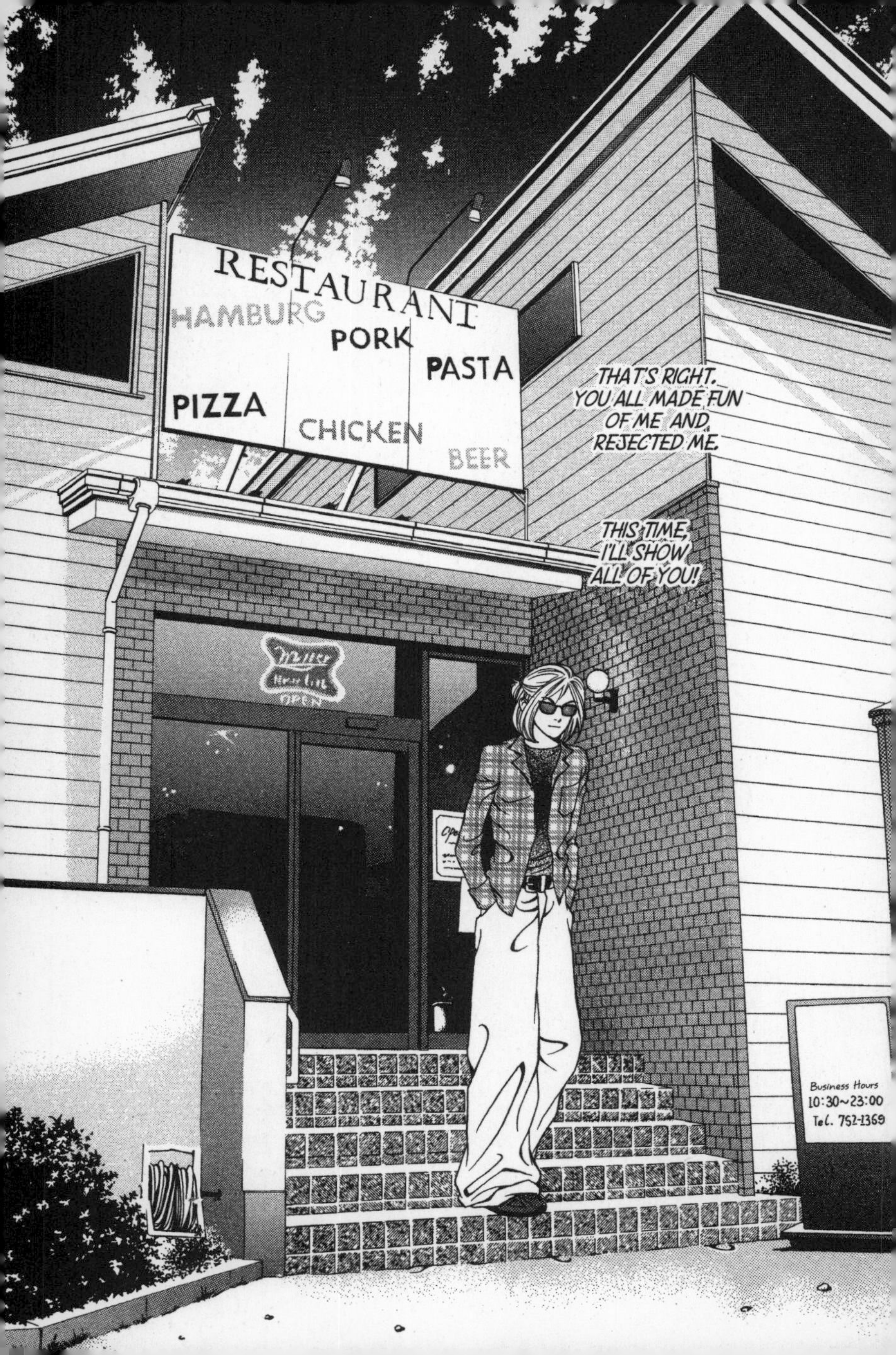
RESTAURANT
HAMBURG
PORK
PASTA
PIZZA
CHICKEN
BEER
THAT'S RIGHT. YOU ALL MADE FUN OF ME AND REJECTED ME.
THIS TIME, I'LL SHOW ALL OF YOU!
OPEN
Business Hours
10:30~23:00
Tel. 752-1369

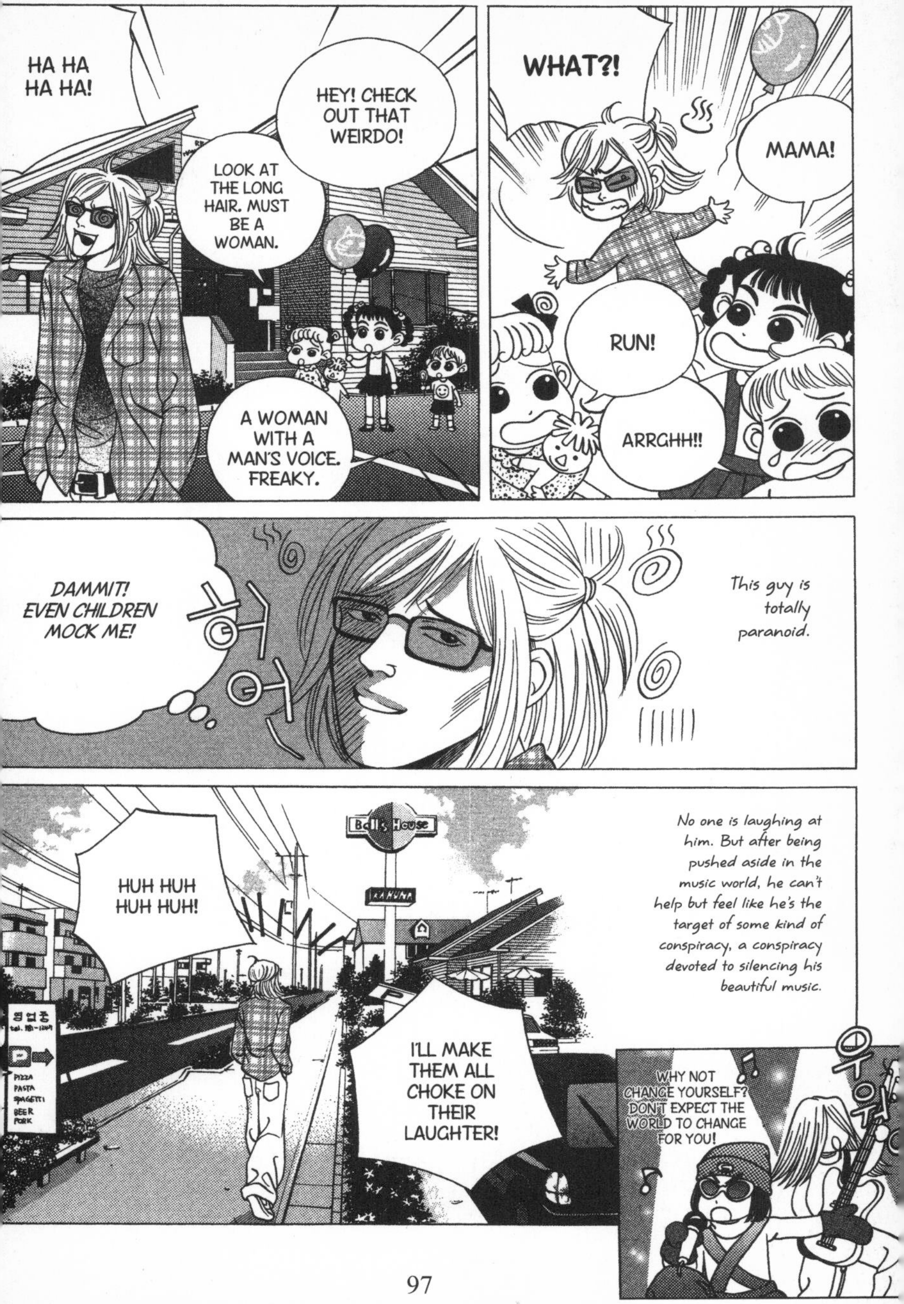
HA HA HA HA!
HEY! CHECK OUT THAT WEIRDO!
LOOK AT THE LONG HAIR. MUST BE A WOMAN.
A WOMAN WITH A MAN'S VOICE. FREAKY.
WHAT?!
MAMA!
RUN!
ARRGHH!!
DAMMIT! EVEN CHILDREN MOCK ME!
This guy is totally paranoid.
HUH HUH HUH HUH!
Ball's House
PIZZA PASTA SPAGETTI BEER PORK
No one is laughing at him. But after being pushed aside in the music world, he can't help but feel like he's the target of some kind of conspiracy, a conspiracy devoted to silencing his beautiful music.
I'LL MAKE THEM ALL CHOKE ON THEIR LAUGHTER!
WHY NOT CHANGE YOURSELF? DON'T EXPECT THE WORLD TO CHANGE FOR YOU!

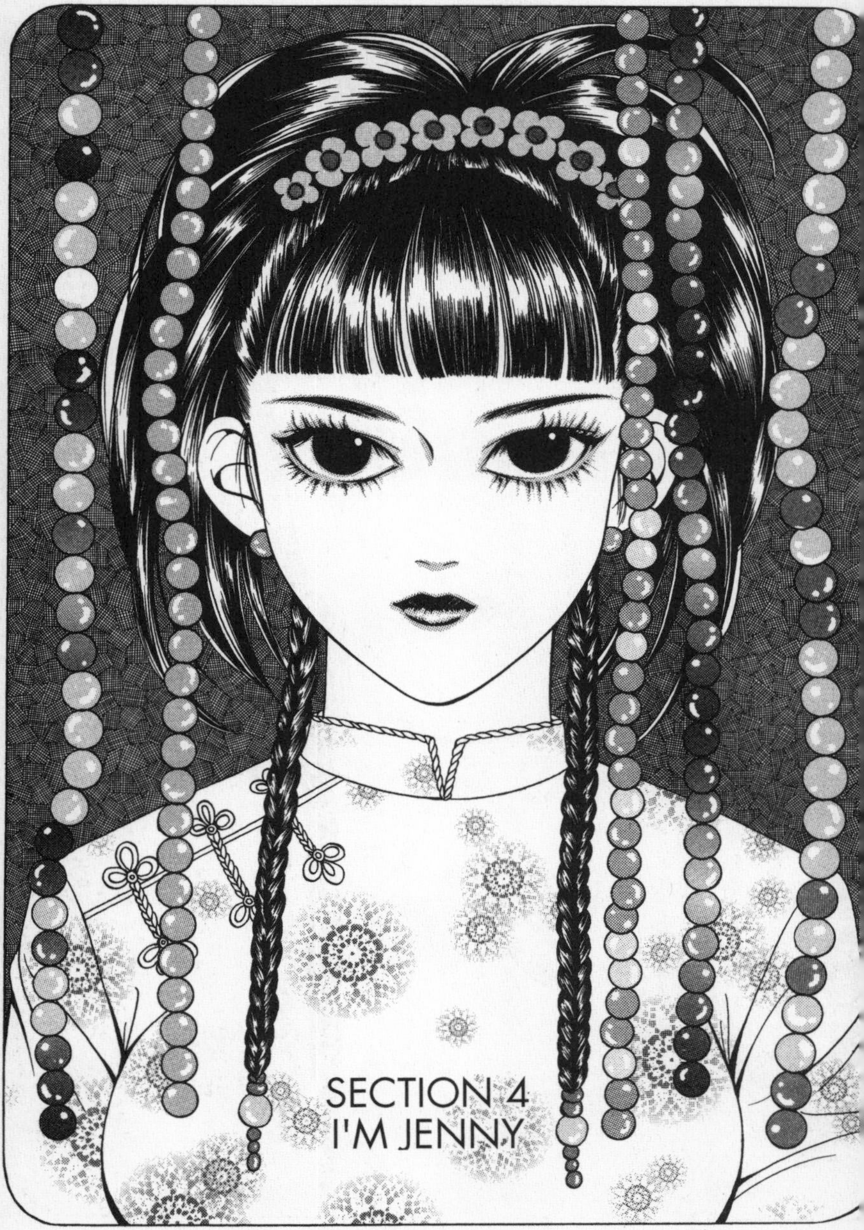
SECTION 4
I'M JENNY

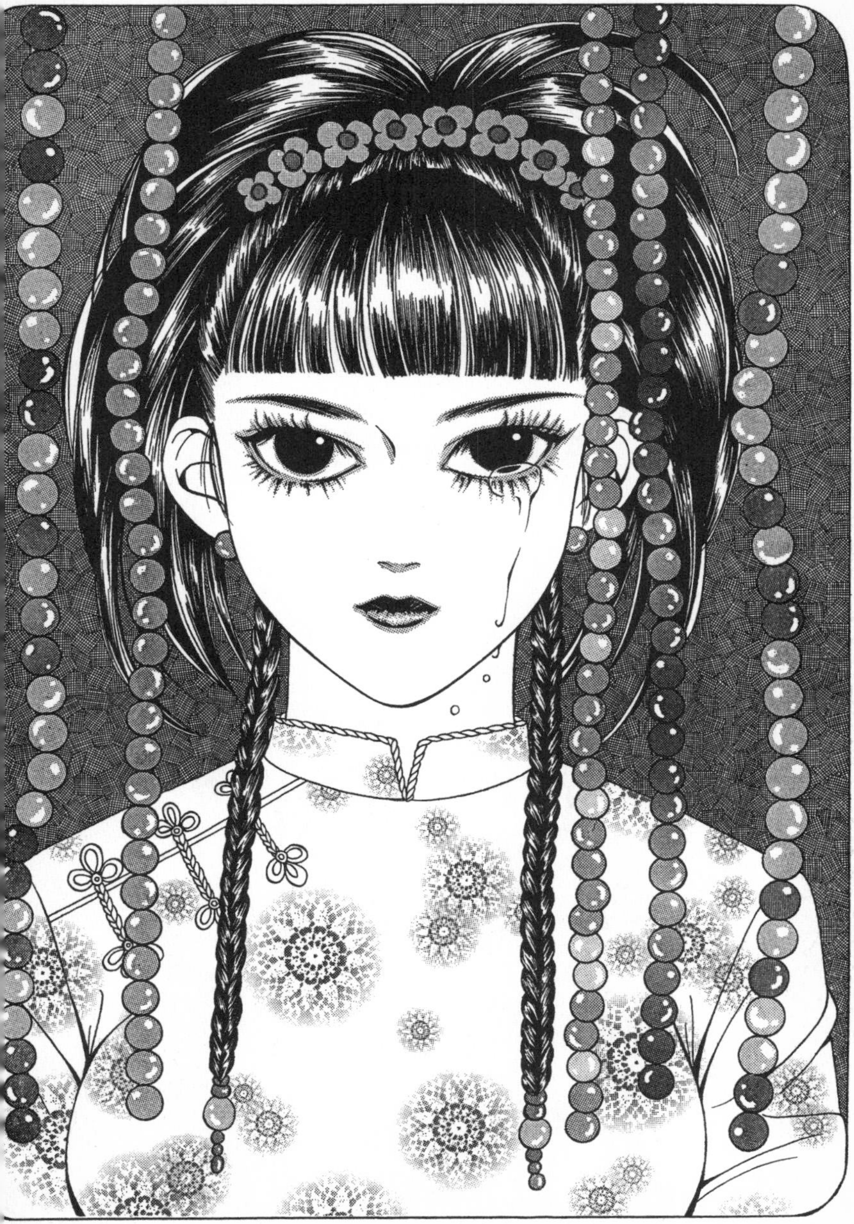

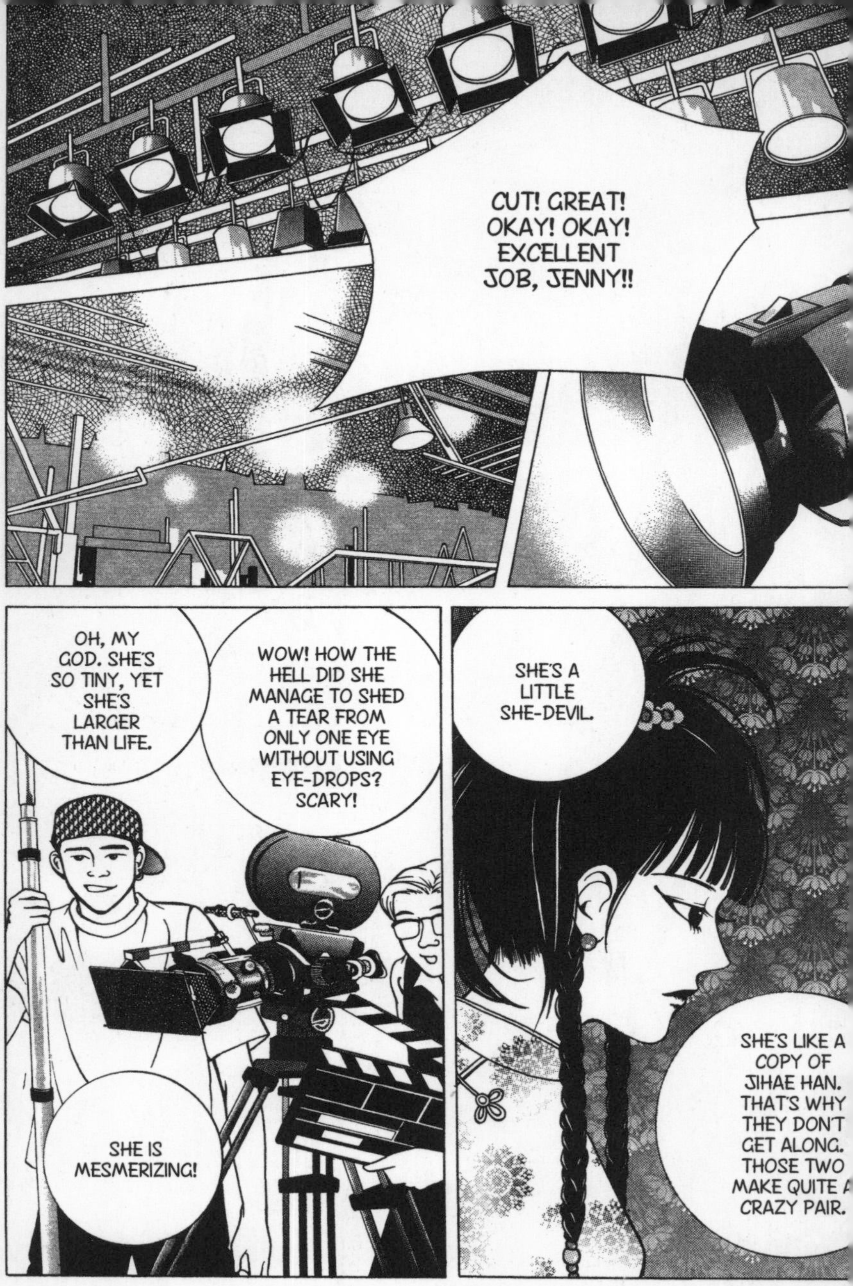
CUT! GREAT! OKAY! OKAY! EXCELLENT JOB, JENNY!!
OH, MY GOD. SHE'S SO TINY, YET SHE'S LARGER THAN LIFE.
WOW! HOW THE HELL DID SHE MANAGE TO SHED A TEAR FROM ONLY ONE EYE WITHOUT USING EYE-DROPS? SCARY!
SHE IS MESMERIZING!
SHE'S A LITTLE SHE-DEVIL.
SHE'S LIKE A COPY OF JIHAE HAN. THAT'S WHY THEY DON'T GET ALONG. THOSE TWO MAKE QUITE A CRAZY PAIR.

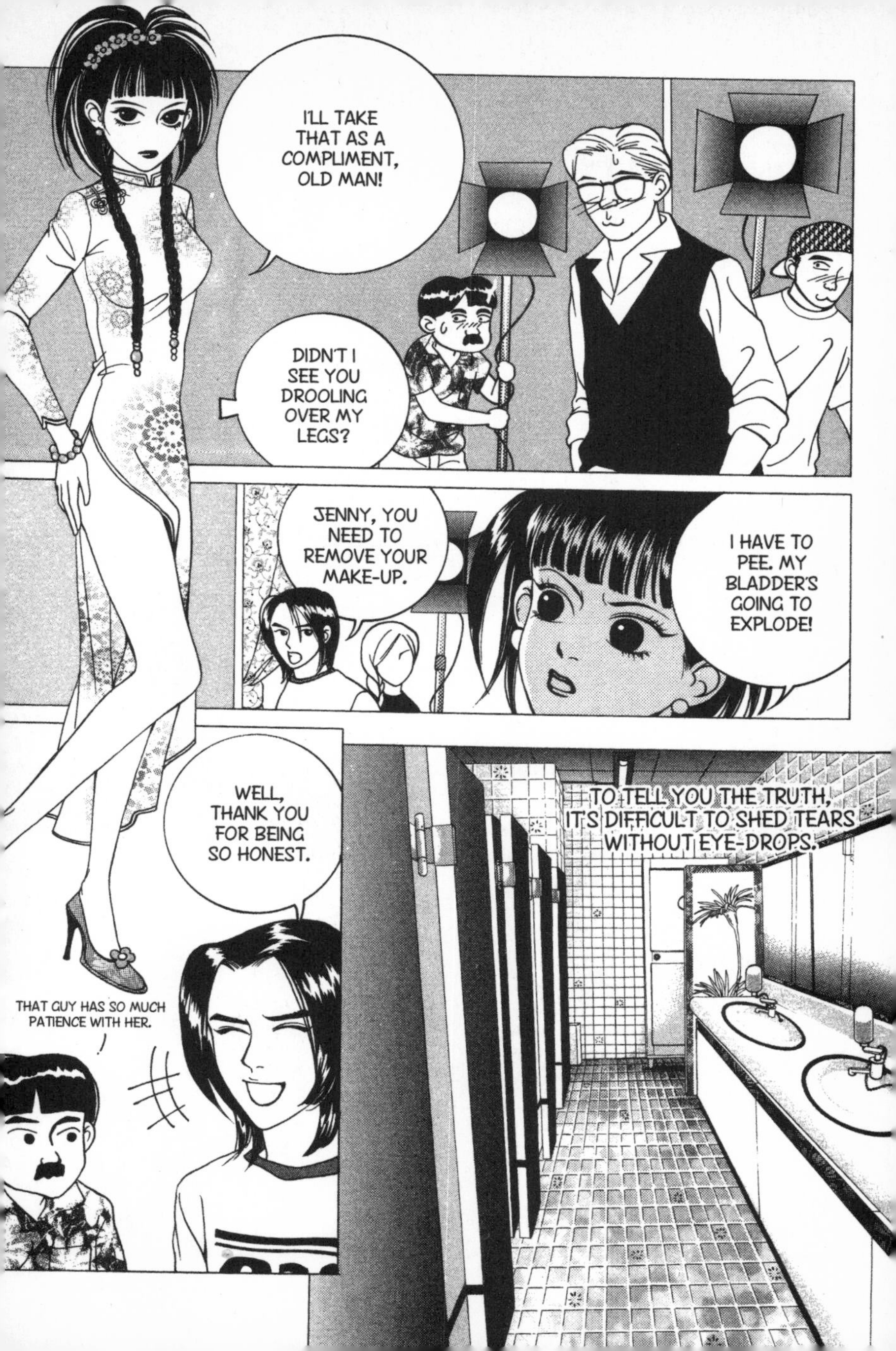
I'LL TAKE THAT AS A COMPLIMENT, OLD MAN!
DIDN'T I SEE YOU DROOLING OVER MY LEGS?
JENNY, YOU NEED TO REMOVE YOUR MAKE-UP.
I HAVE TO PEE. MY BLADDER'S GOING TO EXPLODE!
WELL, THANK YOU FOR BEING SO HONEST.
THAT GUY HAS SO MUCH PATIENCE WITH HER.
TO TELL YOU THE TRUTH, IT'S DIFFICULT TO SHED TEARS WITHOUT EYE-DROPS.

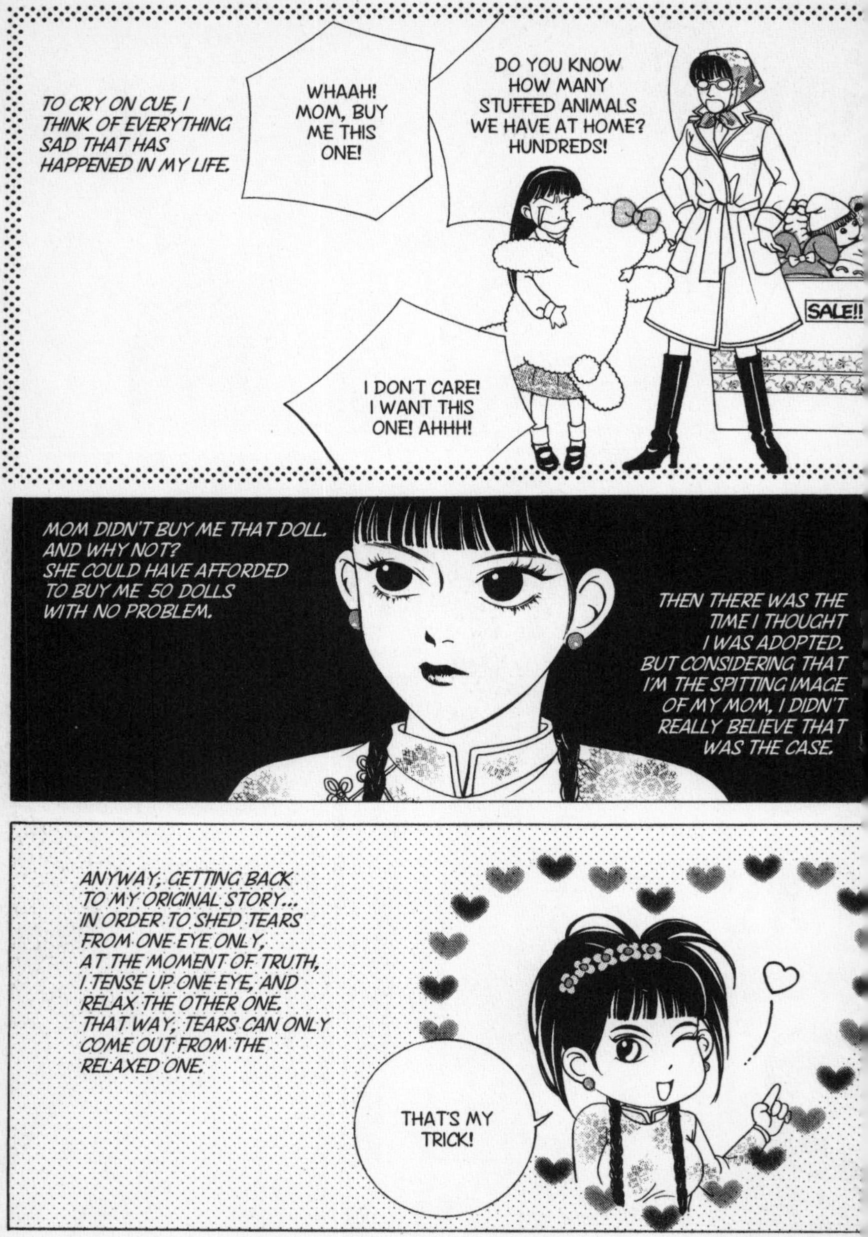
TO CRY ON CUE, I THINK OF EVERYTHING SAD THAT HAS HAPPENED IN MY LIFE.
WHAAH! MOM, BUY ME THIS ONE!
DO YOU KNOW HOW MANY STUFFED ANIMALS WE HAVE AT HOME? HUNDREDS!
SALE!!
I DON'T CARE! I WANT THIS ONE! AHHH!
MOM DIDN'T BUY ME THAT DOLL. AND WHY NOT? SHE COULD HAVE AFFORDED TO BUY ME 50 DOLLS WITH NO PROBLEM.
THEN THERE WAS THE TIME I THOUGHT I WAS ADOPTED. BUT CONSIDERING THAT I'M THE SPITTING IMAGE OF MY MOM, I DIDN'T REALLY BELIEVE THAT WAS THE CASE.
ANYWAY, GETTING BACK TO MY ORIGINAL STORY... IN ORDER TO SHED TEARS FROM ONE EYE ONLY, AT THE MOMENT OF TRUTH, I TENSE UP ONE EYE, AND RELAX THE OTHER ONE. THAT WAY, TEARS CAN ONLY COME OUT FROM THE RELAXED ONE.
THAT'S MY TRICK!

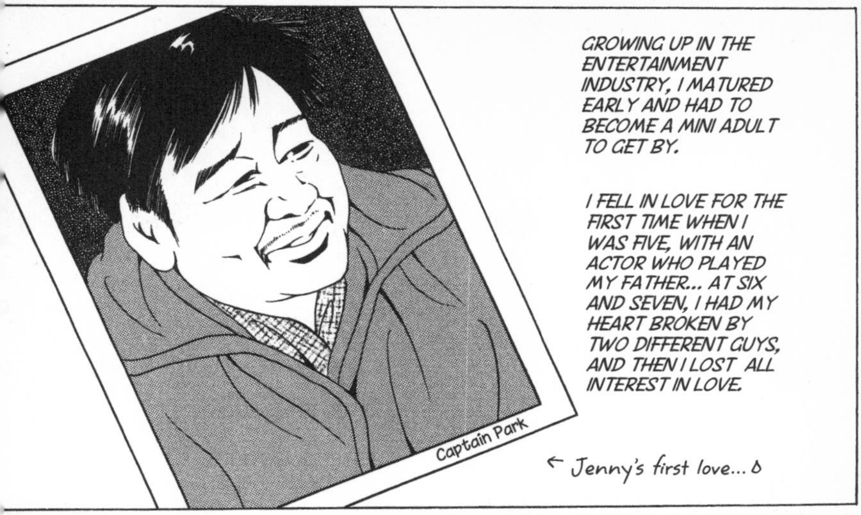
GROWING UP IN THE ENTERTAINMENT INDUSTRY, I MATURED EARLY AND HAD TO BECOME A MINI ADULT TO GET BY.
I FELL IN LOVE FOR THE FIRST TIME WHEN I WAS FIVE, WITH AN ACTOR WHO PLAYED MY FATHER... AT SIX AND SEVEN, I HAD MY HEART BROKEN BY TWO DIFFERENT GUYS, AND THEN I LOST ALL INTEREST IN LOVE.
Captain Park
← Jenny's first love...

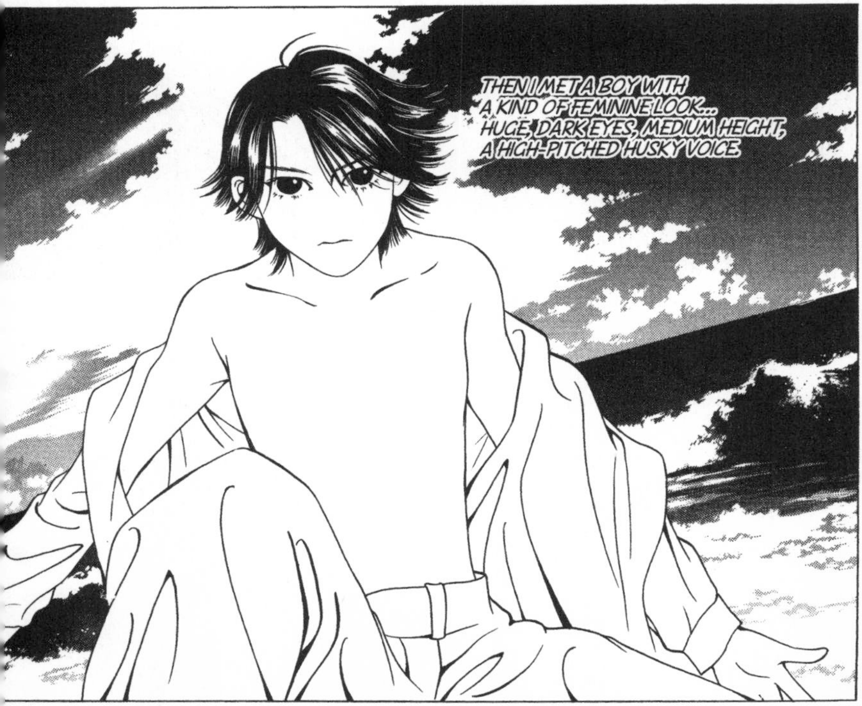
THEN I MET A BOY WITH A KIND OF FEMININE LOOK... HUGE, DARK EYES, MEDIUM HEIGHT, A HIGH-PITCHED HUSKY VOICE.

I FELT A SHUDDER....
...IT WAS A SIGN THAT OUR SOULS WERE LINKED TO EACH OTHER...
HE AND I ARE DESTINED TO BE TOGETHER.
JENNY, ARE YOU GOING NUMBER TWO? YOU'RE TAKING A LONG TIME.

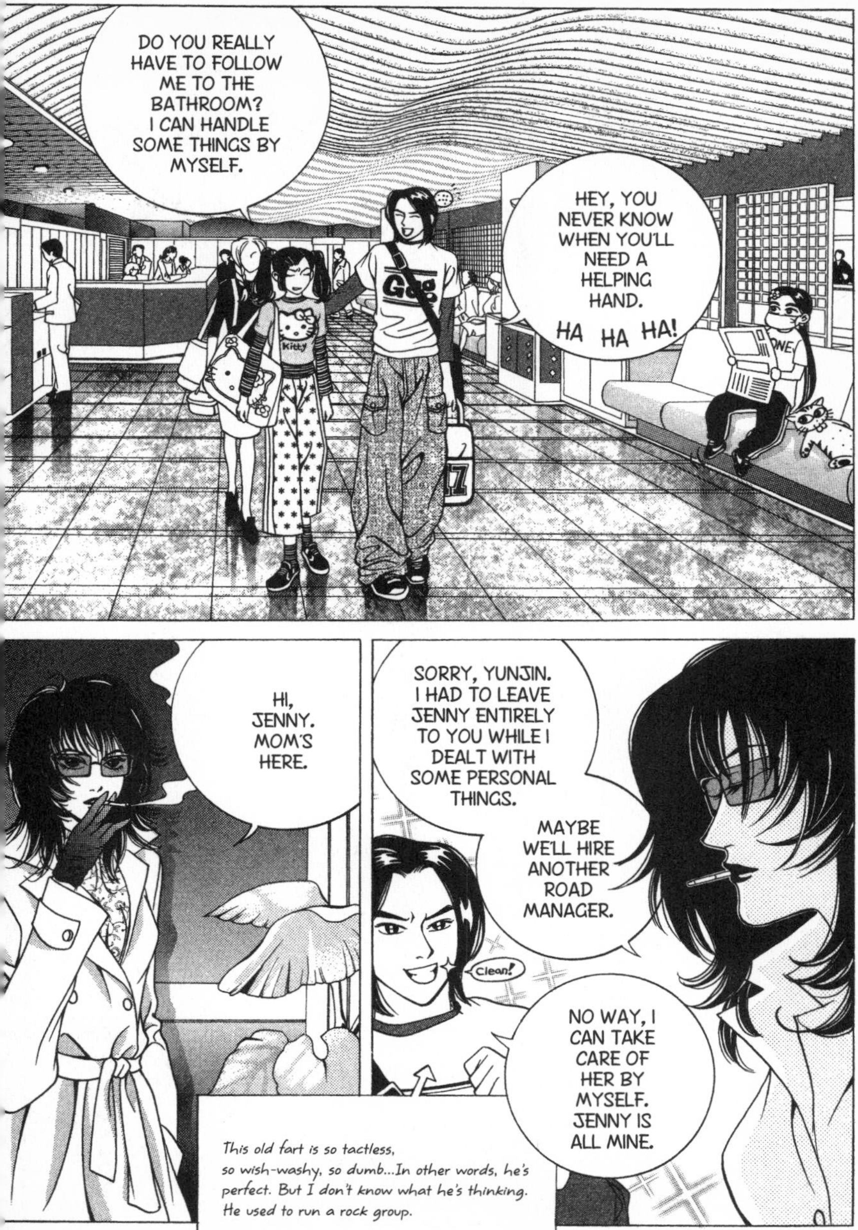
DO YOU REALLY HAVE TO FOLLOW ME TO THE BATHROOM? I CAN HANDLE SOME THINGS BY MYSELF.
HEY, YOU NEVER KNOW WHEN YOU'LL NEED A HELPING HAND.
HA HA HA!
HI, JENNY. MOM'S HERE.
SORRY, YUNJIN. I HAD TO LEAVE JENNY ENTIRELY TO YOU WHILE I DEALT WITH SOME PERSONAL THINGS.
MAYBE WE'LL HIRE ANOTHER ROAD MANAGER.
Clean!
NO WAY, I CAN TAKE CARE OF HER BY MYSELF. JENNY IS ALL MINE.
This old fart is so tactless, so wish-washy, so dumb...In other words, he's perfect. But I don't know what he's thinking. He used to run a rock group.

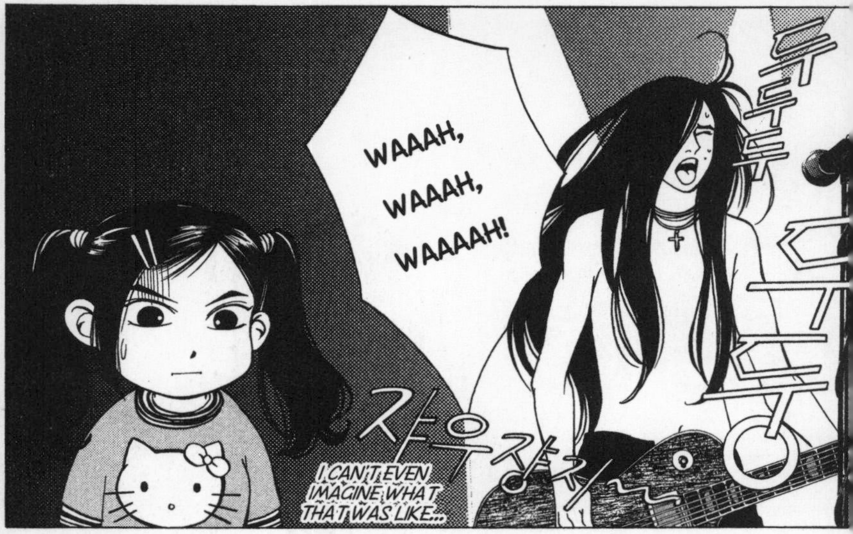
WAAAH, WAAAH, WAAAAH!
I CAN'T EVEN IMAGINE WHAT THAT WAS LIKE...

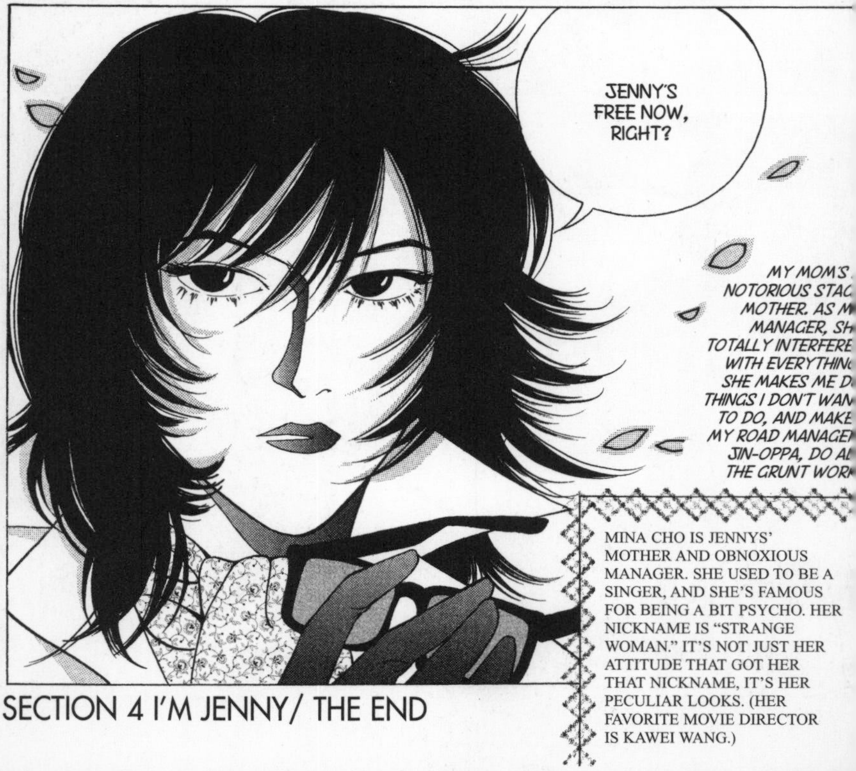
JENNY'S FREE NOW, RIGHT?
MY MOM'S NOTORIOUS STAC MOTHER. AS M MANAGER, SH TOTALLY INTERFERE WITH EVERYTHIN SHE MAKES ME D THINGS I DON'T WAN TO DO, AND MAKE MY ROAD MANAGE JIN-OPPA, DO A THE GRUNT WOR

MINA CHO IS JENNYS' MOTHER AND OBNOXIOUS MANAGER. SHE USED TO BE A SINGER, AND SHE'S FAMOUS FOR BEING A BIT PSYCHO. HER NICKNAME IS "STRANGE WOMAN." IT'S NOT JUST HER ATTITUDE THAT GOT HER THAT NICKNAME, IT'S HER PECULIAR LOOKS. (HER FAVORITE MOVIE DIRECTOR IS KAWEI WANG.)

SECTION 4 I'M JENNY/ THE END

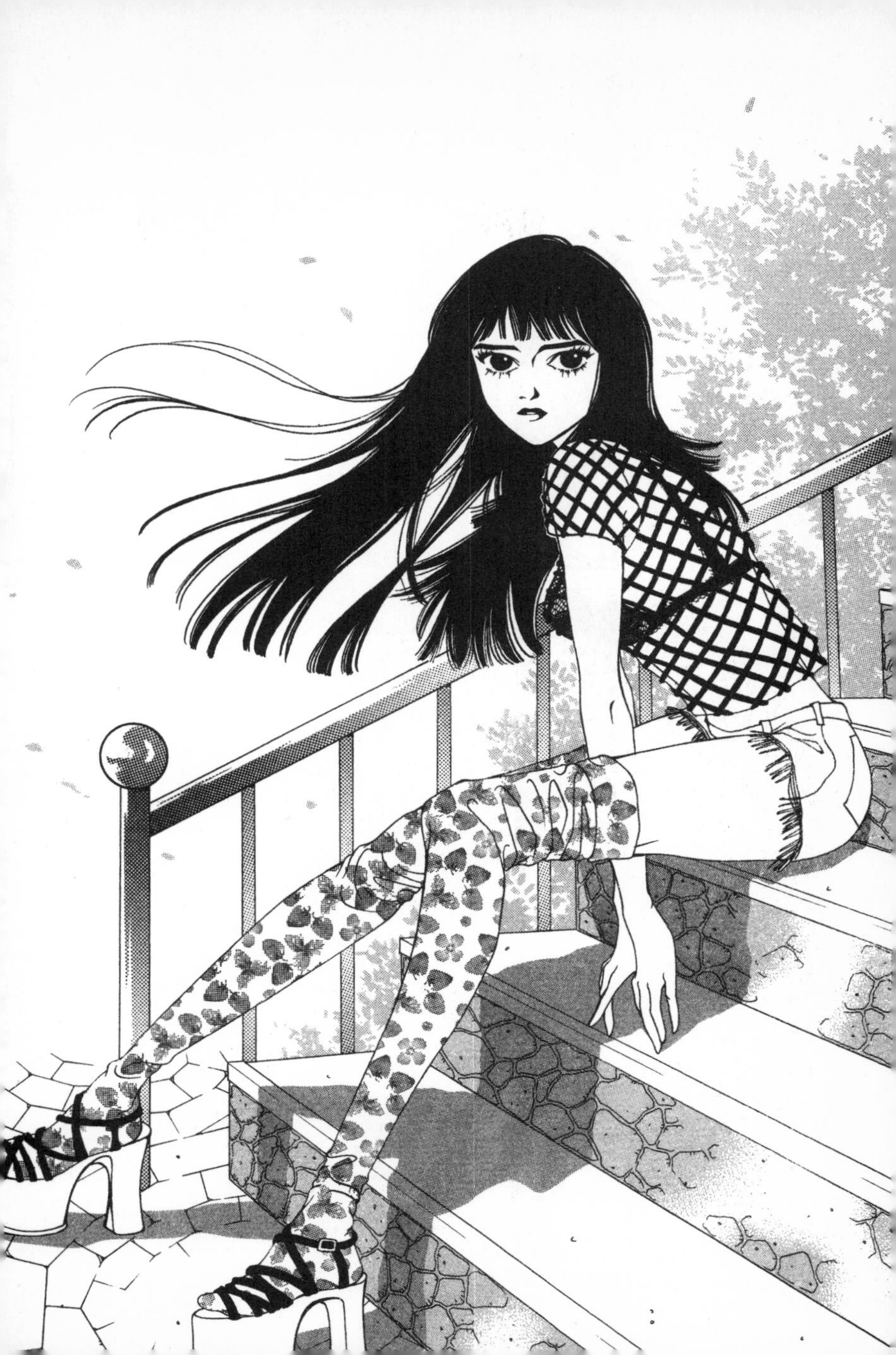

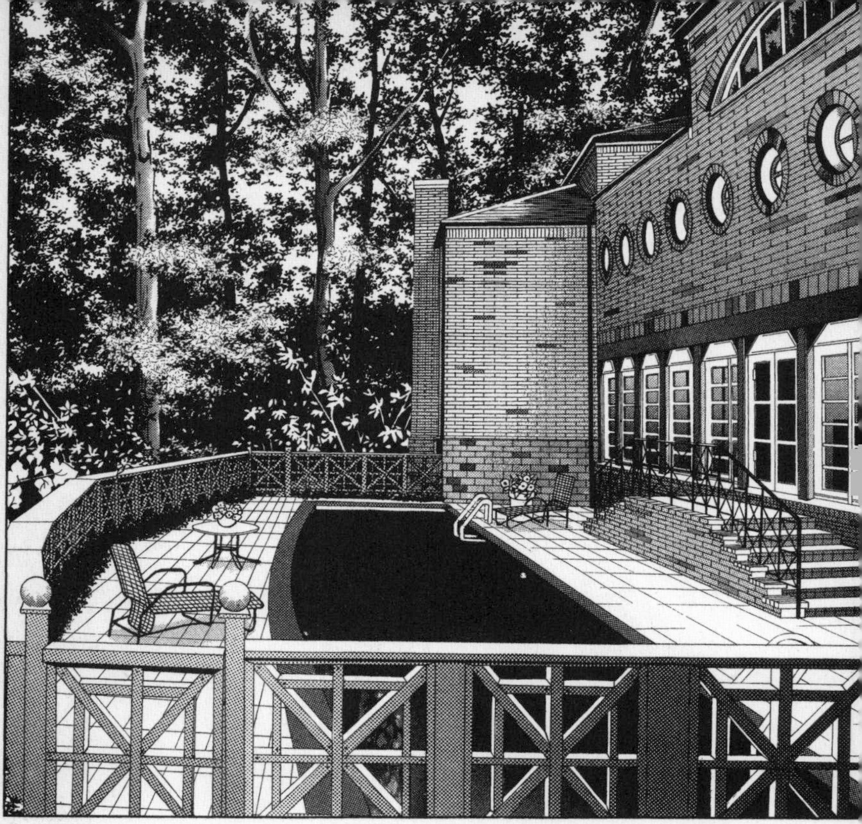

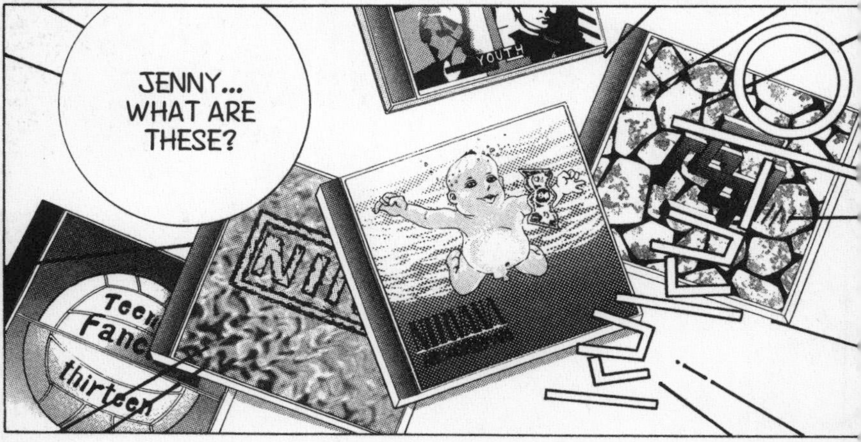
JENNY... WHAT ARE THESE?
YOUTH
thirteen

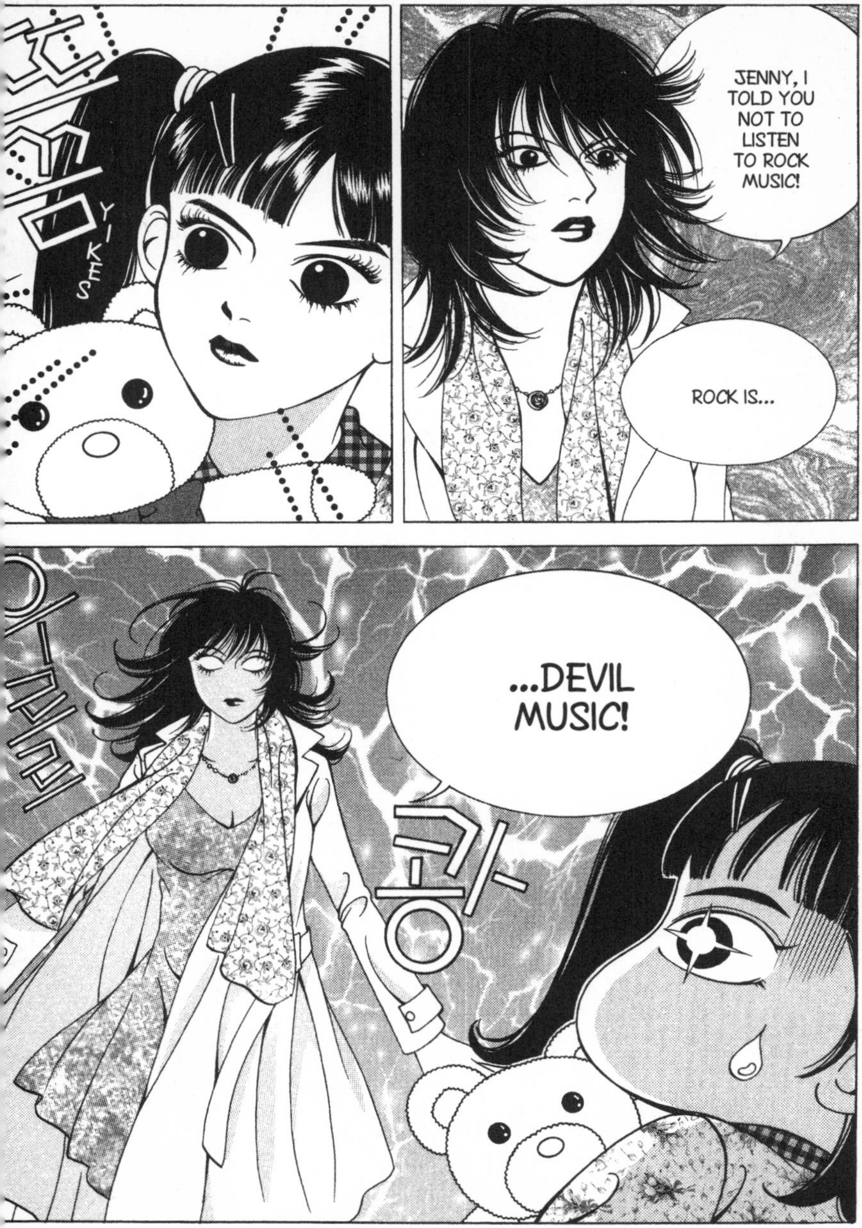
YIKES
JENNY, I TOLD YOU NOT TO LISTEN TO ROCK MUSIC!
ROCK IS...
...DEVIL MUSIC!

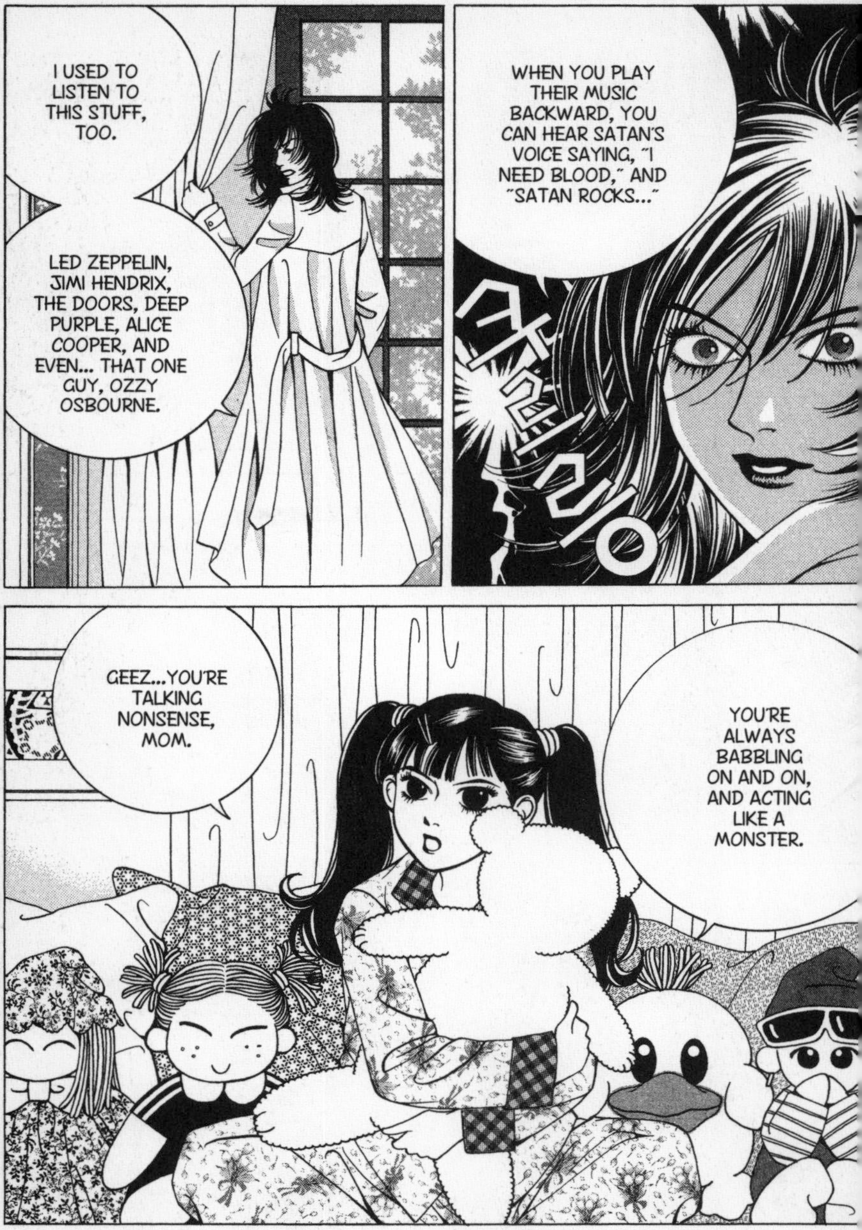
I USED TO LISTEN TO THIS STUFF, TOO.
LED ZEPPELIN, JIMI HENDRIX, THE DOORS, DEEP PURPLE, ALICE COOPER, AND EVEN... THAT ONE GUY, OZZY OSBOURNE.
WHEN YOU PLAY THEIR MUSIC BACKWARD, YOU CAN HEAR SATAN'S VOICE SAYING, "I NEED BLOOD," AND "SATAN ROCKS..."
GEEZ...YOU'RE TALKING NONSENSE, MOM.
YOU'RE ALWAYS BABBLING ON AND ON, AND ACTING LIKE A MONSTER.

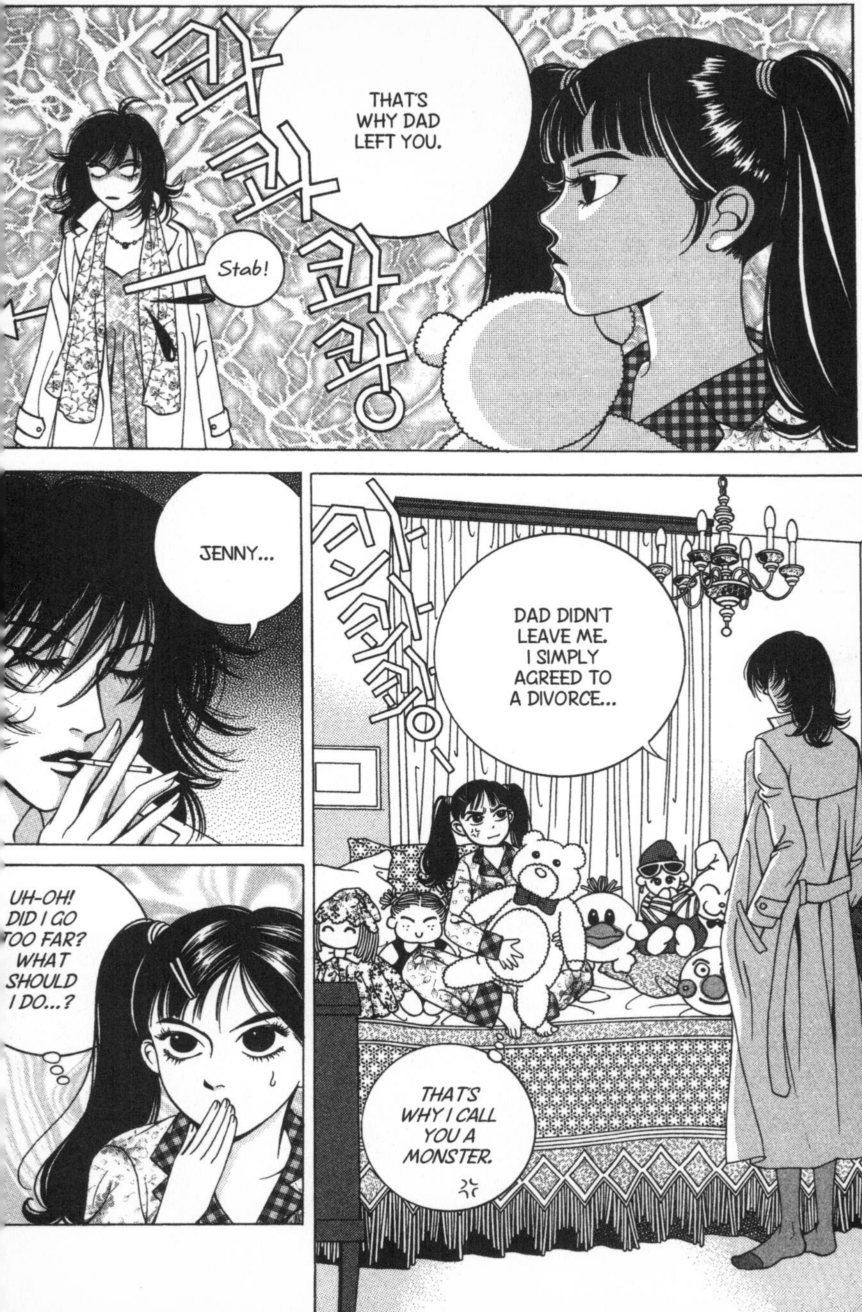
THAT'S WHY DAD LEFT YOU.
Stab!
JENNY...
UH-OH! DID I GO TOO FAR? WHAT SHOULD I DO...?
DAD DIDN'T LEAVE ME. I SIMPLY AGREED TO A DIVORCE...
THAT'S WHY I CALL YOU A MONSTER.

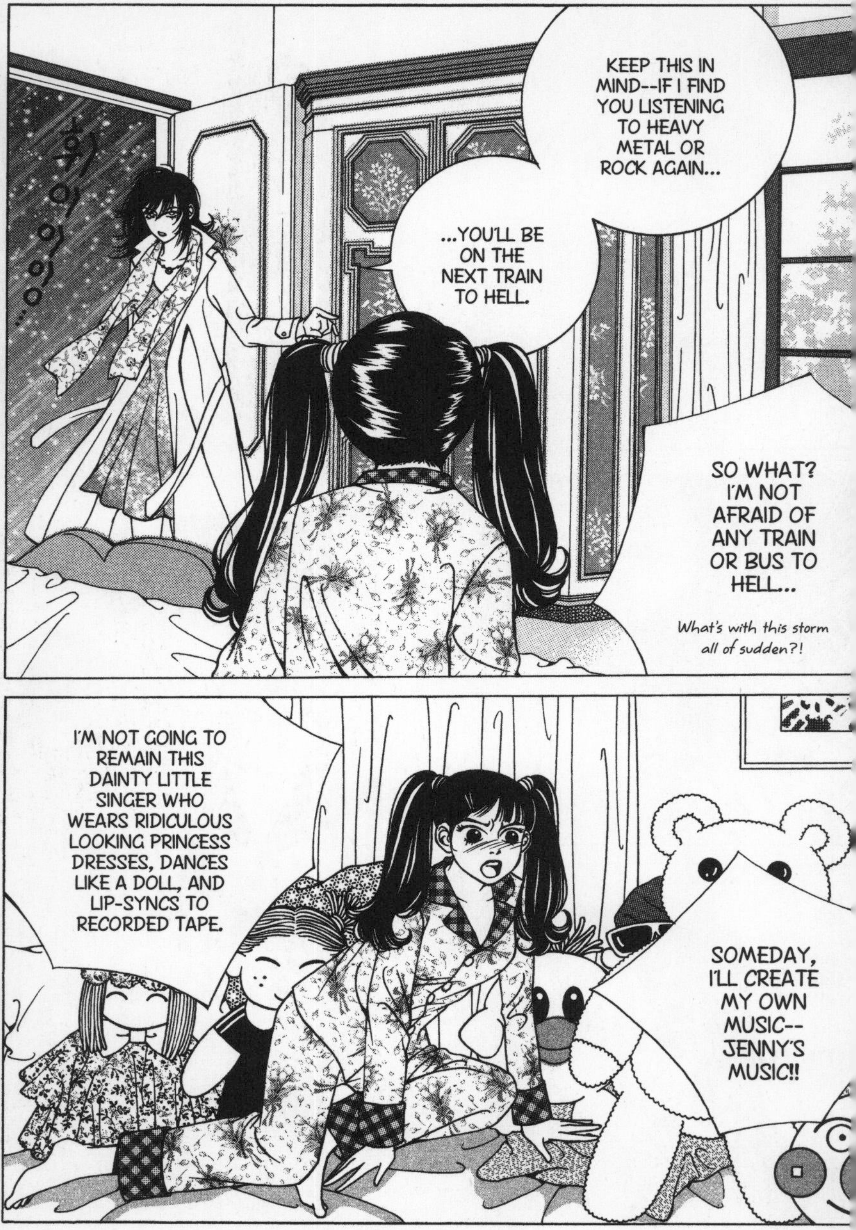
KEEP THIS IN MIND--IF I FIND YOU LISTENING TO HEAVY METAL OR ROCK AGAIN...
...YOU'LL BE ON THE NEXT TRAIN TO HELL.
SO WHAT? I'M NOT AFRAID OF ANY TRAIN OR BUS TO HELL...
What's with this storm all of sudden?!
I'M NOT GOING TO REMAIN THIS DAINTY LITTLE SINGER WHO WEARS RIDICULOUS LOOKING PRINCESS DRESSES, DANCES LIKE A DOLL, AND LIP-SYNCS TO RECORDED TAPE.
SOMEDAY, I'LL CREATE MY OWN MUSIC--JENNY'S MUSIC!!

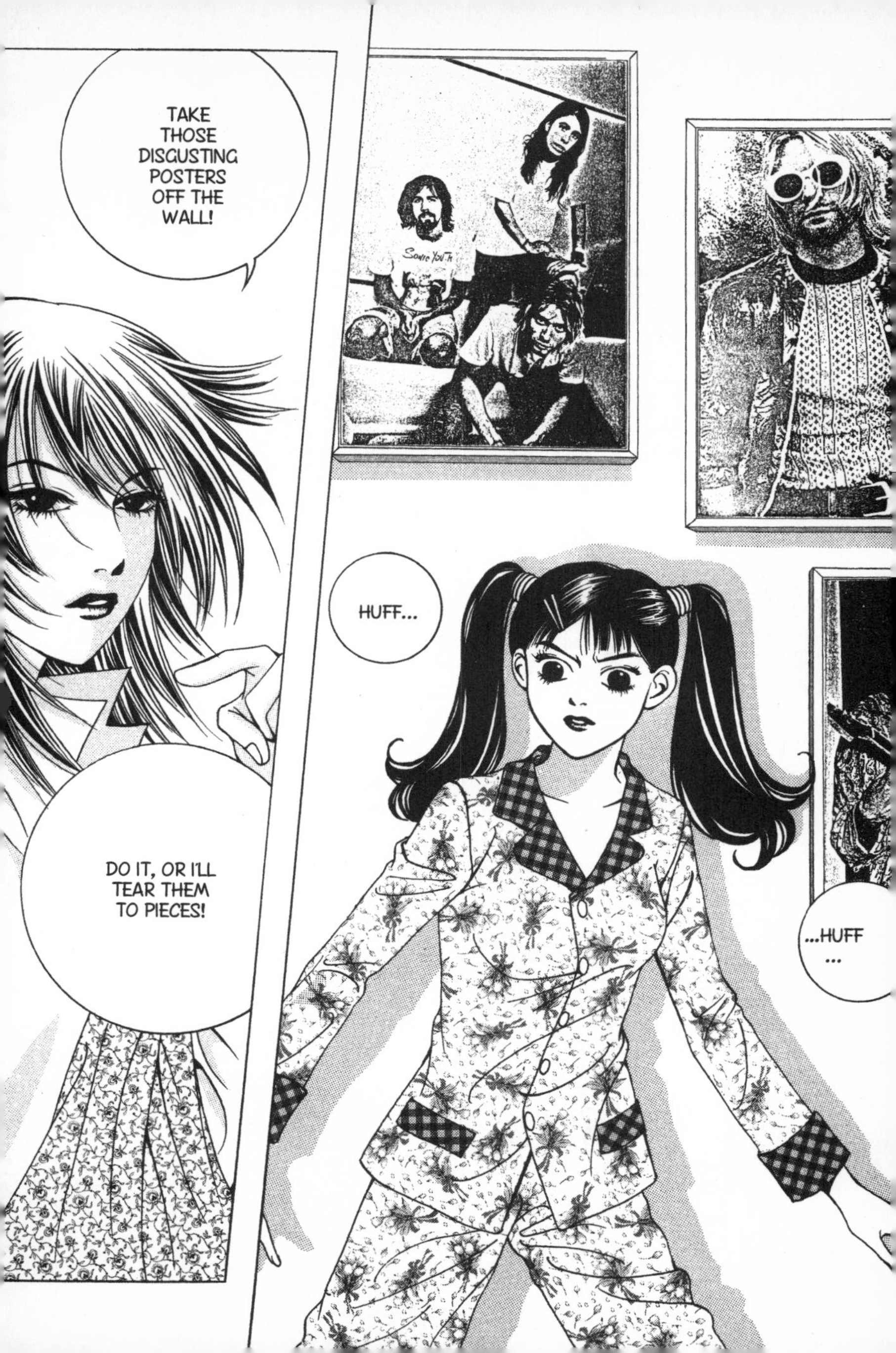
HUFF...
...HUFF ...
TAKE THOSE DISGUSTING POSTERS OFF THE WALL!
DO IT, OR I'LL TEAR THEM TO PIECES!

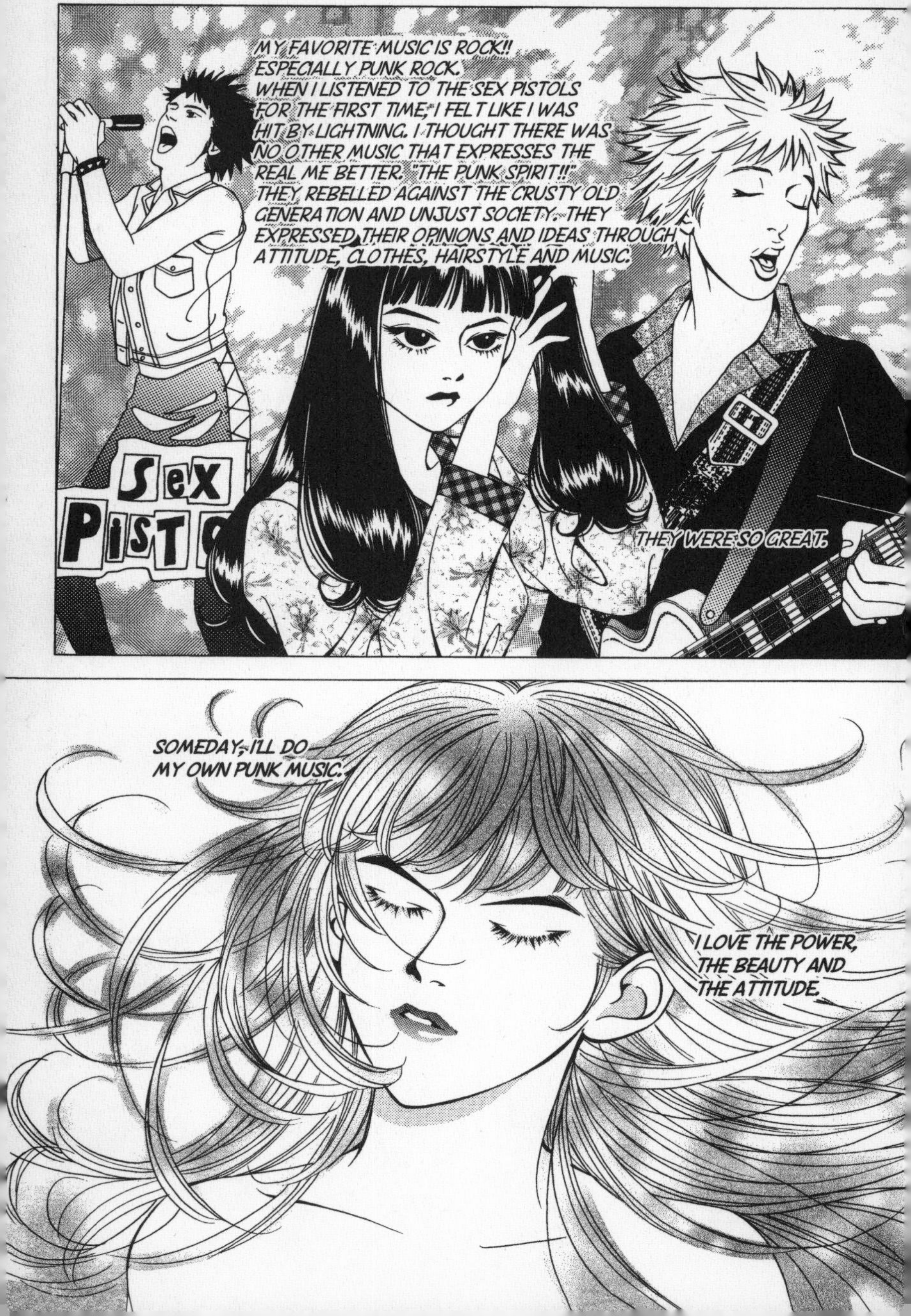
MY FAVORITE MUSIC IS ROCK!!
ESPECIALLY PUNK ROCK.
WHEN I LISTENED TO THE SEX PISTOLS FOR THE FIRST TIME, I FELT LIKE I WAS HIT BY LIGHTNING. I THOUGHT THERE WAS NO OTHER MUSIC THAT EXPRESSES THE REAL ME BETTER. "THE PUNK SPIRIT!!"
THEY REBELLED AGAINST THE CRUSTY OLD GENERATION AND UNJUST SOCIETY. THEY EXPRESSED THEIR OPINIONS AND IDEAS THROUGH ATTITUDE, CLOTHES, HAIRSTYLE AND MUSIC.
SEX PISTO
THEY WERE SO GREAT.
SOMEDAY, I'LL DO MY OWN PUNK MUSIC.
I LOVE THE POWER, THE BEAUTY AND THE ATTITUDE.

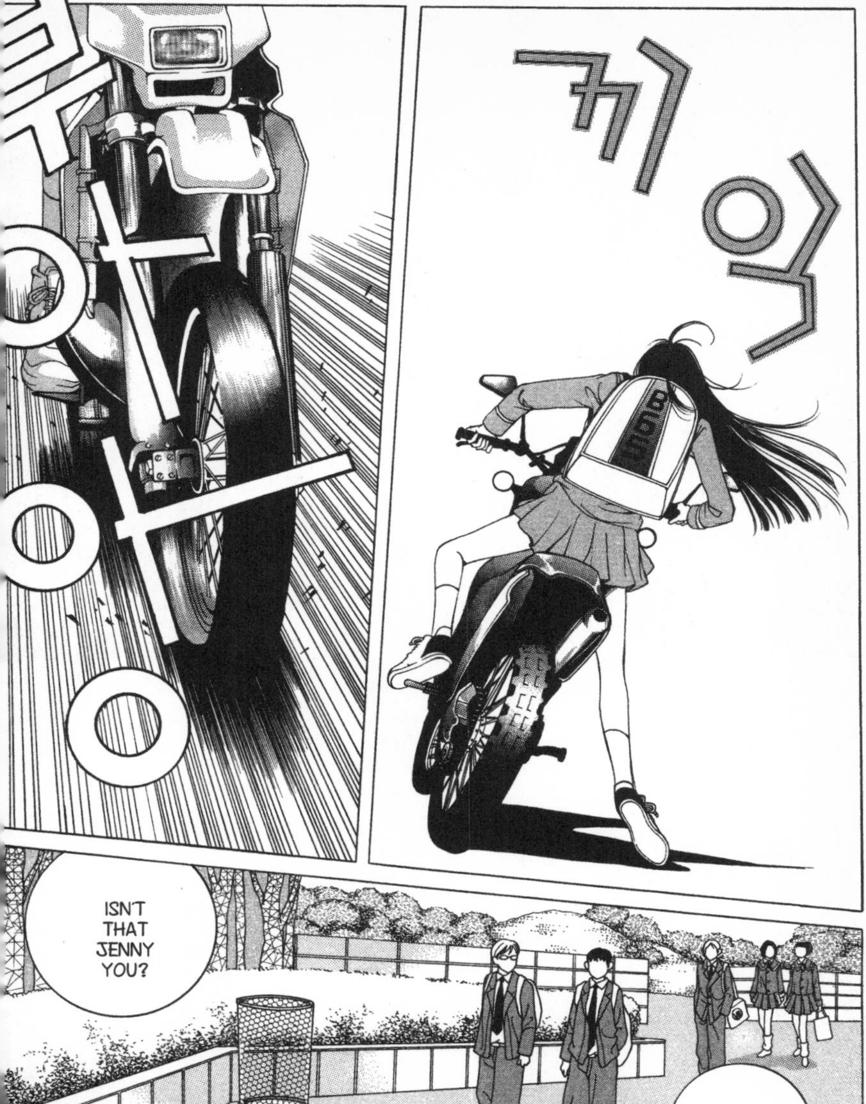
ISN'T THAT JENNY YOU?
CAN'T BE.

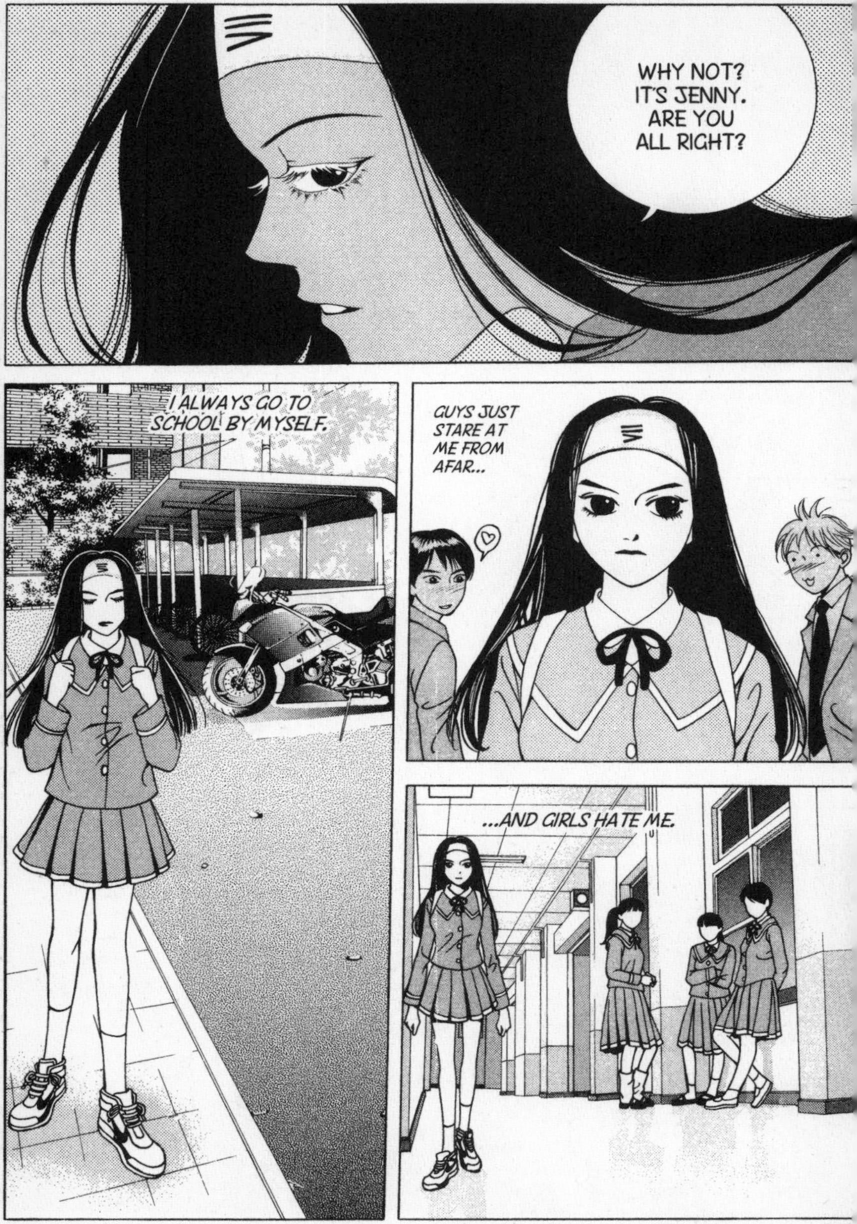
WHY NOT? IT'S JENNY. ARE YOU ALL RIGHT?
I ALWAYS GO TO SCHOOL BY MYSELF.
GUYS JUST STARE AT ME FROM AFAR...
...AND GIRLS HATE ME.

AT SCHOOL, ALMOST NOBODY TALKS TO ME.

THEY JUST WATCH ME AS IF I'M A PRETTY MONKEY IN A ZOO.

I EAT LUNCH ALONE, AND SOMETIMES GET BULLIED.

I HAVE NO FRIENDS AT ALL.

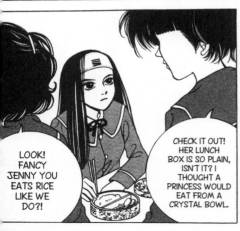

LOOK! FANCY JENNY YOU EATS RICE LIKE WE DO?!

CHECK IT OUT! HER LUNCH BOX IS SO PLAIN, ISN'T IT? I THOUGHT A PRINCESS WOULD EAT FROM A CRYSTAL BOWL.

SO I EAT RICE AND GO TO THE TOILET JUST LIKE YOU. IS THERE A PROBLEM?

ACTUALLY, I HARDLY HAVE TIME TO EAT BECAUSE OF MY HECTIC SCHEDULE. IT'S VERY RARE THAT I EAT LUNCH AT SCHOOL.

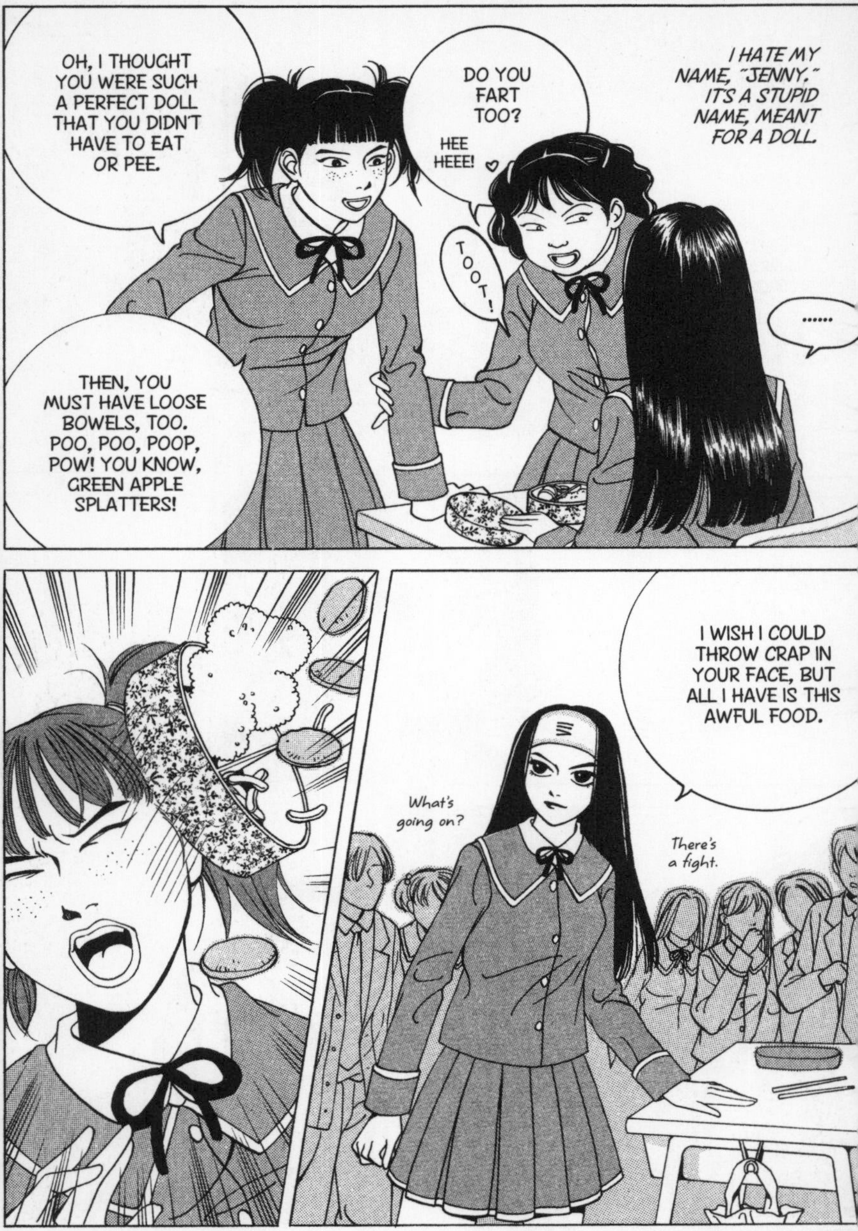

OH, I THOUGHT YOU WERE SUCH A PERFECT DOLL THAT YOU DIDN'T HAVE TO EAT OR PEE.
DO YOU FART TOO?
HEE HEEE!
TOOT!
I HATE MY NAME, "JENNY." IT'S A STUPID NAME, MEANT FOR A DOLL.
......
THEN, YOU MUST HAVE LOOSE BOWELS, TOO. POO, POO, POOP, POW! YOU KNOW, GREEN APPLE SPLATTERS!
I WISH I COULD THROW CRAP IN YOUR FACE, BUT ALL I HAVE IS THIS AWFUL FOOD.
What's going on?
There's a fight.

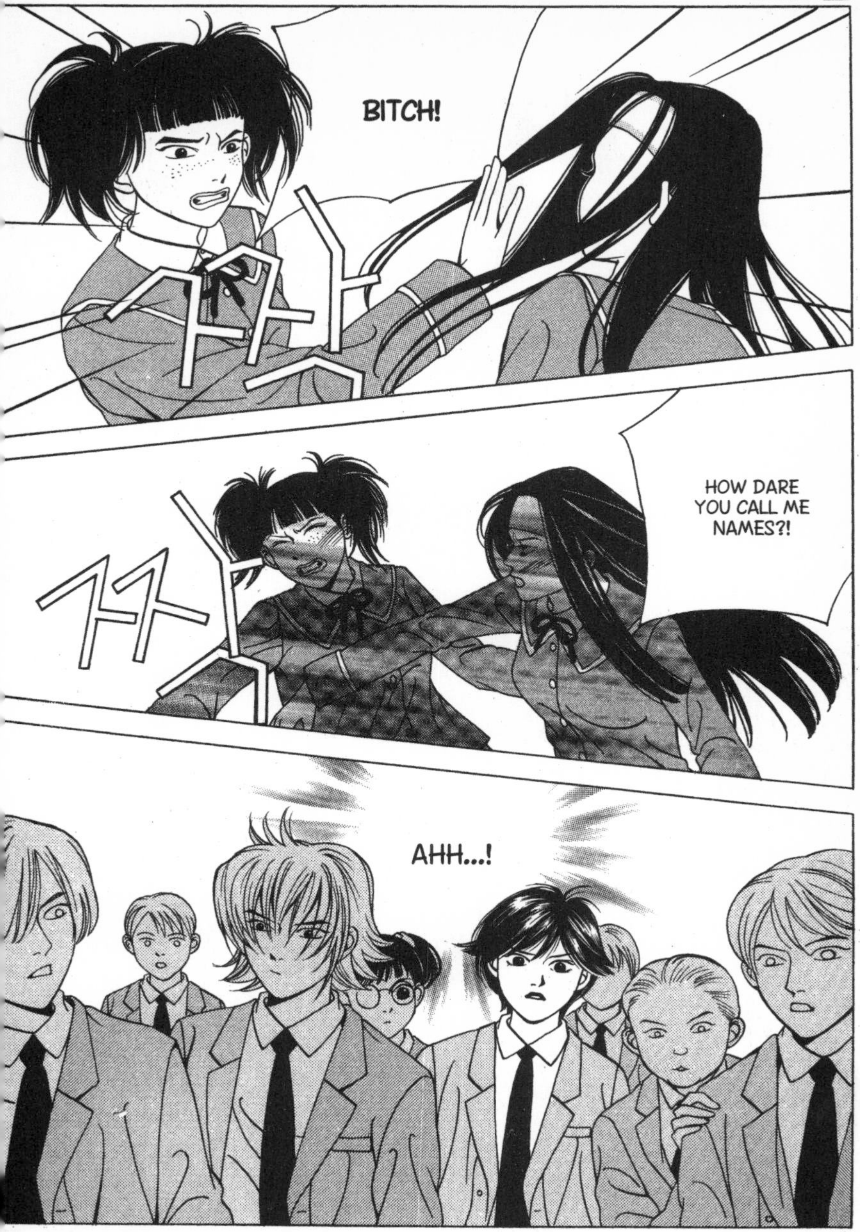
BITCH!
HOW DARE YOU CALL ME NAMES?!
AHH...!

DON'T LOOK AT ME! I DON'T WANT TO BE SEEN LIKE THIS!

I HATE MY LIFE!

HEY! YOU GIRLS ARE BEING KINDA HARSH.

Twins

(Iru)

(Ino)

HA ROCK, IRU, INO! DON'T TELL ME YOU'RE TAKING HER SIDE?

HEY! WHERE YOU GOING?! STOP RIGHT THERE!

DIDN'T YOU SEE? SHE ACTED LIKE A TOTAL BITCH!

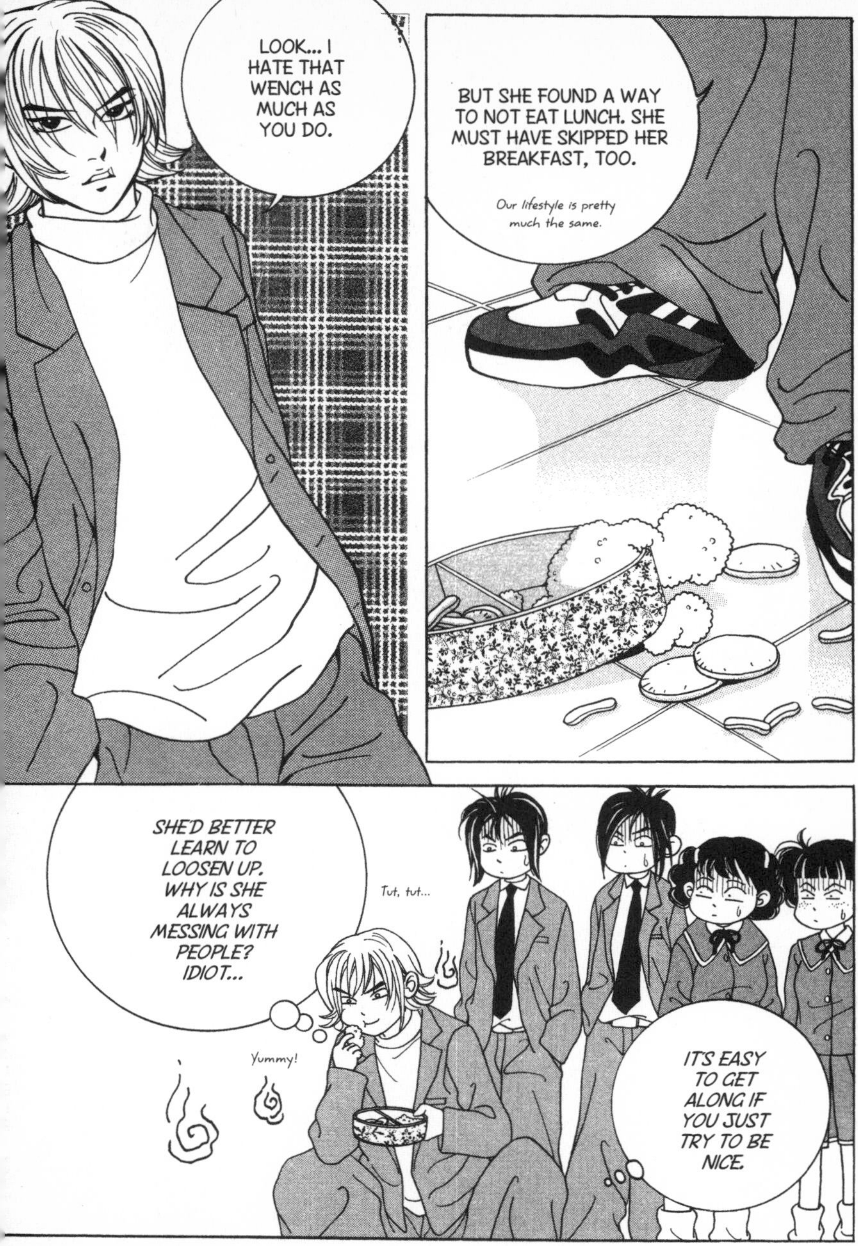
LOOK... I HATE THAT WENCH AS MUCH AS YOU DO.
BUT SHE FOUND A WAY TO NOT EAT LUNCH. SHE MUST HAVE SKIPPED HER BREAKFAST, TOO.
Our lifestyle is pretty much the same.
SHE'D BETTER LEARN TO LOOSEN UP. WHY IS SHE ALWAYS MESSING WITH PEOPLE? IDIOT...
Tut, tut...
Yummy!
IT'S EASY TO GET ALONG IF YOU JUST TRY TO BE NICE.

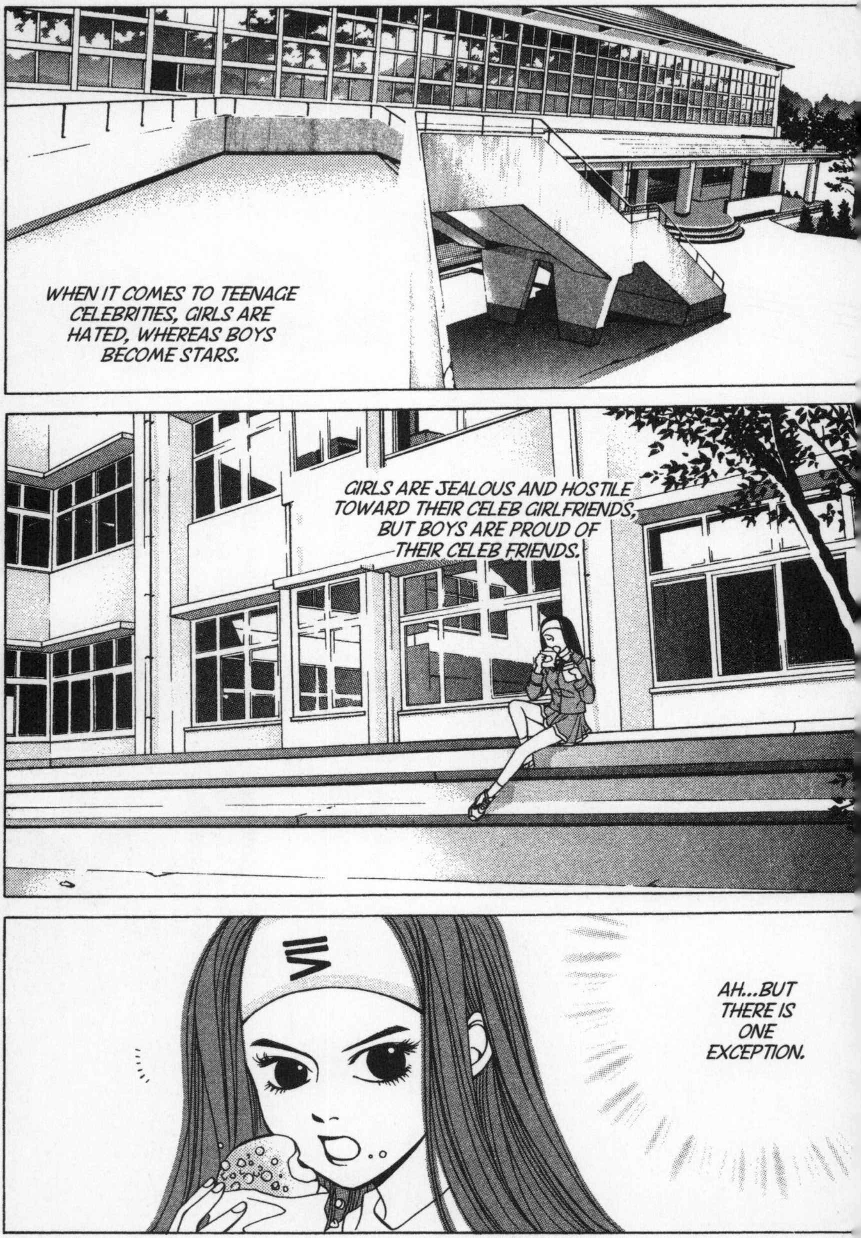
WHEN IT COMES TO TEENAGE CELEBRITIES, GIRLS ARE HATED, WHEREAS BOYS BECOME STARS.
GIRLS ARE JEALOUS AND HOSTILE TOWARD THEIR CELEB GIRLFRIENDS, BUT BOYS ARE PROUD OF THEIR CELEB FRIENDS.
AH...BUT THERE IS ONE EXCEPTION.

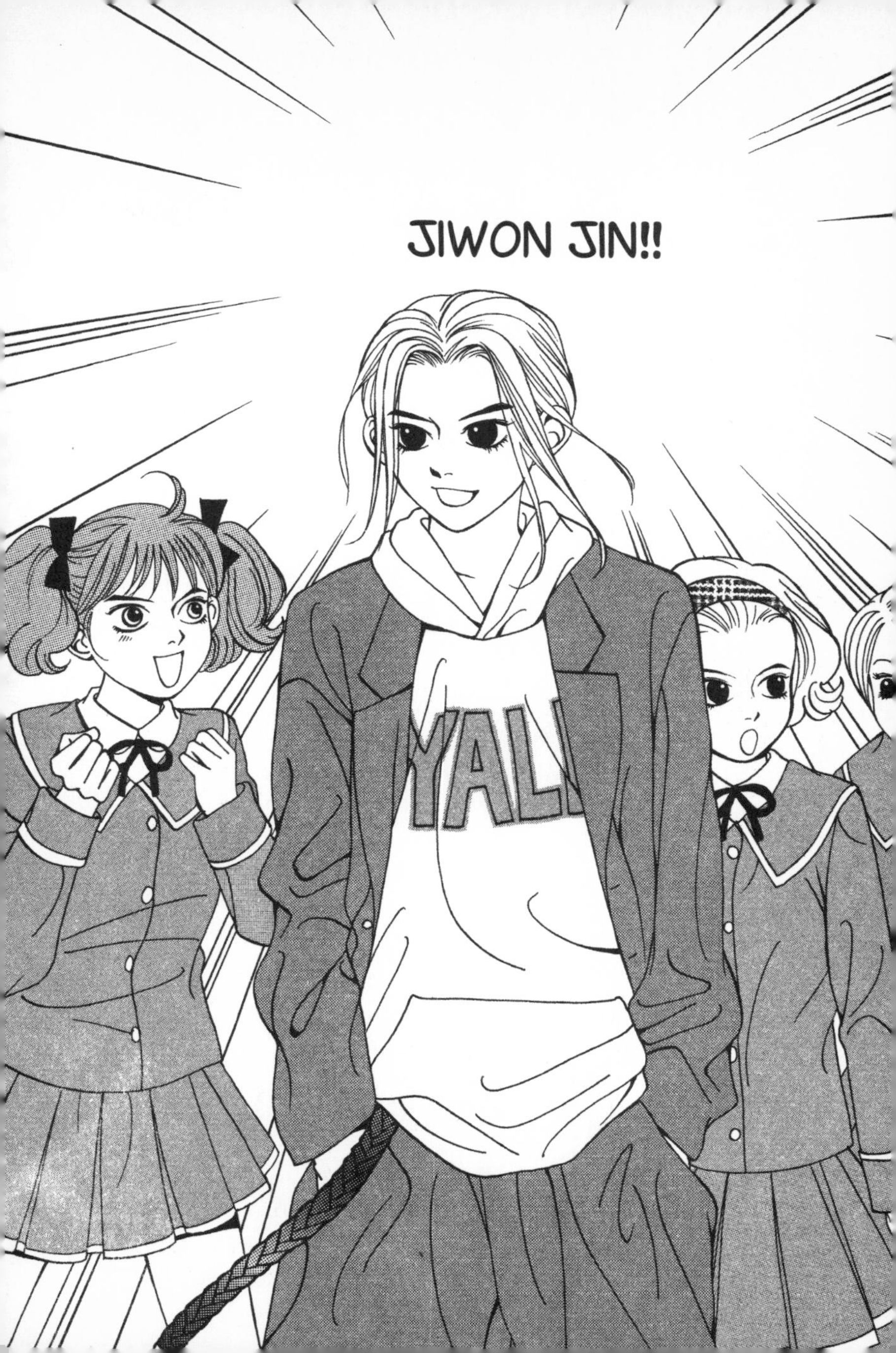
JIWON JIN!!
YALE

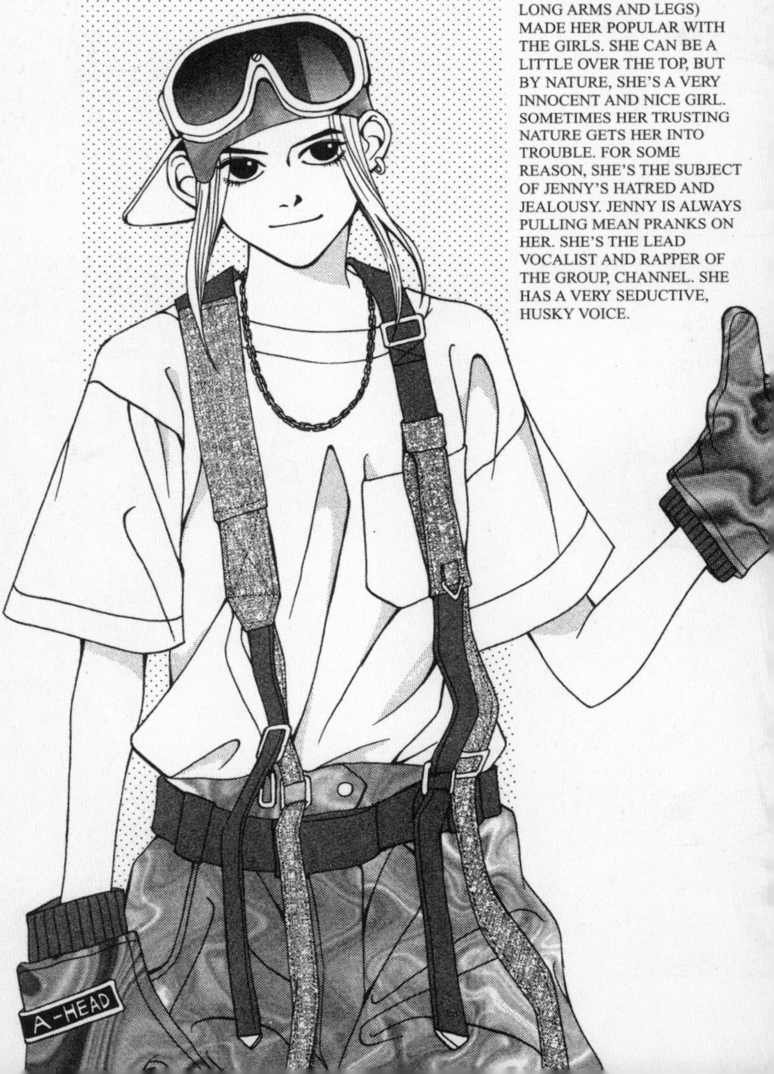
A-HEAD

JIWON JIN
(FEMALE: 17)
BLOOD-TYPE: O. HOROSCOPE SIGN: AQUARIUS.
SHE'S A GIRL WHO DRESSES LIKE A BOY. HER CROSS-DRESSING WAS THE THING THAT MADE HER POPULAR. THE SCHOOL GAVE HER SPECIAL PERMISSION TO WEAR A BOY'S UNIFORM. HER CUTE FACE AND BOYISH APPEARANCE (SHE HAS LONG ARMS AND LEGS) MADE HER POPULAR WITH THE GIRLS. SHE CAN BE A LITTLE OVER THE TOP, BUT BY NATURE, SHE'S A VERY INNOCENT AND NICE GIRL. SOMETIMES HER TRUSTING NATURE GETS HER INTO TROUBLE. FOR SOME REASON, SHE'S THE SUBJECT OF JENNY'S HATRED AND JEALOUSY. JENNY IS ALWAYS PULLING MEAN PRANKS ON HER. SHE'S THE LEAD VOCALIST AND RAPPER OF THE GROUP, CHANNEL. SHE HAS A VERY SEDUCTIVE, HUSKY VOICE.

JENNY... EATING LUNCH ALONE? OUT HERE?

WHAT DO YOU CARE WHETHER OR NOT I EAT ALONE?

JIWON JIN IS A PERVERT-- A GIRL DRESSED LIKE A BOY.

GIRLS WHO LIKE SUCH A PERVERT ARE PERVS THEMSELVES.

BESIDES, JIWON HAS NO BRAINS OR ORIGINAL THOUGHTS. SHE'S JUST A SIMPLETON. SHE'S CLUMSY, AND MESSES UP ALL THE TIME.

MY GOD! WHAT AN IDIOT.

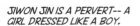

ARE YOU GOING TO THE TOP 21 COUNTDOWN SHOW THIS AFTERNOON? I'M GOING. MY GROUP IS RANKED THIRD.

FOOL! THE P.D.s AND PRODUCTION MANAGERS FORCED YOUR SONG ON THE PROGRAM. YOU REALLY THINK YOU DESERVE TO BE NUMBER THREE?

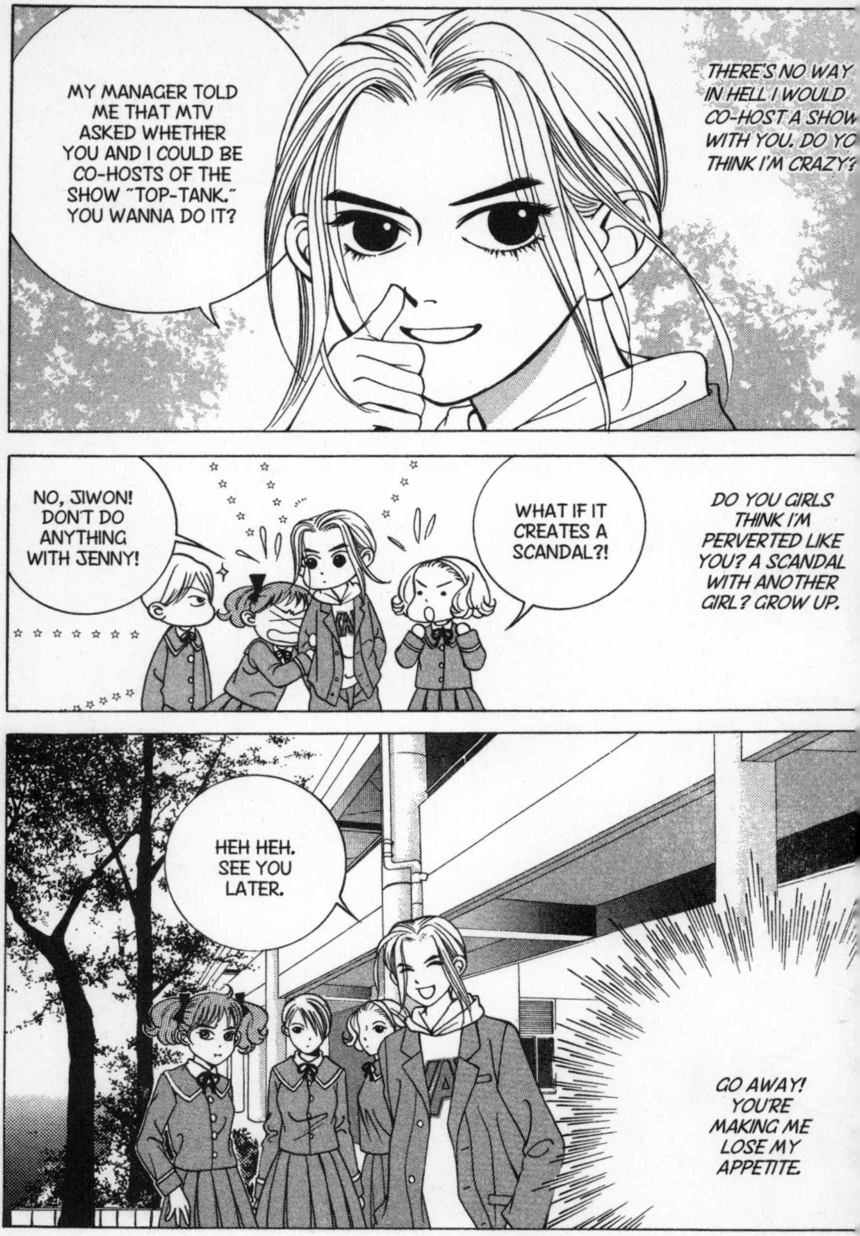

MY MANAGER TOLD ME THAT MTV ASKED WHETHER YOU AND I COULD BE CO-HOSTS OF THE SHOW "TOP-TANK." YOU WANNA DO IT?
THERE'S NO WAY IN HELL I WOULD CO-HOST A SHOW WITH YOU. DO YO THINK I'M CRAZY?
NO, JIWON! DON'T DO ANYTHING WITH JENNY!
WHAT IF IT CREATES A SCANDAL?!
DO YOU GIRLS THINK I'M PERVERTED LIKE YOU? A SCANDAL WITH ANOTHER GIRL? GROW UP.
HEH HEH. SEE YOU LATER.
GO AWAY! YOU'RE MAKING ME LOSE MY APPETITE.

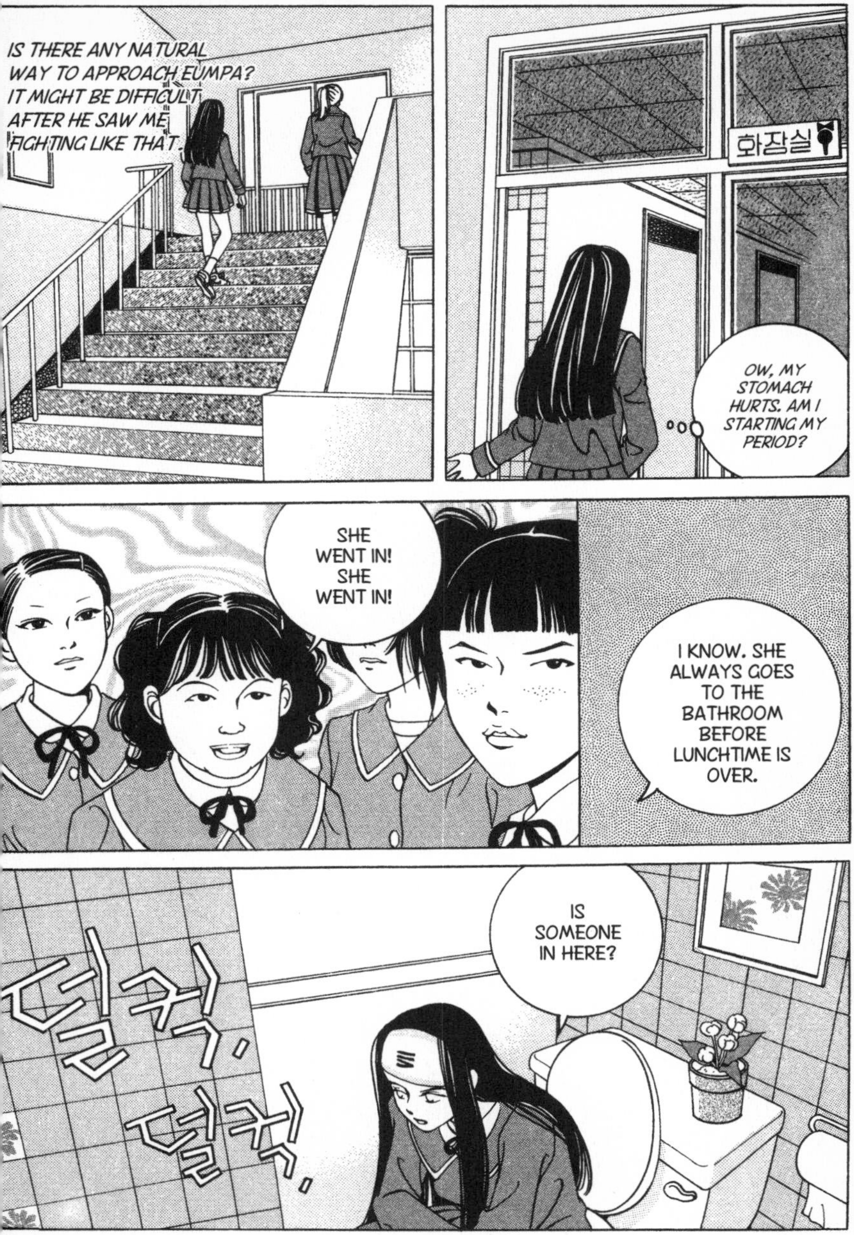
IS THERE ANY NATURAL WAY TO APPROACH EUMPA? IT MIGHT BE DIFFICULT AFTER HE SAW ME FIGHTING LIKE THAT.
화장실
OW, MY STOMACH HURTS. AM I STARTING MY PERIOD?
SHE WENT IN! SHE WENT IN!
I KNOW. SHE ALWAYS GOES TO THE BATHROOM BEFORE LUNCHTIME IS OVER.
덜컥, 덜컥,
IS SOMEONE IN HERE?

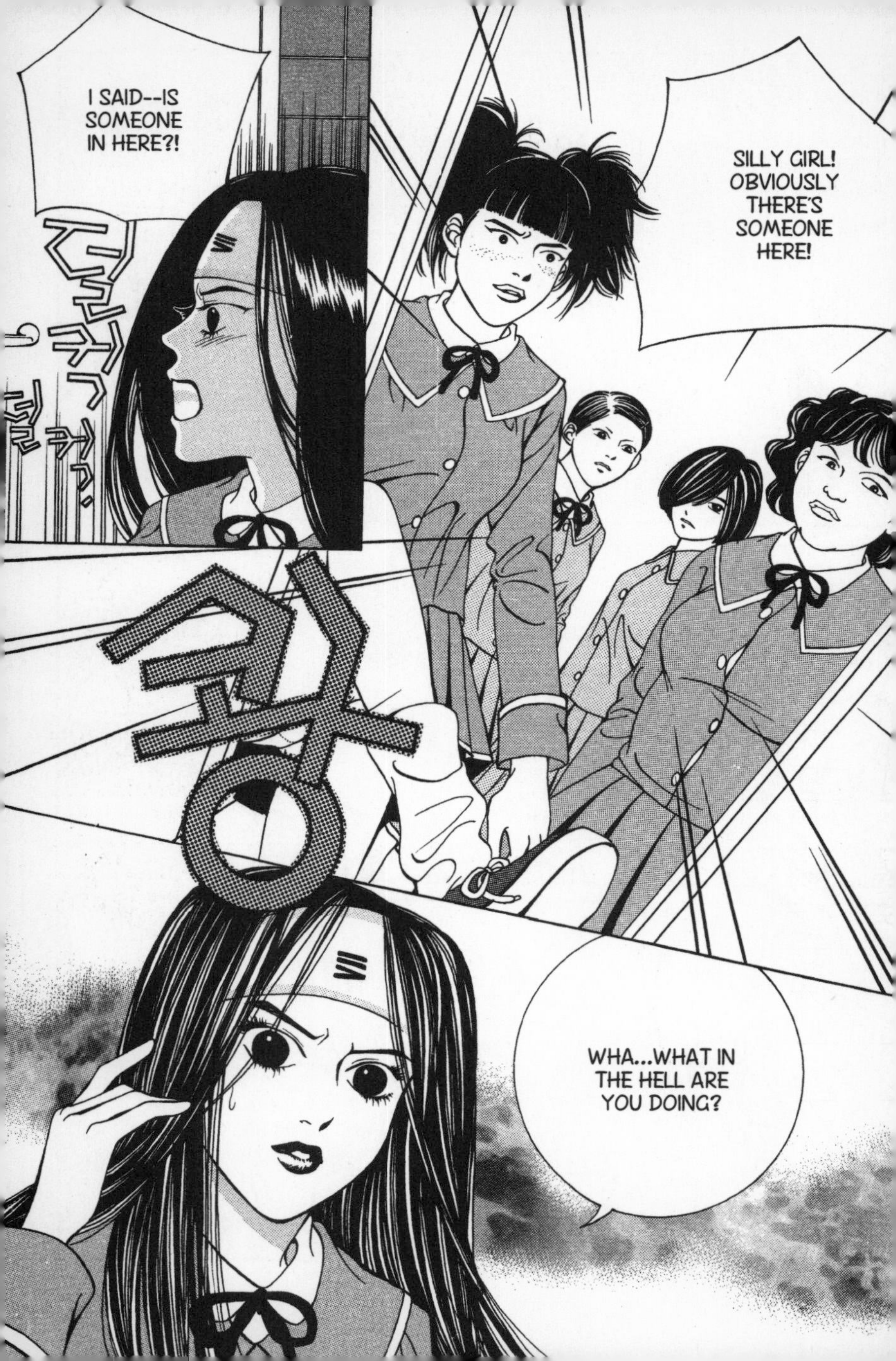
I SAID--IS SOMEONE IN HERE?!
SILLY GIRL! OBVIOUSLY THERE'S SOMEONE HERE!
WHA...WHAT IN THE HELL ARE YOU DOING?

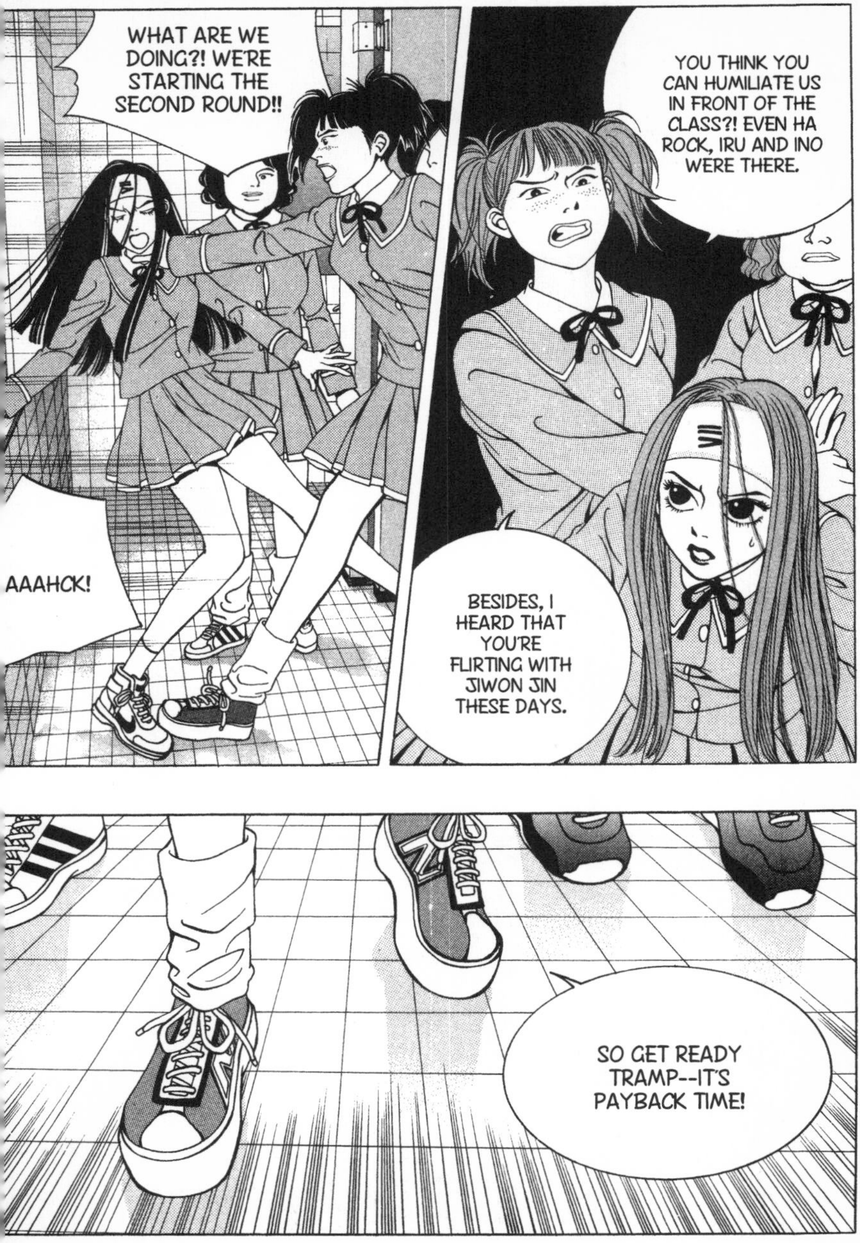
WHAT ARE WE DOING?! WE'RE STARTING THE SECOND ROUND!!
AAAHCK!
YOU THINK YOU CAN HUMILIATE US IN FRONT OF THE CLASS?! EVEN HA ROCK, IRU AND INO WERE THERE.
BESIDES, I HEARD THAT YOU'RE FLIRTING WITH JIWON JIN THESE DAYS.
SO GET READY TRAMP--IT'S PAYBACK TIME!

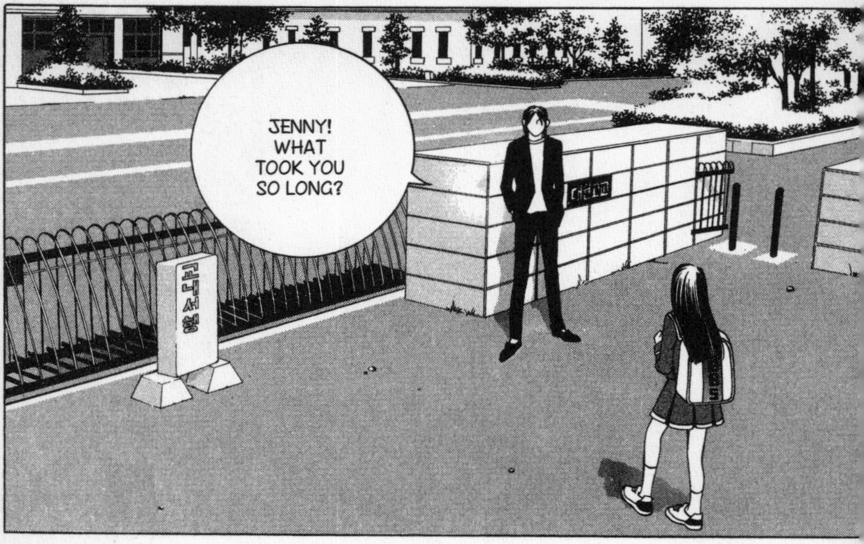
JENNY! WHAT TOOK YOU SO LONG?

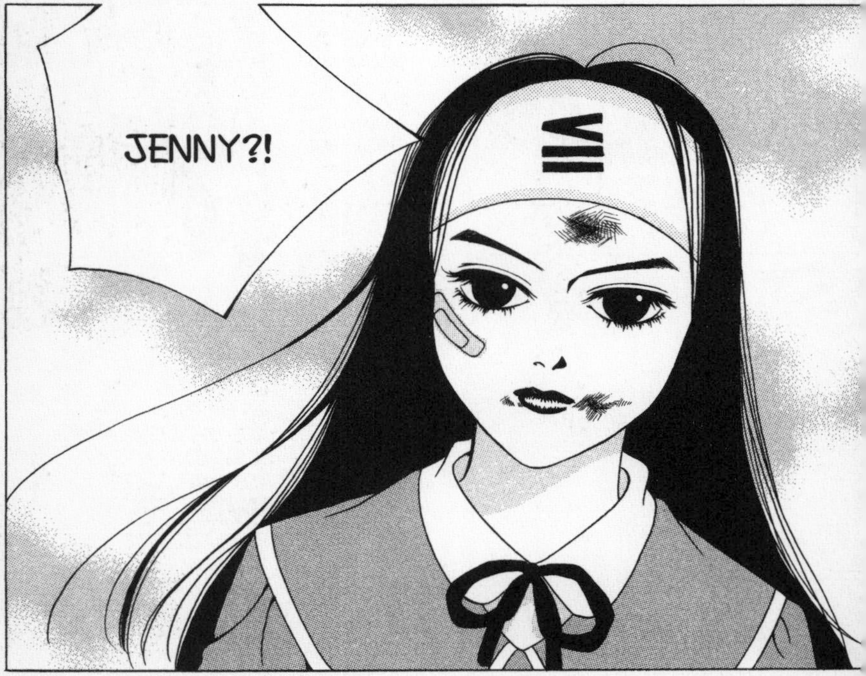
JENNY?!

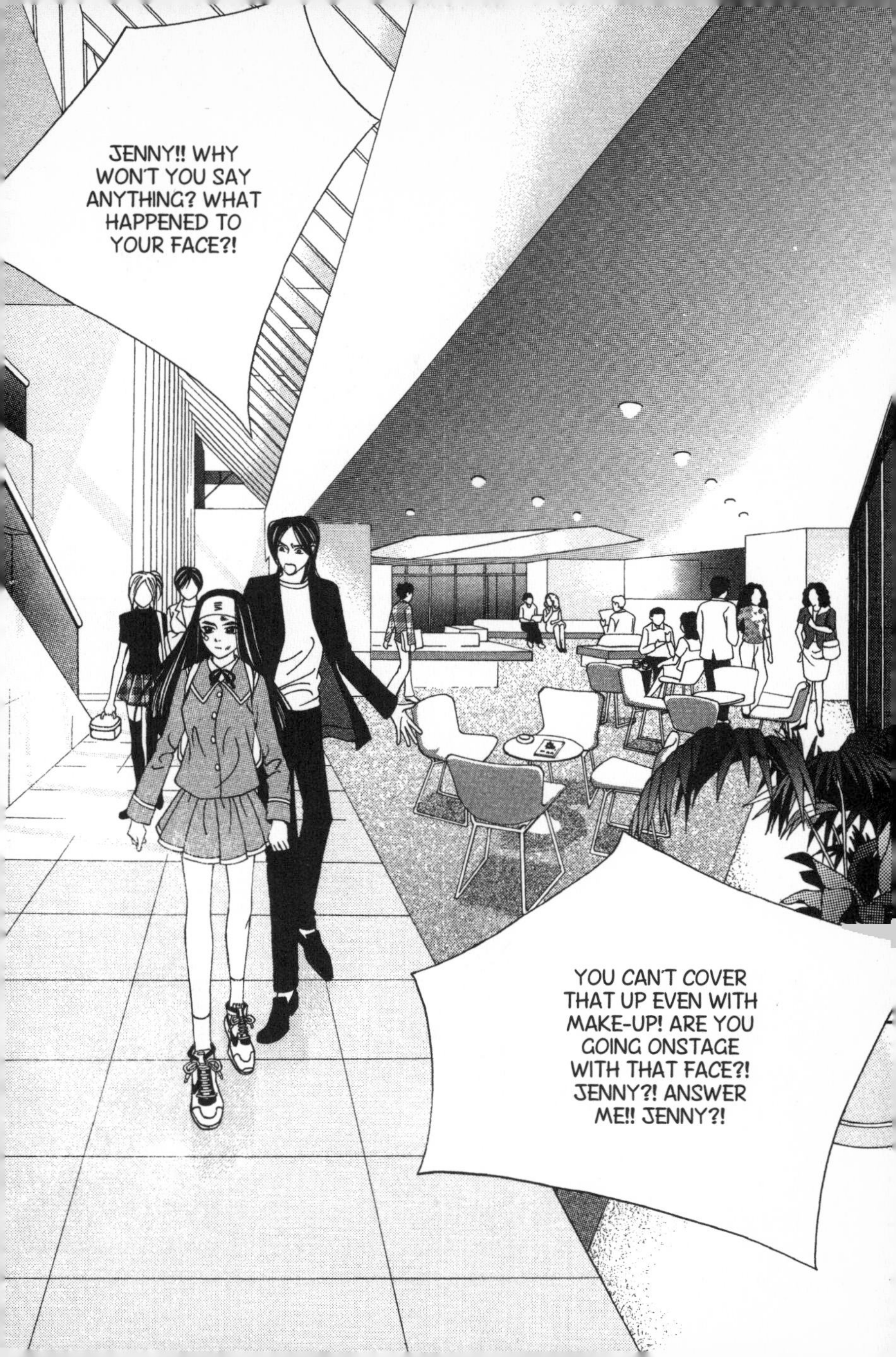
JENNY!! WHY WON'T YOU SAY ANYTHING? WHAT HAPPENED TO YOUR FACE?!
YOU CAN'T COVER THAT UP EVEN WITH MAKE-UP! ARE YOU GOING ONSTAGE WITH THAT FACE?! JENNY?! ANSWER ME!! JENNY?!

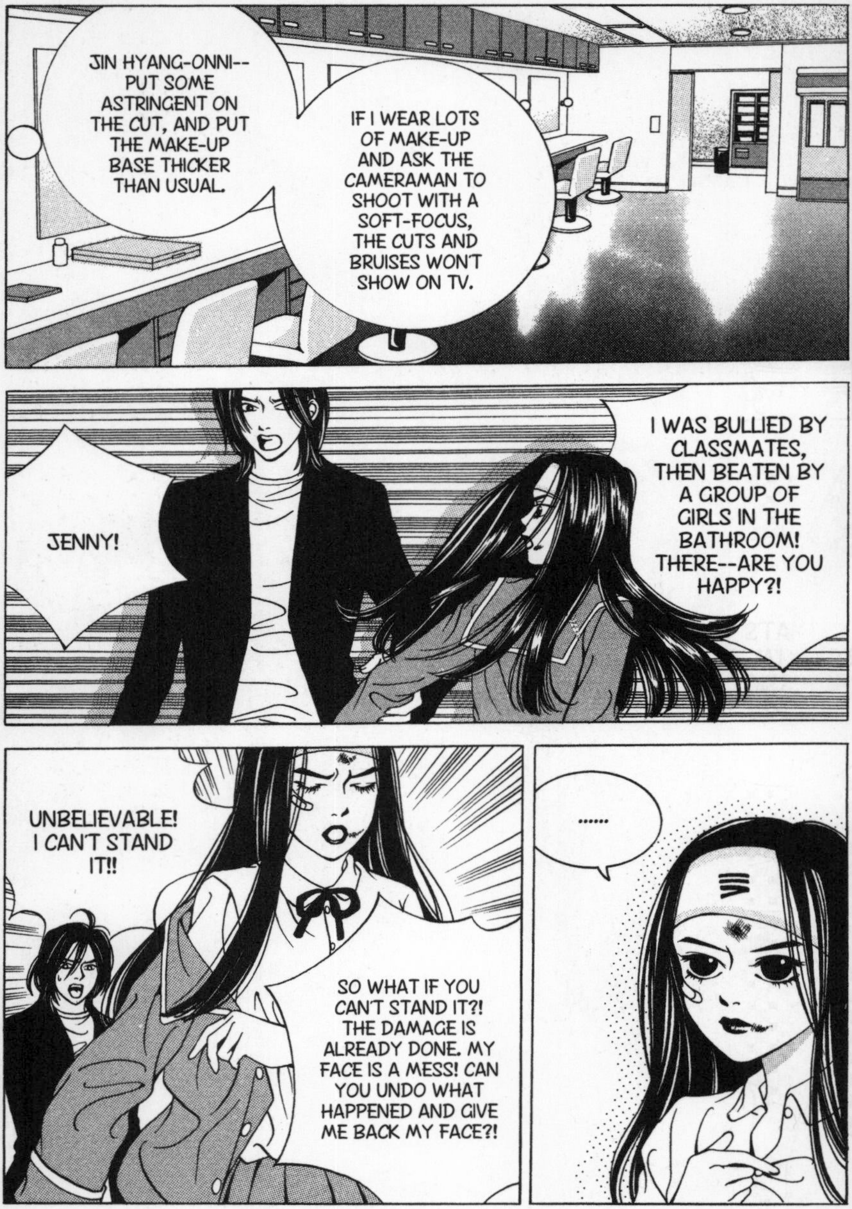
JIN HYANG-ONNI-- PUT SOME ASTRINGENT ON THE CUT, AND PUT THE MAKE-UP BASE THICKER THAN USUAL.
IF I WEAR LOTS OF MAKE-UP AND ASK THE CAMERAMAN TO SHOOT WITH A SOFT-FOCUS, THE CUTS AND BRUISES WON'T SHOW ON TV.
JENNY!
I WAS BULLIED BY CLASSMATES, THEN BEATEN BY A GROUP OF GIRLS IN THE BATHROOM! THERE--ARE YOU HAPPY?!
UNBELIEVABLE! I CAN'T STAND IT!!
SO WHAT IF YOU CAN'T STAND IT?! THE DAMAGE IS ALREADY DONE. MY FACE IS A MESS! CAN YOU UNDO WHAT HAPPENED AND GIVE ME BACK MY FACE?!
......

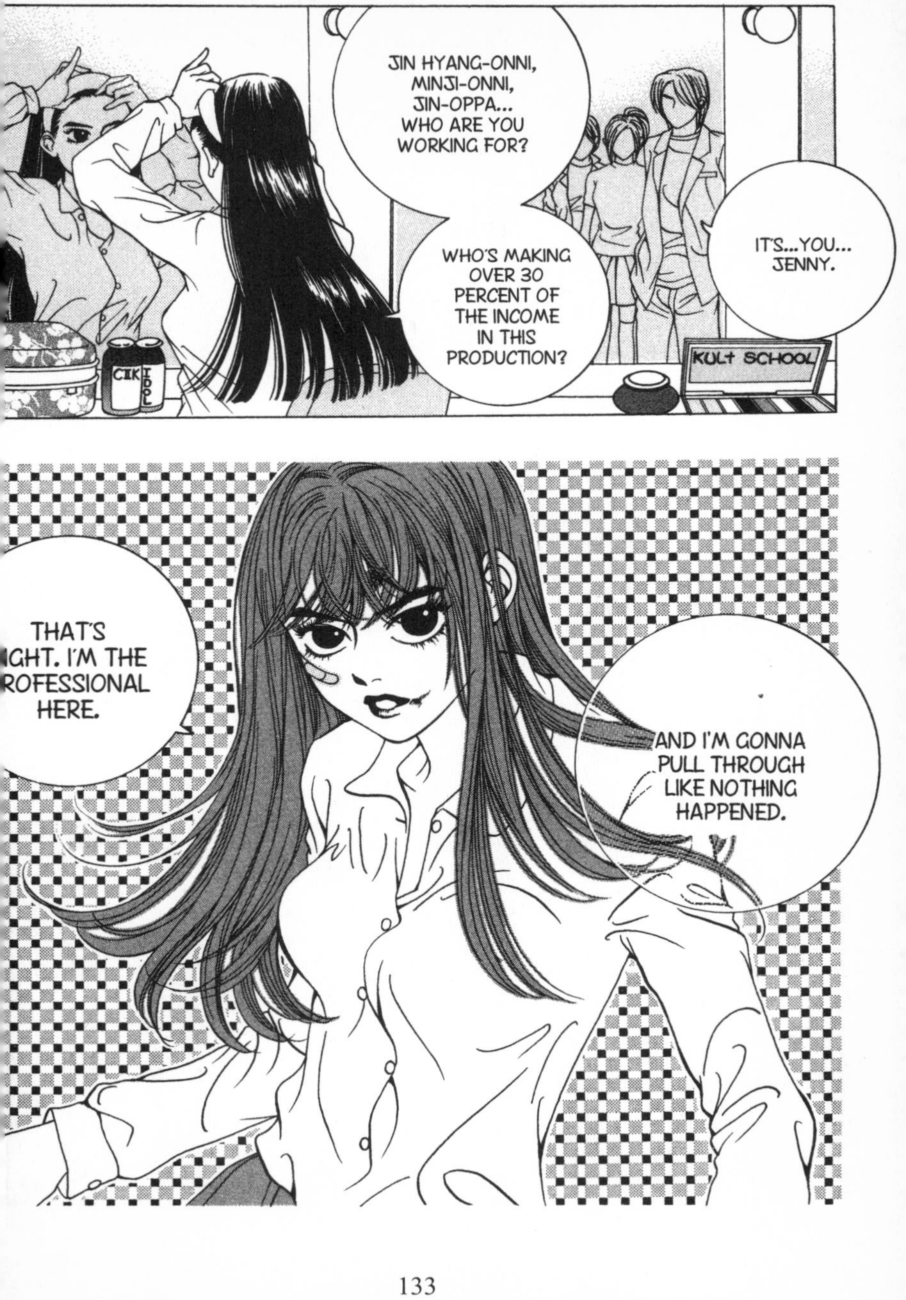
JIN HYANG-ONNI, MINJI-ONNI, JIN-OPPA... WHO ARE YOU WORKING FOR?
WHO'S MAKING OVER 30 PERCENT OF THE INCOME IN THIS PRODUCTION?
IT'S...YOU... JENNY.
THAT'S GHT. I'M THE ROFESSIONAL HERE.
AND I'M GONNA PULL THROUGH LIKE NOTHING HAPPENED.

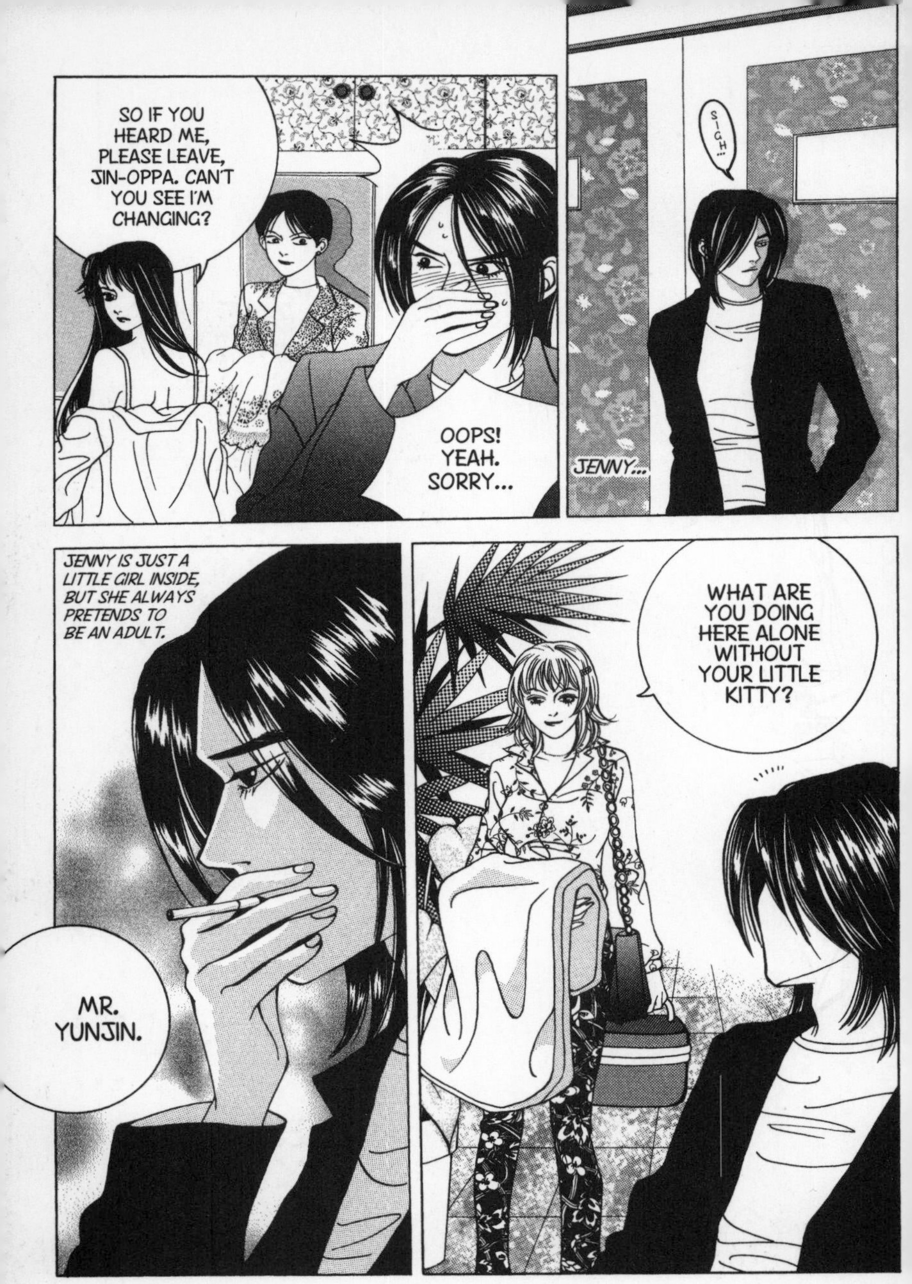
SO IF YOU HEARD ME, PLEASE LEAVE, JIN-OPPA. CAN'T YOU SEE I'M CHANGING?
OOPS! YEAH. SORRY...
SIGH...
JENNY...
JENNY IS JUST A LITTLE GIRL INSIDE, BUT SHE ALWAYS PRETENDS TO BE AN ADULT.
MR. YUNJIN.
WHAT ARE YOU DOING HERE ALONE WITHOUT YOUR LITTLE KITTY?

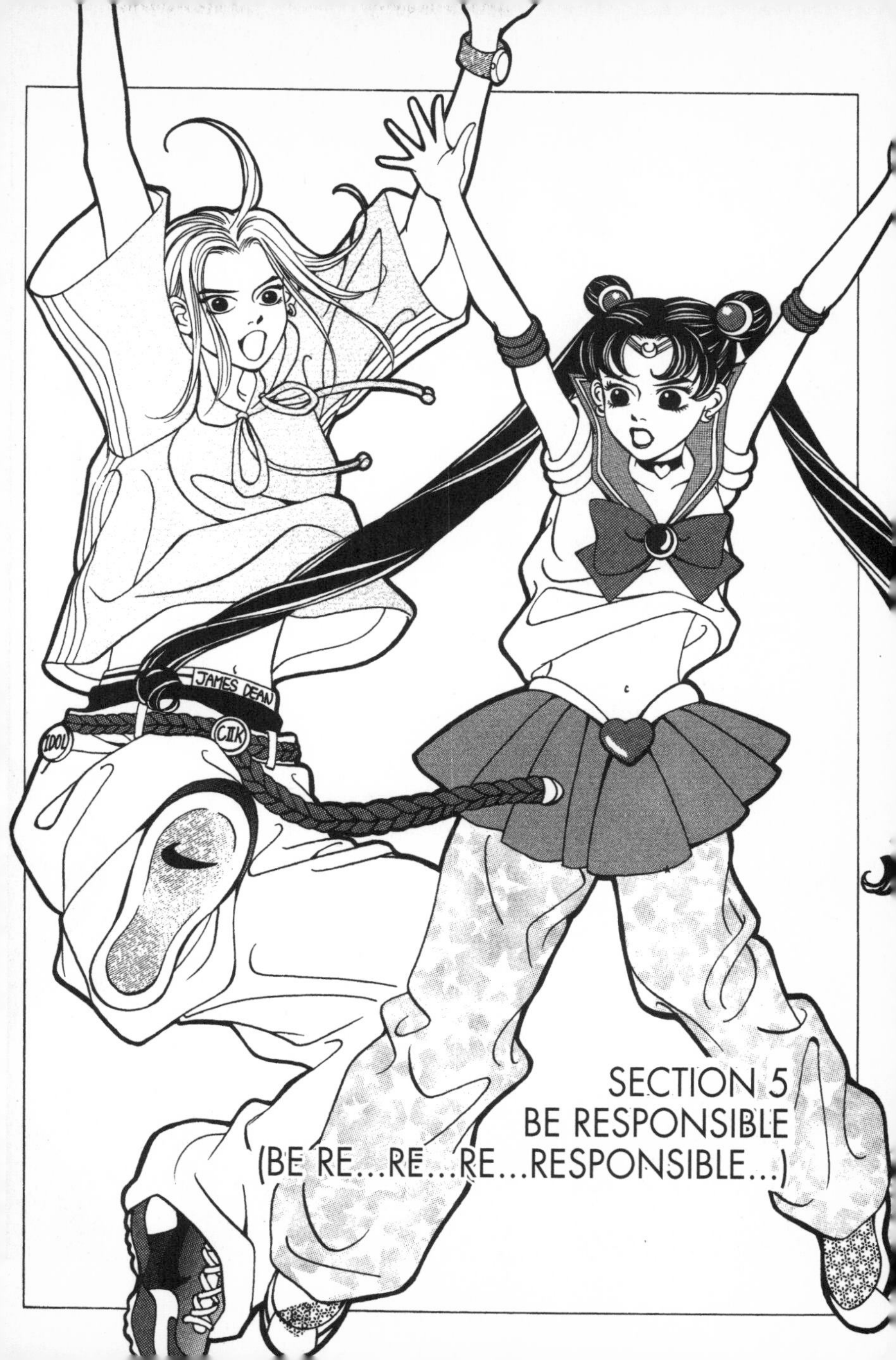
JAMES DEAN
IDOL

SECTION 5
BE RESPONSIBLE
(BE RE...RE...RE...RESPONSIBLE...)

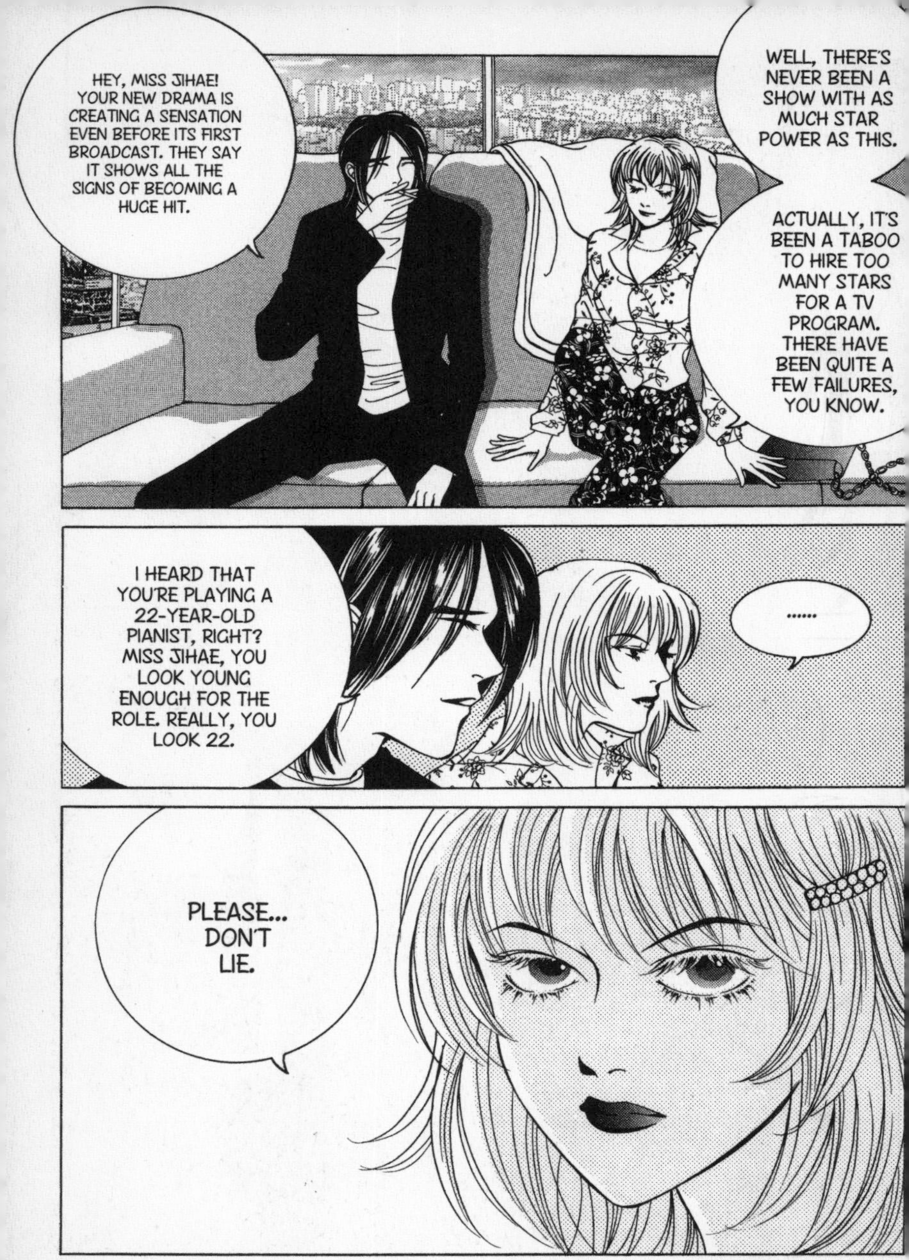
HEY, MISS JIHAE! YOUR NEW DRAMA IS CREATING A SENSATION EVEN BEFORE ITS FIRST BROADCAST. THEY SAY IT SHOWS ALL THE SIGNS OF BECOMING A HUGE HIT.
WELL, THERE'S NEVER BEEN A SHOW WITH AS MUCH STAR POWER AS THIS.
ACTUALLY, IT'S BEEN A TABOO TO HIRE TOO MANY STARS FOR A TV PROGRAM. THERE HAVE BEEN QUITE A FEW FAILURES, YOU KNOW.
I HEARD THAT YOU'RE PLAYING A 22-YEAR-OLD PIANIST, RIGHT? MISS JIHAE, YOU LOOK YOUNG ENOUGH FOR THE ROLE. REALLY, YOU LOOK 22.
......
PLEASE... DON'T LIE.

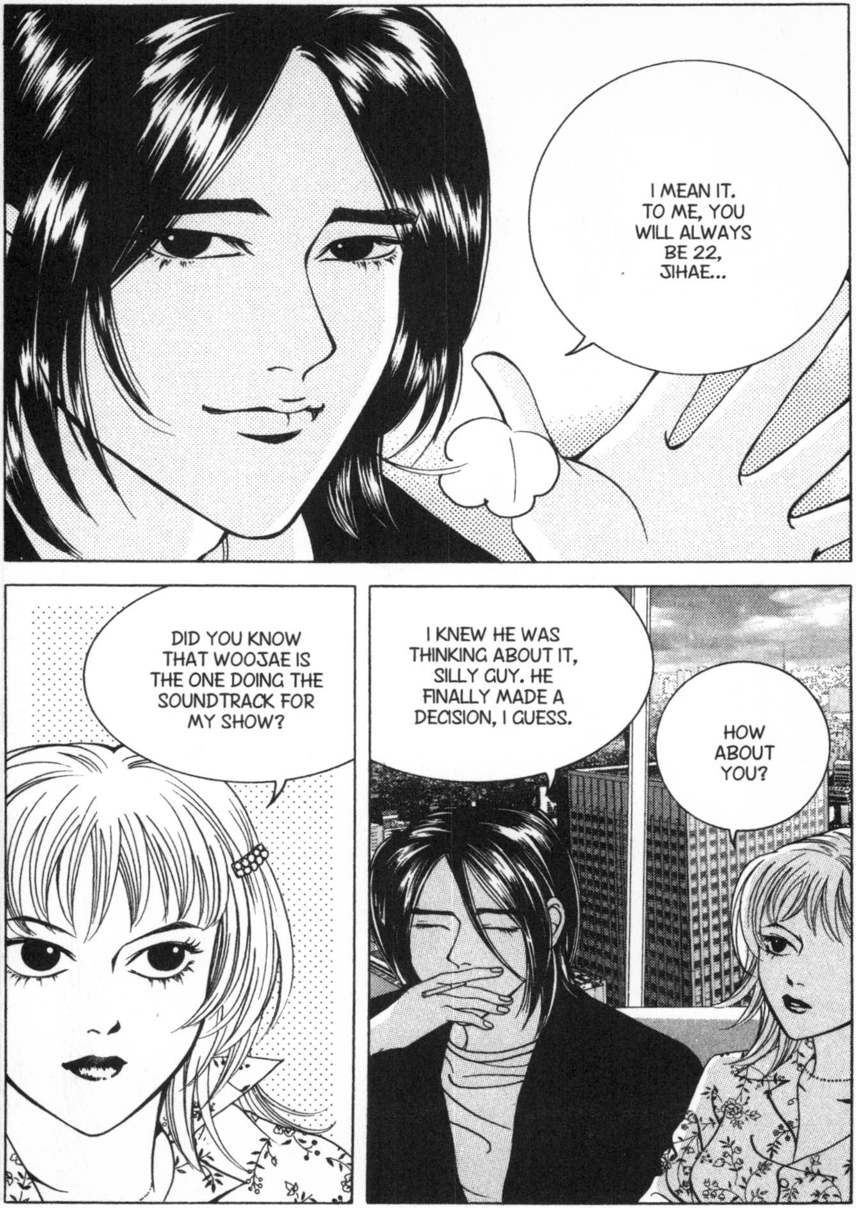
I MEAN IT. TO ME, YOU WILL ALWAYS BE 22, JIHAE...
DID YOU KNOW THAT WOOJAE IS THE ONE DOING THE SOUNDTRACK FOR MY SHOW?
I KNEW HE WAS THINKING ABOUT IT, SILLY GUY. HE FINALLY MADE A DECISION, I GUESS.
HOW ABOUT YOU?

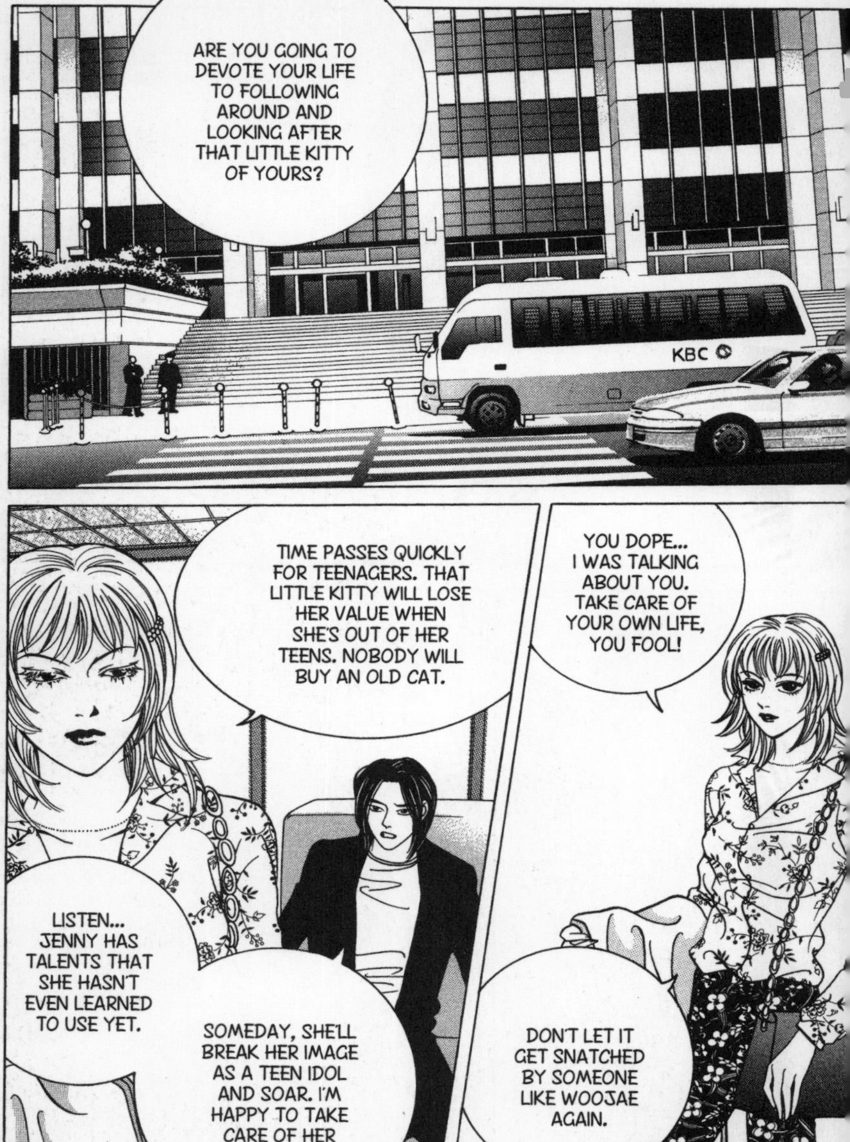
ARE YOU GOING TO DEVOTE YOUR LIFE TO FOLLOWING AROUND AND LOOKING AFTER THAT LITTLE KITTY OF YOURS?
KBC
TIME PASSES QUICKLY FOR TEENAGERS. THAT LITTLE KITTY WILL LOSE HER VALUE WHEN SHE'S OUT OF HER TEENS. NOBODY WILL BUY AN OLD CAT.
LISTEN... JENNY HAS TALENTS THAT SHE HASN'T EVEN LEARNED TO USE YET.
SOMEDAY, SHE'LL BREAK HER IMAGE AS A TEEN IDOL AND SOAR. I'M HAPPY TO TAKE CARE OF HER UNTIL THEN.
YOU DOPE... I WAS TALKING ABOUT YOU. TAKE CARE OF YOUR OWN LIFE, YOU FOOL!
DON'T LET IT GET SNATCHED BY SOMEONE LIKE WOOJAE AGAIN.

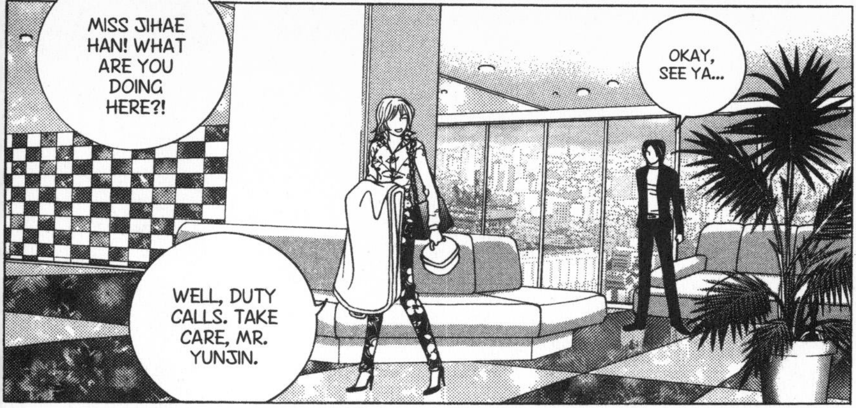
MISS JIHAE HAN! WHAT ARE YOU DOING HERE?!
OKAY, SEE YA...
WELL, DUTY CALLS. TAKE CARE, MR. YUNJIN.

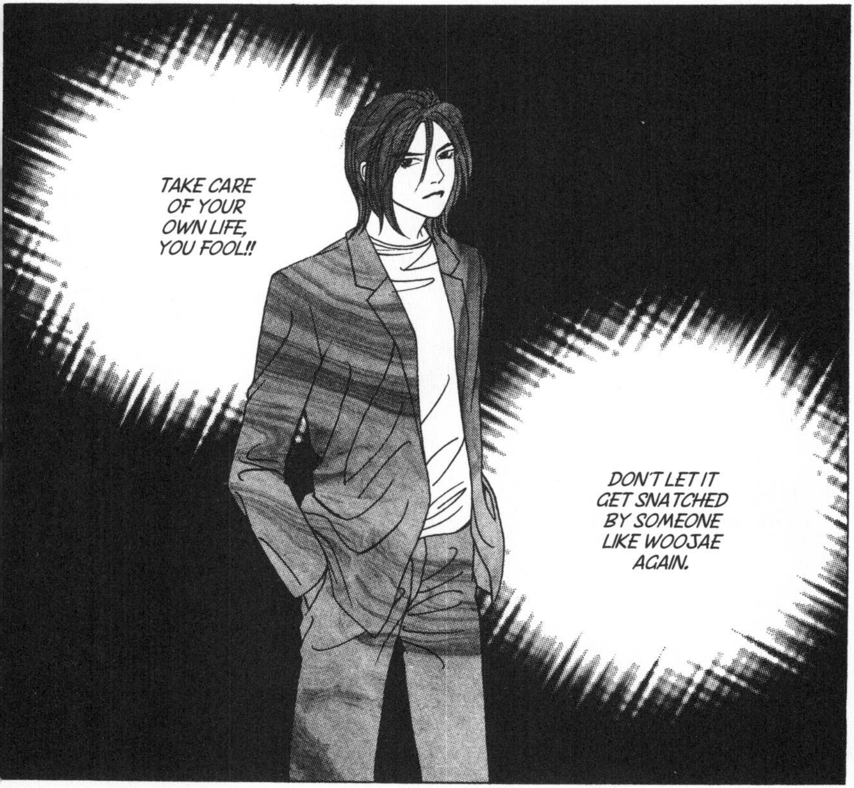
TAKE CARE OF YOUR OWN LIFE, YOU FOOL!!
DON'T LET IT GET SNATCHED BY SOMEONE LIKE WOOJAE AGAIN.

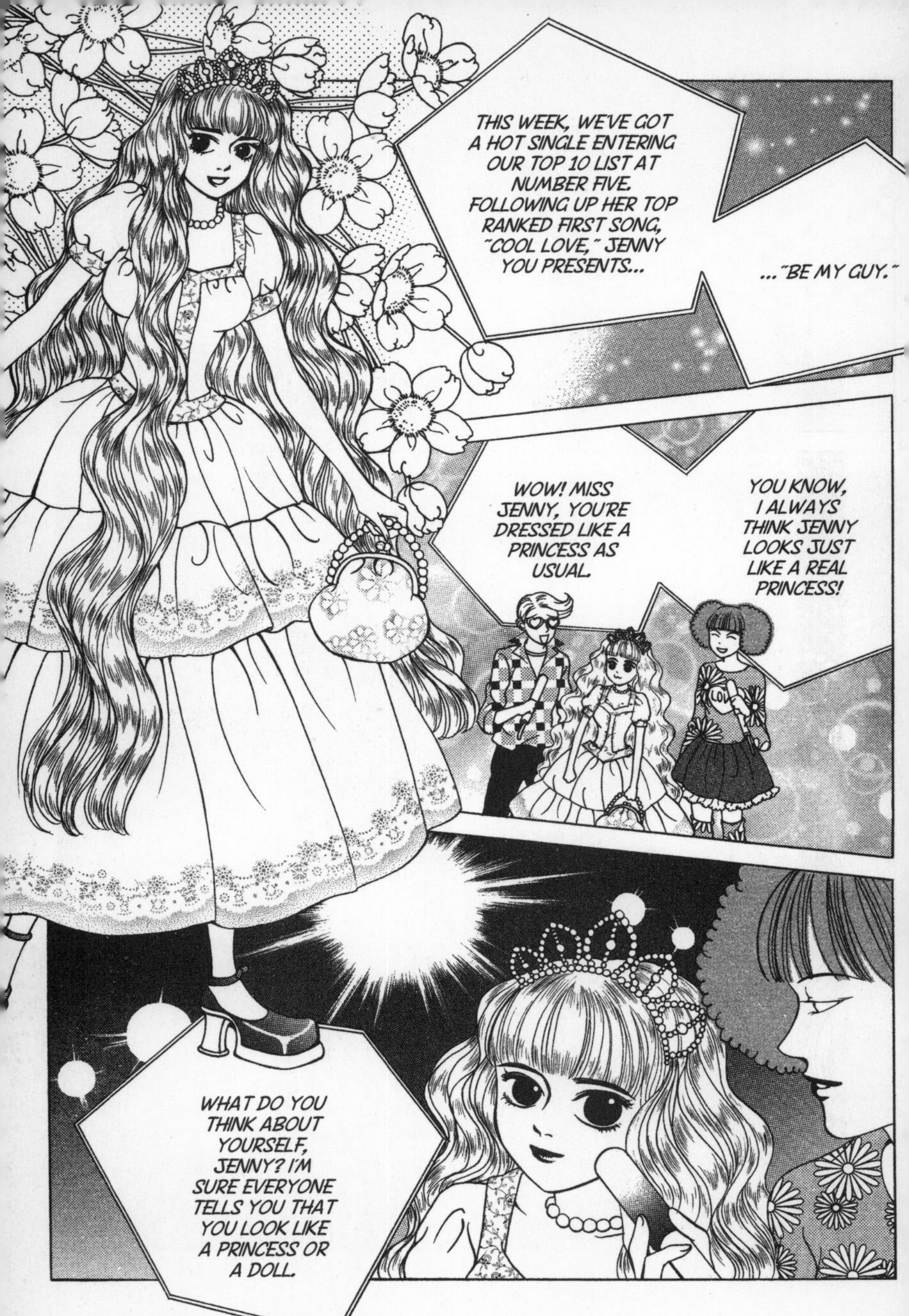
THIS WEEK, WE'VE GOT A HOT SINGLE ENTERING OUR TOP 10 LIST AT NUMBER FIVE. FOLLOWING UP HER TOP RANKED FIRST SONG, "COOL LOVE," JENNY YOU PRESENTS...
..."BE MY GUY."
WOW! MISS JENNY, YOU'RE DRESSED LIKE A PRINCESS AS USUAL.
YOU KNOW, I ALWAYS THINK JENNY LOOKS JUST LIKE A REAL PRINCESS!
WHAT DO YOU THINK ABOUT YOURSELF, JENNY? I'M SURE EVERYONE TELLS YOU THAT YOU LOOK LIKE A PRINCESS OR A DOLL.

WELL, IF I THOUGHT OF MYSELF LIKE THAT, YOU MIGHT SAY I HAVE PRINCESS SYNDROME.

NOW, I DON'T THINK I HAVE PRINCESS SYNDROME, ALTHOUGH...

...I CONSIDER MY FACE A PRODUCT. I THINK IT'S UNFORGIVABLE FOR ANYONE TO DAMAGE THIS PRODUCT.

JENNY YOU, YOU HAVE NO RIGHT TO SAY THINGS LIKE THAT TO US.

YOU'RE RIGHT...

WE HAD TO GO THROUGH A LOT TO KICK HER BUTT...

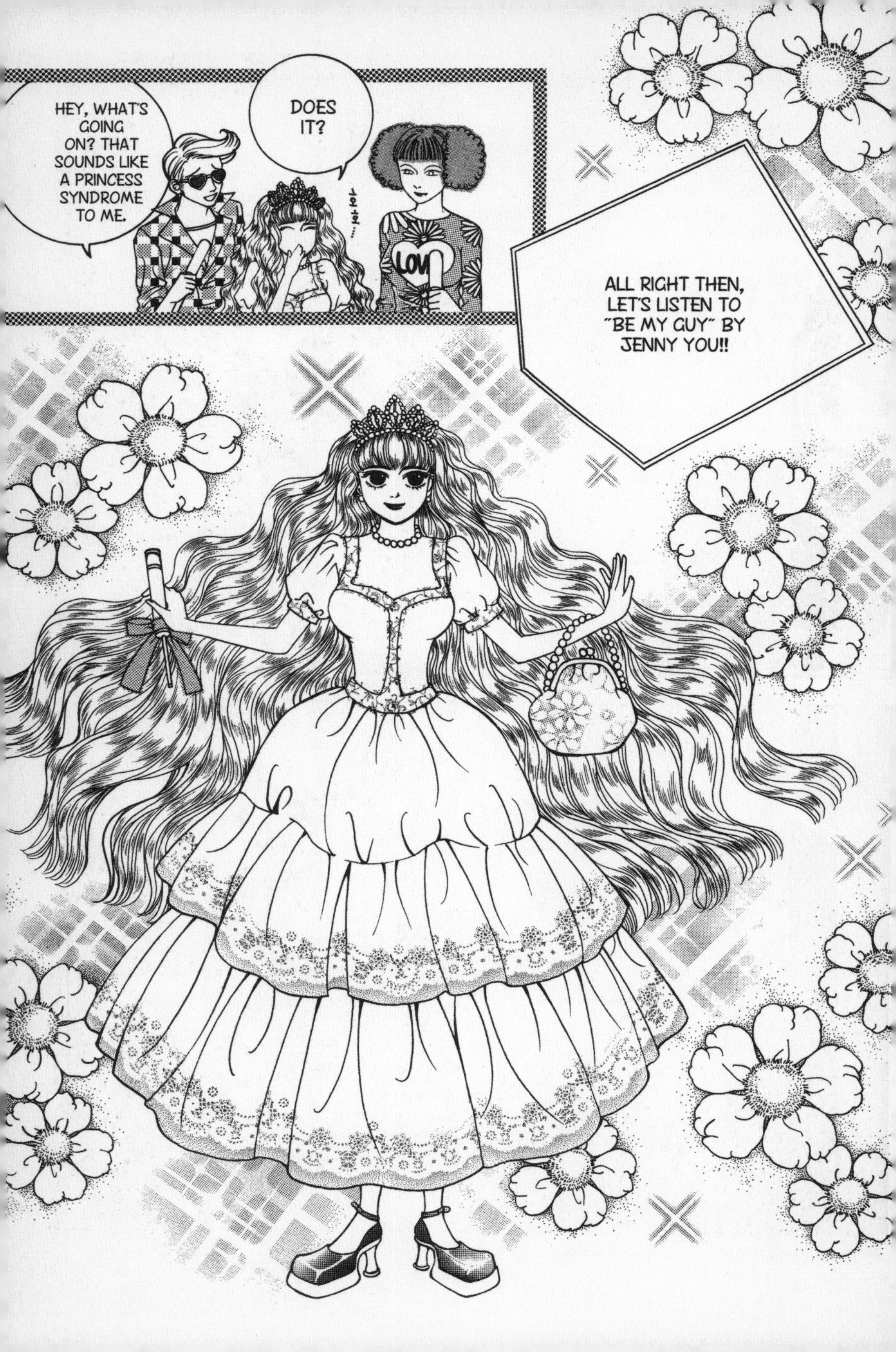
HEY, WHAT'S GOING ON? THAT SOUNDS LIKE A PRINCESS SYNDROME TO ME.
DOES IT?
LOV
ALL RIGHT THEN, LET'S LISTEN TO "BE MY GUY" BY JENNY YOU!!

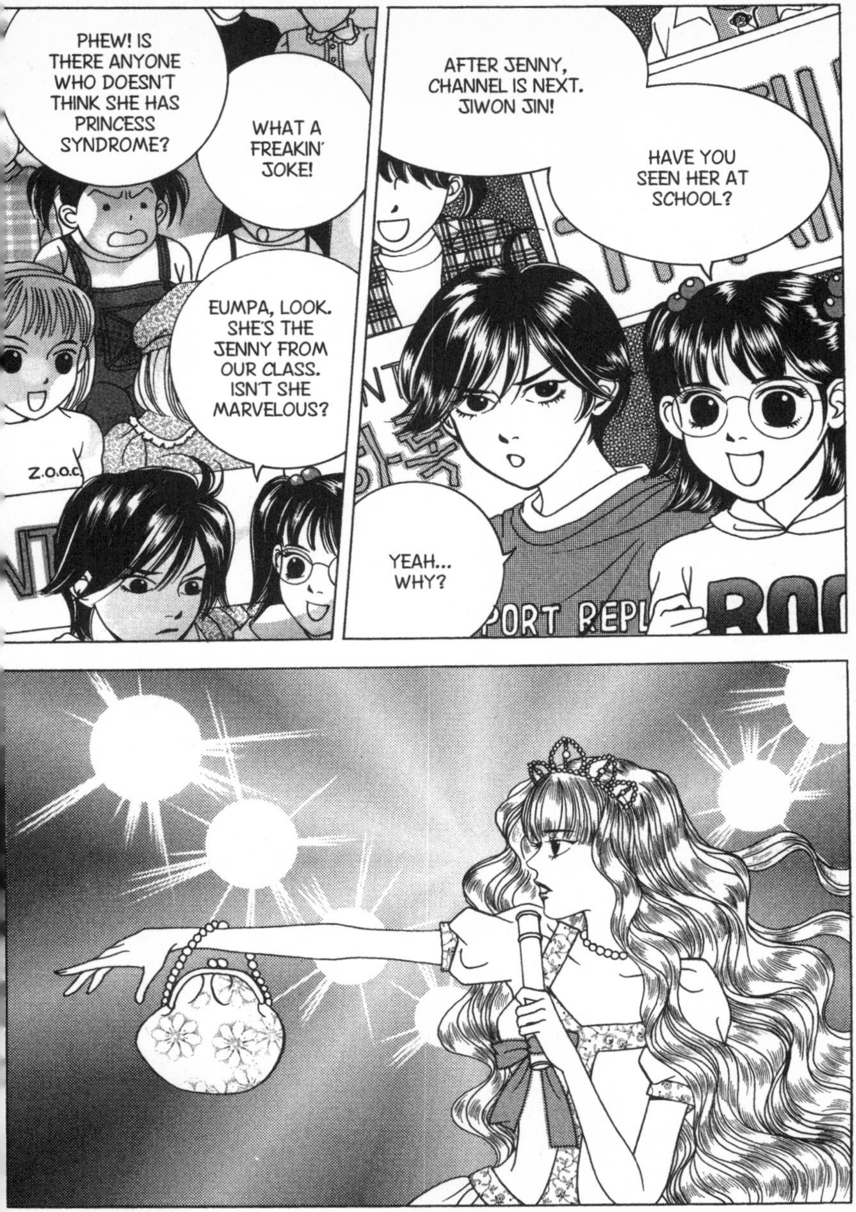
PHEW! IS THERE ANYONE WHO DOESN'T THINK SHE HAS PRINCESS SYNDROME?
WHAT A FREAKIN' JOKE!
Z.O.O.C
EUMPA, LOOK. SHE'S THE JENNY FROM OUR CLASS. ISN'T SHE MARVELOUS?
AFTER JENNY, CHANNEL IS NEXT. JIWON JIN!
HAVE YOU SEEN HER AT SCHOOL?
YEAH... WHY?
PORT REPL

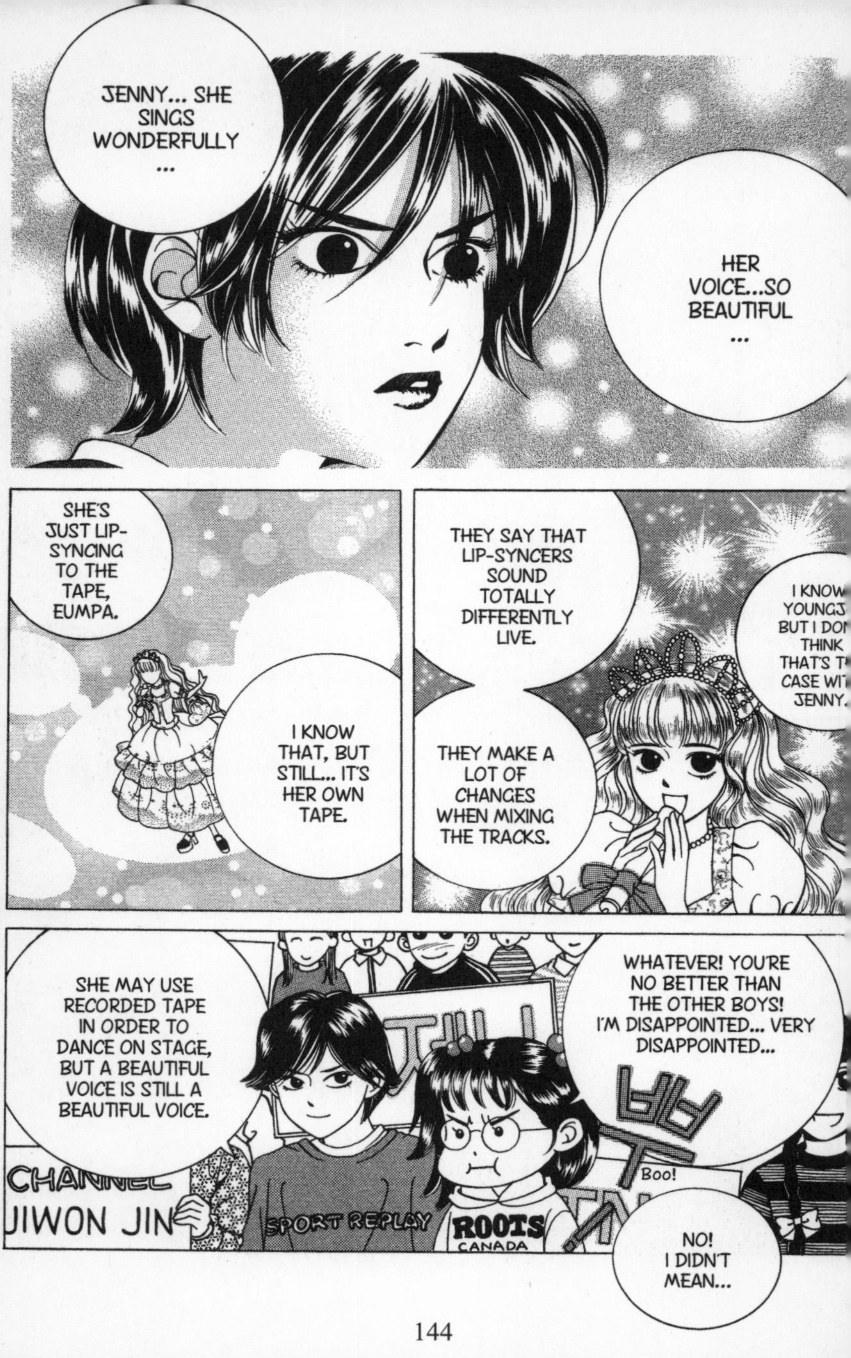

JENNY... SHE SINGS WONDERFULLY ...
HER VOICE...SO BEAUTIFUL ...
SHE'S JUST LIP-SYNCING TO THE TAPE, EUMPA.
I KNOW THAT, BUT STILL... IT'S HER OWN TAPE.
THEY SAY THAT LIP-SYNCERS SOUND TOTALLY DIFFERENTLY LIVE.
THEY MAKE A LOT OF CHANGES WHEN MIXING THE TRACKS.
I KNOW YOUNGJ BUT I DON THINK THAT'S T CASE WIT JENNY.
SHE MAY USE RECORDED TAPE IN ORDER TO DANCE ON STAGE, BUT A BEAUTIFUL VOICE IS STILL A BEAUTIFUL VOICE.
CHANNEL
JIWON JIN
SPORT REPLAY
ROOTS
CANADA
WHATEVER! YOU'RE NO BETTER THAN THE OTHER BOYS! I'M DISAPPOINTED... VERY DISAPPOINTED...
Boo!
NO! I DIDN'T MEAN...

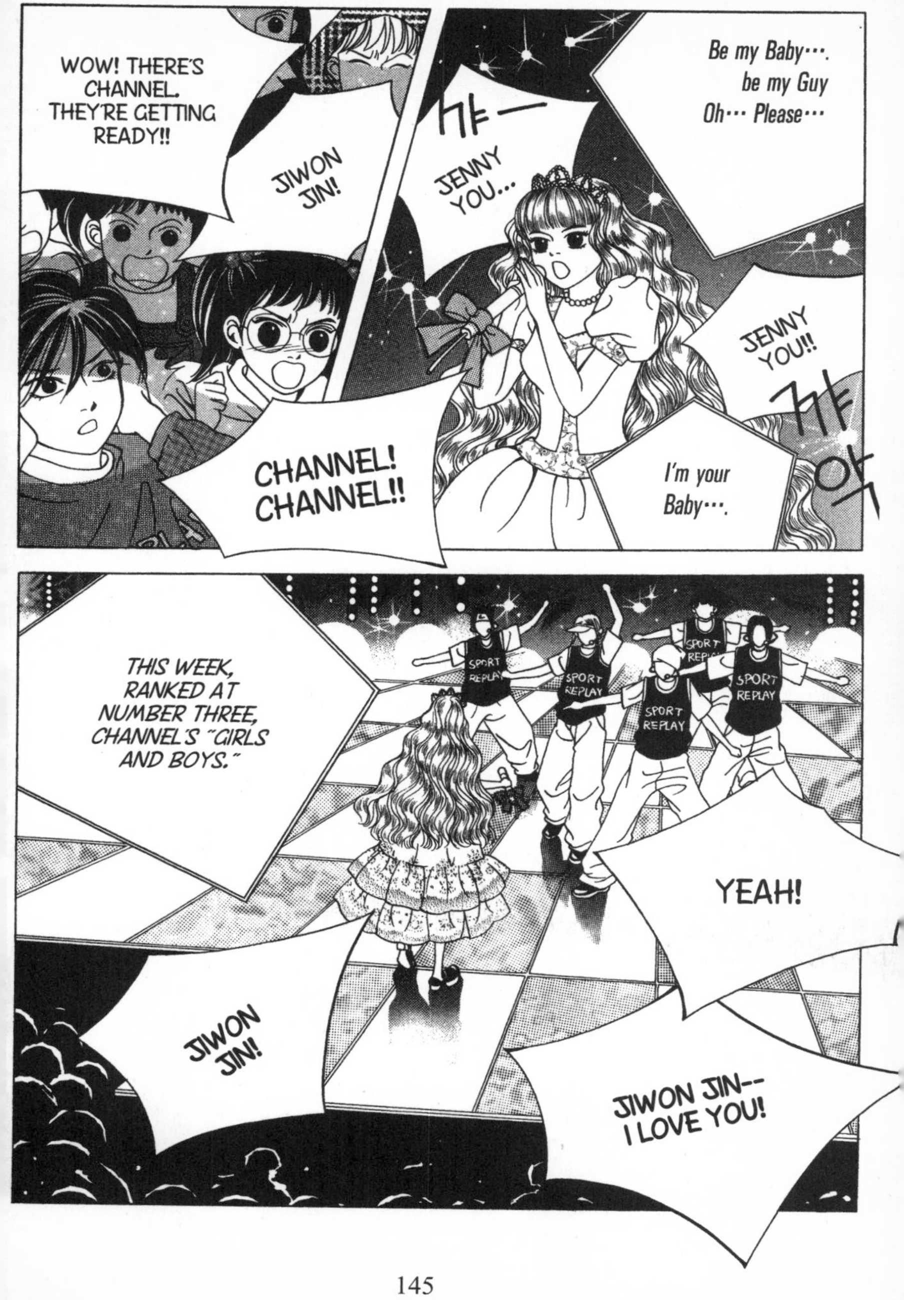
WOW! THERE'S CHANNEL. THEY'RE GETTING READY!!
JIWON JIN!
CHANNEL! CHANNEL!!
JENNY YOU...
Be my Baby…. be my Guy Oh… Please…
JENNY YOU!!
I'm your Baby….
THIS WEEK, RANKED AT NUMBER THREE, CHANNEL'S "GIRLS AND BOYS."
SPORT REPLAY
YEAH!
JIWON JIN!
JIWON JIN-- I LOVE YOU!

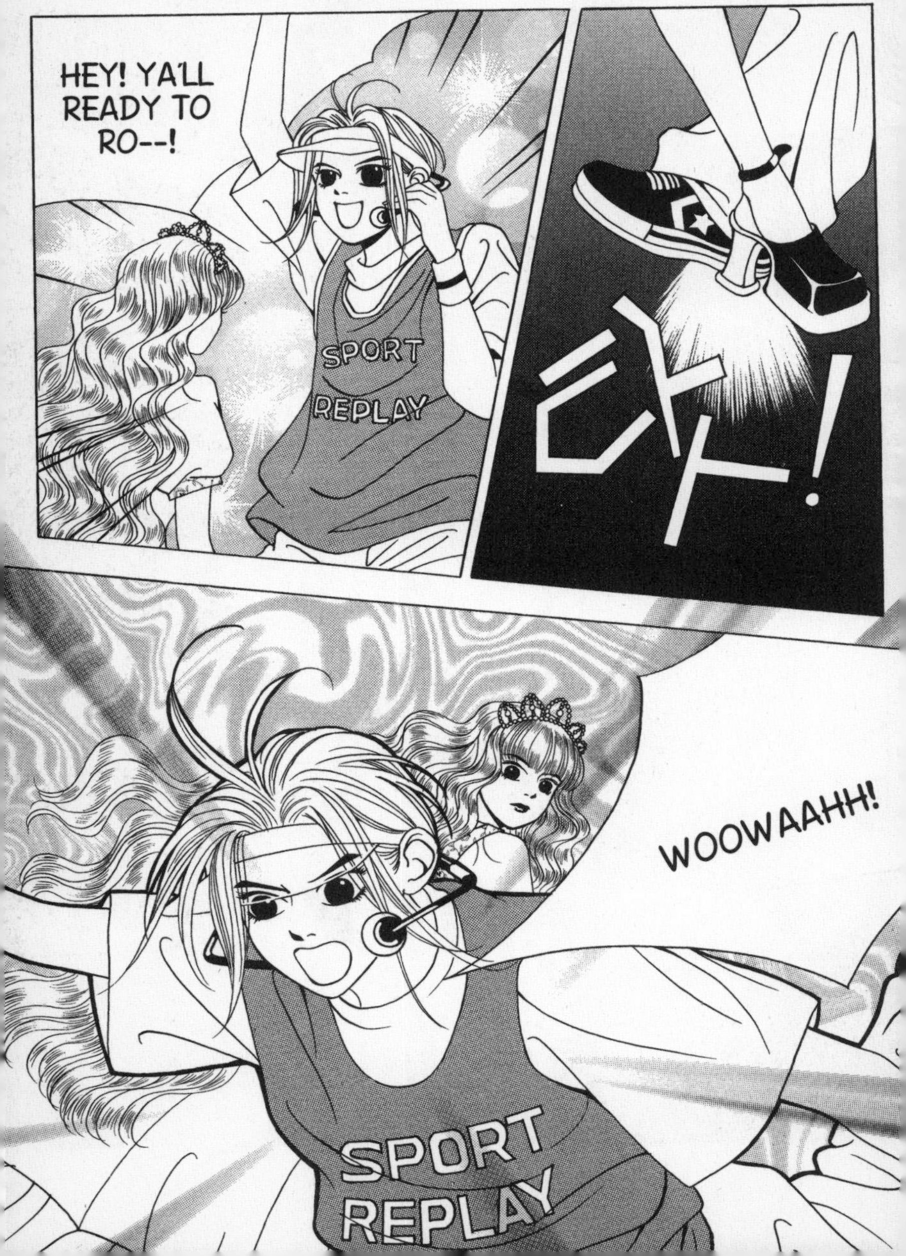
HEY! YA'LL READY TO RO--!
SPORT REPLAY
SPORT REPLAY
WOOWAAHH!

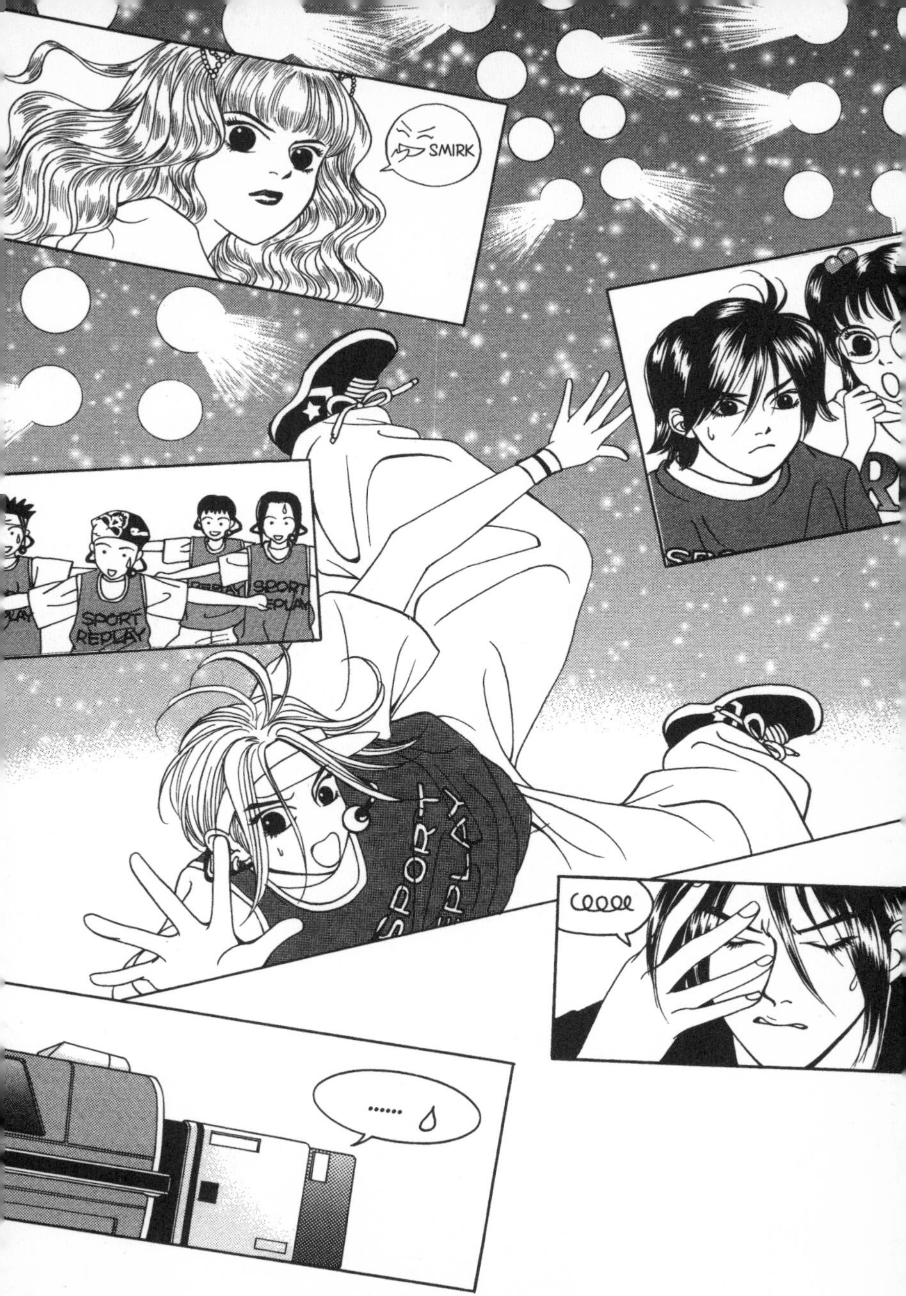
SMIRK
ceeee
......

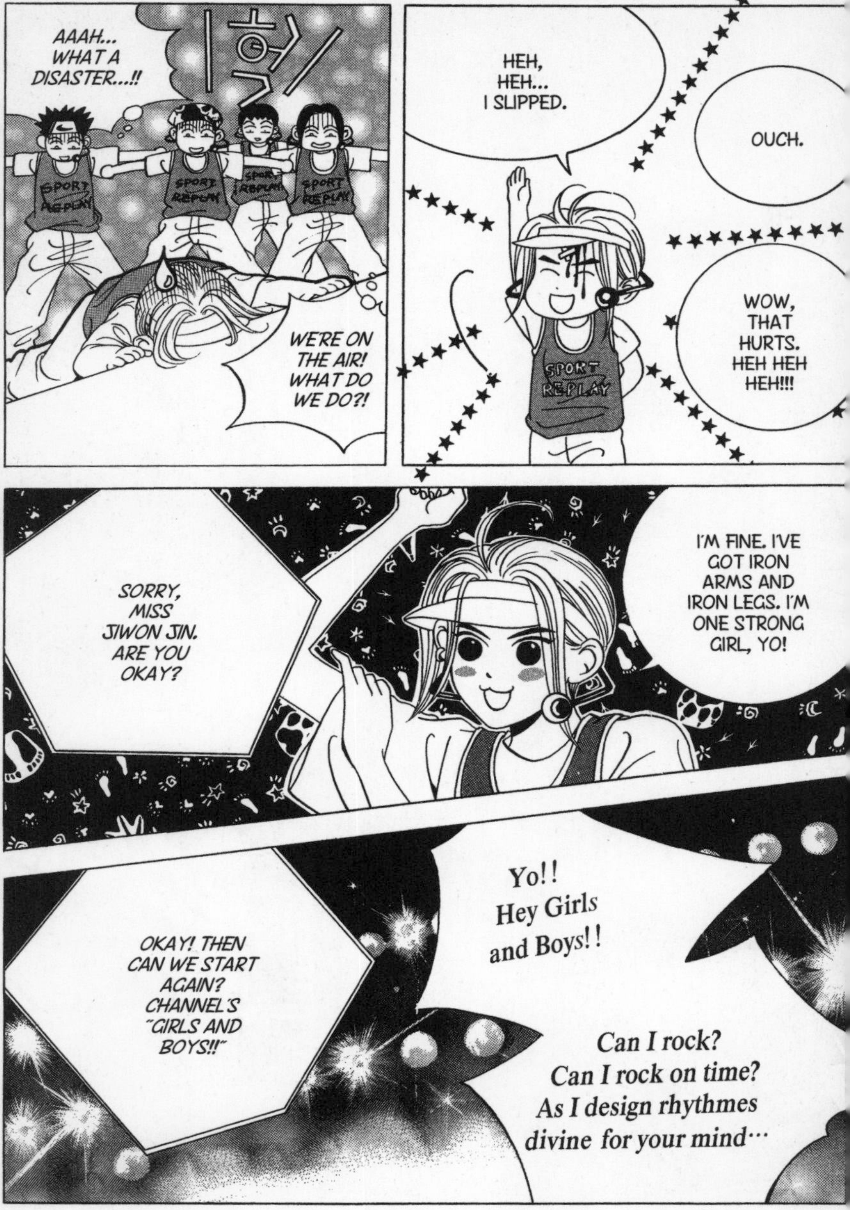
AAAH... WHAT A DISASTER...!!
WE'RE ON THE AIR! WHAT DO WE DO?!
HEH, HEH... I SLIPPED.
OUCH.
WOW, THAT HURTS. HEH HEH HEH!!!
SORRY, MISS JIWON JIN. ARE YOU OKAY?
I'M FINE. I'VE GOT IRON ARMS AND IRON LEGS. I'M ONE STRONG GIRL, YO!
OKAY! THEN CAN WE START AGAIN? CHANNEL'S "GIRLS AND BOYS!!"
Yo!! Hey Girls and Boys!!
Can I rock? Can I rock on time? As I design rhythmes divine for your mind…

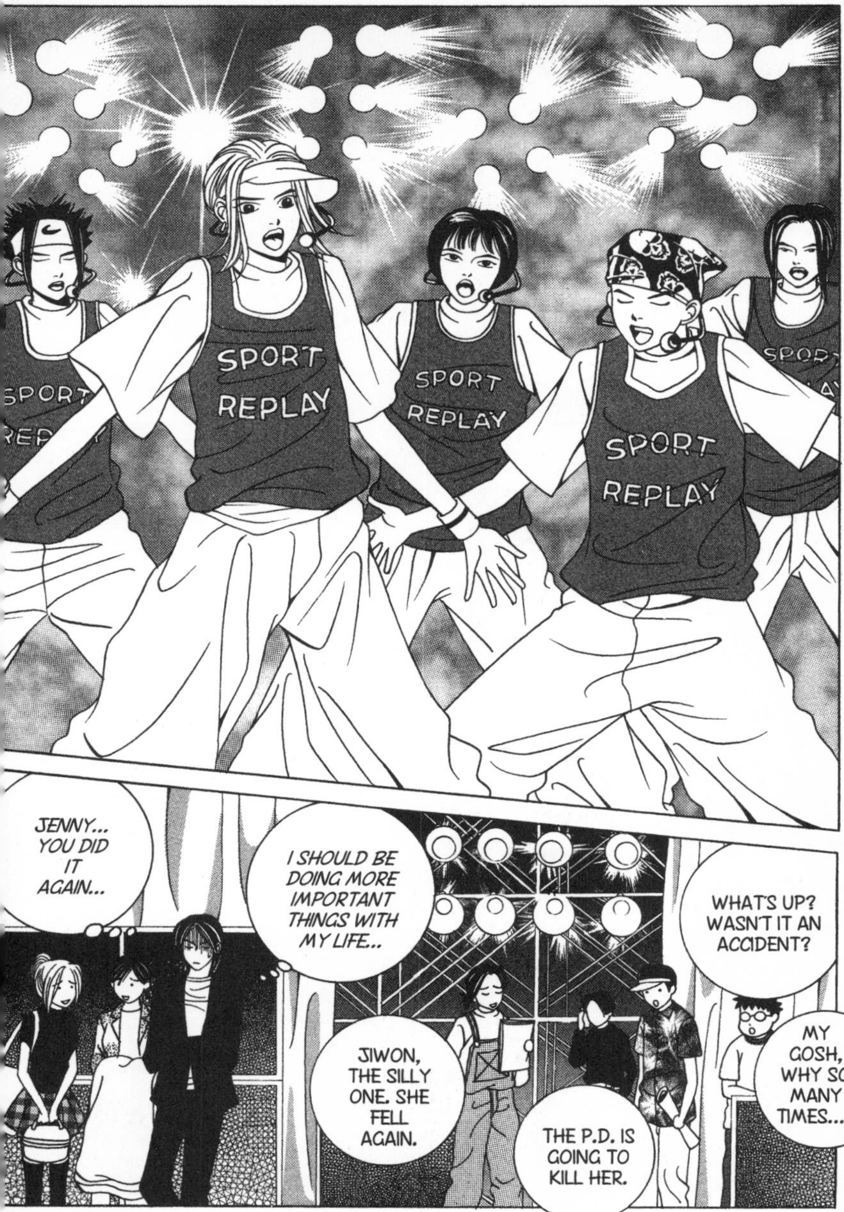
SPORT REPLAY
SPORT REPLAY
SPORT REPLAY
JENNY... YOU DID IT AGAIN...
I SHOULD BE DOING MORE IMPORTANT THINGS WITH MY LIFE...
WHAT'S UP? WASN'T IT AN ACCIDENT?
JIWON, THE SILLY ONE. SHE FELL AGAIN.
THE P.D. IS GOING TO KILL HER.
MY GOSH, WHY SO MANY TIMES...?

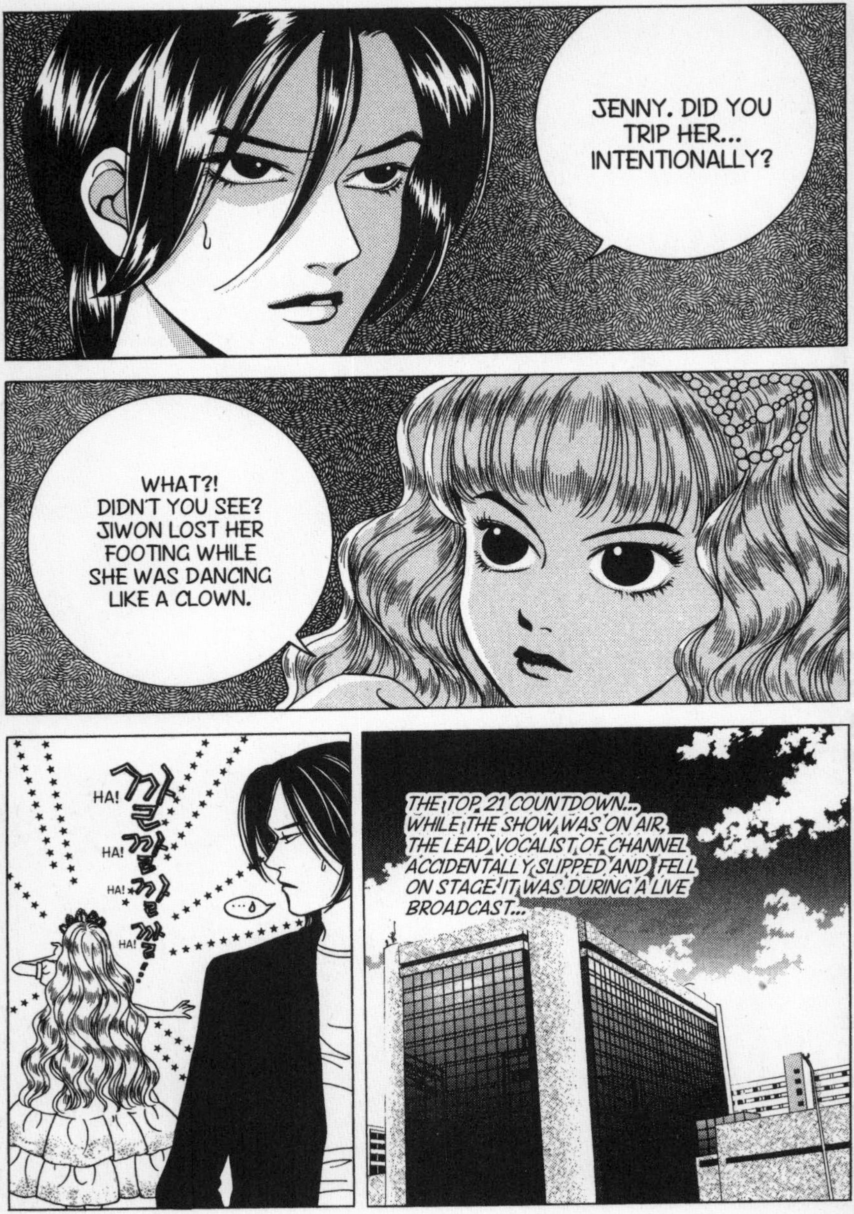
JENNY. DID YOU TRIP HER... INTENTIONALLY?
WHAT?! DIDN'T YOU SEE? JIWON LOST HER FOOTING WHILE SHE WAS DANCING LIKE A CLOWN.
HA!
HA!
HA!
HA!
THE TOP 21 COUNTDOWN... WHILE THE SHOW WAS ON AIR, THE LEAD VOCALIST OF CHANNEL ACCIDENTALLY SLIPPED AND FELL ON STAGE. IT WAS DURING A LIVE BROADCAST...

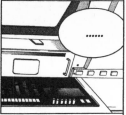

......
......
...BUT MANY PEOPLE IN THE INDUSTRY KNEW...
...IT WAS NO ACCIDENT...
......
......
y Gets a Kick
iwon Jin's Stumble
Have a Nice Trip?"
SPORT
ring a live broadcast of the Top 21 Countdown, won Jin (17), lead vocalist and leader of the popular group Channel, fell on the stage. Surprisingly, it was not an innocent stumble as first believed. Many witnesses testified that they clearly saw Jenny You (17), who is known to be on bad terms with Jiwon, deliberately stick her foot out to trip her.
THERE WAS NO WAY THE MEDIA WOULD KEEP THIS QUIET.
Jenny You and Jiwon Jin go to the same school. Several inside sources stated that, "They don't get along."
O.P.P.A
IDOL CLIK
T.N.T
유제니
T.N.T.
NRG.
Jenny You and Jiwon Jin fight like cats and dogs.
Their friend "Miss A."
In school, Jenny You openly shows her hatred toward Jiwon. Jenny would torment

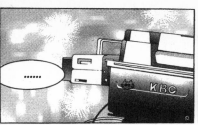

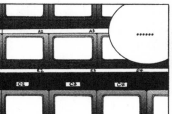

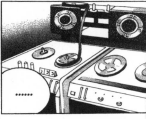

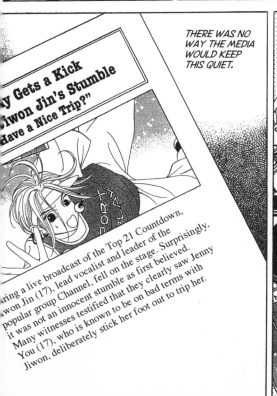

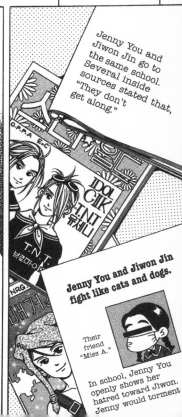

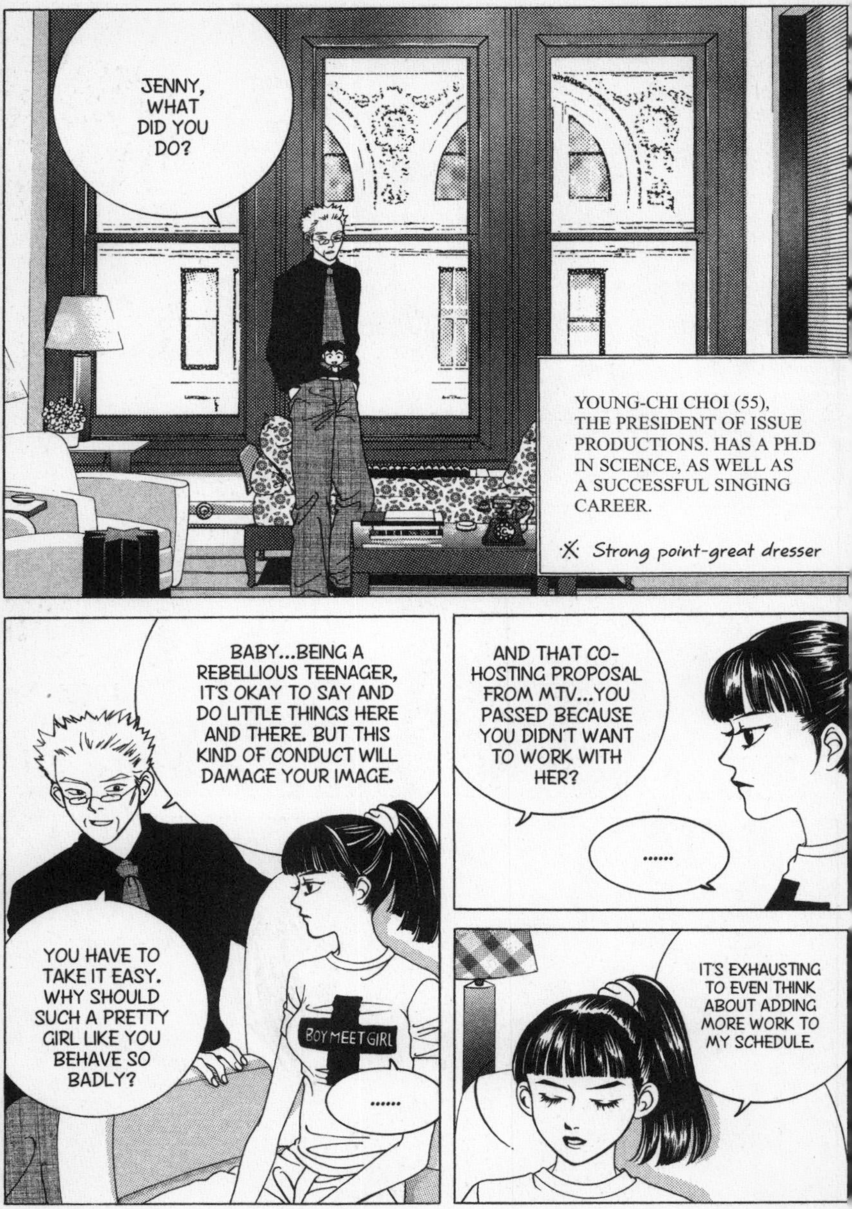
JENNY, WHAT DID YOU DO?
YOUNG-CHI CHOI (55), THE PRESIDENT OF ISSUE PRODUCTIONS. HAS A PH.D IN SCIENCE, AS WELL AS A SUCCESSFUL SINGING CAREER.
※ Strong point-great dresser
BABY...BEING A REBELLIOUS TEENAGER, IT'S OKAY TO SAY AND DO LITTLE THINGS HERE AND THERE. BUT THIS KIND OF CONDUCT WILL DAMAGE YOUR IMAGE.
YOU HAVE TO TAKE IT EASY. WHY SHOULD SUCH A PRETTY GIRL LIKE YOU BEHAVE SO BADLY?
BOY MEET GIRL
......
AND THAT CO-HOSTING PROPOSAL FROM MTV...YOU PASSED BECAUSE YOU DIDN'T WANT TO WORK WITH HER?
......
IT'S EXHAUSTING TO EVEN THINK ABOUT ADDING MORE WORK TO MY SCHEDULE.

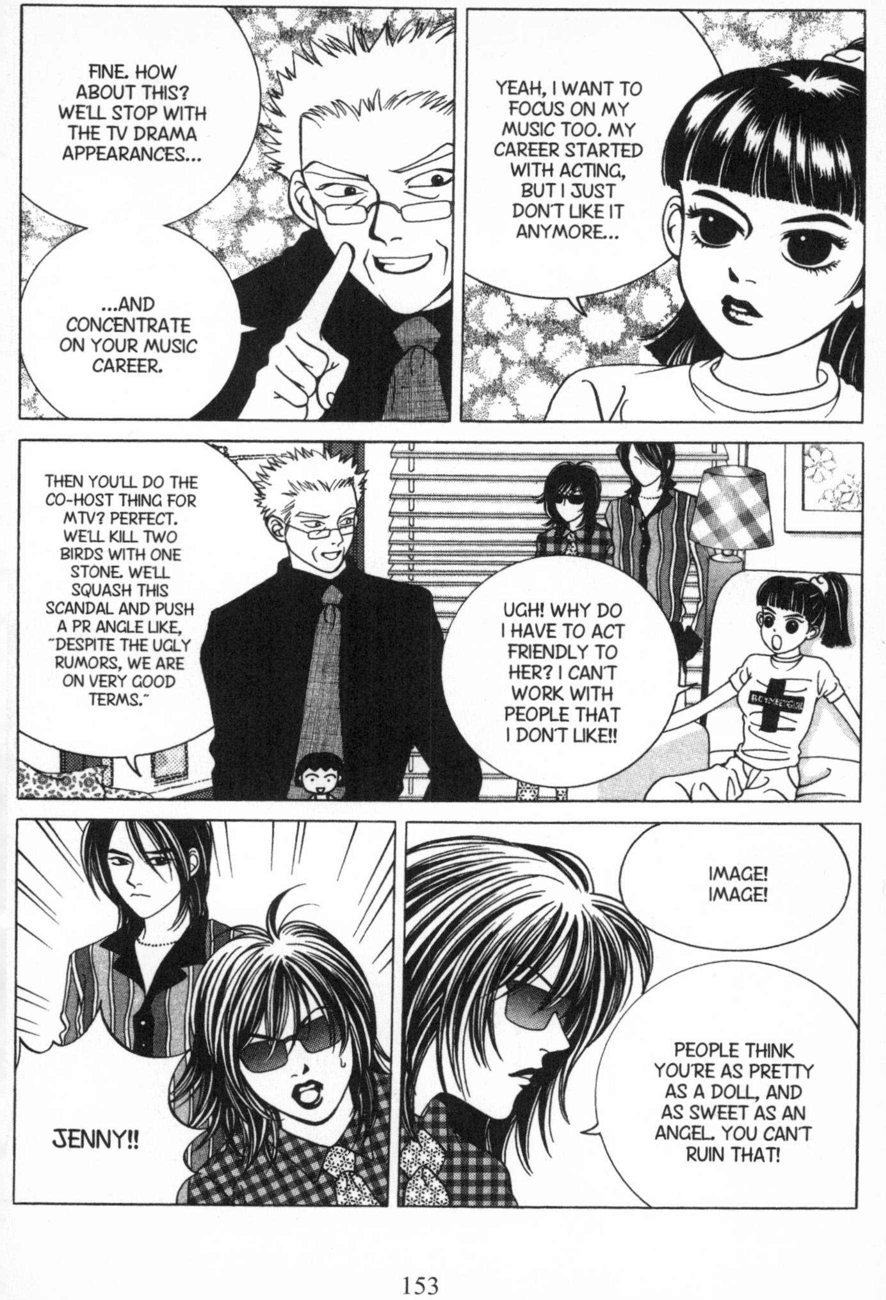
FINE. HOW ABOUT THIS? WE'LL STOP WITH THE TV DRAMA APPEARANCES...
...AND CONCENTRATE ON YOUR MUSIC CAREER.
YEAH, I WANT TO FOCUS ON MY MUSIC TOO. MY CAREER STARTED WITH ACTING, BUT I JUST DON'T LIKE IT ANYMORE...
THEN YOU'LL DO THE CO-HOST THING FOR MTV? PERFECT. WE'LL KILL TWO BIRDS WITH ONE STONE. WE'LL SQUASH THIS SCANDAL AND PUSH A PR ANGLE LIKE, "DESPITE THE UGLY RUMORS, WE ARE ON VERY GOOD TERMS."
UGH! WHY DO I HAVE TO ACT FRIENDLY TO HER? I CAN'T WORK WITH PEOPLE THAT I DON'T LIKE!!
JENNY!!
IMAGE! IMAGE!
PEOPLE THINK YOU'RE AS PRETTY AS A DOLL, AND AS SWEET AS AN ANGEL. YOU CAN'T RUIN THAT!

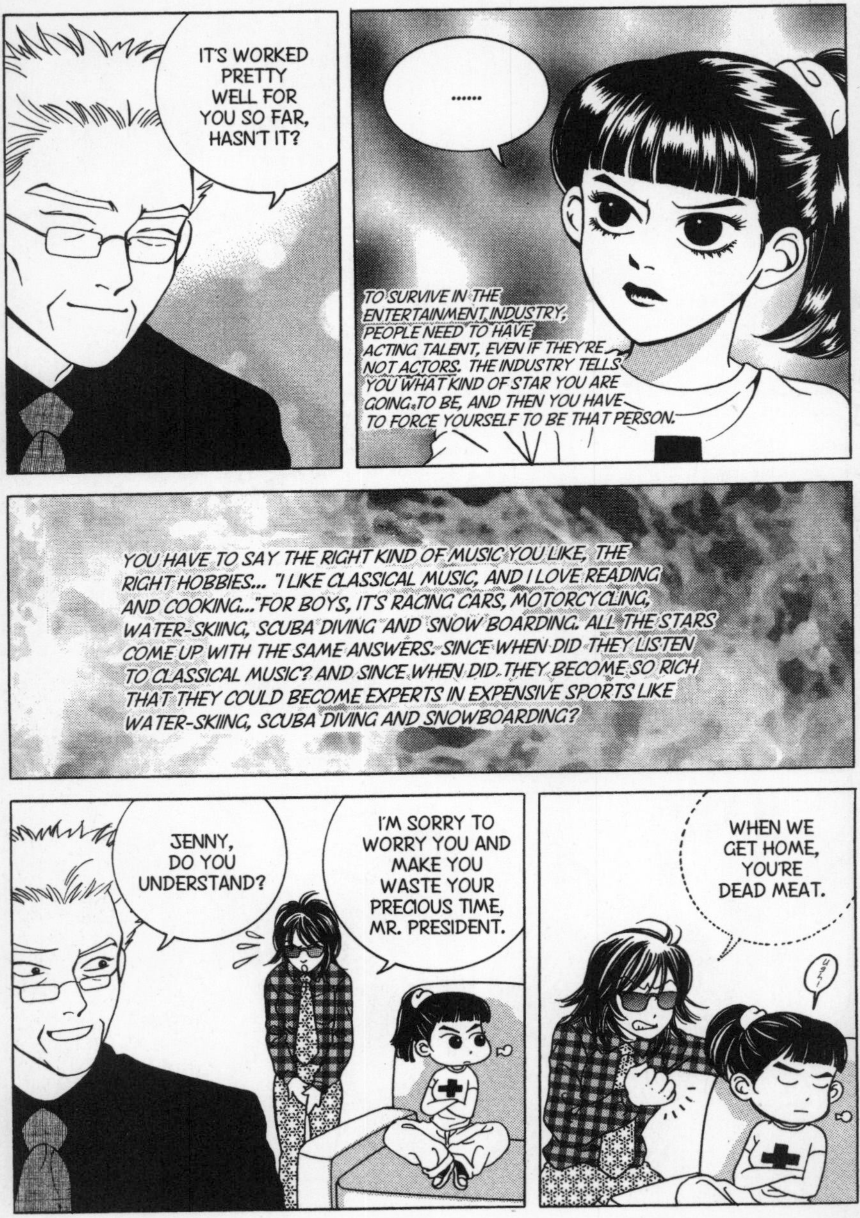
IT'S WORKED PRETTY WELL FOR YOU SO FAR, HASN'T IT?
......
TO SURVIVE IN THE ENTERTAINMENT INDUSTRY, PEOPLE NEED TO HAVE ACTING TALENT, EVEN IF THEY'RE NOT ACTORS. THE INDUSTRY TELLS YOU WHAT KIND OF STAR YOU ARE GOING TO BE, AND THEN YOU HAVE TO FORCE YOURSELF TO BE THAT PERSON.
YOU HAVE TO SAY THE RIGHT KIND OF MUSIC YOU LIKE, THE RIGHT HOBBIES... "I LIKE CLASSICAL MUSIC, AND I LOVE READING AND COOKING..."FOR BOYS, IT'S RACING CARS, MOTORCYCLING, WATER-SKIING, SCUBA DIVING AND SNOW BOARDING. ALL THE STARS COME UP WITH THE SAME ANSWERS. SINCE WHEN DID THEY LISTEN TO CLASSICAL MUSIC? AND SINCE WHEN DID THEY BECOME SO RICH THAT THEY COULD BECOME EXPERTS IN EXPENSIVE SPORTS LIKE WATER-SKIING, SCUBA DIVING AND SNOWBOARDING?
JENNY, DO YOU UNDERSTAND?
I'M SORRY TO WORRY YOU AND MAKE YOU WASTE YOUR PRECIOUS TIME, MR. PRESIDENT.
WHEN WE GET HOME, YOU'RE DEAD MEAT.

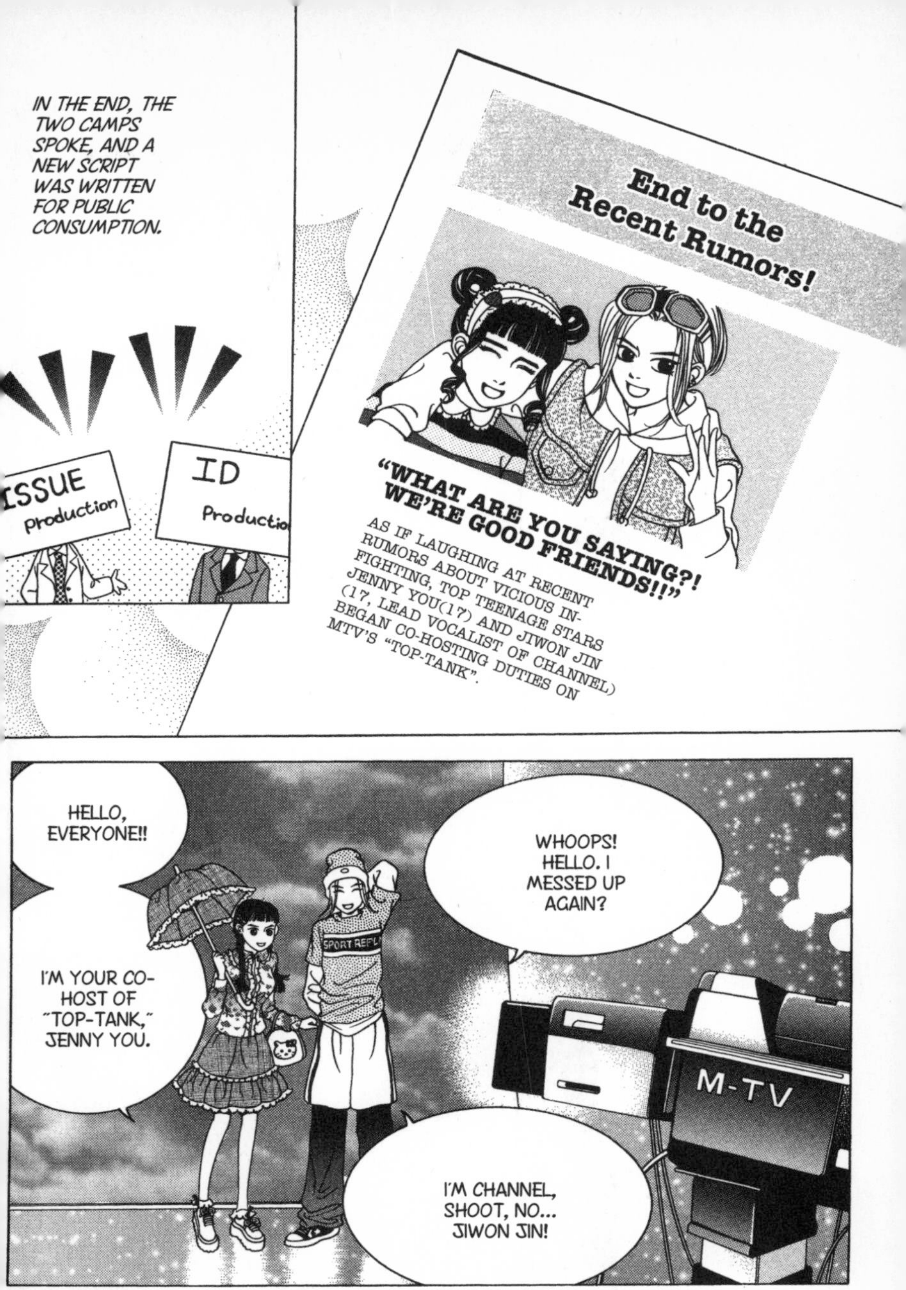
IN THE END, THE TWO CAMPS SPOKE, AND A NEW SCRIPT WAS WRITTEN FOR PUBLIC CONSUMPTION.
ISSUE Production
ID Production
End to the Recent Rumors!
"WHAT ARE YOU SAYING?! WE'RE GOOD FRIENDS!!"
AS IF LAUGHING AT RECENT RUMORS ABOUT VICIOUS IN-FIGHTING, TOP TEENAGE STARS JENNY YOU(17) AND JIWON JIN (17, LEAD VOCALIST OF CHANNEL) BEGAN CO-HOSTING DUTIES ON MTV'S "TOP-TANK".
HELLO, EVERYONE!!
I'M YOUR CO-HOST OF "TOP-TANK," JENNY YOU.
SPORT REPL
WHOOPS! HELLO. I MESSED UP AGAIN?
M-TV
I'M CHANNEL, SHOOT, NO... JIWON JIN!

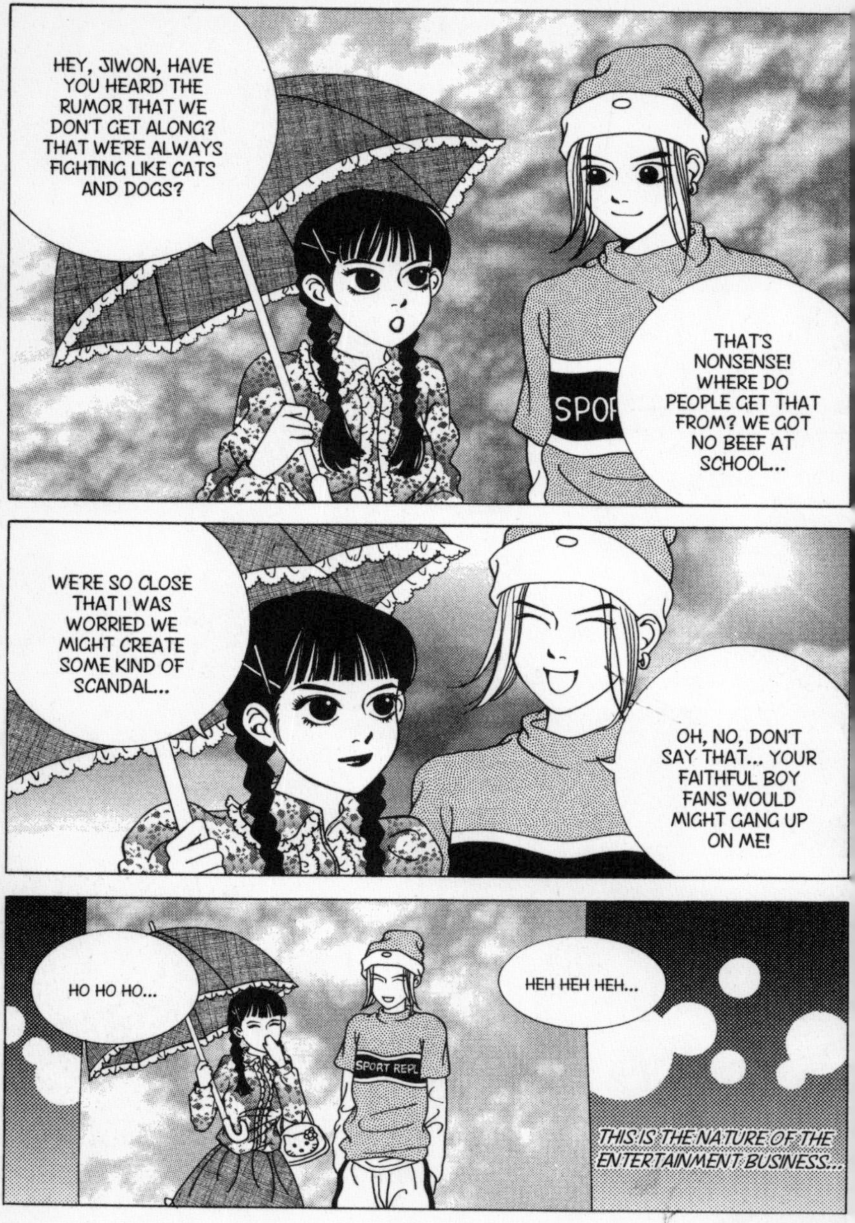
HEY, JIWON, HAVE YOU HEARD THE RUMOR THAT WE DON'T GET ALONG? THAT WE'RE ALWAYS FIGHTING LIKE CATS AND DOGS?
THAT'S NONSENSE! WHERE DO PEOPLE GET THAT FROM? WE GOT NO BEEF AT SCHOOL...
SPOR
WE'RE SO CLOSE THAT I WAS WORRIED WE MIGHT CREATE SOME KIND OF SCANDAL...
OH, NO, DON'T SAY THAT... YOUR FAITHFUL BOY FANS WOULD MIGHT GANG UP ON ME!
HO HO HO...
HEH HEH HEH...
SPORT REPL
THIS IS THE NATURE OF THE ENTERTAINMENT BUSINESS...

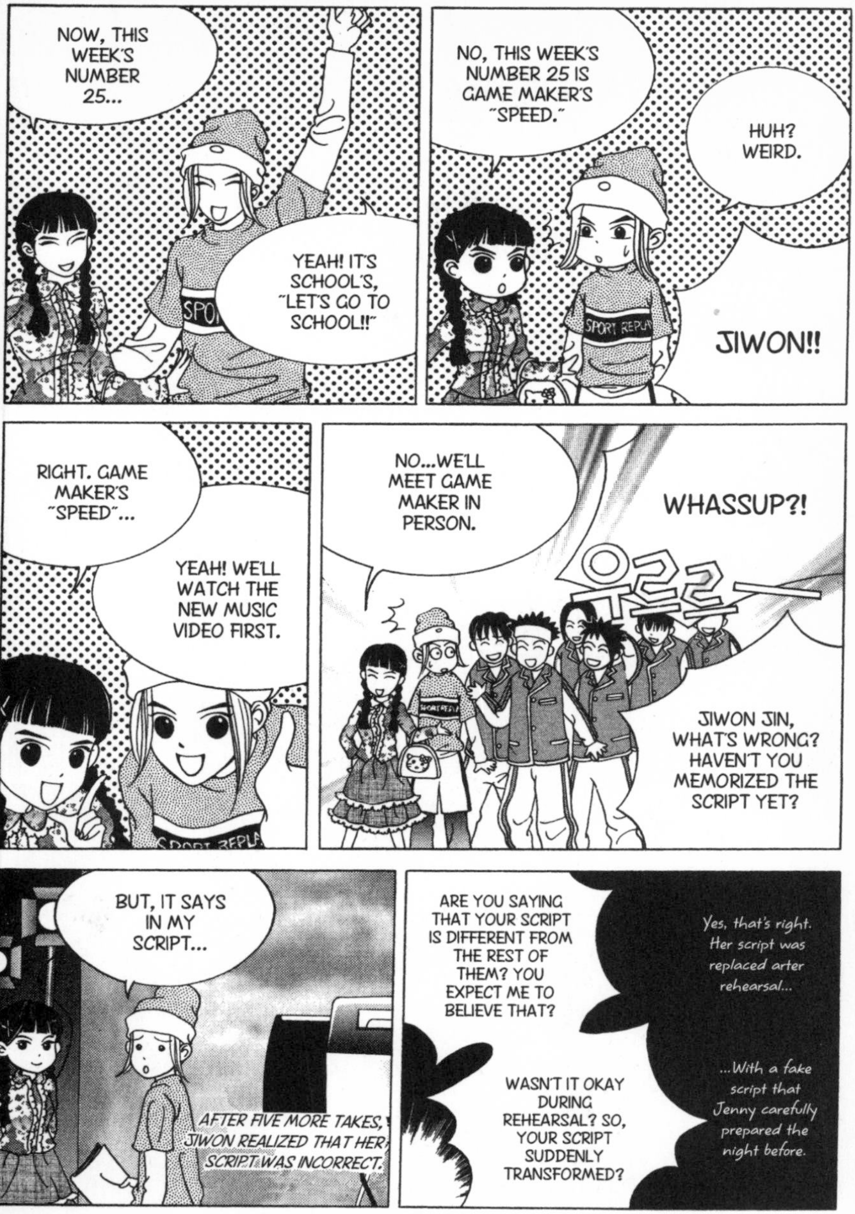
NOW, THIS WEEK'S NUMBER 25...
YEAH! IT'S SCHOOL'S, "LET'S GO TO SCHOOL!!"
NO, THIS WEEK'S NUMBER 25 IS GAME MAKER'S "SPEED."
HUH? WEIRD.
JIWON!!
RIGHT. GAME MAKER'S "SPEED"...
YEAH! WE'LL WATCH THE NEW MUSIC VIDEO FIRST.
NO...WE'LL MEET GAME MAKER IN PERSON.
WHASSUP?!
JIWON JIN, WHAT'S WRONG? HAVEN'T YOU MEMORIZED THE SCRIPT YET?
BUT, IT SAYS IN MY SCRIPT...
AFTER FIVE MORE TAKES, JIWON REALIZED THAT HER SCRIPT WAS INCORRECT.
ARE YOU SAYING THAT YOUR SCRIPT IS DIFFERENT FROM THE REST OF THEM? YOU EXPECT ME TO BELIEVE THAT?
Yes, that's right. Her script was replaced arter rehearsal...
WASN'T IT OKAY DURING REHEARSAL? SO, YOUR SCRIPT SUDDENLY TRANSFORMED?
...With a fake script that Jenny carefully prepared the night before.

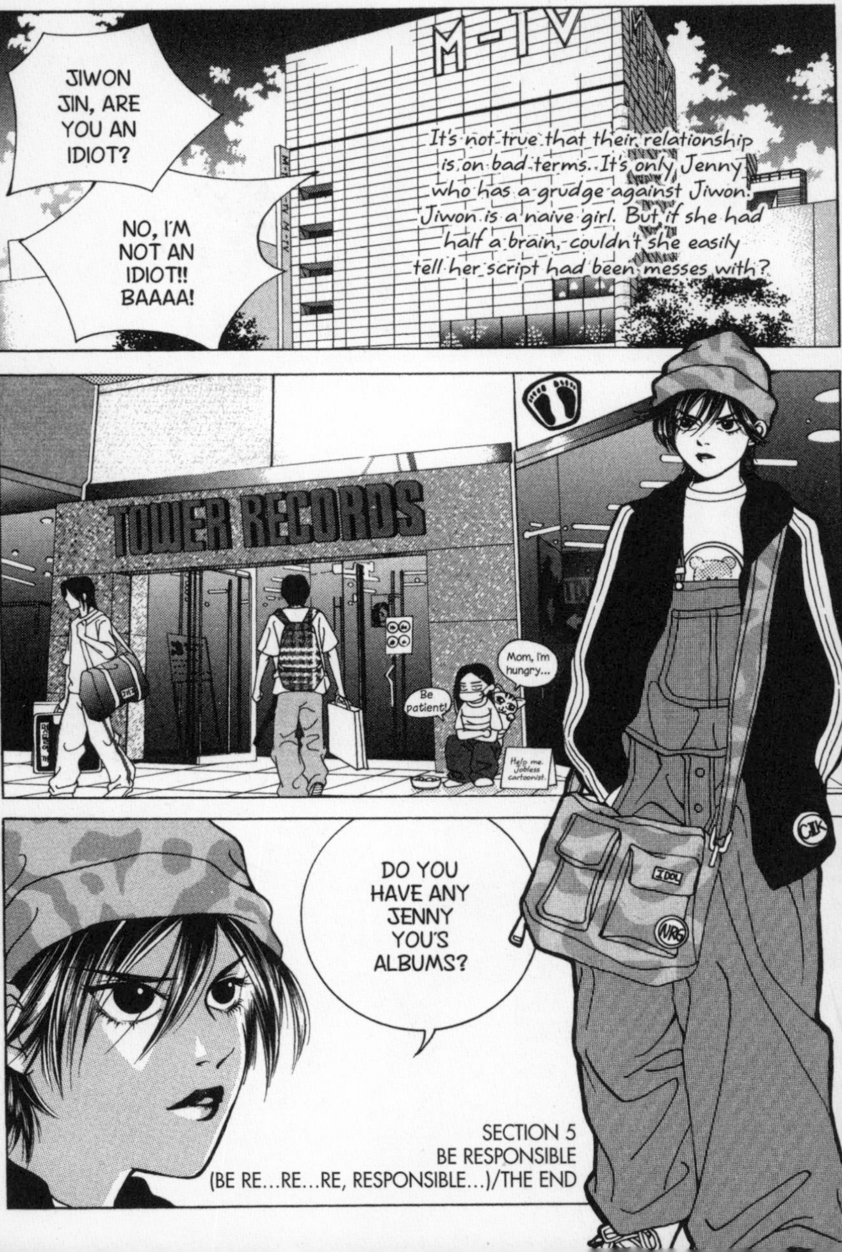
JIWON JIN, ARE YOU AN IDIOT?
NO, I'M NOT AN IDIOT!! BAAAA!
It's not true that their relationship is on bad terms. It's only Jenny who has a grudge against Jiwon. Jiwon is a naive girl. But if she had half a brain, couldn't she easily tell her script had been messes with?
TOWER RECORDS
Be patient!
Mom, I'm hungry...
Help me. Jobless cartoonist.
DO YOU HAVE ANY JENNY YOU'S ALBUMS?
SECTION 5
BE RESPONSIBLE
(BE RE...RE...RE, RESPONSIBLE...)/THE END

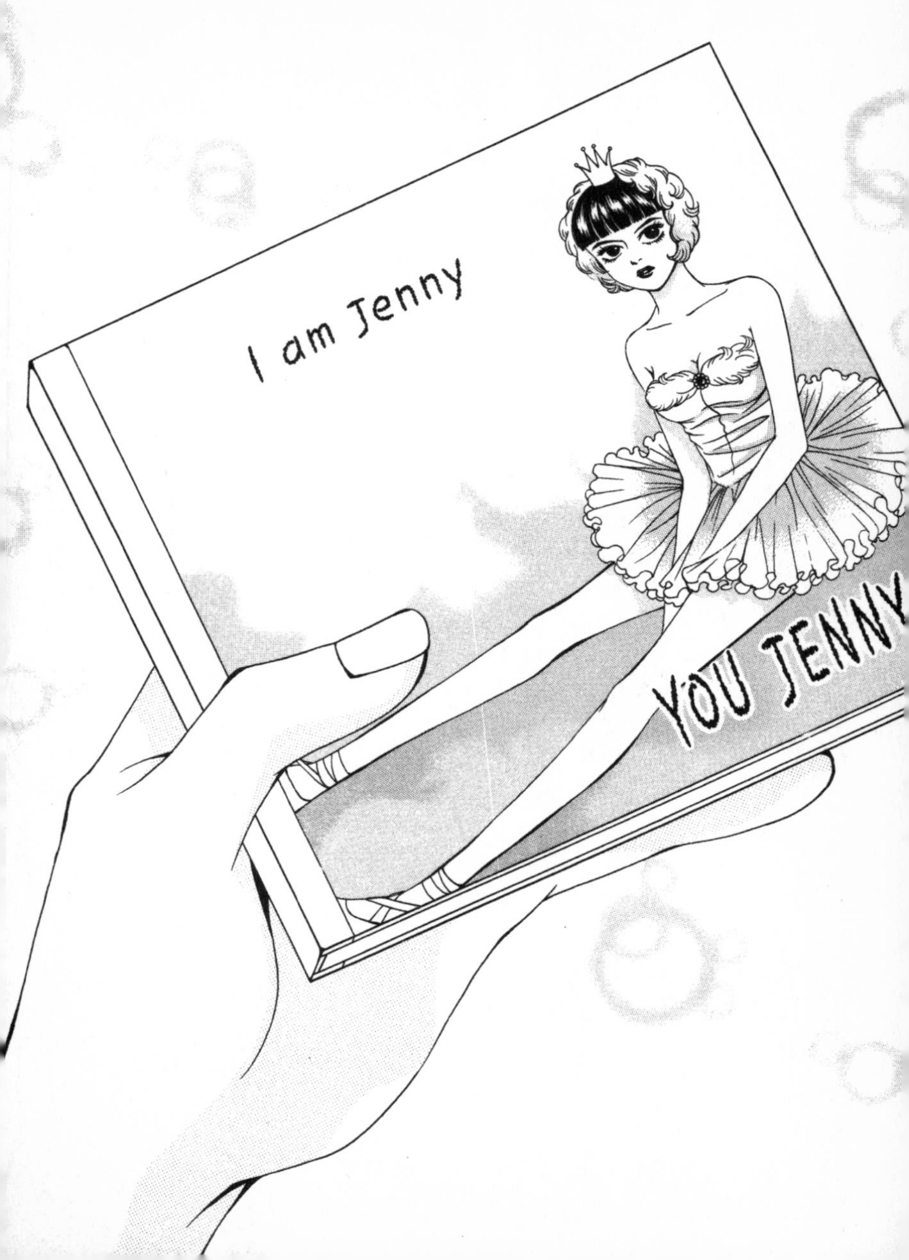
I am Jenny
YOU JENNY

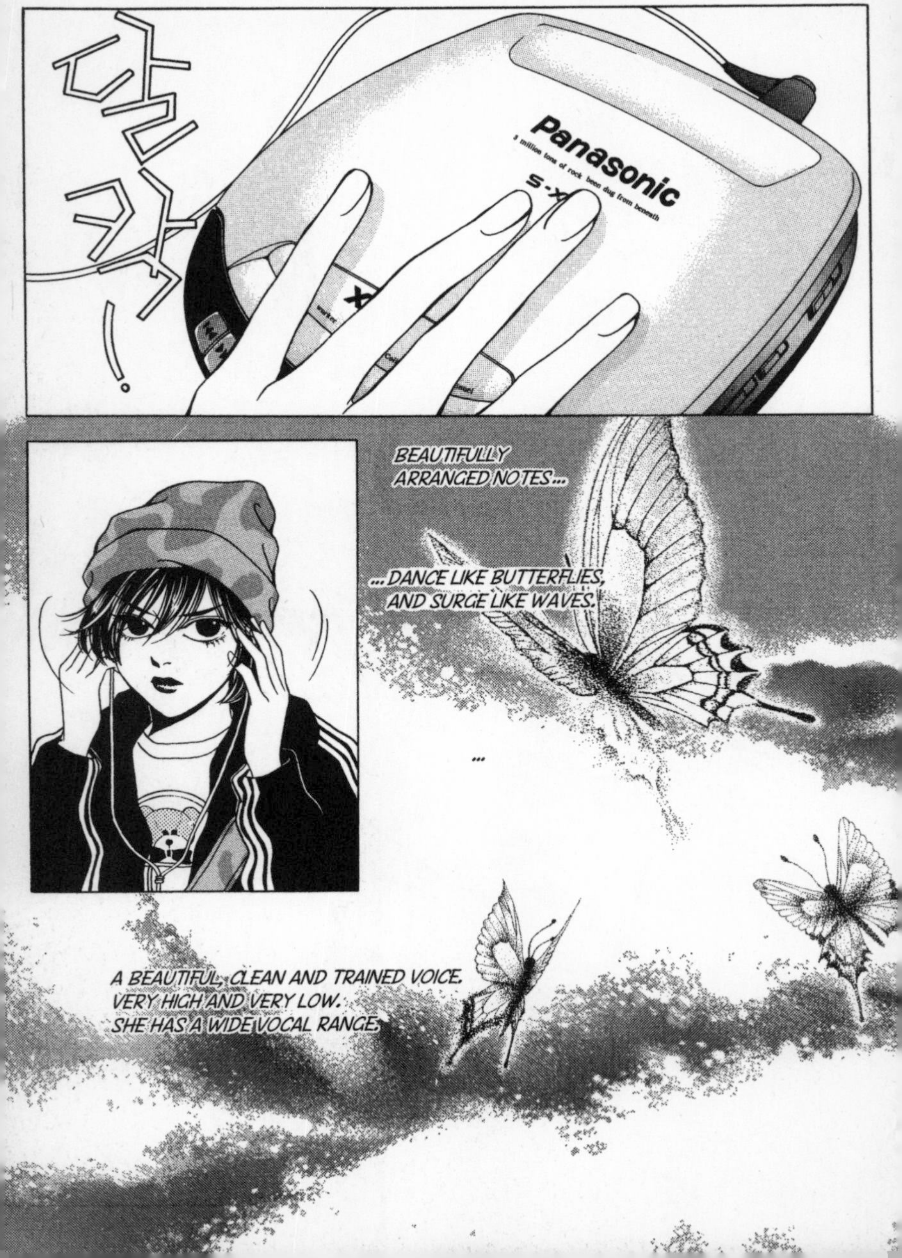
Panasonic
3 million tons of rock been dug from beneath
BEAUTIFULLY ARRANGED NOTES...
...DANCE LIKE BUTTERFLIES, AND SURGE LIKE WAVES.
A BEAUTIFUL, CLEAN AND TRAINED VOICE. VERY HIGH AND VERY LOW. SHE HAS A WIDE VOCAL RANGE.

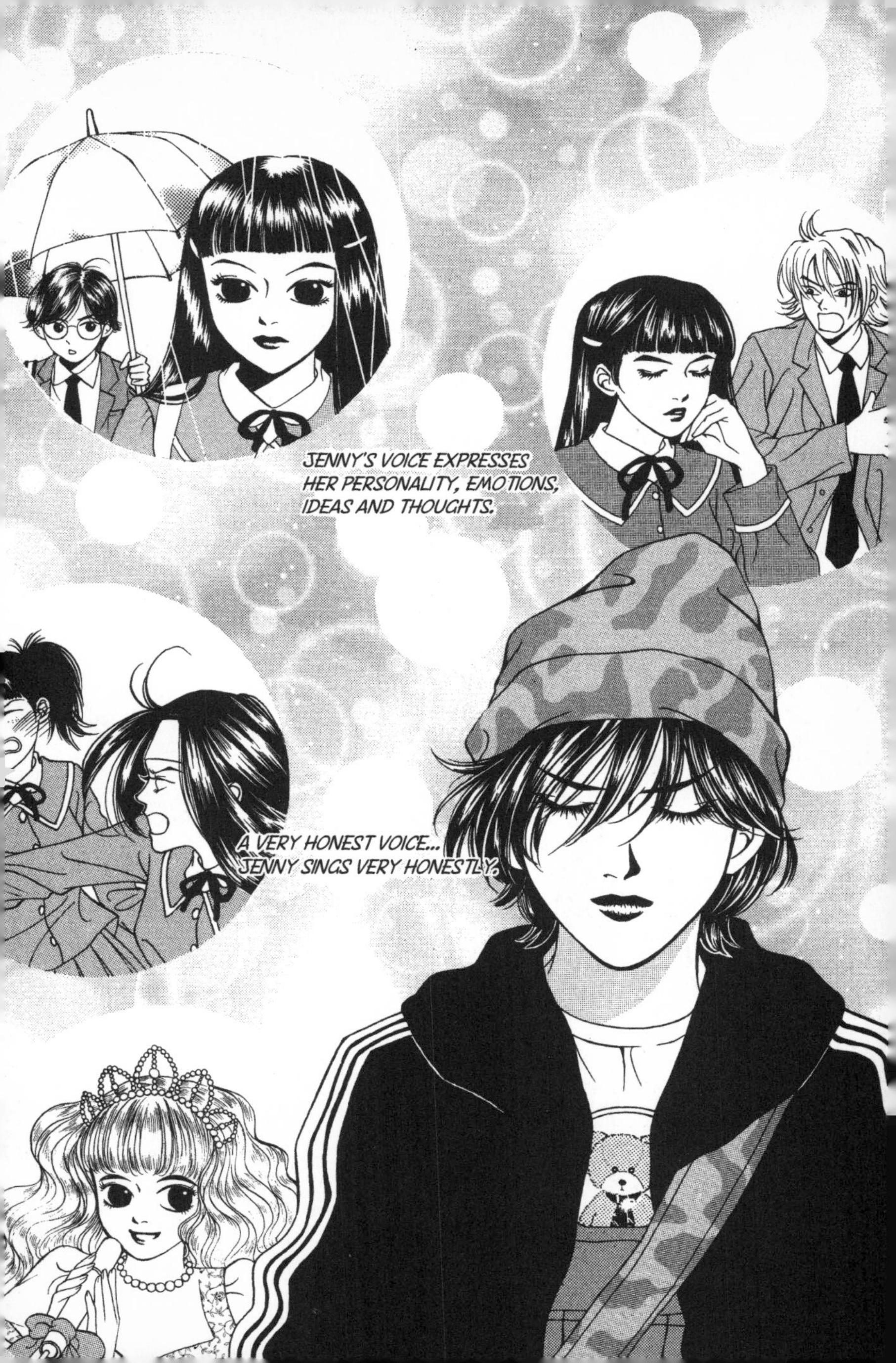
JENNY'S VOICE EXPRESSES
HER PERSONALITY, EMOTIONS,
IDEAS AND THOUGHTS.
A VERY HONEST VOICE...
JENNY SINGS VERY HONESTLY.

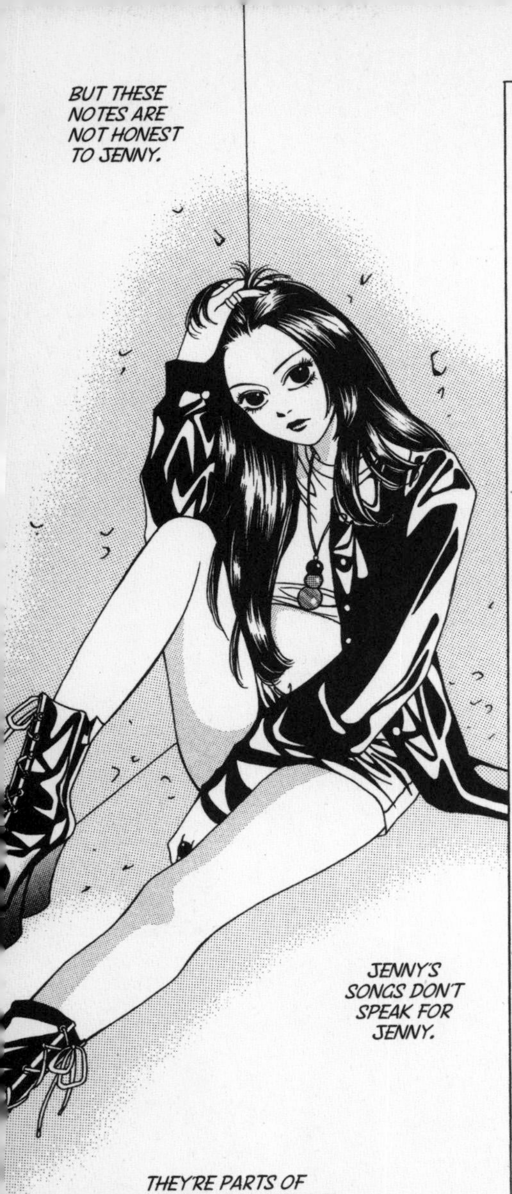
BUT THESE NOTES ARE NOT HONEST TO JENNY.
JENNY'S SONGS DON'T SPEAK FOR JENNY.
THEY'RE PARTS OF JENNY, BUT NOT THE WHOLE JENNY.

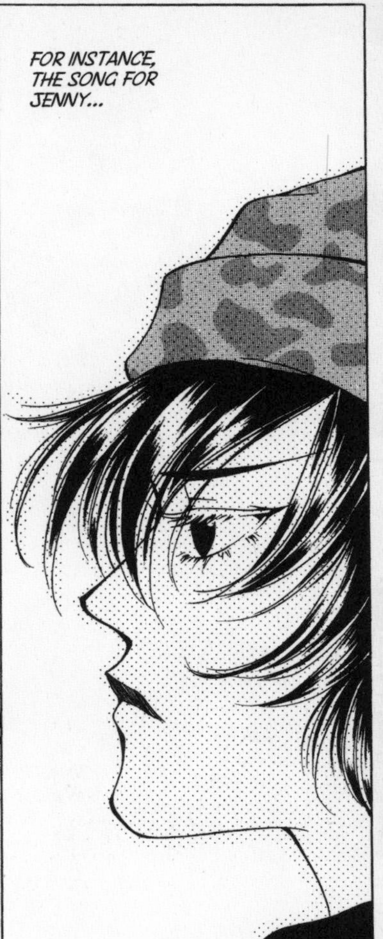
FOR INSTANCE, THE SONG FOR JENNY...
HEY, KID?

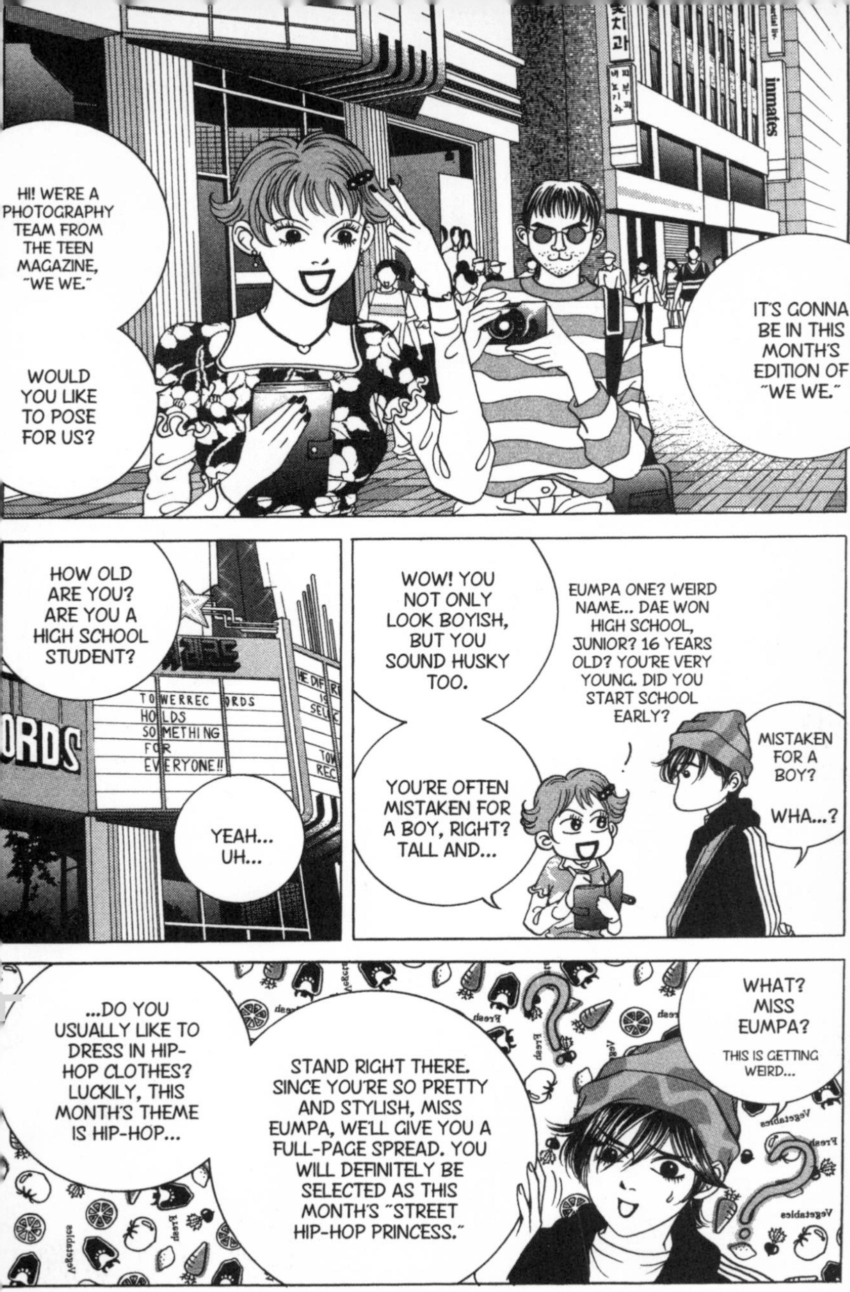
inmates
HI! WE'RE A PHOTOGRAPHY TEAM FROM THE TEEN MAGAZINE, "WE WE."
WOULD YOU LIKE TO POSE FOR US?
IT'S GONNA BE IN THIS MONTH'S EDITION OF "WE WE."
HOW OLD ARE YOU? ARE YOU A HIGH SCHOOL STUDENT?
TOWERRECORDS HOLDS SOMETHING FOR EVERYONE!!
YEAH... UH...
WOW! YOU NOT ONLY LOOK BOYISH, BUT YOU SOUND HUSKY TOO.
YOU'RE OFTEN MISTAKEN FOR A BOY, RIGHT? TALL AND...
EUMPA ONE? WEIRD NAME... DAE WON HIGH SCHOOL, JUNIOR? 16 YEARS OLD? YOU'RE VERY YOUNG. DID YOU START SCHOOL EARLY?
!
MISTAKEN FOR A BOY?
WHA...?
...DO YOU USUALLY LIKE TO DRESS IN HIP-HOP CLOTHES? LUCKILY, THIS MONTH'S THEME IS HIP-HOP...
STAND RIGHT THERE. SINCE YOU'RE SO PRETTY AND STYLISH, MISS EUMPA, WE'LL GIVE YOU A FULL-PAGE SPREAD. YOU WILL DEFINITELY BE SELECTED AS THIS MONTH'S "STREET HIP-HOP PRINCESS."
WHAT? MISS EUMPA?
THIS IS GETTING WEIRD...

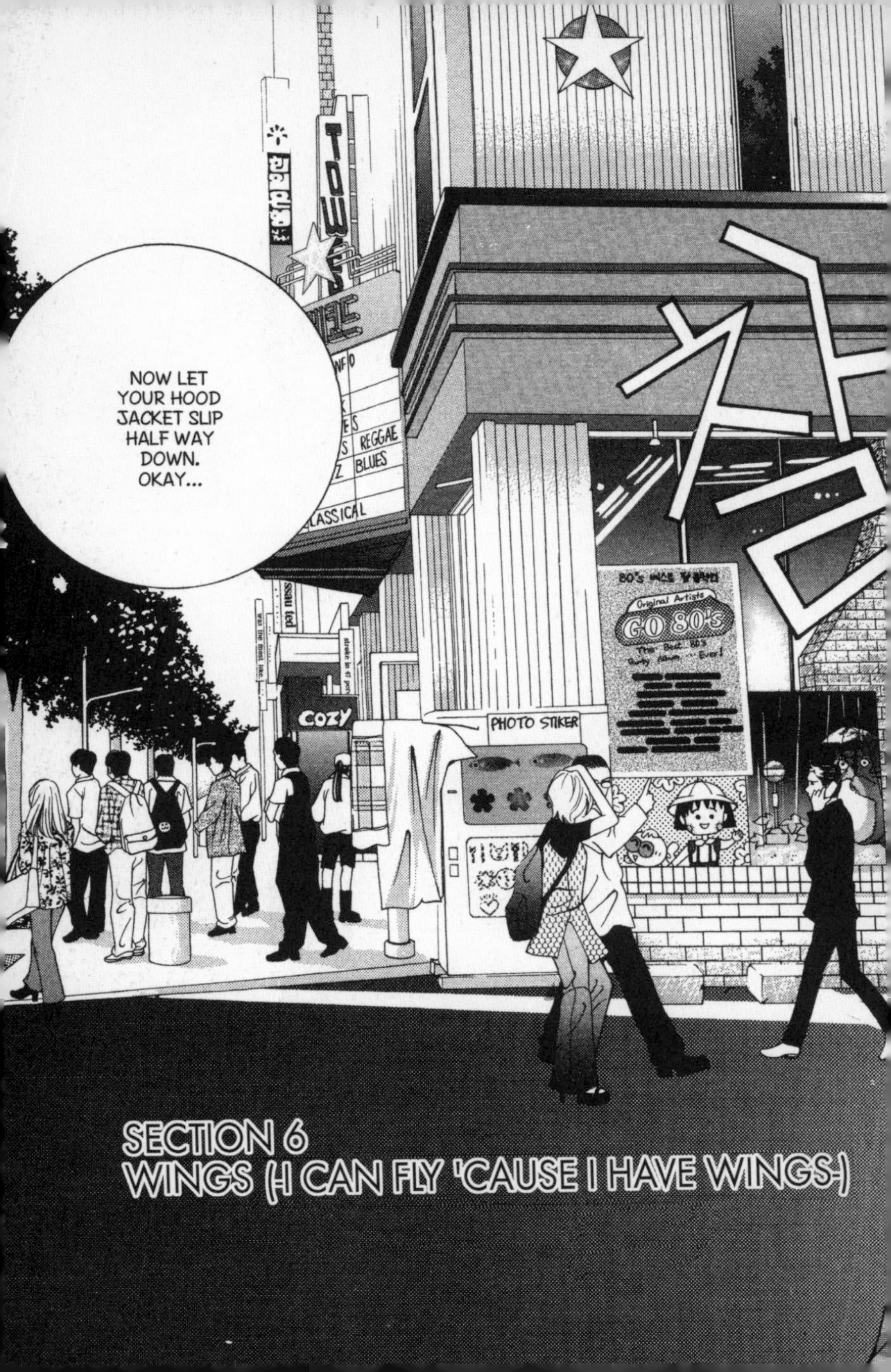
NOW LET YOUR HOOD JACKET SLIP HALF WAY DOWN. OKAY...
REGGAE
BLUES
CLASSICAL
COZY
PHOTO STIKER
Original Artists
GO 80's

SECTION 6
WINGS (-I CAN FLY 'CAUSE I HAVE WINGS-)

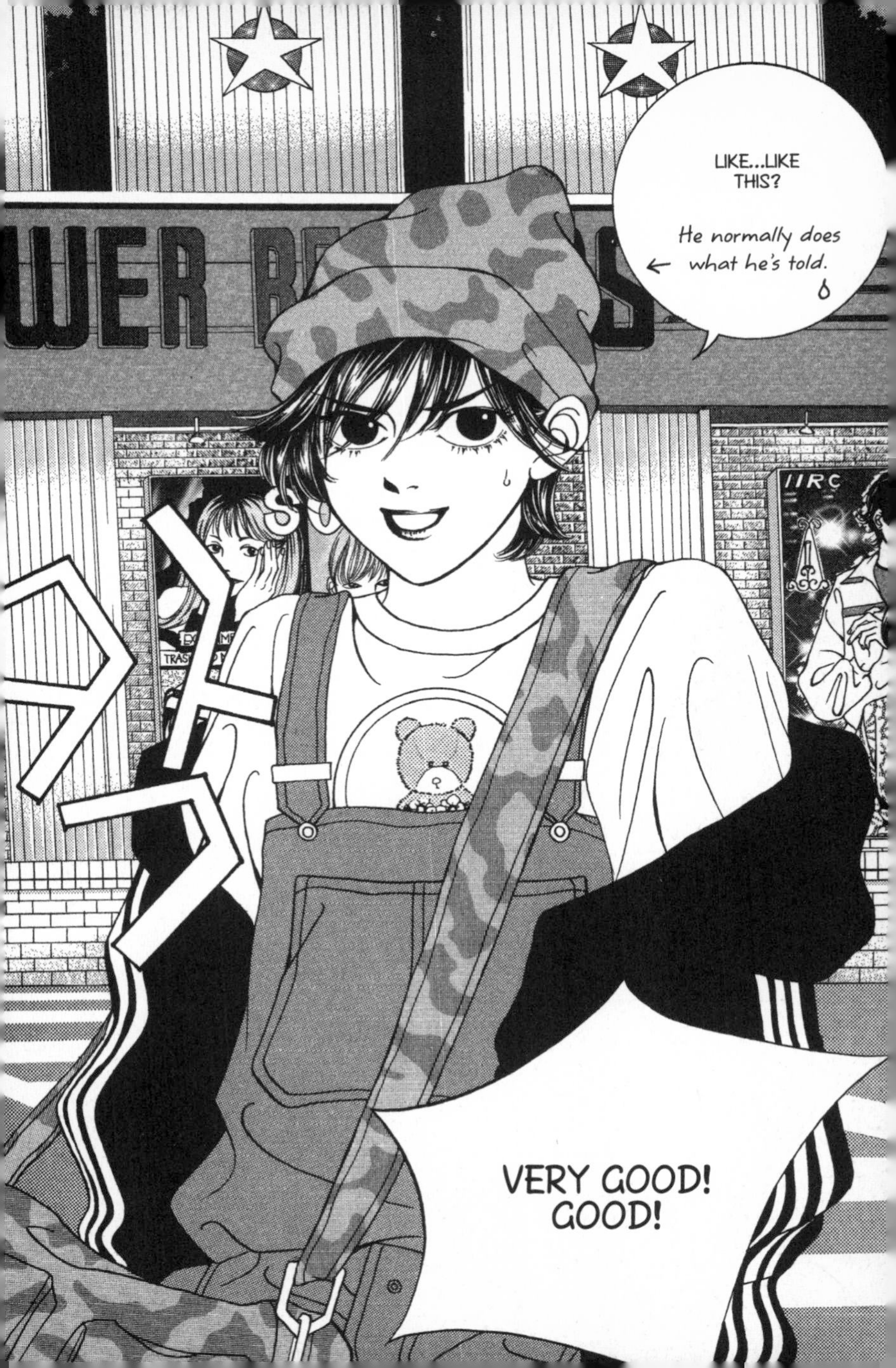
LIKE...LIKE THIS?
He normally does what he's told.
VERY GOOD! GOOD!

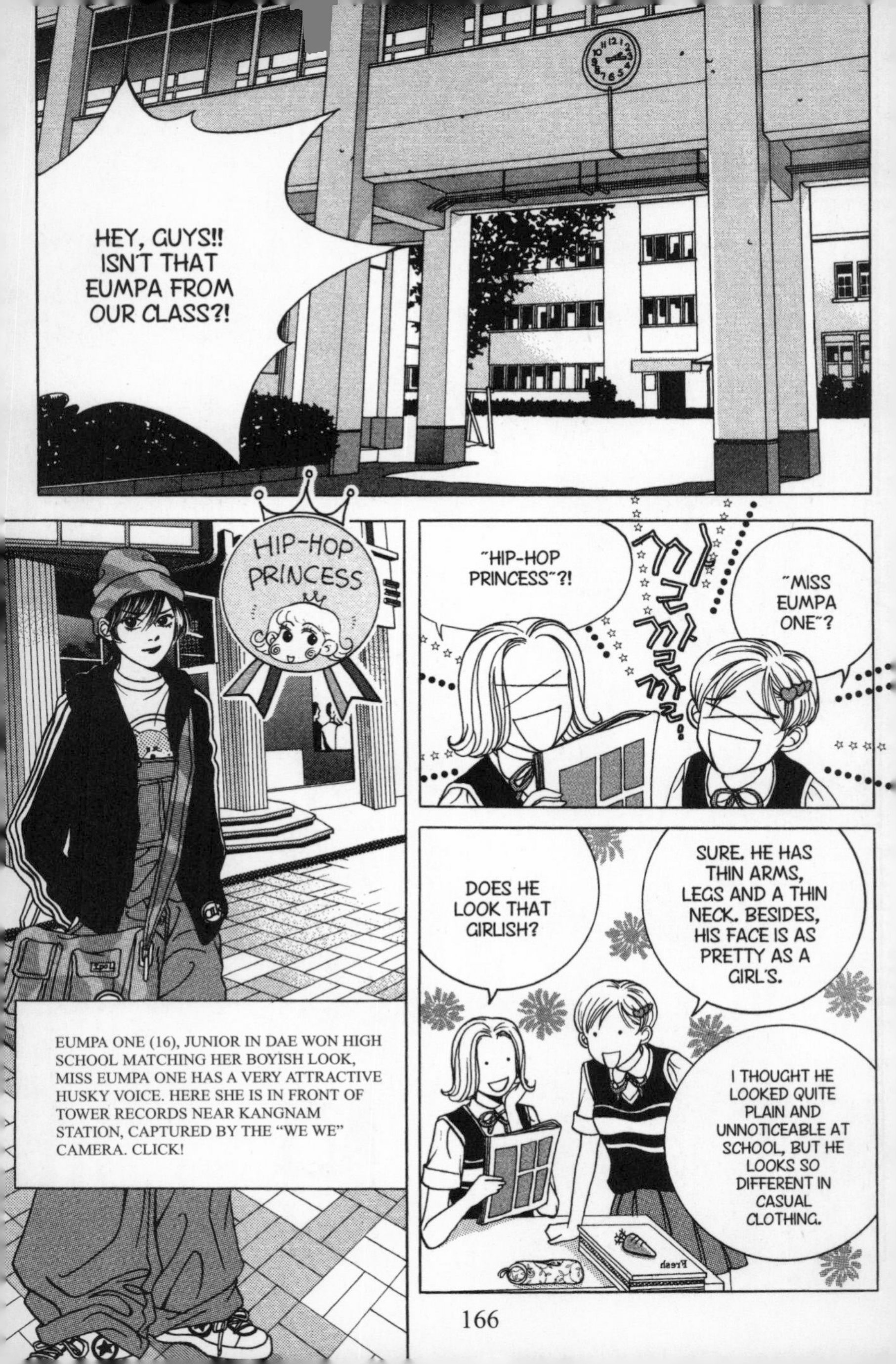
HEY, GUYS!! ISN'T THAT EUMPA FROM OUR CLASS?!
HIP-HOP PRINCESS
EUMPA ONE (16), JUNIOR IN DAE WON HIGH SCHOOL MATCHING HER BOYISH LOOK, MISS EUMPA ONE HAS A VERY ATTRACTIVE HUSKY VOICE. HERE SHE IS IN FRONT OF TOWER RECORDS NEAR KANGNAM STATION, CAPTURED BY THE "WE WE" CAMERA. CLICK!
"HIP-HOP PRINCESS"?!
"MISS EUMPA ONE"?
DOES HE LOOK THAT GIRLISH?
SURE. HE HAS THIN ARMS, LEGS AND A THIN NECK. BESIDES, HIS FACE IS AS PRETTY AS A GIRL'S.
I THOUGHT HE LOOKED QUITE PLAIN AND UNNOTICEABLE AT SCHOOL, BUT HE LOOKS SO DIFFERENT IN CASUAL CLOTHING.

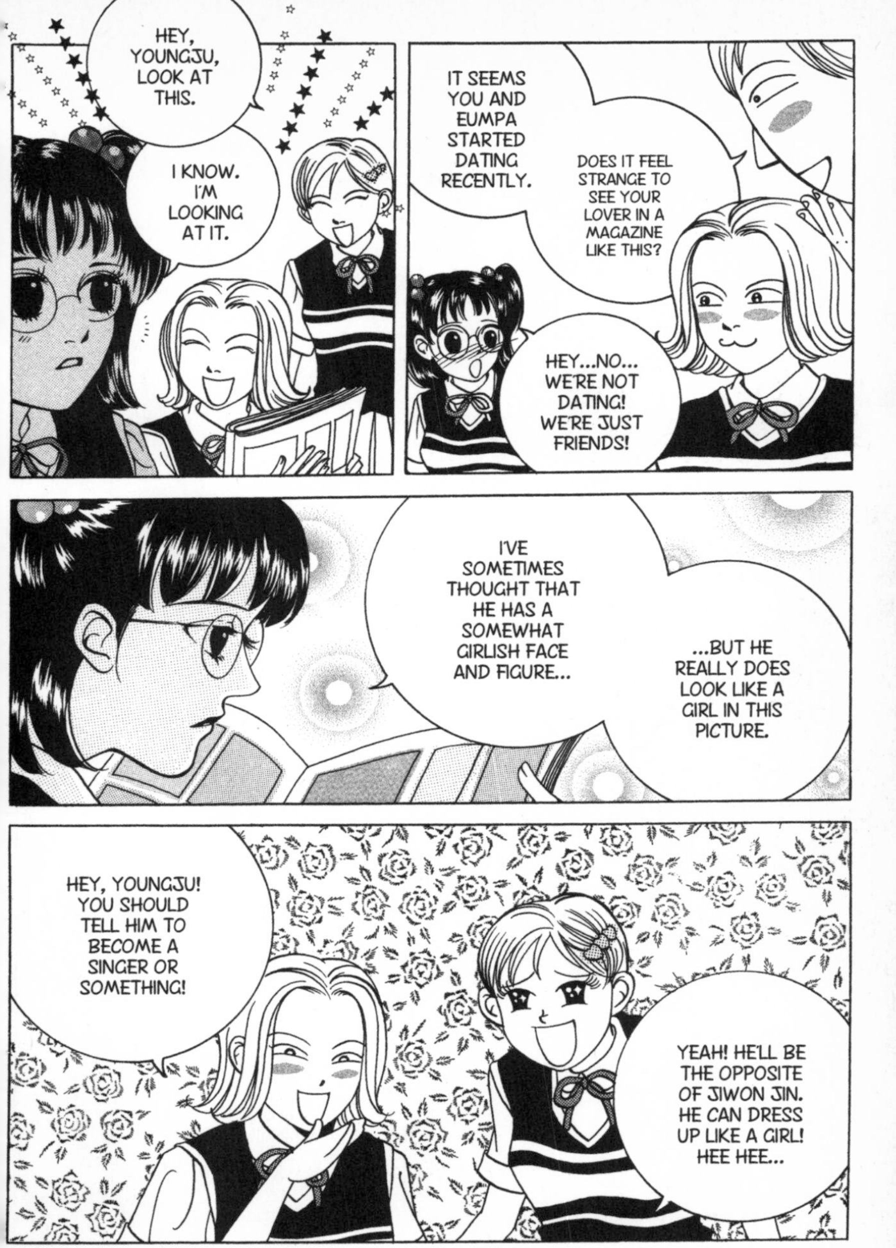
HEY, YOUNGJU, LOOK AT THIS.
I KNOW. I'M LOOKING AT IT.
IT SEEMS YOU AND EUMPA STARTED DATING RECENTLY.
DOES IT FEEL STRANGE TO SEE YOUR LOVER IN A MAGAZINE LIKE THIS?
HEY...NO... WE'RE NOT DATING! WE'RE JUST FRIENDS!
I'VE SOMETIMES THOUGHT THAT HE HAS A SOMEWHAT GIRLISH FACE AND FIGURE...
...BUT HE REALLY DOES LOOK LIKE A GIRL IN THIS PICTURE.
HEY, YOUNGJU! YOU SHOULD TELL HIM TO BECOME A SINGER OR SOMETHING!
YEAH! HE'LL BE THE OPPOSITE OF JIWON JIN. HE CAN DRESS UP LIKE A GIRL! HEE HEE...

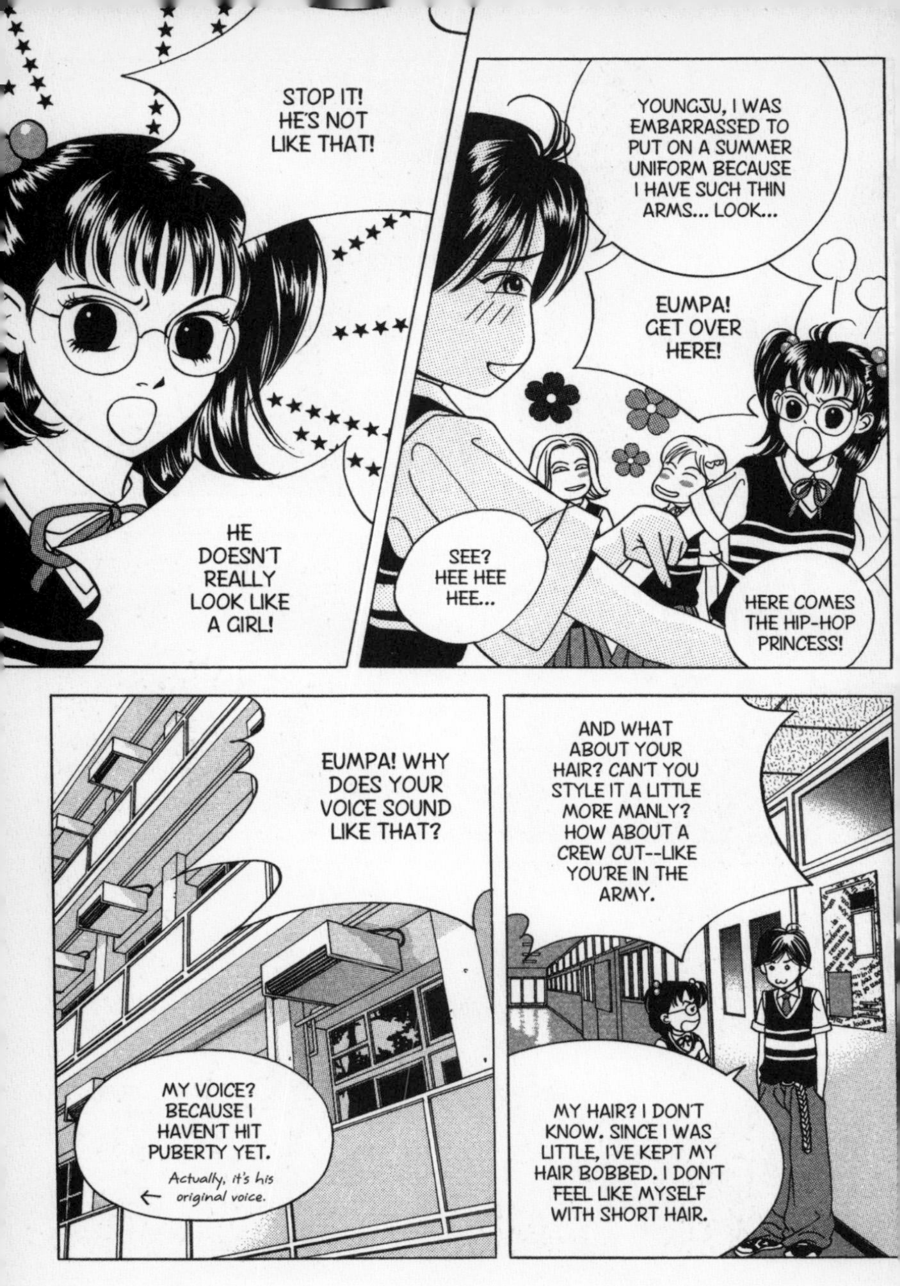
STOP IT! HE'S NOT LIKE THAT!
HE DOESN'T REALLY LOOK LIKE A GIRL!
YOUNGJU, I WAS EMBARRASSED TO PUT ON A SUMMER UNIFORM BECAUSE I HAVE SUCH THIN ARMS... LOOK...
EUMPA! GET OVER HERE!
SEE? HEE HEE HEE...
HERE COMES THE HIP-HOP PRINCESS!
EUMPA! WHY DOES YOUR VOICE SOUND LIKE THAT?
MY VOICE? BECAUSE I HAVEN'T HIT PUBERTY YET.
Actually, it's his original voice.
AND WHAT ABOUT YOUR HAIR? CAN'T YOU STYLE IT A LITTLE MORE MANLY? HOW ABOUT A CREW CUT--LIKE YOU'RE IN THE ARMY.
MY HAIR? I DON'T KNOW. SINCE I WAS LITTLE, I'VE KEPT MY HAIR BOBBED. I DON'T FEEL LIKE MYSELF WITH SHORT HAIR.

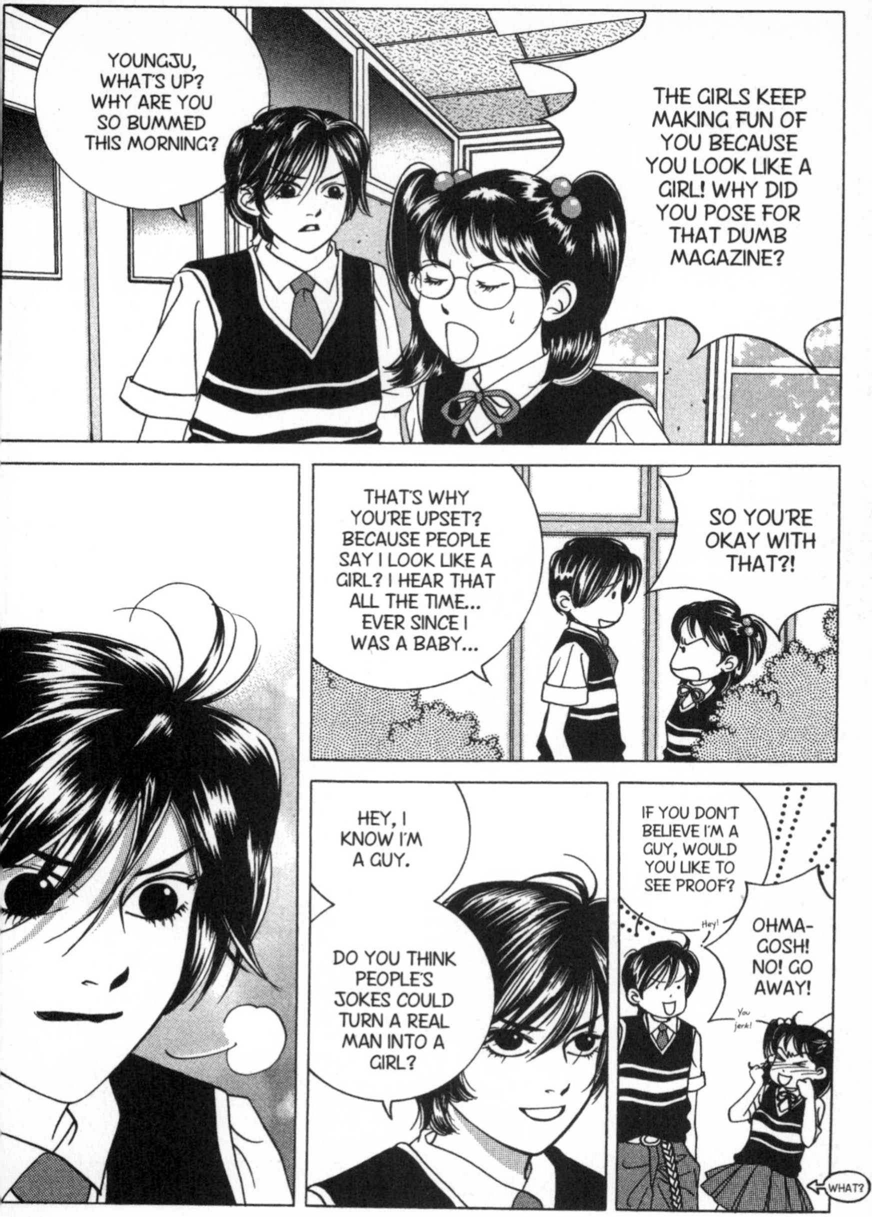
YOUNGJU, WHAT'S UP? WHY ARE YOU SO BUMMED THIS MORNING?
THE GIRLS KEEP MAKING FUN OF YOU BECAUSE YOU LOOK LIKE A GIRL! WHY DID YOU POSE FOR THAT DUMB MAGAZINE?
THAT'S WHY YOU'RE UPSET? BECAUSE PEOPLE SAY I LOOK LIKE A GIRL? I HEAR THAT ALL THE TIME... EVER SINCE I WAS A BABY...
SO YOU'RE OKAY WITH THAT?!
HEY, I KNOW I'M A GUY.
DO YOU THINK PEOPLE'S JOKES COULD TURN A REAL MAN INTO A GIRL?
IF YOU DON'T BELIEVE I'M A GUY, WOULD YOU LIKE TO SEE PROOF?
Hey!
OHMA-GOSH! NO! GO AWAY!
You jerk!
WHAT?

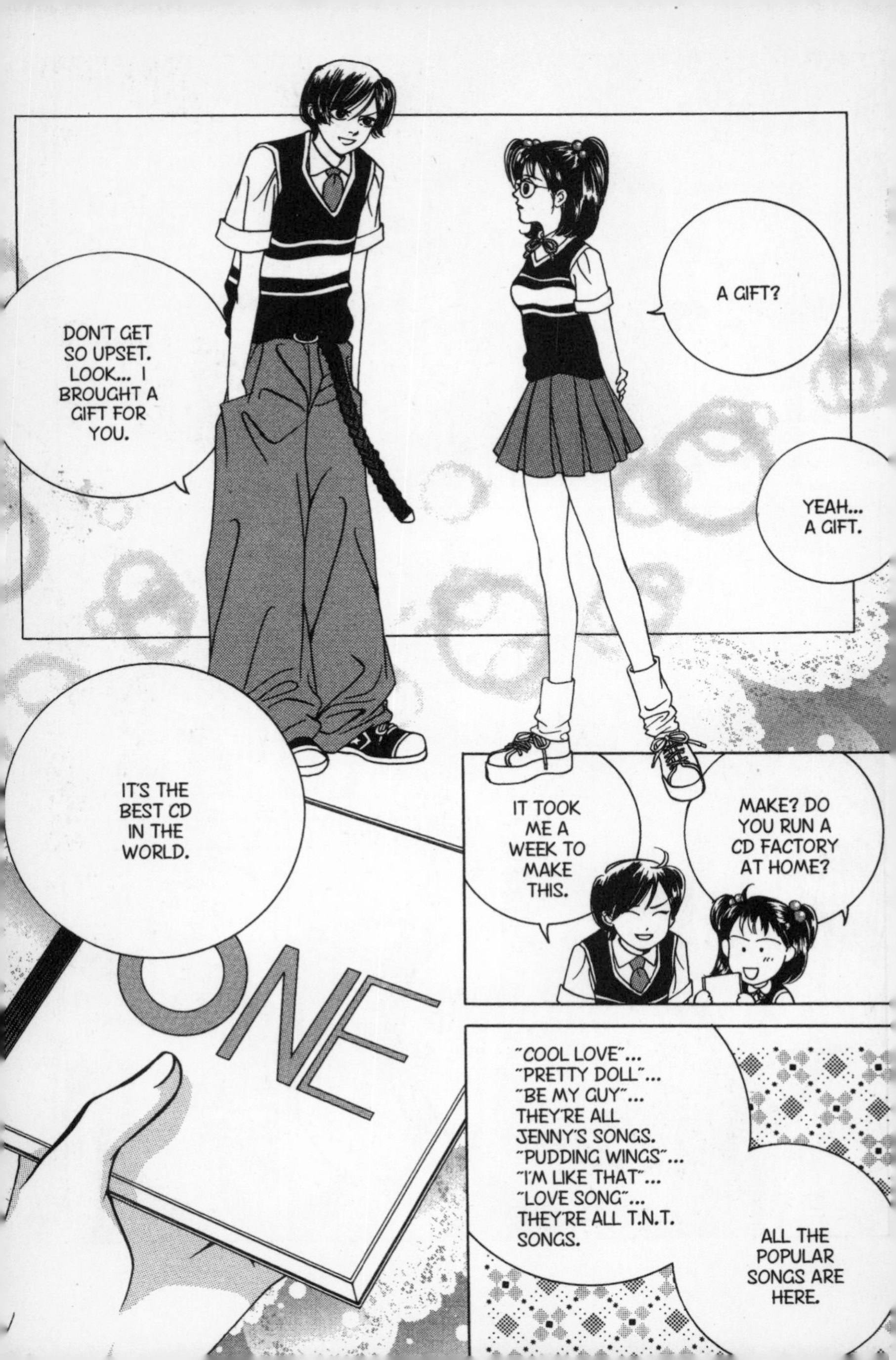
DON'T GET SO UPSET. LOOK... I BROUGHT A GIFT FOR YOU.
A GIFT?
YEAH... A GIFT.
IT'S THE BEST CD IN THE WORLD.
IT TOOK ME A WEEK TO MAKE THIS.
MAKE? DO YOU RUN A CD FACTORY AT HOME?
ONE
"COOL LOVE"... "PRETTY DOLL"... "BE MY GUY"... THEY'RE ALL JENNY'S SONGS. "PUDDING WINGS"... "I'M LIKE THAT"... "LOVE SONG"... THEY'RE ALL T.N.T. SONGS.
ALL THE POPULAR SONGS ARE HERE.

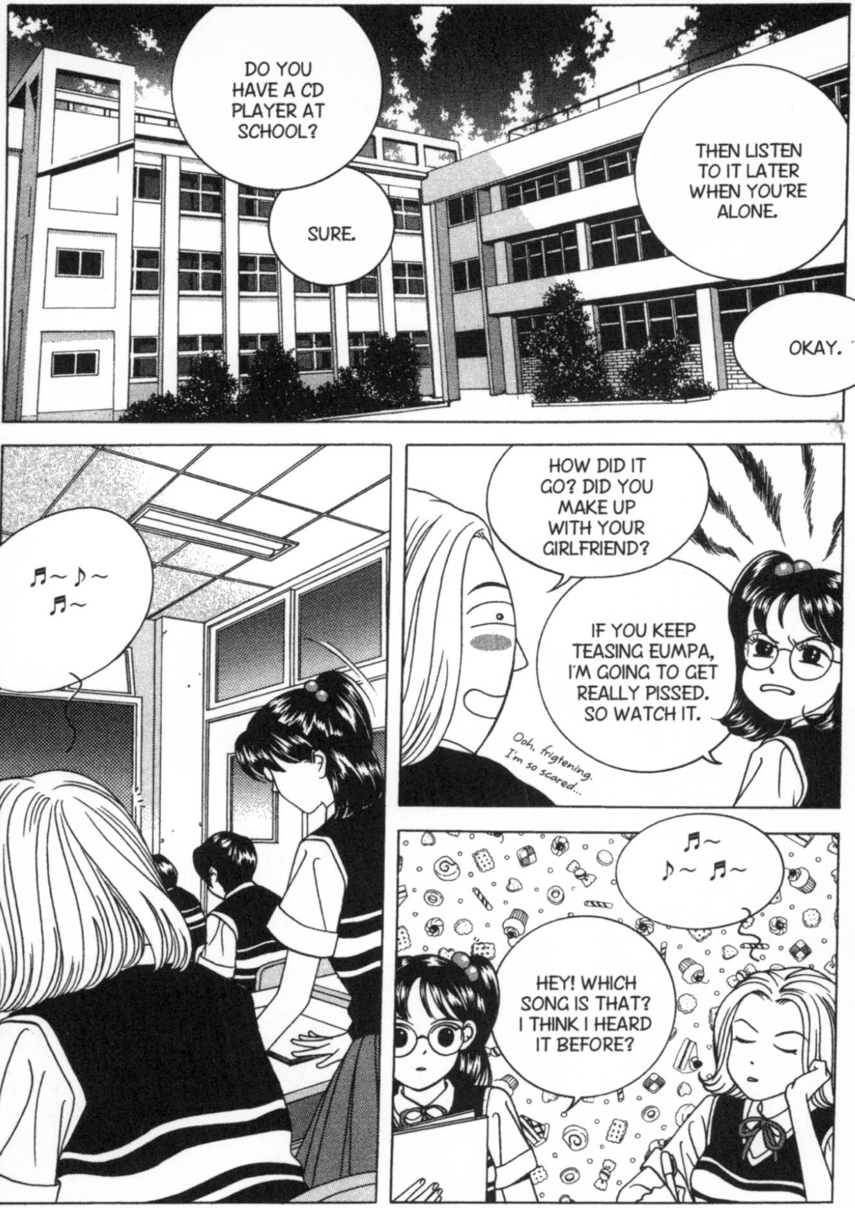
DO YOU HAVE A CD PLAYER AT SCHOOL?
SURE.
THEN LISTEN TO IT LATER WHEN YOU'RE ALONE.
OKAY.
♬~ ♪~ ♬~
HOW DID IT GO? DID YOU MAKE UP WITH YOUR GIRLFRIEND?
IF YOU KEEP TEASING EUMPA, I'M GOING TO GET REALLY PISSED. SO WATCH IT.
Ooh, frigtening. I'm so scared...
♬~ ♪~ ♬~
HEY! WHICH SONG IS THAT? I THINK I HEARD IT BEFORE?

WHAT SONG?

THE ONE YOU'RE HUMMING.

I DON'T KNOW. I HEARD IT THIS MORNING ON THE RADIO ON THE BUS...

WHATEVER I HEAR IN THE MORNING IS STUCK IN MY HEAD ALL DAY.

HEY. IT'S THE THEME SONG OF "YESTERDAY'S LOVE." THE CLOSING THEME...

"YESTERDAY'S LOVE"?

OH, RIGHT! THE NEW DRAMA!

YEAH. JIHAE HAN, SUNGSIK PARK, YUNKI HONG, SUNGEUN KIM, JEONGEUN LEE...ALL THE BIG NAMES ARE IN IT.

THAT THEME SONG IS FOR JIHAE HAN'S CHARACTER "YUNHEE."

HEY! I BET IT'S GONNA BE A BIG DEAL.

SUNGEUN KIM, DON'T YOU THINK HE LOOKS SO SAD THERE? REMINDS ME OF SUNGMU FROM "C.L.S."

SUNGEUN KIM PLAYED A SPOILED, SELFISH BRAT ON HIS LAST SHOW. BUT IN THIS NEW ONE, HE TURNS INTO A TOTALLY DIFFERENT PERSON.

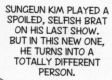

끄악! Yuck!

싫어! Gross!

HEY! JIHAE HAN LOOKS EVEN YOUNGER THAN US. IS SHE USING SOME KIND OF MAGIC MEDICINE? LIKE, THE EXTRACT OF THE PLACENTA?

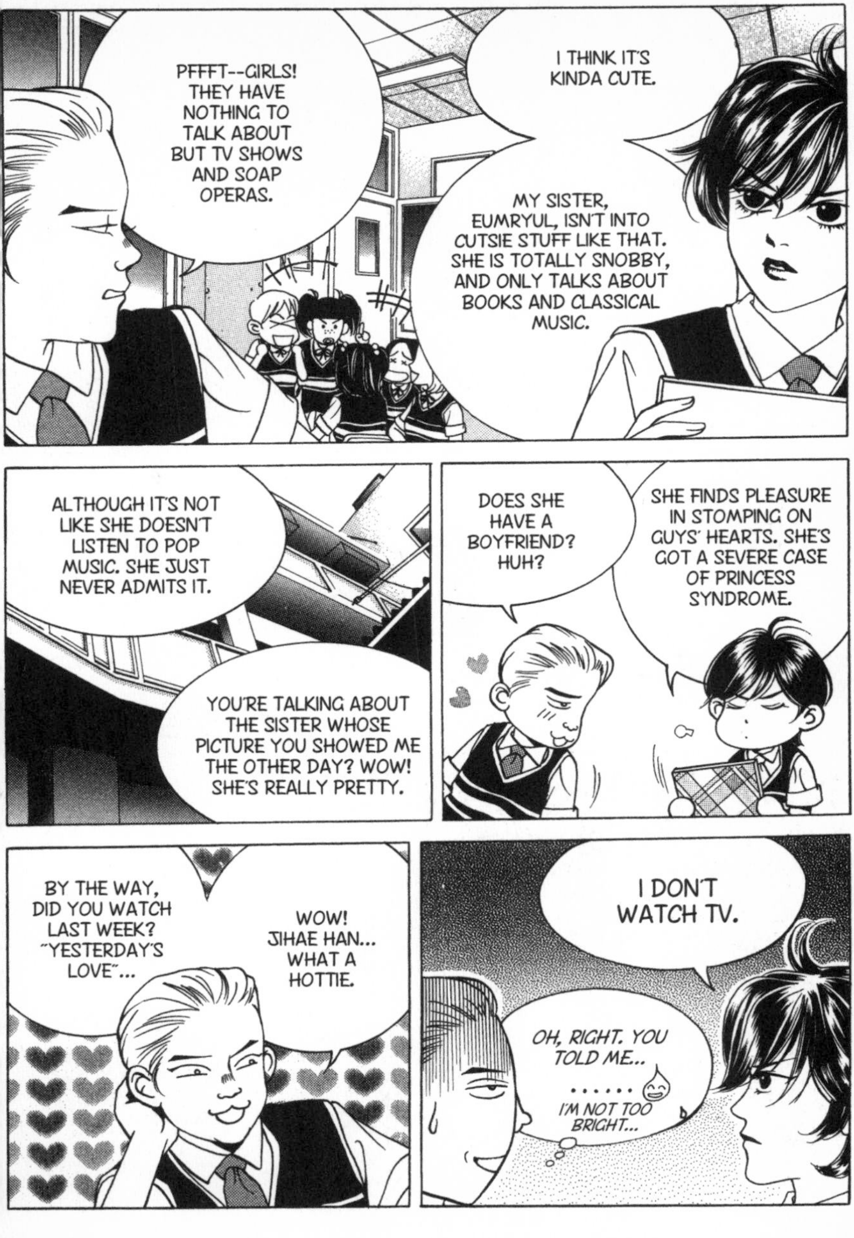

PFFFT--GIRLS! THEY HAVE NOTHING TO TALK ABOUT BUT TV SHOWS AND SOAP OPERAS.
I THINK IT'S KINDA CUTE.
MY SISTER, EUMRYUL, ISN'T INTO CUTSIE STUFF LIKE THAT. SHE IS TOTALLY SNOBBY, AND ONLY TALKS ABOUT BOOKS AND CLASSICAL MUSIC.
ALTHOUGH IT'S NOT LIKE SHE DOESN'T LISTEN TO POP MUSIC. SHE JUST NEVER ADMITS IT.
YOU'RE TALKING ABOUT THE SISTER WHOSE PICTURE YOU SHOWED ME THE OTHER DAY? WOW! SHE'S REALLY PRETTY.
DOES SHE HAVE A BOYFRIEND? HUH?
SHE FINDS PLEASURE IN STOMPING ON GUYS' HEARTS. SHE'S GOT A SEVERE CASE OF PRINCESS SYNDROME.
BY THE WAY, DID YOU WATCH LAST WEEK? "YESTERDAY'S LOVE"...
WOW! JIHAE HAN... WHAT A HOTTIE.
I DON'T WATCH TV.
OH, RIGHT. YOU TOLD ME...
......
I'M NOT TOO BRIGHT...

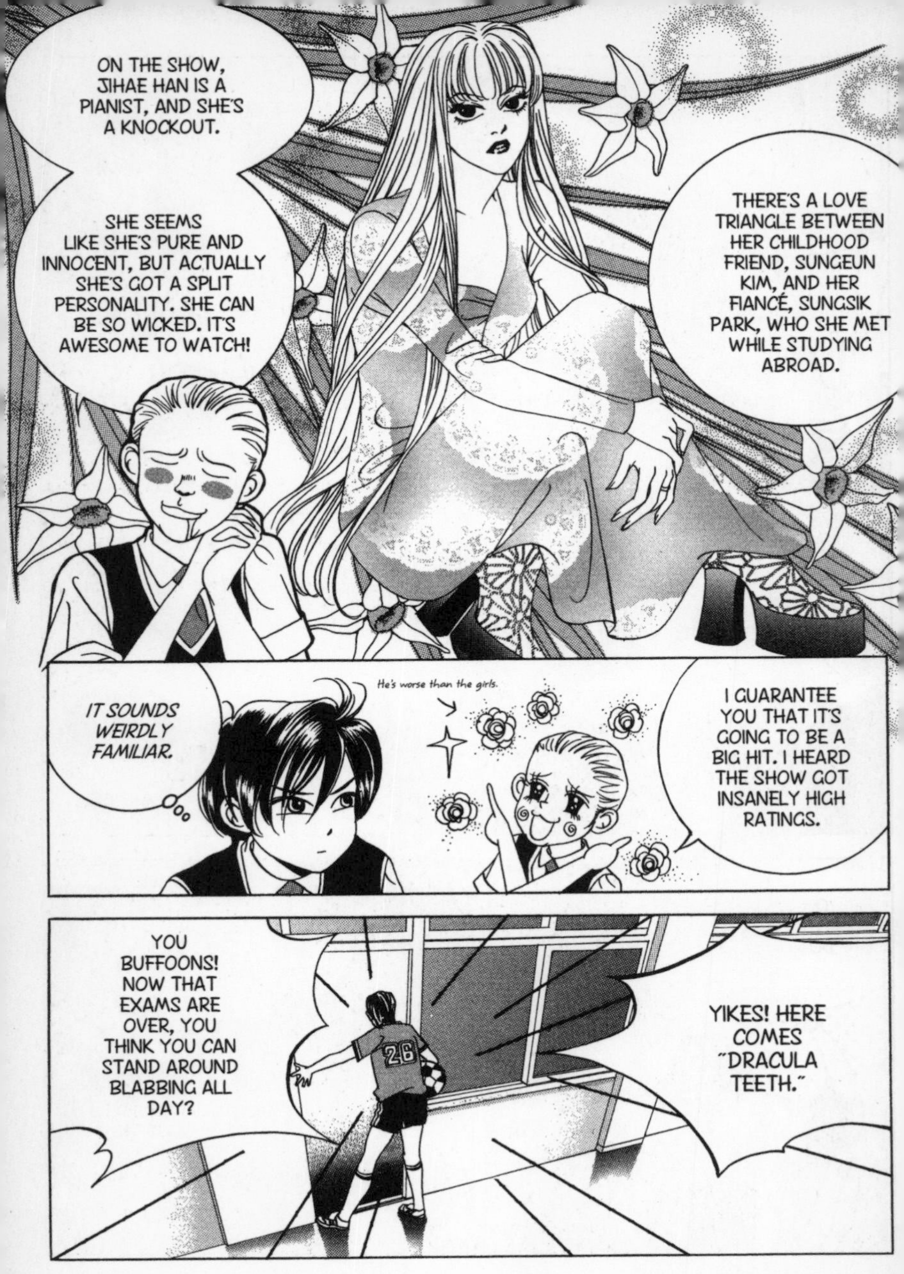
ON THE SHOW, JIHAE HAN IS A PIANIST, AND SHE'S A KNOCKOUT.
SHE SEEMS LIKE SHE'S PURE AND INNOCENT, BUT ACTUALLY SHE'S GOT A SPLIT PERSONALITY. SHE CAN BE SO WICKED. IT'S AWESOME TO WATCH!
THERE'S A LOVE TRIANGLE BETWEEN HER CHILDHOOD FRIEND, SUNGEUN KIM, AND HER FIANCÉ, SUNGSIK PARK, WHO SHE MET WHILE STUDYING ABROAD.
IT SOUNDS WEIRDLY FAMILIAR.
He's worse than the girls.
I GUARANTEE YOU THAT IT'S GOING TO BE A BIG HIT. I HEARD THE SHOW GOT INSANELY HIGH RATINGS.
YOU BUFFOONS! NOW THAT EXAMS ARE OVER, YOU THINK YOU CAN STAND AROUND BLABBING ALL DAY?
26
YIKES! HERE COMES "DRACULA TEETH."

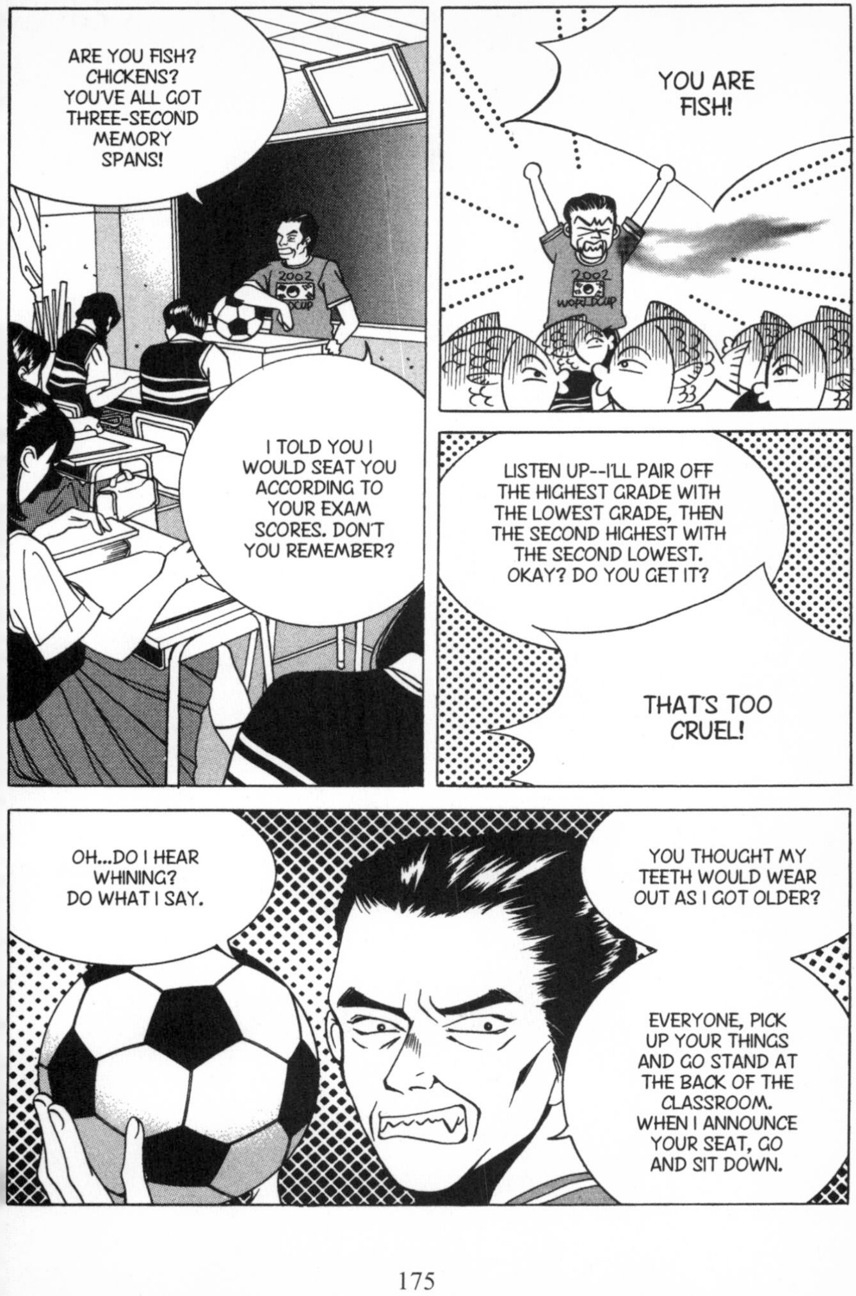

ARE YOU FISH? CHICKENS? YOU'VE ALL GOT THREE-SECOND MEMORY SPANS!
I TOLD YOU I WOULD SEAT YOU ACCORDING TO YOUR EXAM SCORES. DON'T YOU REMEMBER?
YOU ARE FISH!
LISTEN UP--I'LL PAIR OFF THE HIGHEST GRADE WITH THE LOWEST GRADE, THEN THE SECOND HIGHEST WITH THE SECOND LOWEST. OKAY? DO YOU GET IT?
THAT'S TOO CRUEL!
OH...DO I HEAR WHINING? DO WHAT I SAY.
YOU THOUGHT MY TEETH WOULD WEAR OUT AS I GOT OLDER?
EVERYONE, PICK UP YOUR THINGS AND GO STAND AT THE BACK OF THE CLASSROOM. WHEN I ANNOUNCE YOUR SEAT, GO AND SIT DOWN.

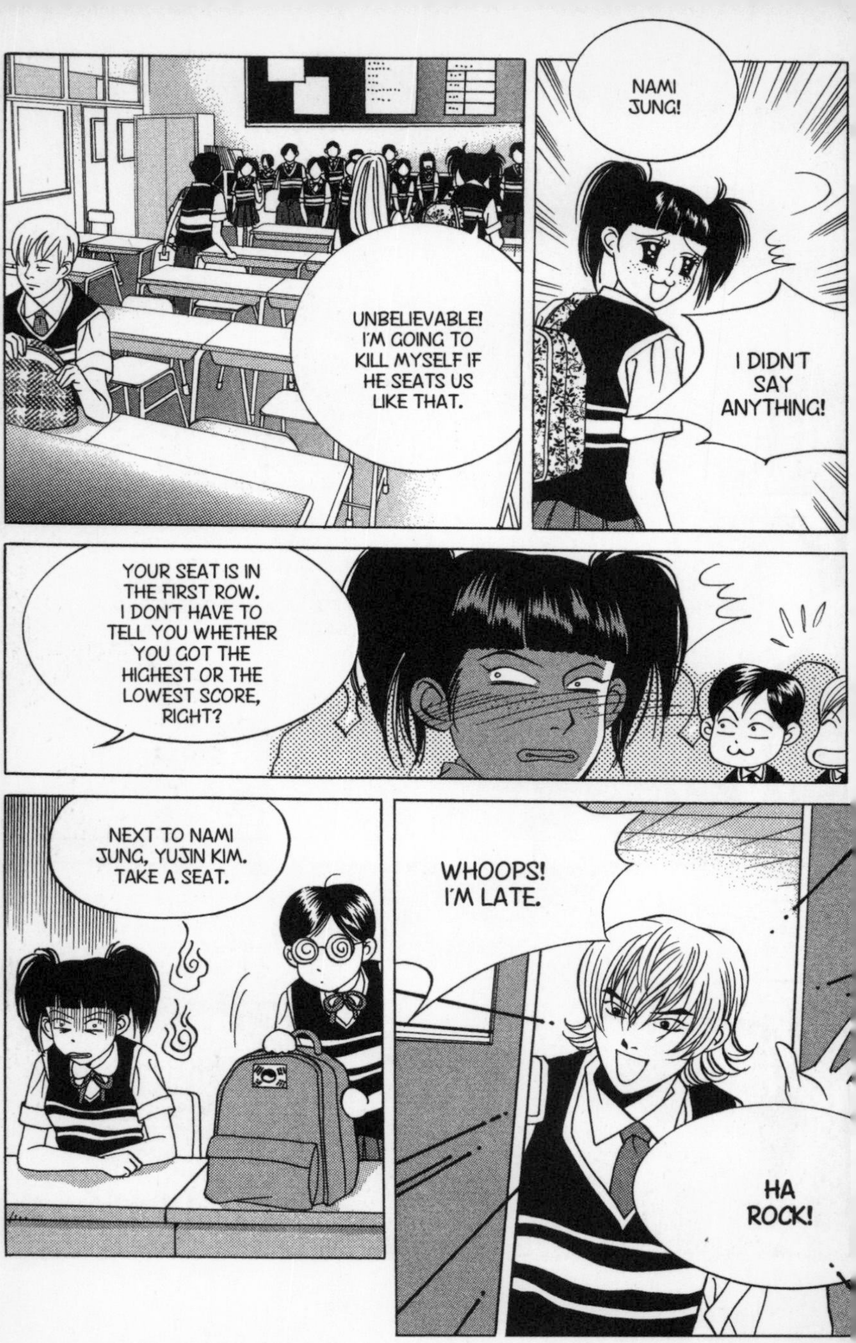
UNBELIEVABLE! I'M GOING TO KILL MYSELF IF HE SEATS US LIKE THAT.
NAMI JUNG!
I DIDN'T SAY ANYTHING!
YOUR SEAT IS IN THE FIRST ROW. I DON'T HAVE TO TELL YOU WHETHER YOU GOT THE HIGHEST OR THE LOWEST SCORE, RIGHT?
NEXT TO NAMI JUNG, YUJIN KIM. TAKE A SEAT.
WHOOPS! I'M LATE.
HA ROCK!

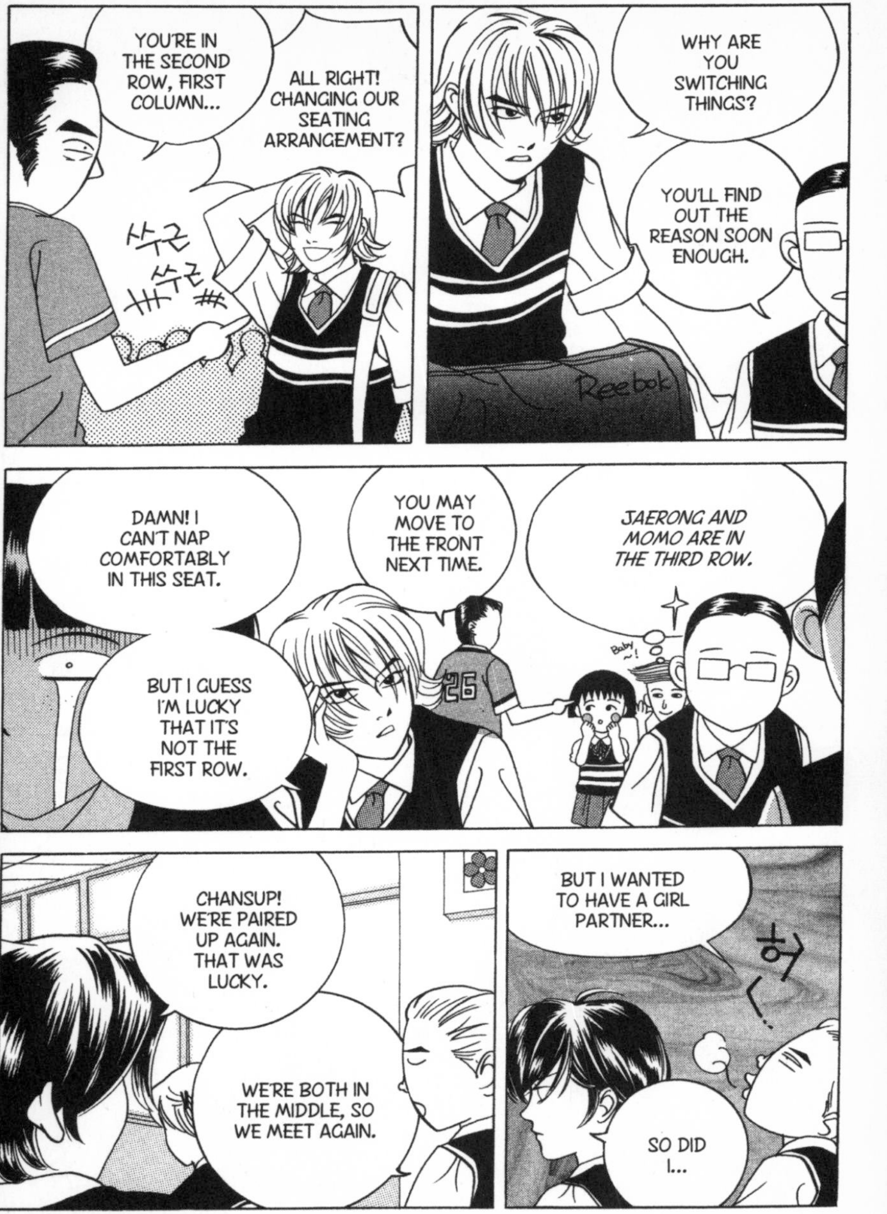
YOU'RE IN THE SECOND ROW, FIRST COLUMN...
ALL RIGHT! CHANGING OUR SEATING ARRANGEMENT?
쑤군 쑤군
WHY ARE YOU SWITCHING THINGS?
YOU'LL FIND OUT THE REASON SOON ENOUGH.
Reebok
DAMN! I CAN'T NAP COMFORTABLY IN THIS SEAT.
BUT I GUESS I'M LUCKY THAT IT'S NOT THE FIRST ROW.
YOU MAY MOVE TO THE FRONT NEXT TIME.
JAERONG AND MOMO ARE IN THE THIRD ROW.
26
Baby ~!
CHANSUP! WE'RE PAIRED UP AGAIN. THAT WAS LUCKY.
WE'RE BOTH IN THE MIDDLE, SO WE MEET AGAIN.
BUT I WANTED TO HAVE A GIRL PARTNER...
SO DID I...

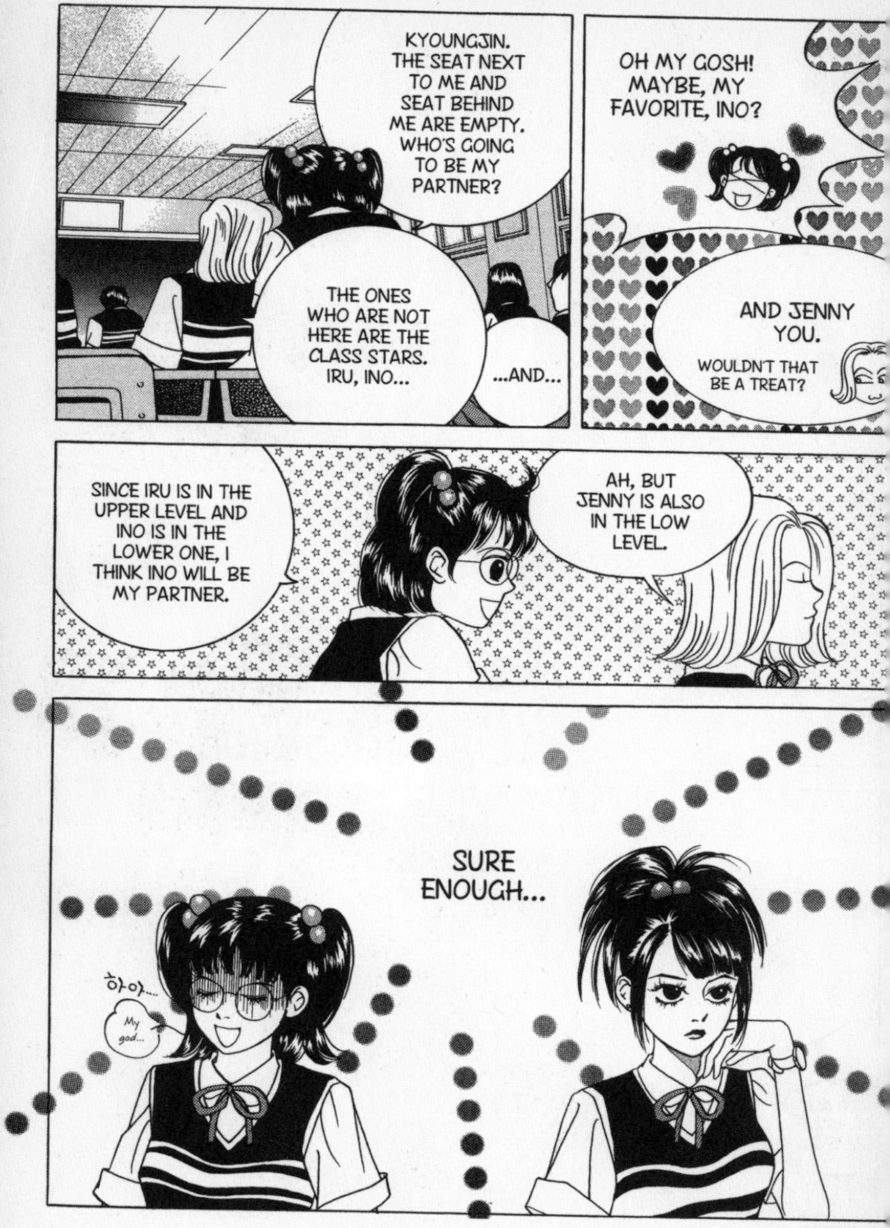
KYOUNGJIN. THE SEAT NEXT TO ME AND SEAT BEHIND ME ARE EMPTY. WHO'S GOING TO BE MY PARTNER?
THE ONES WHO ARE NOT HERE ARE THE CLASS STARS. IRU, INO...
...AND...
OH MY GOSH! MAYBE, MY FAVORITE, INO?
AND JENNY YOU.
WOULDN'T THAT BE A TREAT?
SINCE IRU IS IN THE UPPER LEVEL AND INO IS IN THE LOWER ONE, I THINK INO WILL BE MY PARTNER.
AH, BUT JENNY IS ALSO IN THE LOW LEVEL.
SURE ENOUGH...
하아...
My god...

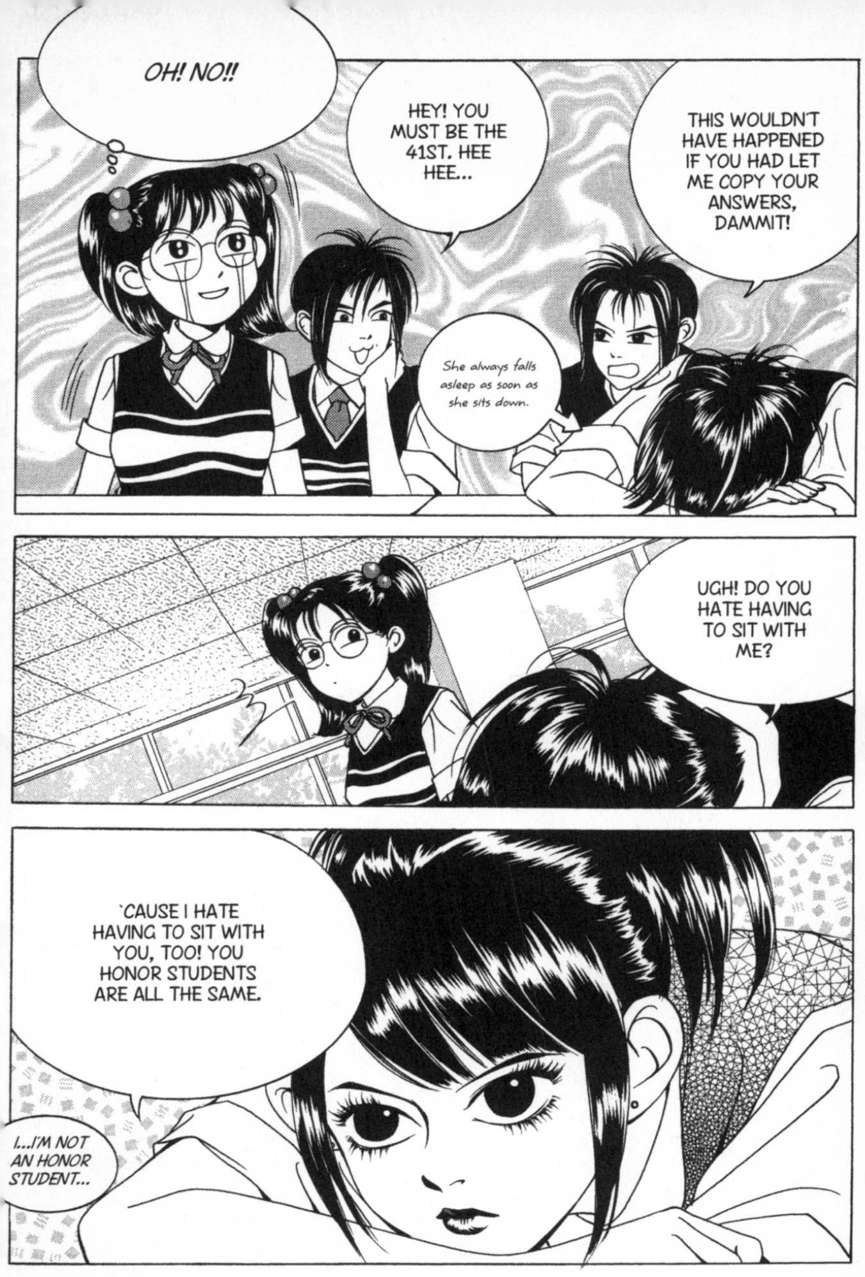
OH! NO!!
HEY! YOU MUST BE THE 41ST. HEE HEE...
She always falls asleep as soon as she sits down.
THIS WOULDN'T HAVE HAPPENED IF YOU HAD LET ME COPY YOUR ANSWERS, DAMMIT!
UGH! DO YOU HATE HAVING TO SIT WITH ME?
`CAUSE I HATE HAVING TO SIT WITH YOU, TOO! YOU HONOR STUDENTS ARE ALL THE SAME.
I...I'M NOT AN HONOR STUDENT...

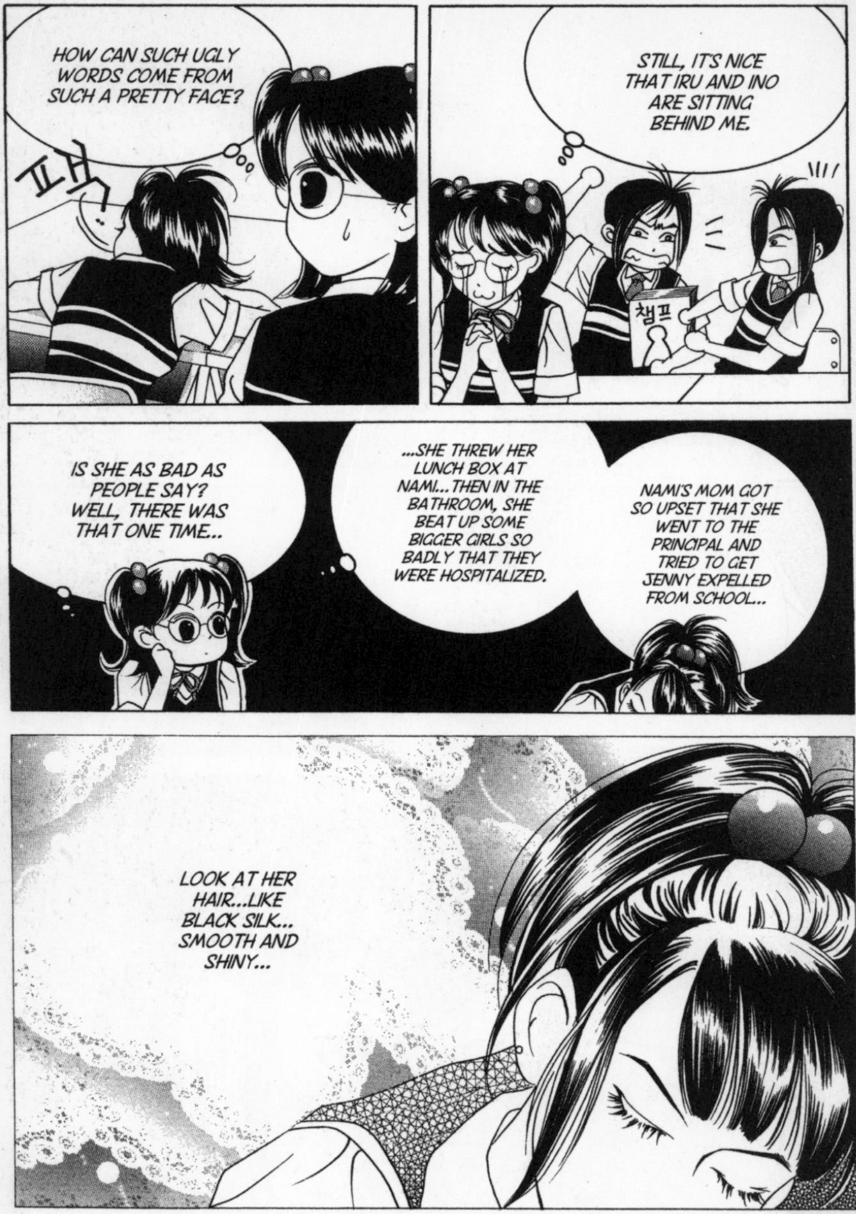
HOW CAN SUCH UGLY WORDS COME FROM SUCH A PRETTY FACE?
STILL, IT'S NICE THAT IRU AND INO ARE SITTING BEHIND ME.
챔프
IS SHE AS BAD AS PEOPLE SAY? WELL, THERE WAS THAT ONE TIME...
...SHE THREW HER LUNCH BOX AT NAMI...THEN IN THE BATHROOM, SHE BEAT UP SOME BIGGER GIRLS SO BADLY THAT THEY WERE HOSPITALIZED.
NAMI'S MOM GOT SO UPSET THAT SHE WENT TO THE PRINCIPAL AND TRIED TO GET JENNY EXPELLED FROM SCHOOL...
LOOK AT HER HAIR...LIKE BLACK SILK... SMOOTH AND SHINY...

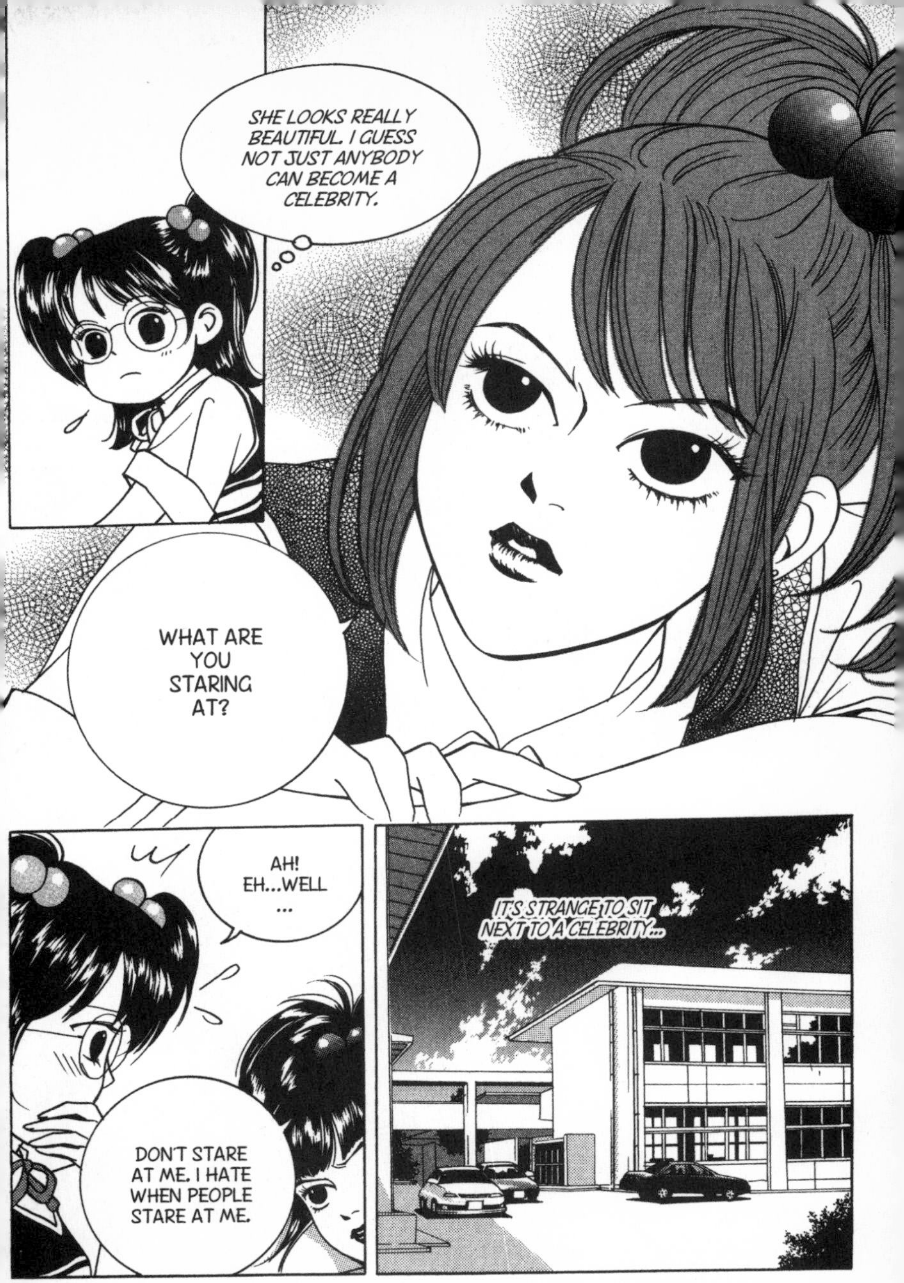
SHE LOOKS REALLY BEAUTIFUL. I GUESS NOT JUST ANYBODY CAN BECOME A CELEBRITY.
WHAT ARE YOU STARING AT?
AH! EH...WELL ...
DON'T STARE AT ME. I HATE WHEN PEOPLE STARE AT ME.
IT'S STRANGE TO SIT NEXT TO A CELEBRITY...

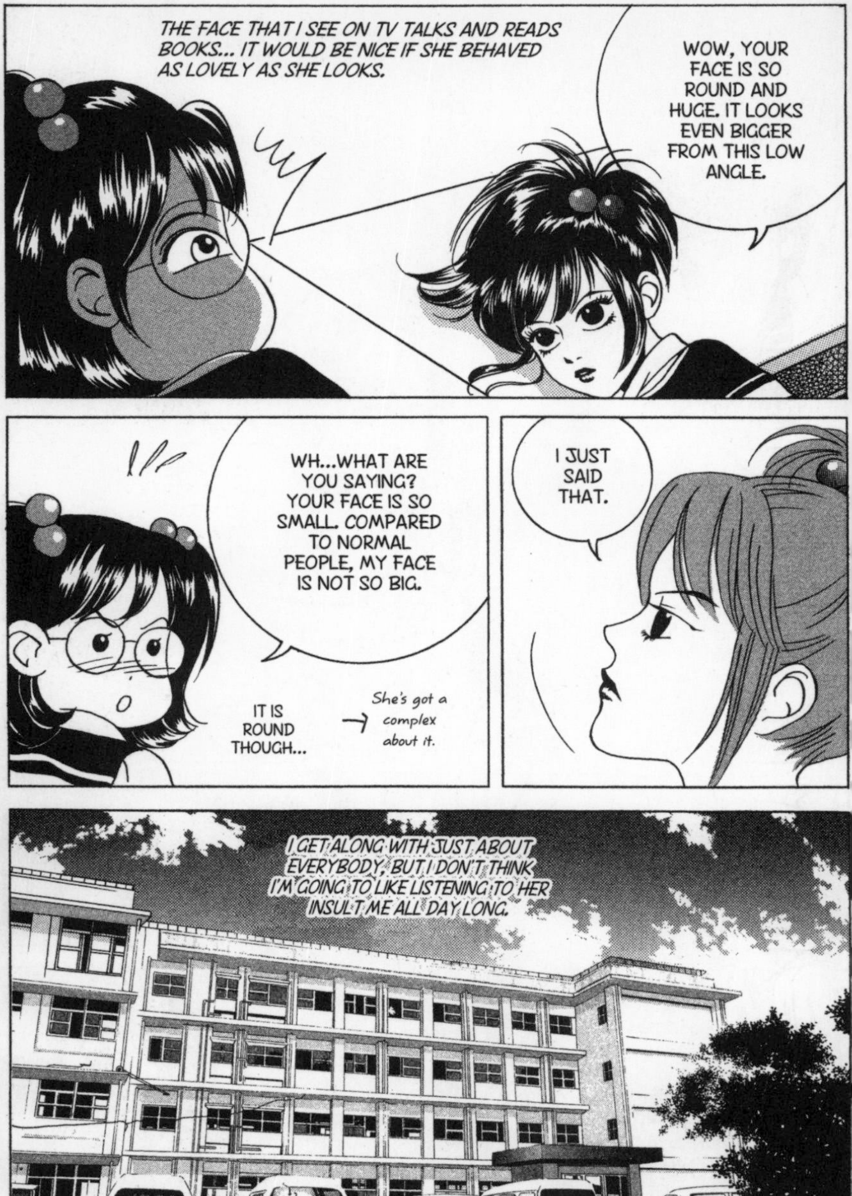
THE FACE THAT I SEE ON TV TALKS AND READS BOOKS... IT WOULD BE NICE IF SHE BEHAVED AS LOVELY AS SHE LOOKS.
WOW, YOUR FACE IS SO ROUND AND HUGE. IT LOOKS EVEN BIGGER FROM THIS LOW ANGLE.
WH...WHAT ARE YOU SAYING? YOUR FACE IS SO SMALL. COMPARED TO NORMAL PEOPLE, MY FACE IS NOT SO BIG.
IT IS ROUND THOUGH...
She's got a complex about it.
I JUST SAID THAT.
I GET ALONG WITH JUST ABOUT EVERYBODY, BUT I DON'T THINK I'M GOING TO LIKE LISTENING TO HER INSULT ME ALL DAY LONG.

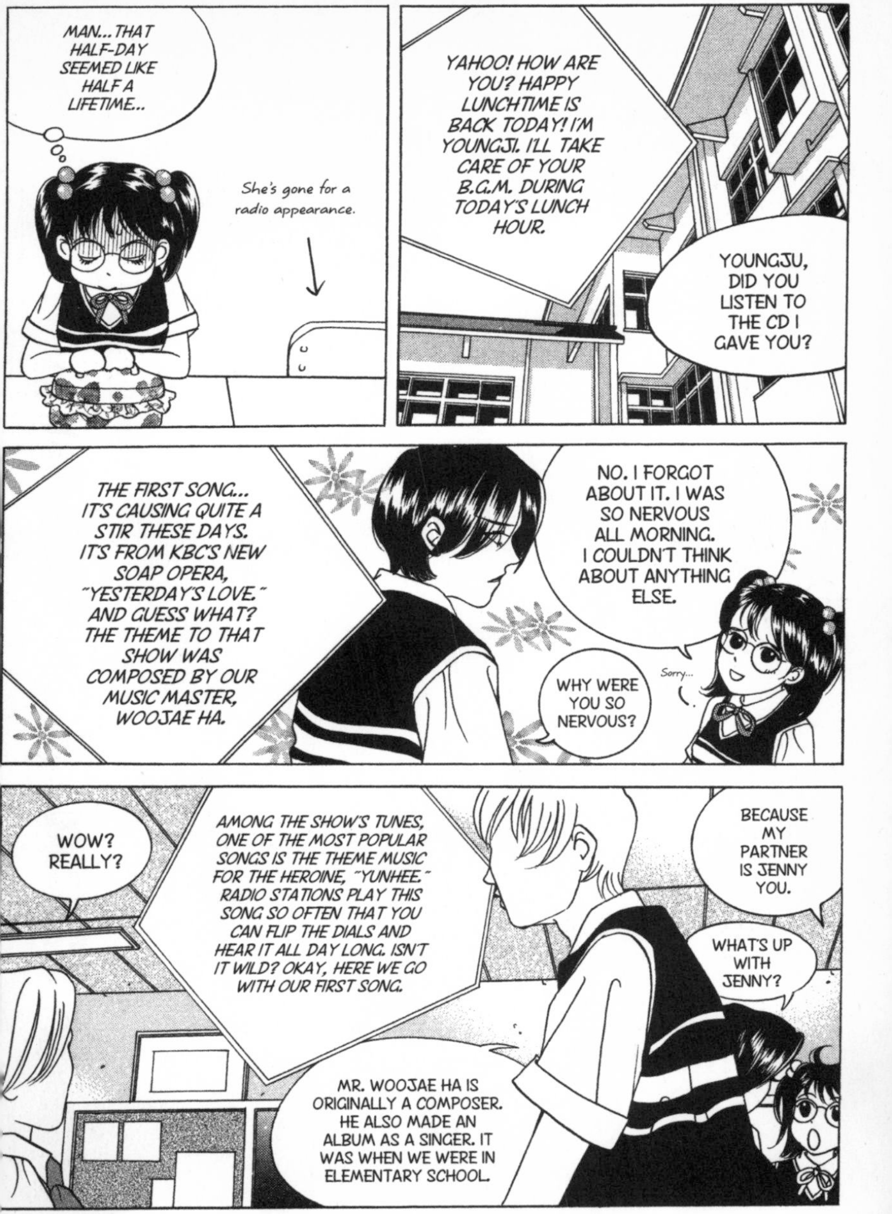
MAN... THAT HALF-DAY SEEMED LIKE HALF A LIFETIME...
She's gone for a radio appearance.
YAHOO! HOW ARE YOU? HAPPY LUNCHTIME IS BACK TODAY! I'M YOUNGJI. I'LL TAKE CARE OF YOUR B.G.M. DURING TODAY'S LUNCH HOUR.
YOUNGJU, DID YOU LISTEN TO THE CD I GAVE YOU?
THE FIRST SONG... IT'S CAUSING QUITE A STIR THESE DAYS. IT'S FROM KBC'S NEW SOAP OPERA, "YESTERDAY'S LOVE." AND GUESS WHAT? THE THEME TO THAT SHOW WAS COMPOSED BY OUR MUSIC MASTER, WOOJAE HA.
NO. I FORGOT ABOUT IT. I WAS SO NERVOUS ALL MORNING. I COULDN'T THINK ABOUT ANYTHING ELSE.
Sorry...
WHY WERE YOU SO NERVOUS?
WOW? REALLY?
AMONG THE SHOW'S TUNES, ONE OF THE MOST POPULAR SONGS IS THE THEME MUSIC FOR THE HEROINE, "YUNHEE." RADIO STATIONS PLAY THIS SONG SO OFTEN THAT YOU CAN FLIP THE DIALS AND HEAR IT ALL DAY LONG. ISN'T IT WILD? OKAY, HERE WE GO WITH OUR FIRST SONG.
BECAUSE MY PARTNER IS JENNY YOU.
WHAT'S UP WITH JENNY?
MR. WOOJAE HA IS ORIGINALLY A COMPOSER. HE ALSO MADE AN ALBUM AS A SINGER. IT WAS WHEN WE WERE IN ELEMENTARY SCHOOL.

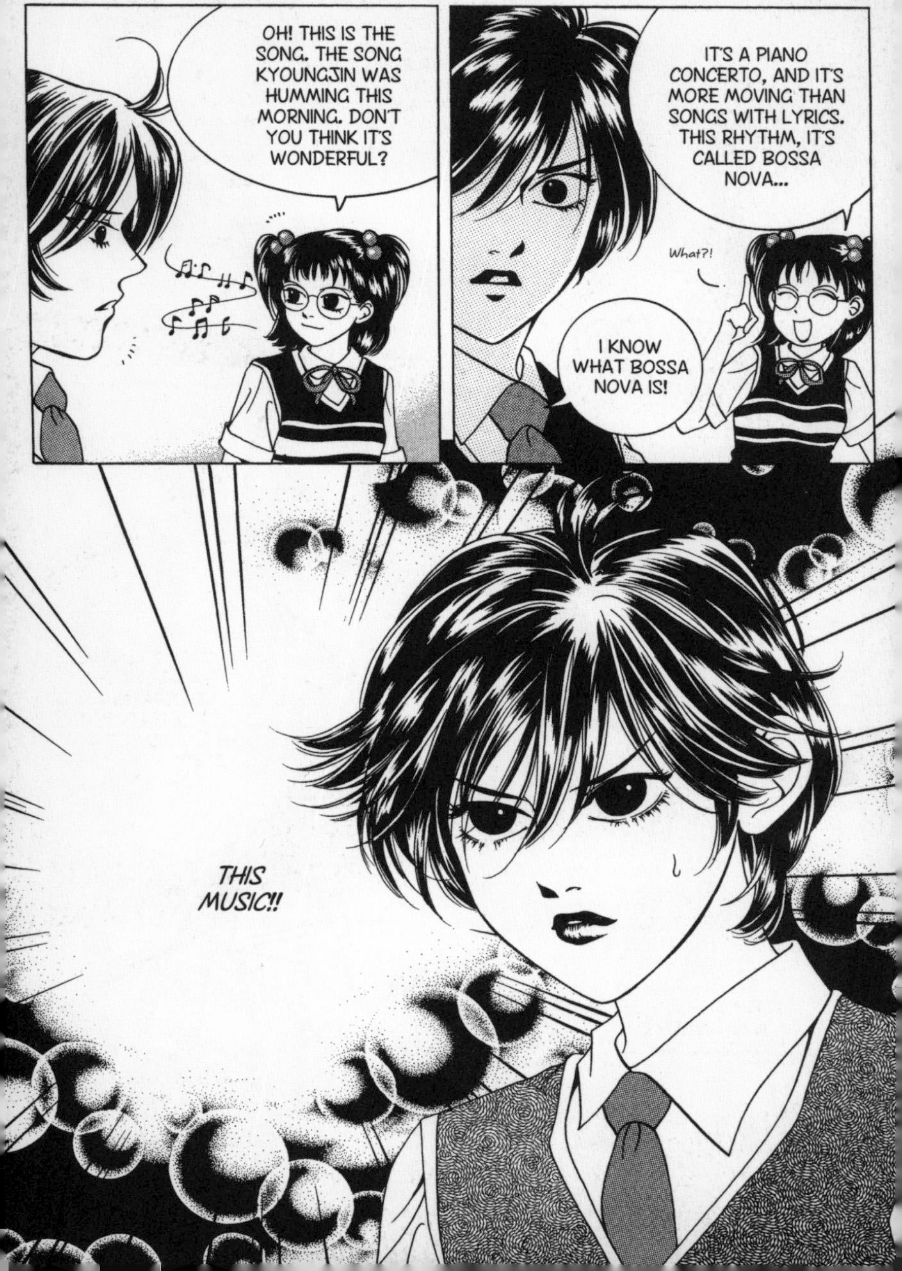
OH! THIS IS THE SONG. THE SONG KYOUNGJIN WAS HUMMING THIS MORNING. DON'T YOU THINK IT'S WONDERFUL?
IT'S A PIANO CONCERTO, AND IT'S MORE MOVING THAN SONGS WITH LYRICS. THIS RHYTHM, IT'S CALLED BOSSA NOVA...
What?!
I KNOW WHAT BOSSA NOVA IS!
THIS MUSIC!!

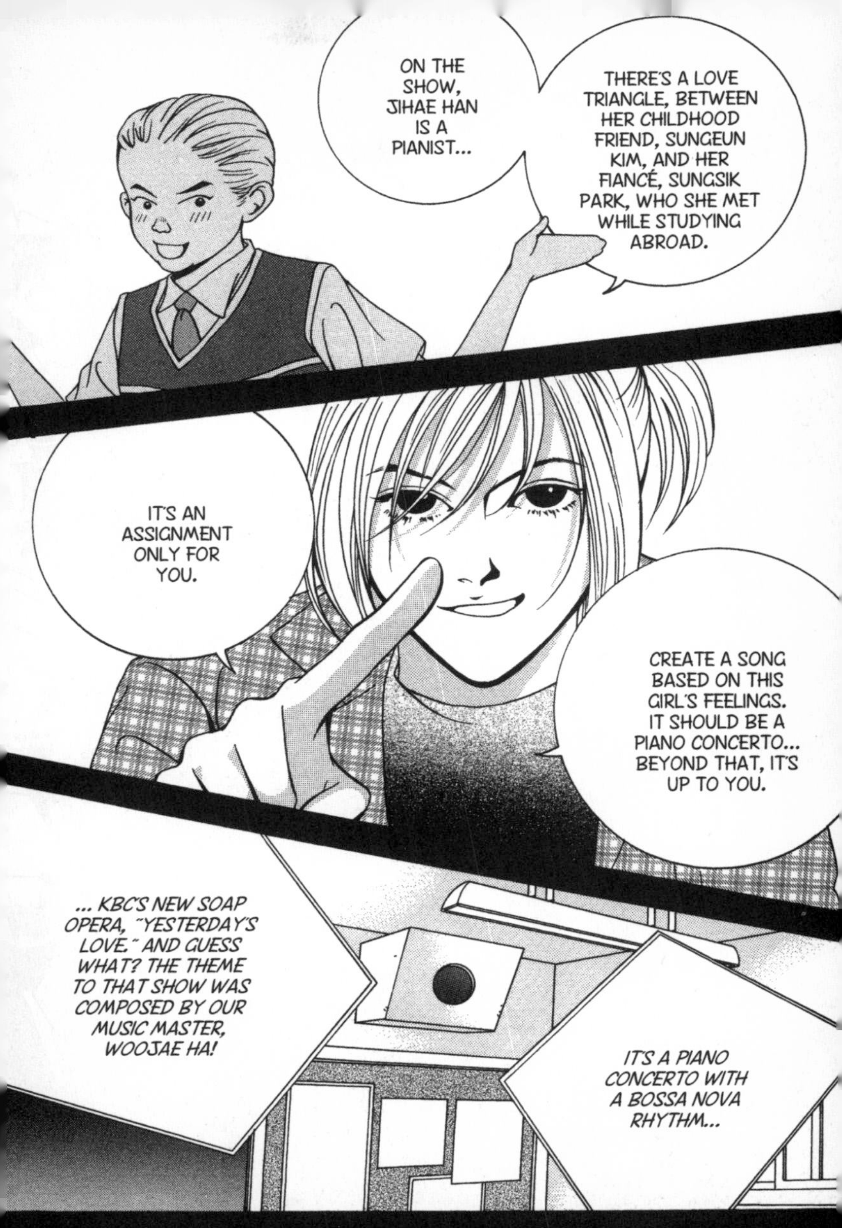
ON THE SHOW, JIHAE HAN IS A PIANIST...
THERE'S A LOVE TRIANGLE, BETWEEN HER CHILDHOOD FRIEND, SUNGEUN KIM, AND HER FIANCÉ, SUNGSIK PARK, WHO SHE MET WHILE STUDYING ABROAD.
IT'S AN ASSIGNMENT ONLY FOR YOU.
CREATE A SONG BASED ON THIS GIRL'S FEELINGS. IT SHOULD BE A PIANO CONCERTO... BEYOND THAT, IT'S UP TO YOU.
... KBC'S NEW SOAP OPERA, "YESTERDAY'S LOVE." AND GUESS WHAT? THE THEME TO THAT SHOW WAS COMPOSED BY OUR MUSIC MASTER, WOOJAE HA!
IT'S A PIANO CONCERTO WITH A BOSSA NOVA RHYTHM...

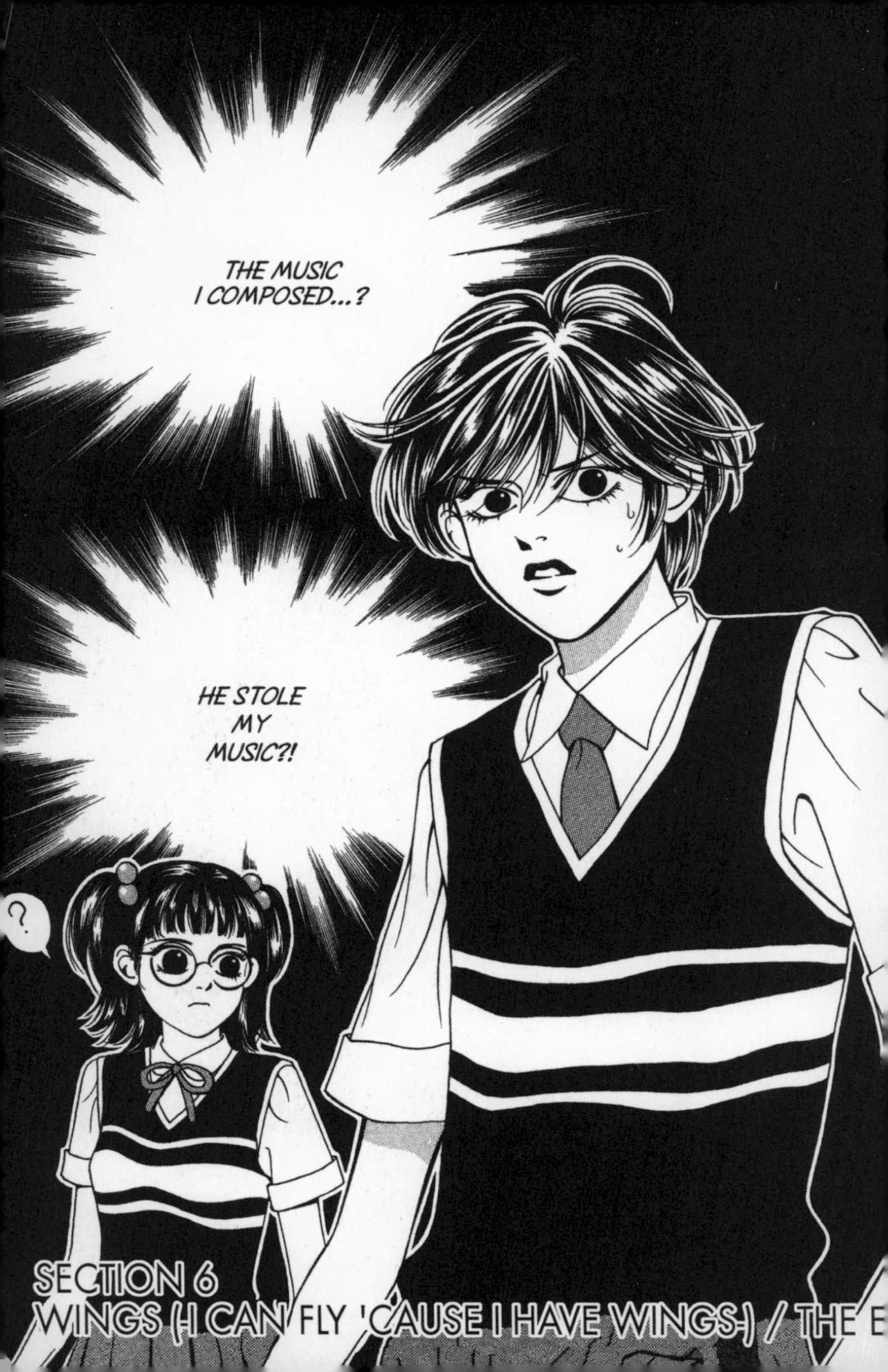
THE MUSIC I COMPOSED...?
HE STOLE MY MUSIC?!
?
SECTION 6
WINGS (I CAN FLY 'CAUSE I HAVE WINGS) / THE E

ONE VOLUME 1 THE END

The Hits Keep Coming in the Next Volume of...

With Jenny and Youngju paired off in class, Eumpa and the girls begin to form an odd emotional triangle. And as Jenny becomes more enamored with Eumpa she urges him to take his musical talent to the public. But our reluctant hero wants no part of fame and fortune, until certain revelations from Jenny—and a shocking admission by Mr. Ha—cause him to reconsider.

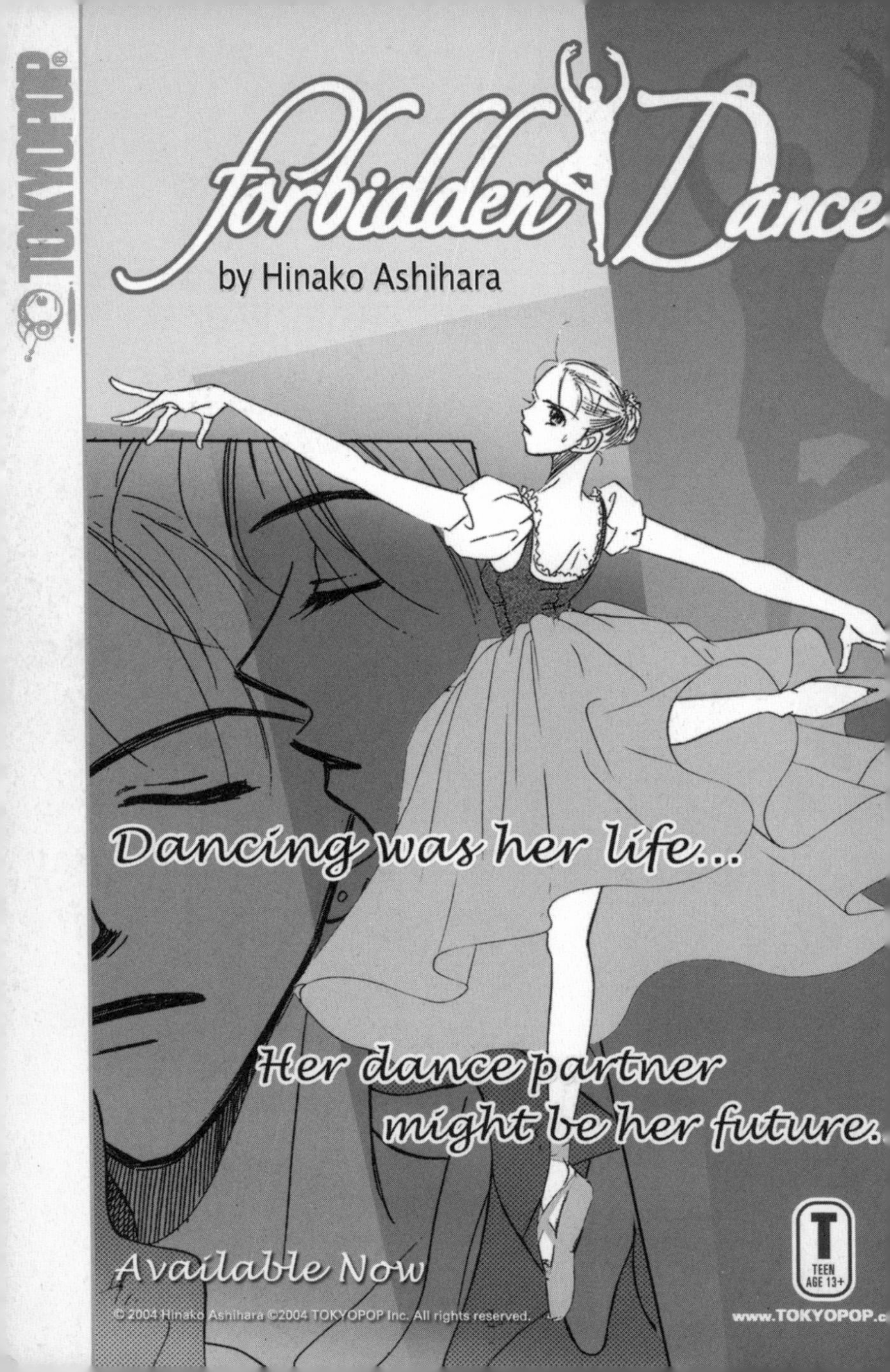

TOKYOPOP
Forbidden Dance
by Hinako Ashihara
Dancing was her life...
Her dance partner
might be her future.
Available Now
T
TEEN
AGE 13+
© 2004 Hinako Ashihara ©2004 TOKYOPOP Inc. All rights reserved.
www.TOKYOPOP.c

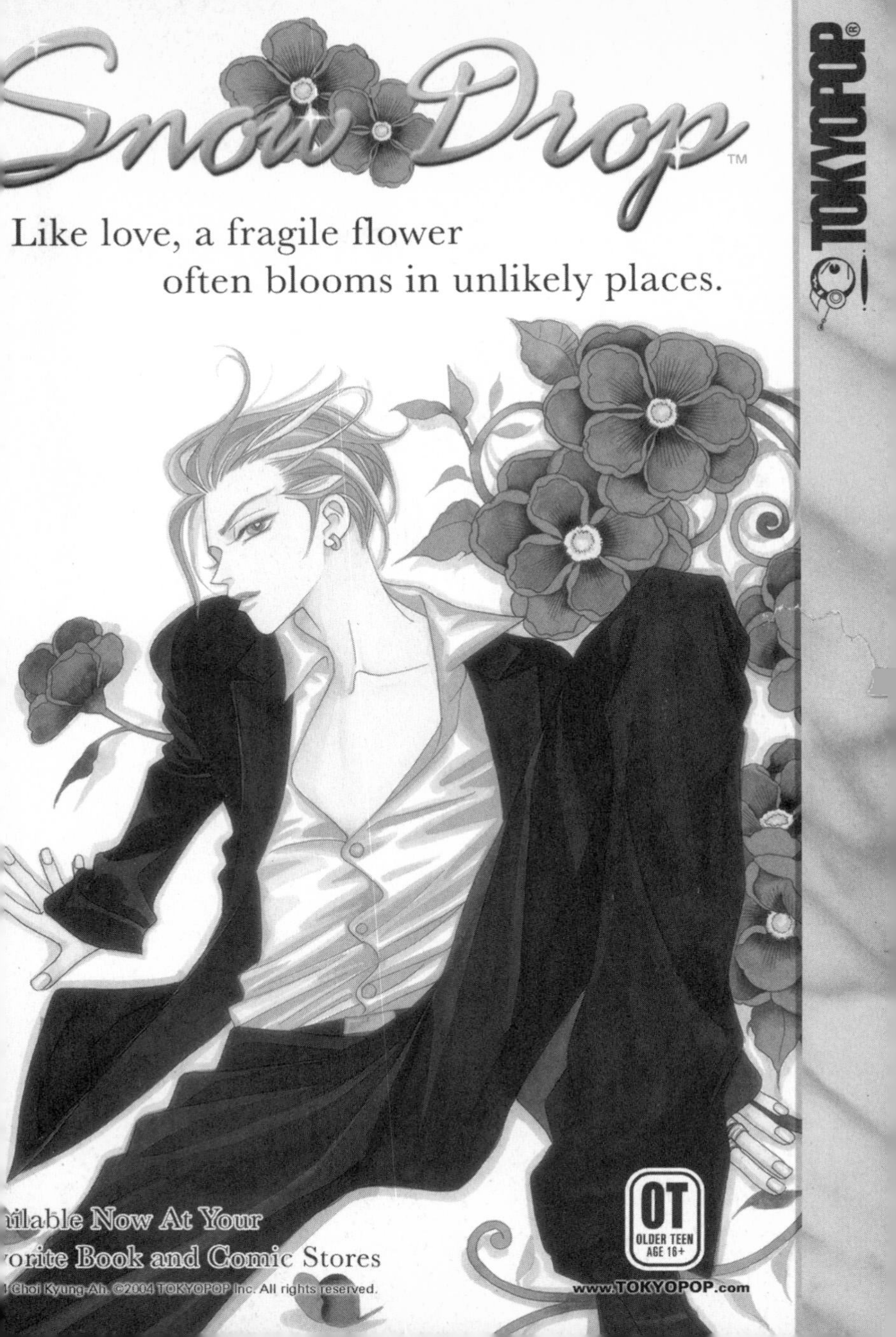
Snow Drop™
Like love, a fragile flower
often blooms in unlikely places.
TOKYOPOP®
OT
OLDER TEEN
AGE 16+
ailable Now At Your
vorite Book and Comic Stores
Choi Kyung-Ah. ©2004 TOKYOPOP Inc. All rights reserved.
www.TOKYOPOP.com

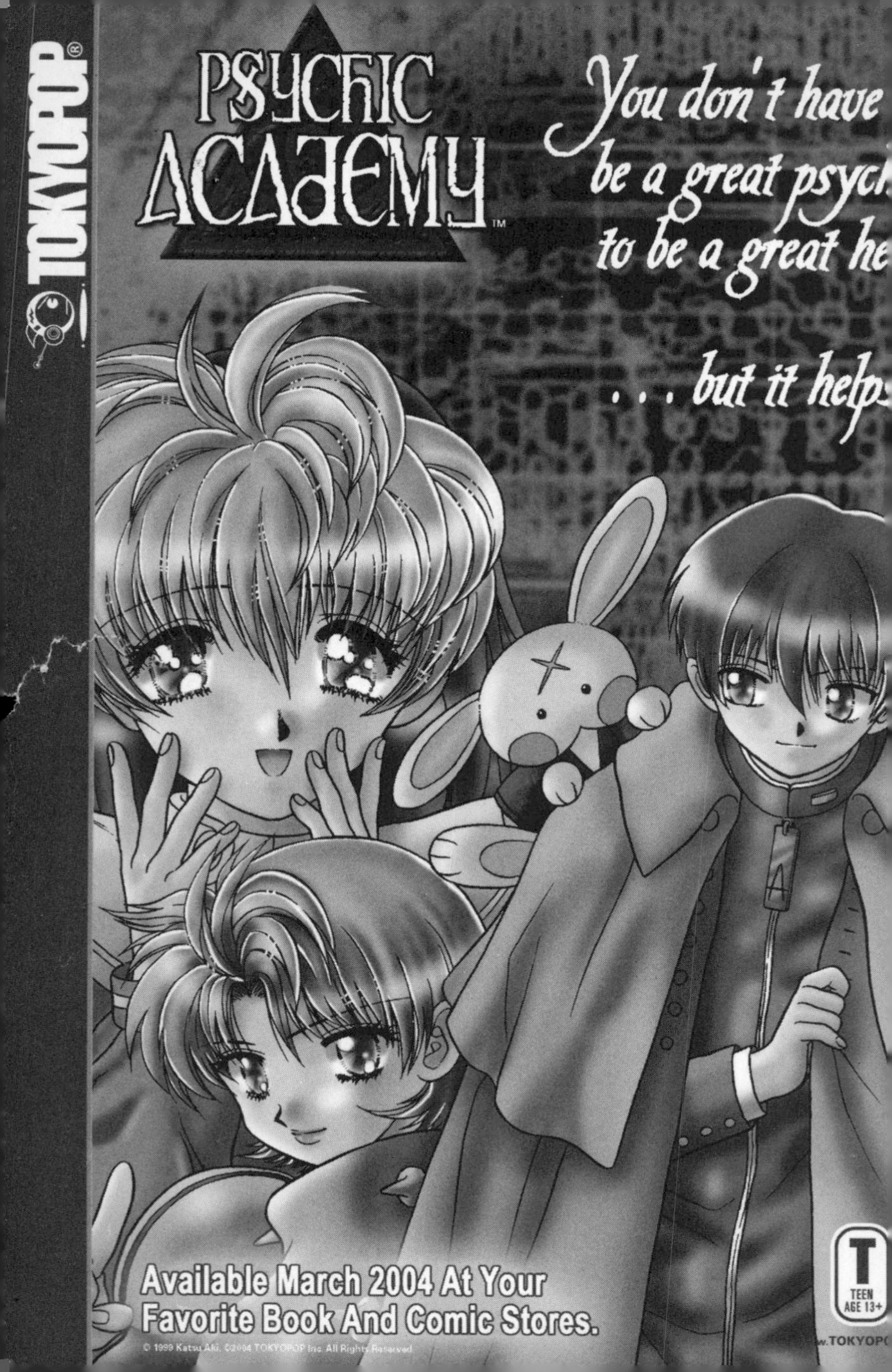
TOKYOPOP®
PSYCHIC ACADEMY™
You don't have
be a great psych
to be a great he
. . . but it helps
T
TEEN
AGE 13+
Available March 2004 At Your
Favorite Book And Comic Stores.
© 1999 Katsu Aki. ©2004 TOKYOPOP Inc. All Rights Reserved.
w.TOKYOP